# Southern Gambit

CAMPAIGNS & COMMANDERS

GREGORY J. W. URWIN, SERIES EDITOR

CAMPAIGNS AND COMMANDERS

# Southern Gambit

## Cornwallis and the British March to Yorktown

Stanley D. M. Carpenter

University of Oklahoma Press | Norman

This book is published with the generous assistance of
The McCasland Foundation, Duncan, Oklahoma.

Library of Congress Cataloging-in-Publication Data

Names: Carpenter, Stanley D. M., author.
Title: Southern gambit : Cornwallis and the British march to Yorktown / Stanley D. M. Carpenter.
Description: Norman : University of Oklahoma Press, [2018] | Series: Campaigns and commanders ; volume 65 | Includes bibliographical references and index.
Identifiers: LCCN 2018027374 | ISBN 978-0-8061-6185-3 (hardcover : alk. paper)
Subjects: LCSH: Southern States—History—Revolution, 1775–1783—Campaigns. | Cornwallis, Charles Cornwallis, Marquis, 1738–1805. | United States—History—Revolution, 1775–1783—British forces.
Classification: LCC E267 .C27 2018 | DDC 973.3/37—dc23
LC record available at https://lccn.loc.gov/2018027374

*Southern Gambit: Cornwallis and the British March to Yorktown* is Volume 65 in the Campaigns and Commanders series.

The paper in this book meets the guidelines for permanence and durability of the Committee on Production Guidelines for Book Longevity of the Council on Library Resources, Inc. ∞



1 2 3 4 5 6 7 8 9 10

*With respect and admiration to*
*Christopher M. Armitage, Bruce P. Lenman,*
*Richard Soloway, and Richard L. Greaves*

# Contents

# Illustrations

## Figures

## Maps

# Preface

A strange thing happened at the Guilford Court House National Battlefield Park on a balmy Sunday afternoon in 1963. My parents regularly took the two younger brothers and myself on expeditions to battlefield parks and museums; this trip was my first to the Guilford Court House site in Greensboro, North Carolina. While I was enamored with the museum articles and artifacts, stories of what occurred at specific locations, dioramas depicting the action, and so on, I came away with one overarching impression—a fascination with Lieutenant General Charles, 2nd Earl Cornwallis and the eighteenth-century British Army. This might have been unusual for a ten-year-old North Carolina kid in the 1960s, but there it was. Perhaps the fact that my North Carolina ancestors on both sides of my family had been committed Loyalists played into the equation. Maybe my Scottish Highland ancestry, of which my maternal family from Moore County were intensely proud, had some bearing. Perhaps, my father, a university professor and amateur historian of old Tryon County, North Carolina, who enthralled us with the exploits of a Loyalist ancestor who fought for King and Country and was wounded in combat, had some influence. Whatever the cause, from that day on I was hooked on the unfortunate earl, the British Army, and the Southern Campaign of the War of American Independence. That then is the origin of this book.

The truth be told, this is not the first attempt. I fully imagined that my doctoral dissertation in British military history would be the story of Cornwallis and the Southern Campaign from the British perspective. It was not to be. After two years of meeting all the coursework requirements, I was walking from class with my major professor and dissertation adviser when he asked what I proposed as the topic. I proudly responded. He promptly rejected. It was not that he objected to the topic, far from it. Professor Greaves simply could not serve as adviser for a dissertation past 1714 or on a purely military topic. He had valid reasons in that both areas were out of his bailiwick and he did not believe it fair to the student for him to go that far afield. But he said that if at least two of the department's military historians sat on the committee, then he would be good to go as advisor. Therefore, I wound up with a case-study analysis on military leadership in the British Civil Wars of 1638–51. I cannot complain—two books and a score of articles resulted from the dissertation. His Lordship still awaited, however, and now after half a century, that project has come to fruition.

One may ask why is another study of the British strategic perspective in the War of American Independence needed. There is a simple and utterly practical answer. In a world rife with conflict and tension, how does a distant great power prosecute an irregular war within the context of a regional struggle all within a global competitive environment? How does that distant power craft an effective strategy (or strategies) and resultant operations to prevail in this "war within a war within a war"? Three U.S. administrations have struggled with that question since the 9/11 terrorist attacks in New York and Washington, D.C. Moreover, British civil and military authorities wrestled in the 1770s with that same problem. The British strategic conundrum during the American War (as they called it) and the elements of strategic decision making and operational execution are as topical today as they were more than two hundred years ago. At the U.S. Naval War College, we teach students how to think strategically, analytically, and critically using historical case studies that illustrate the enduring lessons of conflict and highlight the difficulties in crafting effective strategies. The British Southern Campaign is an ideal laboratory for analyzing and studying strategic thinking in an overwhelmingly difficult contextual environment.

There is an argument that the earl's time is due. Various historians over the past half century, including Piers Mackesy, Jeremy Black, William Willcox, Ira Gruber, Don Higginbotham, Theodore Thayer, and more recently Andrew O'Shaughnessy, have all examined the dynamics of British strategic planning and execution during the Southern Campaign in various journal articles, conference papers, and broader analyses of the war. Where this study differs is that it represents a full-length monograph dedicated specifically to the British strategic perspective. It pulls together the scholarship of historians over decades to provide a causative explanation for the utter collapse of Britain's Southern Strategy that culminated on Surrender Field near a tiny village on the York River in Virginia, resulting in the birth of the United States of America.

There is another reason for this work. Lord Charles Cornwallis was a seminal figure in the founding of the nineteenth-century British Empire through his governor generalship of British India and as lord lieutenant of Ireland. He was, in short, an important and influential player. The man deserves many biographical scribblings. When I undertook my graduate studies, I heard that there were three reasons for a new history on a topic—new primary-source material, new interpretations of well-known material, or a passage of twenty-five years. I am not sure how valid the third element really is, but since the last comprehensive biography of the earl, Franklin and Mary Wickwire's two-volume study, *Cornwallis: The American Adventure* and *Cornwallis: The Imperial Adventure,* is pushing fifty years, I will gladly accept it as a justification. At any rate, the man is owed a new biographical work, especially one that has instructive value for future generations of professional crafters of strategy and operations dealing with a harsh, unfriendly world.

I am most grateful to those who have supported this project over the years, whether by happily providing their thoughts and suggestions, by providing resources, and by reading this historian's wandering words. I would especially like to thank the following friends, colleagues, and mentors, without whom this project could never have been completed, for their inspiration, opinions, and suggestions—Jeremy Black, Ira Gruber, Larry Babits, Kevin Delamer, Jim McIntyre, Richard L. Greaves, and Bruce P. Lenman. I am most appreciative of the kind curators and librarians at the British National Archives at Kew, London, and at the Suffolk Records Office, Bury St Edmunds, for their assistance and in allowing me access to original documents and records. I humbly thank Ms. L. Robinson and the administration of Culford School in Suffolk, the ancestral home of the Cornwallis family, for their special assistance. Map and image assistance was kindly provided by Peter Harrington of the Brown University Library, Anne S. K. Brown Military Collection; Lieutenant Colonel (Ret.) Raymond Hrinko of the Department of History, U.S. Military Academy, West Point; Bob Cembrola of the U.S. Naval War College Foundation Museum; and Gale Munro of the Naval History and Heritage Command. Finally, I am grateful to the U.S. Naval War College administration, particularly Professors Bill Spain, Tim Jackson, Jay Hickey, Walt Wildemann, Tim Garrold, and Doug Smith, for allowing me the time and wherewithal to produce this book. I could not have undertaken the research in Britain without the Naval War College Faculty Development funding so graciously provided in 2006 and 2010. Many thanks to all.

# Southern Gambit

INTRODUCTION

# "Gain the Hearts and Subdue the Minds of America"

## *British Strategic Leadership and the Southern Campaign*

> The most far-reaching act of judgment that the statesman and commander have to make is to establish . . . the kind of war on which they are embarking; neither mistaking it for, nor trying to turn it into, something that is alien to its nature. This is the first of all strategic questions.
>
> —Carl von Clausewitz, *On War*

With the War of American Independence stalemated in the northern and middle colonies by 1778, Britain needed a new military and political strategy, particularly after French intervention turned the colonial affair into a global, great-power, maritime conflict. From this new security dynamic emerged the Southern Strategy. Relying on a massive outpouring of Loyalist support in the Carolinas, Georgia, and the two Floridas (East and West, British colonies since 1763), Great Britain launched the campaign in the South aimed at pacifying and reestablishing imperial rule one colony at a time from Georgia northward. Yet this grandiose plan ended in disaster at Yorktown, Virginia, three years later. Could the strategy have succeeded despite being handicapped by a lack of cohesion, inadequate leadership characterized by a breakdown in command and control, a concept based on flawed assumptions, and a misunderstanding of the nature of the war in the South? Was it a good strategy badly executed or simply a bad strategy? This study examines the Southern Campaign in light of these questions and provides a narrative of the major events from the Crown (British and Loyalist American) perspective, arguing that the British strategy represented a sound concept theoretically. The operational execution proved faulty, however, particularly the critical aspects of unity of command and effort, strategic leadership, and logistics, resulting in a profound failure. Ultimately, from the British perspective, the lack of strategic coherence between the key decision makers—Lord George Germain, the secretary of state for the colonies in London; General Sir Henry Clinton, the commander in chief in North America in New York; and Lieutenant General Charles, 2nd Earl Cornwallis in the field—ineffective command and control, and a profound misunderstanding of the nature of the war in the South all contributed to the series of cascading failures that led to the defeat of Lord Cornwallis and the Southern Strategy in 1778–81.

Military historians and analysts have well established that the concept of a formal national military strategy with all that it entails—including the elements of planning, defining command relationships, diplomacy, logistical administration, and so forth—would not have been a prescribed process by civil and military authorities in the late eighteenth century. While this is the case, it is also irrelevant. Regardless of the spatial, temporal, or cultural dynamic, every human action, reaction, or interaction involves policy objectives, strategic planning, operational execution, and tactics. There is always a desired objective or end state, which in modern strategic thinking is simply the "ends." To establish the conditions whereby the policy goal can be achieved is the "means." The execution of a strategy is embodied in the operations; the actions undertaken represent the tactics.

Here is a simple and somewhat humorous but highly illustrative example demonstrating this strategic universality that might be used in a graduate history seminar. The moderator points to a student, who has brought into the classroom a cup of coffee, and asks the following questions: What is your policy objective? What is your strategy? What are your operations? What is the tactic? The student offers the following answers: to stay awake during this three-hour seminar (policy objective); to caffeinate (strategy); to go to the minimart and purchase the coffee (operation); and to periodically take a sip (tactic).

Modern concepts of strategy, operational art, principles of war, joint operations, and so on largely developed in the twentieth century. Nonetheless, through wartime experience, education, and reading the great numbers of books on military affairs available in the period, senior officers such as Clinton and Cornwallis had a robust understanding of military art and science. In short, while they may not have been able to provide a modern definition of strategy, operational art, or principles of war, these highly skilled and experienced professional officers understood and practiced the concepts. Additionally, they were familiar with the irregular warfare then common on the European continent called *petite guerre*, or "small war," which used formations of light troops to raid, harass, ambush, interdict communications, and generally create havoc for the enemy's regular forces conducting linear, conventional operations. A good example of these "small warriors" were the "pandours," typically Croats and Slovenes serving the Hapsburg Austrian armies. Given this dynamic, the activities of southern partisans, such as Francis Marion and Thomas Sumter, encountered by Cornwallis and his subordinate officers were neither unique nor new. Indeed, Cornwallis's southern forces used German Jägers, riflemen mostly from southern German states skilled and experienced in operating and skirmishing in rough, wooded terrain while utilizing nonlinear tactics. In short, a lack of an understanding of strategic concepts was not the cause for the ultimate failure of the Southern Campaign. How British commanders chose strategies and executed resultant operations is the story of their ultimate failure to pacify the South and restore allegiance to the Crown.[1]

While British military and civil authorities may not have had a well-developed, articulated, staffed, and planned military or political strategy in the modern sense, there clearly existed a definitive policy objective to end the rebellion and restore colonial allegiance to the Crown. The eminent military historian Jeremy Black sees the overarching British strategy as "pacification."[2] The search for the right pacification strategy drove British civil and military authorities toward a military solution combined with a civil accommodation as illustrated by the actions of the Howe brothers at New York in 1776, the 1778 efforts of the Carlisle Commission to grant all of the colonial demands of 1775 save only political independence, and the attempts to restore royal civil governance in the South. In the eighteenth century, pacification meant that the authorities had to crush the rebellion by brute military force and round up or at least neutralize its leadership. Above all, the strategic imperative lay in destroying the rebels' ability to fight. With their military capability eliminated, the rebels would return to their senses and negotiate an end to the uprising, or so ran the theory.

Ultimately, any pacification strategy demanded an initial military component, particularly following the Declaration of Independence in July 1776, an event that dramatically changed the Patriot policy objective. The several Jacobite risings in support of a restoration of the Stuart monarchy from 1689 through 1746 had all been dealt with in this manner—crush the rebel military power, then implement pacification in whatever form, negotiated or enforced. It is no wonder then that civil authorities in London and military commanders in Boston in 1775 shared this attitude toward putting down a rebellion or civil insurrection. Therefore, the strategic solution would be brute military coercion initially regardless of the ultimate civil pacification efforts.

Various strategies for accomplishing that policy objective emerged during the American War, among them crushing the Continental Army, capturing New

York and negotiating a settlement, occupying the entire Hudson Valley–Lake Champlain corridor to divide and conquer the rebellious colonies, imposing a North American naval/maritime blockade, and fomenting a Loyalist reclamation of the southern colonies. Yet these resulted in a series of failed operations: Lieutenant General Sir William Howe's New York–New Jersey Campaign of 1776, Sir Guy Carleton's Lakes Offensive of 1776, Major General John Burgoyne's Hudson Valley Campaign of 1777, Howe's Philadelphia Campaign of 1777, and the Southern Campaign of 1778–81.

Often these operations ran aground on the "rocks and shoals" of what is now called "hybrid warfare," a blended operational concept in which a weaker combatant employs a combination of regular and irregular methods to wear down the ability or will of the stronger opponent in a war of attrition or exhaustion. Hybrid warfare in the War of American Independence encompassed the conventional doctrine and tactics of linear battle between regular, professional troops combined with auxiliary and irregular support common to the period. Using irregular forces to wage unconventional warfare against an opponent often occurred in eighteenth-century Europe, but in North America the typically brutal, guerrilla-style terror tactics injected an element that Crown authorities could neither cope with nor find an effective counterstrategy against. British forces encountered to a limited degree such combat modes in the northern and middle colonies from the opening stages in 1775 to the end of the struggle. But the Southern Campaign represented the zenith of a complex struggle between forces ranging from conventional troops of the regular British/Provincial and Continental armies down to the partisan bands and local Loyalist and Patriot militias, which were in many cases simply armed mobs.[3] In short, the inability of Crown authorities to find a successful pacification strategy for restoring allegiance led to multiple operations and stratagems throughout the struggle. Naturally enough, strategic incoherence followed.

How did the Southern Campaign, which began with such promise for strategic success characterized by often brilliant British operational artistry, come to such utter and ruinous failure? What aspects of British strategy proved beyond the capability of British arms? What dynamics coalesced to undercut the British effort to restore allegiance? An analytical framework that often yields interesting and enlightening results is the counterfactual, or "what if," approach. In modern service colleges, this approach is an inherent pedagogy in the strategy curricula. Many counterfactual questions might be put forward in a study of the British strategic perspective in the Southern Campaign. For example, what if Cornwallis had returned to South Carolina following the Battle of Guilford Court House instead of charging on to Virginia? What if Clinton had dispatched a rescue operation well before the Franco-American forces fully executed their siege at

Yorktown? What if Rear Admiral Sir Thomas Graves had taken control of the mouth of the Chesapeake Bay in September 1781? Finally, what if Cornwallis had comprehended the broader strategic picture as did his foe, Maj. Gen. Nathanael Greene, and not committed the error of operationalizing strategy?[4] These and other counterfactuals, or "strategic alternatives," are useful in any analysis of strategic thinking and decision making.

Many excellent works address the war in the northern and middle colonies during 1775–78 from the strategic perspective. This study looks at the last chapter in the American War of Independence drama—the Southern Campaign of 1778 to October 1781, with a focus on the actions, decisions, and strategic/operational leadership of Lieutenant General Cornwallis and his command relations with superiors and subordinates. In this regard it is both a biography and a narrative history. It is also a strategic analysis since understanding the dynamics and manner in which British civil and military authorities formulated, coordinated, and communicated military strategy to field commanders bears particular scrutiny when considering the campaign's viability. Ultimately, this study proposes some explanatory conclusions for Cornwallis's ultimate failure.

Why is another analysis of the War of American Independence necessary or even desired? There is a simple response. The British experience three centuries ago provides insights for contemporary strategic and operational planners and decision makers, particularly in terms of how a great power conducts a distant irregular or hybrid war characterized by insurgency, rebellion, and internal civil strife, all complicated by a severe resource constraint. The twenty-first century security environment demands such strategic and operational analysis; the Southern Campaign provides a robust laboratory for that analysis.

## British Strategic Failure

In examining the underlying causes of the eventual British strategic failure, there are many possible courses of action. This study examines a number of critical dynamics that illustrate both the strategic and the operational aspects of the campaign with evidence drawn from the particular events. In essence, British strategic planners and operational commanders failed to understand the true nature of the conflict in the South. They misinterpreted the ability and motivation of southern Loyalists to support Crown field forces, particularly their willingness to engage the rebels and provide logistical support. British authorities assumed that the campaign would conform to their operational and tactical concepts. Called "scriptwriting," this potentially fatal flaw lulls strategists into believing that a campaign will unfold as they forecast, completely ignoring such fundamental dynamics of war as "fog and friction" and the opponent's interaction and adaptation. Cornwallis and his peers assumed a vast Loyalist outpouring of troops and resources, but their planning and execution in terms of manpower and matériel proved woefully inadequate to the operational mission. Moreover, they assumed that Major General Greene would be as inept a field commander as previous Continental Army officers in the Southern Department (encompassing Virginia, the Carolinas, and Georgia), notably Maj. Gen. Horatio Gates. Events soon proved the fallacy of that assumption.

Moreover, the Royal Navy failed to gain and maintain command of the sea. Rear Admiral Graves's failure to secure the mouth of the Chesapeake Bay allowed uncontested French naval movement in support of the land force and complicated similar British movements. Conversely, Cornwallis failed to capitalize on the British naval advantage. In moving inland in pursuit of regular Continental forces, he negated the mobility and logistical advantage that British naval power provided. In general, the overall defensive maritime posture adopted by Frederick, Lord North's ministry in 1778, maintaining a strong fleet in home waters to prevent an invasion as France actively intervened in the conflict, set the stage for the ultimate loss of command of the sea. Consequently, British naval forces on American station were weak relative to the enemy once a French squadron broke out of the Mediterranean and arrived in the West Indies.

Crown military and civil authorities failed to ensure unity of command and unity of effort. In exercising ultimate authority over his field commander, Clinton allowed Cornwallis too much free rein and thus lost control of events. The four essential entities charged with the campaign's strategic direction—Lord Germain; Clinton; Vice Admiral Sir Marriott Arbuthnot (North American Royal Navy commander) and his successor, Graves; and Cornwallis—often worked at cross-purposes. This dynamic compromised joint coordination between the British Army and Royal Navy, which chronically hampered British efforts throughout the rebellion, including the Southern Strategy. For the strategy to succeed, "fog and friction" had to be minimized. Yet the lack of strategic coherence and unity of command and effort severely crippled any chance for success.

British authorities placed potential neutrals on "death ground." In issuing provocative proclamations, they often forced neutrals and paroled rebels to swear a loyalty oath or be regarded as in rebellion. The resultant outpouring of Patriot support stymied pacification efforts, particularly in South Carolina. For Loyalists, the offer to captured rebels of parole without punishment for insurrection angered many and often diminished their enthusiasm and willingness to turn out for either active military service or to provide logistical support for Crown forces.

British officers often "operationalized strategy." Cornwallis believed that operational and tactical brilliance would overcome all strategic difficulties, an attitude that ultimately led to the abandonment of hard-won gains in South Carolina and Georgia. This flawed concept eventually led to the disastrous march into Virginia in April 1781 following the costly engagement at Guilford Court House that March.

Taken as a whole, these faults ultimately doomed Crown efforts to restore the South to allegiance. While the strategic concept might have been valid, the operational execution failed. The Southern Strategy can be neatly expressed as "clear and hold." Simply put, once Patriot forces, both regular and irregular, were destroyed, removed, or otherwise neutralized in a specific geographic area, Crown regular forces would move on to the next targeted region. Local Loyalists would then take over, restore royal government, and provide security against any rebel resurgence. In essence then, "clear and hold" represented the ideal pacification strategy when given the limited British resources available due to active French and later Spanish military intervention. But the "clear and hold" method came to naught. Faced with a flawed conception of the nature of the southern colonies combined with an inappropriate and incoherent strategy hampered by inadequate logistics and a breakdown in command and control, Cornwallis and his subordinates proved unable to end the rebellion in the South and restore Crown authority by force of arms.

In the broader strategic sense, British authorities, both civil and military, can be accused of "strategic drift." As the war bogged down in the northern and middle colonies, they tried several stratagems, none of which solved the conundrum of how to restore the North American colonies to allegiance. Ira Gruber nicely captures this in his analysis of how Crown authorities "pursued a variety of strategies: isolating and crushing resistance in the most disloyal provinces, combining an overwhelming display of force with conciliatory gestures, destroying the Continental Army in a climactic battle, and raising loyalist forces to help recover the colonies piecemeal."[5]

In the Southern Campaign, "clear and hold" encompassed two of these British stratagems—crushing the opponent militarily and recovering the colonies by using Loyalists to reestablish security and royal governance. Cornwallis sought the decisive battle first against Gates, then against Greene. At Camden, South Carolina, in August 1780, he achieved his military goal with the utter destruction of Gates's mixed force of Continental regulars and Patriot militia. This victory supported the "clear" aspect of the overall strategy. He attempted a repeat performance several months later at Guilford Court House, North Carolina, against the far more strategically astute Greene. While in technical and tactical terms the earl won the day at Guilford, he failed to destroy the Patriot force. In retrospect, Cornwallis never achieved the essential "clear" requirement that would allow for local Loyalists to restore Crown authority in the South and to suppress any latent Patriot misbehavior once the main British force moved on. The failure of this element of the strategy prevented the conditions whereby the "hold" component could develop. As this narrative and its analysis of British strategic failure in the South and Cornwallis's role as the field commander unfolds, the failure of the "clear and hold" strategy becomes apparent for several reasons, primarily the misunderstanding of the nature of the war in the South but also a profound lack of strategic cohesion and a breakdown in British command and control, most notably within logistics.

## Strategic Concepts: The Analytical Framework

Before undertaking a chronological narrative and analysis of events within the framework of the above dynamics, it is useful to include some definitions. Military readers will certainly recognize terms such as "unity of effort and command," "center of gravity," "joint operations," "force concentration," "logistical sustainment," "strategic leadership," and so on. But this look at the British strategic perspective on the Southern Campaign is not just for a military audience. Analysts and historians are always on the hunt for causative explanations—causes and effects—of past events. Likewise, this look at the closing years of the War of American Independence focuses on several reasons for the eventual outcome—after all, any credible historical analysis must address not only the who, what, when, and where of human events but also must consider the why. Analysts and historians need a framework for their studies. These strategic concepts provide that framework under which the actions, decisions, options proposed and those taken, and prejudices and perceptions of the central characters are addressed and outcomes evaluated.

For the general reader more interested in the narrative flow, these concepts provide a broader understanding of why things happened as they did and why particular persons chose particular pathways or made specific decisions. Hopefully, readers will come away with a broader understanding of the historical events and a greater appreciation for the why and wherefore of the flow of events. Perhaps they may view events so often cloaked in mythology and legend from a new perspective.

Some technical terms used by practitioners of strategy will be used throughout but will be defined for clarity. Readers should keep in mind these key concepts as they examine the Southern Campaign from the British perspective and, in particular, the decisions and actions of the key Crown players. They include "strategic coherence," "strategic leadership," the "theory of victory," and "desired strategic effects." Additionally, a brief examination of the eighteenth-century

British constitutional system as it pertained to warfare is helpful since it was a major driver of the strategic incoherence and the inability to establish unity of command or effort for Crown forces in North America. Its influence on strategic and operational decision making as well as the genesis of the Southern Strategy are provided to orient the reader to the context within which the major players operated.

### *Strategic Coherence*

Strategic coherence implies an orderly, rational, and logical arrangement of all the elements of a military strategy that, if successful, will foster the desired strategic effects on the adversary and ultimately establish the conditions whereby the policy objectives can be achieved. Conversely, strategic incoherence implies that certain elements of the decision-making process are flawed or incompatible with the whole, thus inducing friction and possibly impeding the development of a successful strategy. In other words, the strategic decision-making process is handicapped from the outset. This dynamic can be a function of such elements as poor intelligence and net assessment, leading to erroneous assumptions and estimates and a flawed understanding of the nature of the conflict; a clumsy or inefficient command-and-control structure; strategic planning that fails to comprehend matériel or resource constraints; and geographic conditions that impede communications between decision makers. A factor as simple as a personality conflict may lead to such dissonance. A critical subset of strategic coherence, and a major determinant of its absence, consists of the operational concepts of unity of command and unity of effort. Both will be considered in this analysis of British strategic incoherence in the Southern Campaign, particularly the inability to empower a single decision maker who could enforce unity of effort if not unity of command.

## Strategic Leadership: Traits and Characteristics

Strategic leadership implies effectiveness at all levels of conflict—strategic, operational, and tactical. While a debate has long raged over the precise nature of effective leadership, ranging from the more traditional focus on individual traits and characteristics to the social-science concepts of cultural behaviors and group dynamics, for the purposes of this study, strategic leadership will be viewed as an amalgam of an individual's inherent characteristics and resultant behaviors. Accordingly, the primary players' actions can be considered in terms of their leadership traits and behaviors. Several aspects of strategic leadership during the Southern Campaign will be highlighted, including civility, aggressiveness, and martial superiority.

Civility is the adherence to a code of conduct that regulates actions such as the treatment of prisoners and noncombatants in accordance with the standards of the period. The decline of the medieval code of chivalry during the sixteenth- and seventeenth-century religious wars and the attendant barbarity, particularly against civilians, gave rise to new codes of military conduct. The Dutch political philosopher Hugo Grotius addressed the decline of long-established restraints on soldiers' behavior by the end of the sixteenth century. He viewed religion, formerly a governor on such actions, as having become the justification for savagery. In his work on conduct in war, *De jure belli ac pacis libri tres* (On the Law of War and Peace; 1625), Grotius attempted to come to terms with the new moral paradigm of his day and established behavioral conventions based on the reality of warfare in the early modern age. His limits included killing prisoners, slaughtering and terrorizing civilians, and devastating land and property. Although most rational men avoided these excesses as a matter of moral concern, the low standards of Grotius's era justified such actions during times of conflict. Incidents of cruelty and devastation in the Thirty Years' War (1618–48) eventually caused European public opinion to reject these standards and adopt the earlier medieval concept of honor and civility in warfare. By the mid-seventeenth century, various "Articles of War" emerged that memorialized and codified these renewed restraints on combatants. More than a century later, events in the American South quickly deteriorated into barbarity, pitting neighbor against neighbor, Loyalist against Patriot, and both sides against neutrals, those who merely wanted to survive and move on with their lives and businesses. Once conventional British and Continental forces moved out of an area, the rebellion often devolved into civil war. In the Carolinas this period has come down in the popular consciousness as the "Tory War." Cornwallis suffered from the public perception of British cruelty, oppression, and barbarism stimulated by the excesses—either supposed or real—of Lieutenant Colonel Banastre Tarleton and other subordinates.

Aggressiveness consists of risk, boldness, and initiative as modified by prudence. Military commentators since antiquity have stressed the primacy of aggression for battlefield success. Carl von Clausewitz, the early nineteenth-century Prussian military theorist, pointed out that "no military leader has ever become great without audacity." He additionally characterized aggressiveness as boldness and asserted that "a distinguished commander without boldness is unthinkable." Further, it "has its own prerogative . . . a genuinely creative force."[6]

Most military commentators advocate audacity, boldness, and risk taking as necessary characteristics of a successful leader. The moral force of aggressiveness and risk gives one the ability to motivate men despite the human factors of fear and lack of confidence. Adm. John Paul Jones captured the essence of risk taking in advice to the Russian Imperial Navy, noting, "in human affairs . . . it seems to be a law inflexible and inexorable that he who will not risk cannot win."[7] Nevertheless, such gambles cannot be foolhardy. The element of prudence must moderate a commander's actions lest he commit an ill-advised act that leads to a tragic conclusion. An aggressive but prudent commander not only exhibits appropriate daring and a willingness to engage the enemy, an offensive spirit that expresses great vitality, energy, and swiftness of decision and action, but also practices prudence, such as intelligence gathering prior to committing to action. In premodern warfare, the commander who understood the nature of the enemy, gathered a realistic assessment of the spatial battlefield, processed the information quickly, and issued appropriate orders enjoyed a distinct advantage. Prudence implies both caution and the acquisition of battlefield knowledge as well as information on the state of the enemy forces prior to committing to combat, thus serving as a necessary moderator of uncontrolled aggressiveness.

The contrast between Cornwallis in the field and Clinton in his New York headquarters starkly illustrates the hazards risk taking and audacity pose in terms of a coherent and ultimately successful strategy. Cornwallis advocated a highly aggressive strategy of annihilation, meaning the use of offensive military actions to destroy the opponent's ability to continue the fight, and chose to pursue and engage Continental forces whenever and wherever possible. Clinton, on the other hand, after the debacle of the 1777 Hudson Valley Campaign, advocated a different pathway—that of a strategic defensive characterized by an "enclave strategy," whereby Crown forces would hold key ports and outposts, such as Charleston, New York, and later the Chesapeake Bay, while confronting the emergent French and later Spanish threat to British imperial interests. The contrasting strategic concepts of the principal commanders—one offensively oriented and highly aggressive, the other more defensive and cautious—established the basis for a profound lack of coherence in British operations.

Martial superiority includes tactical acumen, operational artistry, strategic vision, battlefield management, and intuition. Tactics are the art of fighting once the enemy is engaged in combat and govern the actions of all manners of units, from individual squads to army groups. Operational art is the employment of forces to attain strategic objectives through the design, organization, integration, and conduct of campaigns. Military strategy represents the disposition of forces, direction of operations, and organization of assets to establish the conditions for achieving the policy objectives of the state or political entity (for example, a revolutionary movement). While tactical acumen, battlefield management, and intuition are critical in determining the outcome of combat once initiated at the field level, without a high degree of all elements of martial superiority, a commander has little hope of ultimate success.

Tactical acumen encompasses numerous qualities, the most important of which is the capability to employ one's forces in a manner that destroys the enemy's ability to wage war. Methods include deception, movement, and pursuit.

The ancient Chinese military philosopher General Sun Tzu advocated that "all warfare is based on deception."[8] A successful commander will feign weakness and disorder, disguise his movements, and entice the enemy to act imprudently. Once the deception is accomplished, he swiftly attacks at an unexpected weak point and, if tactical surprise is achieved, overwhelms the stunned opponent. Bevin Alexander, a prominent military-leadership analyst, advocates the tactical principle of "convergent assault," whereby the successful commander divides his force into two or more bodies and attacks the enemy simultaneously while maintaining close coordination and control. Often one force will hold the enemy in place and distract its attention while the second, through speed, mobility, and maneuver, surprises and overwhelms the adversary. Almost all victorious generals in the late eighteenth century achieved their results by successful movements against an enemy's flanks or rear. At the point of attack, they concentrated their forces against the most vulnerable and important position while employing deceptions to surprise, mislead, and confuse the enemy. The key to this principle is to avoid a headlong charge against an organized and strong defensive position. Once the enemy is beaten, the failure to follow up with a vigorous pursuit often allows the battered adversary to reform and reengage later, making pursuit another essential element of tactical acumen. Alexander provides a useful summation: (1) approach on a line of least resistance, (2) maneuver in the enemy's rear, (3) occupy the central position, (4) employ a "plan with branches," and (5) deliver convergent blows.[9]

A successful commander must be able to overcome the spatial and temporal dimensions of war. This and the ability to overcome the negative aspects of terrain, weather, and geography are inherent characteristics of strategic vision. Clausewitz refers to the ability to grasp the overall situation instantly as a mark of military genius. Referring to this intuition as "*coup d'oeil*" (roughly translated as "flash of the eye"), the highly successful commander overcomes spatial and temporal dynamics by using them to his advantage, while the lesser officer is hampered by geography and conditions.[10] While Cornwallis demonstrated a keen tactical acumen and battlefield-management ability, consistently winning engagements according to the concepts of victory in that era, when compared to his chief opponent, Nathanael Greene, the earl came up short in his strategic vision, particularly in terms of overcoming spatial and temporal domains. Greene, on the other hand, while not as tactically adept as his opponent, nonetheless showed a profound sense of strategic vision in terms of the spatial and temporal battlefields of the colonial South.

In the premodern age the distinction between operational artistry and strategic vision is not sharply defined. Even Clausewitz blurs this distinction; what he typically terms "strategy" is usually defined as the operational level of war in modern analysis. As Basil H. Liddell Hart points out, the term "strategy" only appeared in military literature in the early eighteenth century.[11] A limited ability to conduct war much beyond the visual limits of the immediate battlefield coupled with a tendency of an ultimate political and strategic authority (for example, Frederick the Great) to command physically in the field essentially limited broad strategic planning before this time. Yet as Martin van Creveld argues, the strategic level of war has always existed, whether or not recognized as such. Once a war commenced, a commander charged with conducting operations in a specific geographic area had to make strategic decisions such as going on the offensive or the defensive or whether to conduct a strategy of annihilation or a strategy of attrition, often through small actions and harassment. In this regard strategic vision, like leadership effectiveness itself, is universal and enduring. It is thus "eternal and has changed hardly at all from the Stone Age to our time."[12] Accordingly, the strategic vision of the major field commanders of the Southern Campaign—Greene, Clinton, and Cornwallis—will form a major analytical element of this study. Therefore, operational artistry and strategic vision are examined simultaneously and as symbiotically related within the broader context of martial superiority. This perspective essentially analyzes the ability to manage the many branches of a complex campaign while discerning, if not completely articulating, some sense of strategic coherence in support of national policy objectives.

A central ingredient in the ability to manage the battlefield is flexibility, the capacity to respond to changing dynamics or to recover from and surmount setbacks. The ability to control battlefield events at any level of conflict and to alter one's plan without an attendant loss of control is a mark of martial superiority. Given the nature of the fighting during the War of American Independence, a successful field commander had to possess broad tactical ability as well as the capacity to manage the battlefield in a variety of diverse conditions and operational situations. In addition, the ability to remain calm in the face of calamity with a personal presence and energy that inspires and steadies wavering troops or rallies panicked men are part of the battlefield-management skills of successful leaders.

Finally, there is the element of intuition. This encompasses the ability to be at the right place at the right time with a grasp of the context and realities of the situation at hand. It is not always blind luck and often is the result of a firm knowledge of events, terrain, and the nature of the enemy and one's own troops. Additionally, intuition is the ability to know the precise moment to strike or commence a tactical movement based on an understanding of the situation and an inherent sense of timing. Some amount of innate ability to know instinctively when and how to act is fundamental to effective strategic leadership; no amount of training or experience can compensate for its lack. Learned skills can partially mitigate but cannot compensate for its absence. Intuition acts as a governor for the other martial-superiority traits. Thus, the dynamics that compose strategic leadership weave their way through the narrative of events as the Southern Campaign unfolds.

A successful commander must exhibit a strong sense of strategic vision. This implies that he understands how military activity will establish the conditions whereby the political objective can be attained.[13] This concept forms a major element of this analysis of the Southern Campaign, particularly as to the strategic decision making of Clinton, Greene, and Cornwallis. The southern conflict experienced warfare on multiple levels, from conventional linear battle such as at Yorktown, Charleston, Camden, and Guilford Court House; to the use of irregular forces (essentially local militia) in conjunction with regular troops in a conventional engagement (for example, Cowpens, Guilford Court House, and Camden); to pure insurgency warfare characterized by hit-and-run raids on detachments and logistics trains. The scope of the conflict ranged from a global alliance of France and the United States versus the British Empire down to a bitter and brutal partisan-based internecine civil war often fought over local issues of political and economic power compounded by personal rivalries and vendettas. As will be seen, Patriot commanders such as Greene and his principal subordinate, Brig. Gen. Daniel Morgan, proved highly adept at molding the disparate forms of warfare into successful strategies, while the ever-conventional but tactically skilled Cornwallis suffered from a lack of this vital skill required in "hybrid" warfare. When combined with the British breakdown in command and control and logistics, a profound misreading of the nature of the conflict, and the attendant strategic incoherence, the outcome could only be strategic failure and ultimately defeat for Crown interests.

A caution is in order. As with all subjects of this nature, the concept of what composes strategic leadership is by nature subjective. Therefore, the definition of strategic leadership in this study is proposed as a framework for analysis rather than as a comprehensive definition. Readers will naturally assign their own concepts of strategic leadership based on their experiences and perceptions.

### *Theory of Victory and Desired Strategic Effects*

Brad Lee of the U.S. Naval War College has proposed a framework for analyzing a nation or political entity's thoughts and assumptions in terms of their chosen course(s) of action and how that will translate into the projected successful outcome. Termed "theory of victory," this concept essentially means that strategic assumptions, if correct, will lead to strategic success and thus the achievement of overall policy objectives. The desired strategic effects, as generated by the course(s) of action, are the ways in which they play out in the enemy's political system. These effects encompass all aspects of a society, including its economy, psychology, morale, and so forth. All directly influence political decision making. How they play out in the governments of each participant then leads to the actual events, outcomes, and decisions in war, including those by other parties (neutrals, opponents, allies, and others). In short, if one achieves the desired strategic effects and the theory of victory is valid, then the likelihood of achieving strategic success is high.

A strategic assumption and a desired strategic effect are intimately related; one flows from the other. The assumption is some expected or anticipated result from one's actions or the assumed ramifications of one's actions. The effect is the situation that causes the opponent to act in a particular manner. For example, if facing a strongly defended front, one attacks the opponent's rear. The assumption is that the opponent will rotate forces to deflect or confront the attack. The desired strategic effect, then, is that this action will cause the defender to weaken his front and allow the attacker to assault there with better success and fewer casualties. The logic can be taken to any level, such as an operational assumption or a desired tactical effect; the logic flow is the same. It can be applied to practically any human endeavor. Think of a chess match—the original game of strategy—that is nothing if not assumptions and desired effects.

Throughout the Southern Campaign, Clinton, Cornwallis, and other Crown commanders constantly made strategic assumptions that they thought would bring about the desired policy objective (that is, achieve the desired strategic effect): the restoration of the southern colonies to allegiance by pacification efforts. Throughout this study of the Southern Campaign, this framework for analysis is used to explain the ultimate British strategic assumptions and operational failures, even down to the tactical level in specific events.

In terms of the Southern Strategy of 1778–81, the overall British theory of victory can be stated as follows:

1. By conducting aggressive, offensive operations in the southern colonies—Georgia, North and South Carolina, and ultimately Virginia—vast Loyalist support in the region would materialize.
2. Loyalists would provide the logistical needs of the engaged conventional forces as well as develop additional irregular forces themselves.
3. The capture of key cities, including Savannah, Georgia, and Charleston, South Carolina, through joint army-navy amphibious operations, would establish safe operating bases from which to launch offensive actions into the interior.

4. Loyalists would then retake political control of areas lost previously to the rebels, reestablish Crown law and authority, and maintain security against any rebel resurgence.
5. Reestablishing Crown control in the South would undercut the export of key commodities, including naval stores, rice, tobacco, and indigo, the principal rebel sources of income.
6. Reestablishing Crown control in the South would also place immense pressure on the middle and New England colonies to agree to a negotiated settlement.

From this theory of victory flowed the British desired strategic effects, which in essence entailed the following:

1. As British arms advanced, Continental Army and rebel irregular forces would be defeated in detail, undercutting the colonists' military ability to continue the rebellion.
2. Resultantly, Loyalists, no longer fearful for their property and persons, would rise in great numbers and reestablish Crown authority as well as supply logistical aid and manpower to Crown forces.
3. Once the forces secured the South, both political and military pressure would be placed on the remaining colonies for a negotiated settlement.
4. Seeing the inevitability of rebel defeat, France would withdraw its naval and land forces and cease material and political support of the rebellious colonies.
5. Once a negotiated settlement was concluded, Britain could redirect those naval and military forces engaged in North America toward the global war with France, especially in the West Indies theater.[14]

## Britain's Strategic Concept

The "clear and hold" strategic concept that evolved by 1778 called for retaking each colony in turn from south to north while establishing the conditions whereby local Loyalists could restore Crown authority and civil government. In so doing, the regular British Army presence would overawe and intimidate the rebellious troublemakers into submission. But conditions and a lack of manpower overturned the British theory of victory. The colonials failed to cooperate. Though Continental Army forces consistently lost major conventional engagements, Patriot partisans and irregulars successfully continued the resistance. By engaging in hit-and-run guerilla-style warfare characterized by small-unit actions, ambushes, rapid movements and escapes, intimidation of civilians and Loyalists and so on, rebel bands prevented the implementation of such a pacification strategy.[15] Frustrated, Cornwallis eventually viewed the key to victory as the destruction of regular Continental forces, an attitude that led to two separate invasions of North Carolina, the chase of Greene's army into southern Virginia, and major engagements at Camden and Guilford Court House. In a tactical sense he won both engagements; in the overall strategic sense, however, he suffered devastating losses, especially at Guilford Court House, where he ultimately lost the strategic initiative to Greene. Finally, with the backing of Lord Germain and in direct opposition to Clinton's strategic desires, Cornwallis advanced into Virginia, an act that precipitated the collapse of Crown efforts to restore allegiance. The British theory of victory proved a thin reed. The framework upon which it rested—the Southern Strategy—proved unreliable and flawed.

This study explores the operational events of the Southern Campaign of 1778–81 through the lens of these fundamental concepts—strategic coherence, strategic leadership, and theory of victory and desired strategic effects—to address the question of how the Crown's cause came to such ruin and failed to achieve its political objective. Through the chronological narrative, characteristics and traits such as boldness, risk taking, aggressiveness, martial superiority (tactical acumen, operational artistry, strategic vision, battlefield management, and intuition), and so on will be highlighted to build portraits of the individual central players. This analysis will go a long way toward explaining why particular officers failed or succeeded. Through the narrative and analysis of the central events and strategic decision points, a definitive pattern develops. Essentially, plagued by strategic incoherence; a profound misunderstanding of the nature of the war in the southern colonies; the failure of logistics and an attendant breakdown in command and control, particularly unity of command and effort; and undone by a singular failure of strategic leadership saddled with a flawed theory of victory, the British campaign to win back the southern colonies ultimately lay beyond a realistic hope for success.

This is not to say that strategic success was unattainable. Many elements of the Southern Strategy were indeed sound, hence the argument that at least in theory, the strategy was rational and might have worked had the operational execution been flawless and the theory of victory assumptions proven accurate. Success relied upon an almost perfect campaign, with little "friction" and a great abundance of simple good fortune. A longstanding perception is the charge of military and political incompetency on the part of the primary players, most notably Lord Germain, General Clinton, General Cornwallis, Lord North, Lord Sandwich, and King George III himself. Andrew Jackson O'Shaughnessy has fundamentally challenged that view; this historian agrees with his assertion.[16]

These were professional soldiers and statesmen who had risen to the pinnacle of military and political power because they possessed or displayed certain critical traits, characteristics, and behaviors needed in their time. But they were human, and they exhibited the normal human flaws of misperception, arrogance, jealousy, mistrust, stubbornness, lack of imagination, fear of the unknown, excessive caution or boldness, and others. Perhaps they were not the right minister or general for the moment and in a different environment would have flourished (as Cornwallis eventually did in India and Ireland). Perhaps they suffered from the bad fortune to face some extraordinarily adept and talented opponents.[17] Were they that incompetent, or were they saddled with an intractable and almost impossible mission? Were the geographic, spatial, and temporal dynamics and environment simply beyond their knowledge, education, training, and experience? The reader can reach his or her own conclusions.

It is equally important to remember that the American rebellion at its heart and soul represented a conservative reaction, not a radical rearranging of society such as the later French or Russian Revolutions. When men such as George Washington, Benjamin Franklin, Thomas Jefferson, George Mason, and John Adams spoke of the "rights of free Englishmen," they meant exactly that—the rights of a free society of independent citizens charged with determining its own destiny as opposed to the centralization of political, military, and economic power inherent in an autocratic monarchy. These rights had been won, with much blood and treasure expended, in the previous century with the long struggle of the British Civil Wars and the eventual establishment of parliamentary sovereignty by 1689. These men sought not to overturn the social order; rather, they struggled to be the masters of their own destinies. Might the rebellion of 1775–83 be called the "American Evolution" as opposed to "Revolution"? Might one look at the events and outcome more as the gradual flowering of the constitutional, political, social, and economic ideas that had evolved in Europe (primarily Britain and France) during the Enlightenment? Traditionally, this process of evolution has been called the "Whiggish" theory of history, which argues for the inevitable progress of Western democracy in a republican mold, with ultimate sovereignty held by the citizens as expressed through the elected assembly and executive.

Why is this dynamic important for the study of the Southern Campaign? It is a critical element in that many of the key players were of the Whig political faction, which included not only the upper aristocracy but also the growing commercial, mercantile, and industrial middle class. More importantly, Cornwallis and the Howe brothers, Lord Richard and Sir William, were political Whigs. Indeed, many of the senior British officers sympathized with the colonial complaints and concerns. But when the rebels challenged Parliament's authority by force of arms, these men clearly saw their duty to suppress the rebellion with the least amount of cost in blood and treasure. This attitude rippled all through Cornwallis's actions particularly. He saw the need to squash the rebels' ability to wage war and to, as it were, bring them to their senses. From this orientation came his guiding strategic thinking, which, simply put, meant victory through aggressive offensive actions against formed military bodies: destroy the rebel ability to make war and the restoration of peace, civil authority, and royal authority would follow through the "clear and hold" strategy. As will be seen, such a strategy required the utmost in war without fog, friction, and the usual chaos of conflict, a state that Clausewitz might have viewed as an ideal type never achievable in reality.

Complicating Cornwallis's strategy of annihilation was the conundrum of how overly aggressive actions and counterinsurgency tactics might affect public opinion. Many neutrals, as is always the case in an internecine war, wanted simply to be left alone to live unmolested lives, raise their families, and conduct their business. In a moment of strategic clarity, Clinton acknowledged the need for careful measures, proclaiming in February 1776 that Britain must "gain the hearts and subdue the minds of America." He again expressed this sentiment to Germain in June 1781, stating that if "we have not their hearts . . . which I fear cannot be expected in Virginia . . . [then we] may conquer [but] we shall never keep."[18] Yet as the senior officer and a co-commissioner with Arbuthnot for restoring peace in Charleston in late May and early June 1780 prior to his departure for New York, the general issued a series of inflammatory loyalty proclamations bound to cause recently paroled Continental prisoners of war to leap back into the rebellion and to turn otherwise neutral parties toward sympathy with the Patriot cause. As will be seen, the proclamations of May–June 1780 roiled the southern countryside and created a dynamic that Cornwallis and his senior commanders could never overcome. The debacle caused by Clinton's proclamations illustrate one of many breakdowns in the British strategic-leadership triad, particularly unity of command and effort. It also illustrates starkly the profound misunderstanding of the nature of the southern struggle. Thus, as Clinton returned to New York with a great military victory in hand, he left Cornwallis with an almost herculean task, an inadequate force, and an increasingly uncooperative if not outright hostile populace.

A final word on terminology will assist the reader as they examine the strategies of both sides. An annihilation strategy implies the complete destruction of the opponent's military capabilities; in other words, he is no longer able to maintain the fight through force of arms. A good example of this is during World War II in the European theater of operations, where the overarching Allied strategy was to so destroy Germany's military capability such that there could be no continued resistance and thus leading to unconditional surrender. Note that an annihilation strategy does not mean killing the opponent's entire manpower;

rather, it means destroying the enemy's military capability to continue the fight. An attrition strategy, on the other hand, seeks to degrade the opponent's military to the point that the adversary can no longer win. Implied here is the loss of will to continue the struggle on the part of the attrited force. An exhaustion strategy is closely related to this and has many attrition elements, however its essential objective is to attack the will of the opponent's forces, population, or political authority to the point that the value of the object—the overarching war aim—exceeds the costs. In Clausewitzian terms, such a strategy seeks to disrupt that linkage between the people, the government, and the military to the point that pressure is put on the authorities to end the war through withdrawal or negotiation. Such was the case following the Yorktown surrender, when Lord North's Tory government fell due to public pressure, bringing in Lord Rockingham's Whig ministry, which initiated negotiations with the French, Spanish, and Dutch governments as well as the Continental Congress.

In the Southern Campaign one sees elements of all three types of strategies. Clearly, Cornwallis sought an annihilation strategy. In his destruction of Gates's force at Camden and his dogged pursuit of Greene that led to the "Race to the Dan" and the Battle of Guilford Court House, he strove to destroy the military capability and means to fight of all Patriot forces in the South, particularly regulars. On the other hand, Greene employed an attrition strategy to wear down the earl's forces characteristic of a classic Fabian strategy, which depends on a culminating final conventional event to convince the opponent that the cost of continued fighting exceeds the benefit—the value of the object determination. In this manner Greene also carried out an exhaustion strategy that eventually diminished the British will to continue the war, particularly in light of the dangerous global war once France, Spain, and the Dutch entered the fray. Thus, throughout the Southern Campaign, one sees elements of annihilation, attrition, and exhaustion strategies at play.

This study's mission is to present the drama of the Southern Campaign from the British and Loyalist perspective, with all of the decisions and actions, attendant frustrations and perceptions (and, most importantly, misperceptions), from the brilliant operational achievements of Savannah, Camden, and Charleston; through the South Carolina upcountry hills and Low Country wetlands struggles; across the North Carolina hinterland; and finally to ultimate collapse at a little port along Tidewater Virginia's York River. It is a story replete with all the cruelty, barbarity, passion, sacrifice, dedication, zealousness, and nobility that characterize all human military conflicts. It is also a cautionary tale of how not to craft strategy and operations and how a credible understanding of the nature of the conflict in which one is engaged must trump all other strategic considerations.

CHAPTER 1

# "Without Which the Machine Must Fail"

## *British Command and Control and the Southern Strategy*

To understand the context within which each member of the British strategic triad operated, one must comprehend the constitutional limitations and duties inherent in the military and naval system of the late eighteenth century. The period represented a transition from the medieval system of "household" troops, founded on personal obligation to a superior, to the Industrial Age mass-citizen armies based on concepts of nationalism, patriotism, and universal military service. Late-eighteenth-century British forces relied on long-service professional soldiers with long-term enlistments. Many found permanent employment in the armed forces, and thus a cadre of highly skilled, very professional, and competent officers, noncommissioned officers, and other ranks served their careers in the British Army and Royal Navy. As such, maintaining a large force structure entailed a significant and continuing financial investment. Additionally, monarchs were loath to suffer significant casualties that required replacement through expensive recruitment efforts. In wartime, monarchs typically hired foreign troops to fill the need of additional combat units. Ireland and the German states proved to be fertile ground for hired troops, who were generally of a high quality. In Britain, professional soldiers were typically despised by the public, reflecting a civic opposition to a standing army. Five decades of civil war had roiled England, Scotland, and Ireland, culminating in the 1689 settlement that ensured the supremacy of Parliament, particularly in military matters. Standing forces might allow an overarching monarchy the wherewithal to reestablish an absolutist system, which was not acceptable to the British nobility and gentry.[1] As an outgrowth of this contextual dynamic, continuous pleadings for reinforcements by North American commanders came to naught—Britain simply did not have the military manpower. For General Cornwallis, as casualties and attrition ground down his forces, this limitation became especially critical. It greatly influenced his decision to abandon North Carolina after Guilford Court House and march into Virginia.

Efforts to stimulate recruitment created serious problems, both in resources and in domestic politics. Heavy recruitment of Irish Catholics caused turmoil in Scotland and England and contributed to the Gordon Riots in London during the summer of 1780 as anti-Catholicism ran high. Authorities debated arming irregular groups as the threat of Bourbon (combined French and Spanish) invasion or interference in Ireland rose after 1778. The Recruiting Act of 1779 allowed men to enlist for a more limited term as opposed to the traditionally long service obligation. These measures illustrate the desperate manpower imperative, especially as the war widened into a global struggle. The effect on Cornwallis and the resource constraints on the Southern Campaign cannot be ignored as a fundamental factor.

Much of the recruitment difficulty came also from opposition to the war itself. Many in the political nation viewed the struggle as an effort by the Crown and the parliamentary majority led by Frederick, Lord North to deny freeborn colonial Britons their inalienable rights under the constitution and traditional common law.[2] While not actively supporting rebellion, many at least sympathized with the cause, a barrier to increased recruitment. Additionally, many men stood ready to enlist in various local volunteer corps to oppose the French and Spanish rather than the regular army, which might be used to subdue the rebellious colonists. The key difference lay in the extent of governmental control. Volunteer formations had little official oversight and thus could not be deployed to North America. The political opposition shared this attitude and, while ready, able, and willing to support the broader global war, resisted the effort against the Americans. Typical of this attitude, particularly among the opposition Whigs, is the statement of Member of Parliament Sir Charles Banbury in the debate over the 1779 bill: "the principle of the Bill . . . was confessedly calculated to recruit our armies for the purpose of carrying on a ruinous, offensive war in America; a war which . . . ought for every reason to be abandoned."[3]

Recruitment difficulties had a direct influence on the Southern Campaign's conduct. Limits on reinforcements from Britain also stimulated the concept that underwrote the Loyalist strategy. Manpower shortages caused British authorities to rely heavily on both German contract troops and Loyalists willing to enlist in the Provincial regiments. Paul H. Smith has calculated that upward of 10,000 Loyalists took up the "king's shilling" in various Provincial military units during the period prior to the Southern Campaign and that a further 9,000 did so by the final end of hostilities.[4]

## "A Very Unstable Base": British Military Administration

The complex system of military administration, operating without a central organizing authority, proved disastrous for the British war effort in America. The modern departmental and cabinet governmental system had not yet fully developed its definitive roles and responsibilities. It should be noted that many officeholders serving the monarchy, cabinet, and the various departments of the state were highly skilled and very professional. There were also long-service professionals and administrators at all levels of government. But the modern civil-service system had not developed; personality drove the government more than other dynamics. In terms of war administration and management, the cabinet, made up of the king's principal ministers, established the national policy, however, it also influenced strategic and operational matters, including what operations or expeditions to conduct, their time frames, and assorted troop allocations. The various secretaries of state (Lord George Germain was secretary of state for the Americas, commonly referred to as the American secretary) actually executed the plans by issuing orders to the Treasury, Admiralty, Ordnance (artillery), and the officer serving as commander in chief (CinC) of the Army. Although these bureaucracies had responsibility for logistics, transportation, manpower, and unit movements, they had little responsibility for operational planning or execution. The monarch, as captain general, served as titular head of the army, but in reality he might delegate a CinC, who commanded the home forces (but not those overseas) and oversaw army administration. No CinC served during the early stages of the war until 1778, with the appointment of Jeffrey, Lord Amherst. A secretary at war, who did not sit in the cabinet but did hold a parliamentary seat, assisted the CinC in matters of military administration, particularly general resources and finance. Yet the secretary at war had dubious authority and an ill-defined mission. Nonetheless, he might exercise great influence depending on his personality and that of the CinC. During the Southern Campaign, Charles Jenkinson held the post and proved to be a competent, engaged, but constantly frustrated administrator.

Actual operational control of the forces came under the cabinet and the secretaries of state. Herein lies the first great determinant to British strategic incoherence. Given the limitations of the evolving governmental system in the eighteenth century, still largely personality driven and only taking on the modern form in the following century, managing a war on the operational as well as strategic level from 3,000 miles' distance proved difficult. A major complicating factor lay in that the American War evolved into an irregular and unconventional struggle ultimately beyond existing British military capabilities. To further compound the difficulties, the CinC had no significant input into strategic or operational determinations in America. Again, though a member of the cabinet and thus a player in determining strategy and operations, Amherst had no direct command role over forces in the colonies. Once the cabinet made strategic and operational decisions as transmitted through the appropriate secretary of state, orders and instructions flowed directly to the field commanders.

The Royal Navy's system differed vastly from the army's. Rather than officials with ill-defined or dubious roles, the Lords Commissioners of the Admiralty, a mix of political appointees and professional naval officers who sat on the Board of Admiralty, controlled all naval functions and decision making. The navy had evolved earlier into a modern institution; the Admiralty structure for command and control dated from the mid-seventeenth century. Led by the first lord of the Admiralty, John Montagu, Earl of Sandwich, with operational command exercised by the senior admiral as first sea lord, the board exercised direct operational and administrative control; the subordinate Navy Board oversaw shipbuilding, supply, and transport. Although the general outline of operations was determined by the cabinet through orders from the secretary of state to the Board of Admiralty, unlike the army, the navy governed its own specific operations. Given this tight institutional control over ships and movements, cooperation with the military proved problematic. For example, the navy typically would hold ships in port for weeks or months, their cargos spoiling, to await sufficient convoy escorts. Since the Royal Navy had deteriorated from its strength in the Seven Years' War to a dangerously low preparedness level by 1775, the Navy Board only reluctantly released vessels from European, Channel, and Mediterranean duties for North American escort operations.[5] Given the relative position of the Admiralty in determining employment of naval assets, there was little that the CinC, secretary at war, or even the secretary of state could do to force the issue. With the rise of the French threat by 1778, it became even more difficult to obtain convoy escorts to America. Clinton in New York summed up the difficulty in supplying his forces and in working with the Royal Navy to William Eden, one of the Carlisle peace commissioners of 1778: "I have no money, no provisions, nor indeed any account of the sailing of the Cork fleet, nor [an] admiral that I can have the least dependence on. In short, I have nothing left but the hope for better times and a little more attention!"[6]

Given that Cornwallis operated deep in the hinterland from late summer 1780 to mid-spring 1781 before eventually arriving at Wilmington, North Carolina, the time delay of supplies from British docks to Charleston, South Carolina, followed by inland transportation under the constant threat of rebel attack, proved debilitating. By operating independently of his waterborne supply line,

Cornwallis compounded an already difficult operational reality. Once he arrived in Tidewater Virginia, logistics improved until the French blockaded Chesapeake Bay and made starvation at Yorktown a key element in his decision to surrender. Cornwallis only fully appreciated the connection between seapower, maritime resupply, and the ability to operate inland much too late in the campaign. Further complicating the problem, given the difficulty in providing logistical support across the Atlantic, British forces in theater relied on local foraging for food and fodder. For Cornwallis, deep into the hinterland and cut off from seaborne supply through Charleston, foraging made his forces subject to ambush and interdiction by partisans and Patriot irregulars. The prominent logistics historian Arthur Bowler nicely summarizes this troublesome connection between the need to forage, the danger of irregular attack, and ultimately the relationship to the local population's loyalties; he also underscores the British misunderstanding of the nature of the war: "To obtain supplies it needed, the British army was forced throughout the war to engage in extensive forage operations. This allowed the often untrained rebel forces to fight the kind of battles for which they were best suited, and the brutality of these operations drove more and more Americans to the rebel side."[7]

A study by the U.S. Army Command and General Staff College captures the essence of the British logistical problem in America caused by distance and organization:

> The organization of the British administrative system was complex and initially ill suited for sustaining a war so far from England. The decentralized, civilian-led bureaucracy that effectively maintained far-flung colonies during times of relative peace was not prepared to support its army in a hostile environment. The lack of integration between the warfighting strategy and logistical design ensured that the army would suffer from a lack of provisions and supplies. Interagency cooperation was nonexistent . . . , which compounded the inefficient use of transportation and other valuable resources. Corruption and profiteering simply made matters worse. These inadequacies formed a very unstable base for the entire logistics framework that extended from London and Cork to British garrisons in the colonies.[8]

Illustrative of the desperate supply situation is the commentary of Captain Robert Rotton in a letter to Lord Amherst: "Our army moulders away amazingly: many die by the sword, many by sickness, brought on by bad provisions. . . . I wish [the] government would look after the contractors, for without we are supplied with wholesome necessaries of life, it cannot be expected we will long fight their battles."[9]

## Powering the War Machine

Given the cabinet and the war-making nature of British government in the late eighteenth century, the key to the effectiveness and efficiency of any military undertaking lay in the talent of the incumbent secretary of state. Historian Piers Mackesy's succinct description captures the essence of the role: "It was they who powered the war machine. They provided at once a Cabinet Secretariat and executive supervision. By their hands, the complex of supply and transport, military movement and naval preparation was drawn together and given life."[10] Unfortunately for Cornwallis as he slogged through the swamps and dense forests of the Carolinas in pursuit of an elusive enemy, Lord George Germain, the secretary of state for the colonies and the official charged with the suppression of the rebellion, lacked the extraordinary capabilities required to achieve victory in an irregular, unconventional, and distant colonial war. Though noted for his administrative ability but not well liked, Germain lacked political support in Parliament, which might have overcome some obstacles. He often refused to cooperate, compromise, or accept expert advice. The secretary felt that he had no role in operational planning or even military strategy and thus typically left such things to the field commanders. Germain saw his role as limited to that of the appointment of commanders, allocation of resources, and organization of movement and supply. Yet he often suggested strategic and operational directions to field commanders, a habit that lacked the precision of definitive orders, further confusing and muddling strategic coherence. In March 1778 he instructed Clinton, "use your own discretion in planning as well as executing all operations which shall appear the most likely means of crushing the rebellion."[11] A proper civil-military relationship requires that the political authority set the overall policy objectives; the military authority then determines strategy as ultimately approved by the civil leadership. Germain, though, having given such instructions to the CinC in North America, typically used hint, innuendo, and references to the king's opinion to inject his strategic and operational wishes, especially as the Southern Campaign unfolded. Clinton felt pressured to conduct operations that he felt neither necessary nor the best use of limited resources. Frustrated with Clinton, the secretary corresponded directly with Cornwallis in the field, further undermining the chain of command. Inevitably, strategic drift resulted, characterized by confused operations and incongruent strategic decisions.

To overcome this lack of direction from London, both Generals Howe and Burgoyne suggested the appointment of a "viceroy" to coordinate operations and military strategy. A common sentiment in London as the rebellion dragged on advocated "One Great Director"—a war leader like William Pitt in the previous conflict—who could direct the machinery of British military administration, strategy, and operations. Though Germain's role was to oversee the war effort, he failed to pull all entities together for the common purpose. Mackesy says of Germain: "For all his talents, he lacked the magic gift of . . . the power to frighten and inspire."[12] Moreover, he suffered from an intense sense of overoptimism. Germain's unrealistic expectations led to his undermanning forces in America while demanding results totally unachievable given the war's nature, context, and geography. This attitude created friction with the field commanders. Clinton constantly complained of the secretary's lack of support for troop needs coupled with his unachievable expectations. While the concepts for destroying the rebellion and returning the colonies to their allegiance in terms of aggressive, offensive operations had worked well in eventually destroying the domestic Jacobite rebellions of the late seventeenth and early eighteenth centuries, Germain never made the connection that the North American colonies were characterized by an entirely different nature and context, thus demanding different strategic thinking, not a heavy-handed police action.[13] George III viewed the war through a similar prism. Therefore, commanders in the field were expected to suppress the rebellion through conventional, offensive military operations aimed at eliminating the ringleaders and the rebel means of resistance—the Continental Army and associated Patriot militia. The king's attitude and that of his American secretary left little room for strategic flexibility and subtlety.

If Clinton found the secretary frustrating and interfering, Germain heartily disapproved of the army commander. The secretary once commented to his assistant, William Knox, that he viewed Clinton as sluggish, needing to be forced to take action, and never aggressive enough in executing an approved plan even in the most favorable of conditions. To compound the problem, Germain decidedly preferred the subordinate field commander, Cornwallis. Consequently, he exchanged numerous secretive reports and letters ("backchannel communications" in modern parlance) with the earl. While Cornwallis often "back briefed" his superior on key issues raised in his sidebar communications with the secretary, the loss of the chain-of-command accountability element undercut Clinton's efforts to manage the war's strategic and operational direction. Therefore, what emerged was a breakdown in the essential command, control, and communications aspect of the war's prosecution in the South, a poisonous recipe for a devastating loss of strategic coherence, as well as unity of command and effort.[14]

Germain's most serious problem lay in his poor relations with the first lord of the Admiralty and the Royal Navy.[15] When the nature of the conflict demanded cooperative, joint army-navy operations and strategic planning, an adversarial relationship dominated. Knox strongly advised him to take more positive control of the naval situation. On the first lord and the inefficiency of the Admiralty Board, Knox commented, "to the insufficiency of their Instructions, when no directions are given them, much of our delays and disappointments are owing and if your Lordship does not determine to give the orders yourself instead of leaving it to Lord Sandwich . . . things will never be better."[16] Perhaps inhibited by his chilly relations with Admiralty, Germain did not press field commanders on details of joint operations until after the war began to go badly in 1778. By this time, the profoundly weakened North government lacked the power to make substantial changes in the status quo and force closer army-navy cooperation.

Complicating the problems of an adversarial, uncooperative joint relationship in the colonies, the less-than-adequate strategic-leadership performance of Vice Admiral Arbuthnot, Royal Navy commander in North America, deserves mention. A prominent twentieth-century historian and Clinton biographer has described the admiral as "vacillating, irascible, and timid; his strategic sense was usually meager, and his tactical ideas, to judge by his one engagement, were in the worst tradition of the period."[17] This is not a high recommendation for the man charged with planning and executing the maritime component of the Southern Strategy. A successful restoration of allegiance in the South relied on a thorough command of the sea—as Rear Adm. Alfred Thayer Mahan would later advocate—or at least local control in support of forces ashore—as British naval and maritime theorist and historian Sir Julian Stafford Corbett has argued.[18] Mahan, in his highly influential work *The Influence of Sea Power upon History* (1890), captures the essence of Britain's rise to imperial and commercial domination through the effective use of maritime power. Essentially, Mahan argues that the fundamental imperative for a great maritime power is to win command of the sea through decisive battle fought between great battle fleets. His work chronicles Britain's rise through this dynamic. Corbett, however, argues that the role of naval power entails winning control of the sea in the specific operational area to support military operations ashore. The Corbettian model might be characterized as winning local sea control as opposed to Mahan's more grandiose concentrate and destroy the enemy's naval power through decisive battle. Arguments have raged for decades over which approach is more applicable to modern navies. The Southern Campaign exhibited elements of both theories of the proper role of naval and maritime power. A dominant Royal Navy allowed for supply and reinforcement of British forces ashore despite the discomfort of the occasional attacks by Continental or French warships and privateers. Equally valuable, the Royal Navy provided expeditionary operational support for troop transport and logistics, which gave British army commanders the ability to strike at almost any point along the Atlantic and Gulf of Mexico seaboard. But a caution is in order. There is great truth in the old aphorism, "he who lives by the sword, dies by the sword." The failure of the Royal Navy to defeat a French squadron off the Virginia Capes in September 1781 prevented either the reinforcement or evacuation of Lord Cornwallis's besieged force at Yorktown. The event nicely illustrates Corbett's concept of naval domination in support of the land battle.

Clinton feuded with Arbuthnot over operational coordination and imperatives for well over a year following the Charleston operation before the Admiralty acceded to his demands to replace the admiral. In an example of this breakdown in unity of command and effort, in late 1780 Arbuthnot proposed sending Rear Admiral Thomas Graves to the West Indies with six ships of the line. Clinton realized that with the French navy engaged in active operations in the Americas, to dilute Crown naval concentration courted disaster, especially with Cornwallis then in South Carolina preparing to invade North Carolina. He wrote to Arbuthnot that the loss of sea superiority would allow the French to land troops in the South, a situation leaving him without the "power to render Lord Cornwallis my assistance against them," precisely the Yorktown conundrum nine months later.[19] The admiral backed down, but the lack of strategic coherence and unity of effort in this and other instances undercut the campaign's desired strategic effects at a time when Clinton's success at Charleston and Cornwallis's victories at Camden, South Carolina, in August 1780 and (to a lesser extent) at Guilford Court House, North Carolina, in March 1781 might have rescued a rapidly deteriorating strategic situation. Illustrative of the poisoned relations between the two commanders, Clinton referred to Arbuthnot as "an Old Dotard."[20]

A major British strategic problem revolved around the lack of definitive lines of authority. Germain frequently bypassed the chain of command by corresponding with subordinate commanders while ignoring recommendations from his commanding generals. Throughout the Southern Campaign, he carried on such conversations with Cornwallis, undercutting the operational chain of command and roiling command relationships between headquarters and the field. Typically, no specific direction emanated from London, and local commanders determined strategy and operational plans. Periodically, the cabinet would make its desires known, which influenced strategic decisions, but neither Lord North as chief minister nor the king engaged in any meaningful strategic-coordinator role. In short, with no real central controlling entity or agency, British strategic decision making became chaotic, uncoordinated, often unrealistic, incoherent, and subject to individual preferences—in a word, random. Added to this stew of troubles, parliamentary opposition led by Charles James Fox and the earl of Shelburne maintained a vibrant and loud criticism of the North ministry's war management. They argued that the Bourbon monarchies would take advantage of Britain's focus on suppressing the rebellion through military offensives, which tied up so much of Britain's resources worldwide.[21]

From a strategic-cohesion viewpoint, British decision making suffered from a secretary at war with ill-defined responsibilities, a CinC with no command authority beyond the British Isles, a secretary of state charged with executing strategic direction but who did not believe in that role and who could not operate in the joint arena, and an Admiralty reluctant to cooperate with cabinet and army officials. The constitutional arrangements for military and strategic matters from the political authority to operational field commanders consistently hobbled efforts to achieve victory. B. D. Bargar, Lord Dartmouth's biographer, addresses the inefficiency and ineffectiveness of the American Department even before Lord Germain arrived: "The American Department continually suffered from certain constitutional defects and personality conflicts which prevented it from becoming a strong, permanent branch of the government. Until colonial policy could be concentrated in a modern Colonial Office, decisions which affected America were often taken in other offices or in cabinet meetings where Dartmouth was only one of five or seven ministers."[22]

As to the overall inadequacy of the cabinet in prosecuting the war, O'Shaughnessy nicely summarizes the problem: "The consequence of North's leadership was a divided Cabinet that postponed decisions and often left military goals nebulous. In what he called government by departments, North was surrounded by strong personalities in the Cabinet who feuded with one another and pursued conflicting initiatives."[23]

Ultimately, the corrosive effect of Germain's strategic mismanagement complicated field operations. Alan Valentine captures the consequences of the secretary's actions: "Thus as the year 1780 drew to an end, Lord George Germain had reduced his last commanding general in America to something like psychotic and military impotence. He had also aroused and stimulated enmity between Clinton and Cornwallis, and had encouraged Cornwallis to feel almost independent of his military commander. . . . If mutual trust and good will between statesmen and generals are essential to victory, Lord George had chosen a curious way to win a war."[24]

John Robinson, the secretary to the lords of the Treasury in 1777, described the essence of the lack of a dominant and talented war leader and the inefficiencies of the chaotic cabinet, stating, "War can't be carried out in departments: there must be a consultation, union, and a friendly and hearty concurrence in all the several parts, which set the springs at work and give efficacy and energy to the movements, without which the machine must fail."[25]

## The Indian and Slave Alliances: A Failed Effort

An Indian alliance represented another potential tool for suppressing the rebellion. British authorities keyed on this dynamic early in the war, with the idea of using Indian warriors as auxiliaries to regular forces, primarily as scouts. Agitated by settlers coming over the mountains and encroaching on traditional lands, the various tribes saw Britain as the defender of their interests and thus represented a potentially potent strategic ally. But Indian attacks and actions in support of British arms were bound to roil the colonists, especially along the frontier. In the South, Crown efforts to employ the tribes in a military alliance failed, nevertheless it is useful to examine briefly their strategic potential.

Formed in 1754 to manage colonial relations with the Indians, particularly land acquisition and trade along the frontier, the Indian Department factored into British thinking from the rebellion's beginnings. Divided into two districts, Northern and Southern, appointed superintendents derived their funding from the North American military commander. Ultimately, Parliament approved these disbursements, which often proved to be hit-or-miss propositions. Twenty tribes came under the sway of the Southern District, including the Choctaw, Cherokee, Creek, Chickasaw, and Catawba. These five along with the many smaller tribes could put 13,000 warriors into the field. With such an asset, British authorities had a significant potential, if controversial, irregular force.

William Legge, Earl of Dartmouth, secretary of state for the colonies in 1775, sent orders to field commanders and department agents initiating the plan to employ Indians as auxiliaries to the regular forces. The original concept conceived of using a limited number in scouting and reconnaissance roles. As the war progressed and moved south and west, the ugliness and cruelty of a traditional Indian war came to full fruition. For example, the department agent in Detroit, Henry Hamilton, became known as the "Hair-Buyer General" due to his policy of bounty payment for Patriot scalps. From the outset of the rebellion, the strategy of suppression by brute, military force envisioned using Indians as part of the force mix. General Thomas Gage advised Dartmouth in June 1775 that he required a 32,000-man force to suppress the revolt, and that force included Indians.

Dartmouth only approved the strategy once he learned that Indians were used in support of the Continental Army. Writing to Gage, he stated, "The steps which you say the rebels have taken for calling in the assistance of Indians, leave no room to hesitate upon the propriety of your pursuing the same measure."[26] Upon the earl's resignation in November 1775, Lord Germain became the American secretary. While Dartmouth had been reticent about using Indians in roles other than scouting and reconnaissance, his successor had no qualms, sending orders to Major General Sir Guy Carleton, commanding in Canada, to employ warriors in military operations. Carleton objected and issued orders to the agents setting geographic boundaries beyond which Indians could not operate.[27]

Relations between the tribes and colonists stood at low ebb by the 1770s primarily due to treaty violations and the inevitable encroachment of settlers into what became the Northwest Territory. The royal proclamation of 7 October 1763 reserved territory acquired from France for the tribes by way of the 1763 Treaty of Paris and excluded settlers from almost all lands north and west of the Appalachian and Allegheny Mountains. The proclamation established a hard boundary between the frontier and tribal lands that further infuriated the colonists while it tied the tribes to the British government for continued enforcement. When the rebellion broke out, tribal leaders had a hard choice—support the Crown, throw in with the Patriots, or remain neutral. Although some tribes such as the New York Oneidas chose the Patriots, most either remained neutral or sided with the Crown. Inevitably, conflict erupted. In the South the first significant event was the Cherokee War of 1776.[28]

In the north the Battle of the Cedars on 19 May 1776, won largely with Indian help, and Burgoyne's Hudson Valley Campaign of 1777 represented the only significant use of Indian allies. In the Northwest Territory, frontier raids organized and encouraged by Agent Hamilton used mixed units of whites and Indians. After Saratoga, actions in the North tended to be small-scale raids organized by Indians rather than coordinated British military operations. Events such as the Wyoming Massacre of 3 July 1778 and the Cherry Valley affair of 11 November created turmoil along the frontier and evoked a response from George Washington—the Sullivan expedition of August–October 1779. Despite destroying numerous villages and food supplies, the campaign failed to suppress the raids, which continued for the rest of the war. From a strategic-effects viewpoint, the British and allied Indians had incompatible objectives. For the Crown, the use of Indians and particularly their small-scale raids had the desired strategic effect of inhibiting frontiersmen from joining Patriot forces in the East and disrupting rebel command, control, and communications. For the Indians, their objectives were to expel interloping settlers, discourage any further westward settlement, and obtain military supplies from Crown stores. For an alliance to succeed, common strategic objectives are usually necessary; they simply did not exist in the northern and middle colonies.

In Canada and along the northern borders of New York and New England, Carleton, wary of using Indians as main forces, refused to employ them except as scouts attached to regular formations. In the South, Superintendent John Stuart also opposed using Indians against the Patriots, arguing that to do so would only provoke the colonists and likely throw neutrals into rebellion. Like Carleton, he allowed Indians to engage only alongside regular formations commanded by Crown officers. But by December 1775 Stuart had lost the argument. He complied with Gage's earlier instructions and ordered subordinates to enlist Cherokee and Creek allies to serve alongside Loyalists. Violence flared in May 1776 over treaty violations; bands of Cherokee struck settlements from the Watauga area of North Carolina down through Georgia, precipitating the Cherokee War. Stuart and the department were thus dragged into the conflict even though the root causes had more to do with land disputes between settlers and Indians than with political disputes between Loyalists and Patriots.

Farther south, Royal Governor Patrick Tonyn of East Florida had more aggressive use of Indian allies in mind. He proposed active alliance participation in coordinated operations led by white officers. Lord Germain and the new CinC in America, General Howe, both approved. In February 1777 the secretary ordered Stuart to cooperate with Hamilton in a campaign of frontier raids from Pennsylvania to Detroit. The military commander in East Florida, Major General Augustine Prevost, and Stuart opposed using Indians in such a manner. Nonetheless, Stuart convened a meeting in Mobile attended by almost 3,000 Choctaw and Chickasaws, who pledged support for the plan. But George Galphin, an Indian commissioner, talked many Lower Creeks out of participating, so no active operations emerged from the conference. Though Stuart eventually managed to convince enough Indian leaders to cooperate, they did not participate in the campaigns of late 1778 and early 1779. On 21 March 1779 Stuart died. Two subordinates, Charles Stuart and Alexander Cameron, replaced the chief agent but little activity against the Patriots occurred. Budget and administrative difficulties essentially undercut any effective military planning or operations.

Spain entered the war as a French ally on 21 June 1779. Operations against British posts in West Florida commenced almost immediately. From their New Orleans base, the Spanish attacked and captured Mobile in February 1780 and then attempted to take Pensacola, capital of West Florida, in March. Indian allies, 2,000 Creeks, assisted in the successful defense and helped save that town from capture. Pensacola, though, represented the last significant allied Indian action in the South. The Choctaw did attempt raids against the Spanish garrison at Mobile but to little avail. Major General John Campbell, military commander at Pensacola, neither liked nor had empathy for the Indians, which they reciprocated. When Spanish royal governor Don Bernardo de Galvéz launched a second attempt on Pensacola in March 1781, only a few hundred Creeks turned out to defend the capital, which this time fell to a siege in May. Farther north the Cherokee attempted another assault against the colonists in late 1780, but an expedition from North Carolina and Virginia counterattacked, destroying key Indian towns. Chastened by their defeats in 1776 and 1780, the Cherokee conducted only intermittent frontier raids thereafter. Farther south Indian allies failed to arrive in time to rescue Augusta, Georgia, lost to Patriot forces in June 1781. The last Indian action was a raid from East Florida into Georgia in August 1782 amid the ongoing Paris peace negotiations.

The Indian alliance, as part of the Southern Strategy, came to naught. Despite potential force multipliers provided by thousands of highly capable warriors,

Crown authorities in the southern colonies never fashioned or executed effective allied operations. In the northern and middle colonies, the Indian alliance proved far more successful in roiling the countryside and maintaining British domination. But by late in the war, the frontier descended into barbarism as each side massacred the other, including noncombatants. Using trade and supplies, primarily food, clothing, ammunition, weapons, and rum, as an inducement to remain on the British side, Crown authorities did prevent almost all the major tribes from siding with the Patriots. As seen with the southern colonies after John Stuart's death, budget and administrative disarray undercut the ability to keep the Indians engaged and active.

Attempts to restrain Indian activities while awaiting combined operations in the North proved frustrating and illusory. The tribes had their own objectives, primarily the prevention of further encroachment westward, which did not align with Crown objectives. Additionally, the British did not have the wherewithal or resources to support the Cherokee in 1776, largely due to the Cape Fear–Charleston expedition's failure and the Moore's Creek Bridge debacle. Another problem that undercut combined operations lay in the method. British authorities, fearful of neutral reaction in support of the Patriots or against the Crown, refused to allow the Indians to conduct traditional raids that terrorized the frontier and insisted that white officers command and control all operations to prevent massacres or other actions that might serve rebel propaganda. While this humanity might be noble, it undercut any real military effectiveness by precluding the greatest effects of traditional Indian warfare, which were more psychological than physical. Four factors undercut any successful strategic effects from the alliances in the South: Crown authorities more tightly controlled Indian activities than in the northern and middle colonies; John Stuart and General Prevost's reluctance to use Indian allies except in an auxiliary role; the inhibiting effects of the Cherokee War, which utterly defeated that tribe and drove them farther west; and the administrative drift that occurred following Stuart's death in 1779. In short, as a component of the overall Southern Strategy, the Indian alliance remained only a potential, never a kinetic, dynamic.[29]

Similar to the American Indians as a strategic ally, British authorities advocated using freed and escaped African American slaves as a force multiplier. Yet this also failed to have a significant operational effect. Lord Dunmore, royal governor of Virginia, in November 1775 raised the Ethiopian Regiment, which fought in the Battle of Great Bridge on 9 December. Evacuated with the rest of the Loyalist forces, the unit disbanded in September 1776 at Staten Island, with members distributed to other units, notably the Black Pioneers and the irregular Black Brigade. In April 1776, upon Clinton's arrival at Cape Fear, roughly fifty escaped slaves joined British forces and were placed under the command of a marine officer. Captain Allan Stewart, a North Carolina Loyalist, who later commanded the Black Pioneers, which became the only black unit placed on the official Provincial establishment. The unit served in the northern colonies and at Charleston throughout the war and was evacuated from New York in 1783 to Nova Scotia. As pioneers, the men undertook engineering projects, including camp sanitation, fortification construction, siege-works construction, and so forth.

Throughout the war, blacks, both freedmen and escaped slaves, volunteered for and served in various Provincial units, including the 1st Battalion of De Lancey's Brigade (Brigadier Oliver de Lancey of New York, sometimes seen as Delancey's). Some served in the King's American Regiment. In March 1777, General Howe ordered that all blacks, mulattos, Indians, and sailors should be discharged from the Provincial organizations, yet blacks continued to serve as regimental musicians, a tradition long-established in the British Army. Some units such as the King's American Regiment and the Volunteers of Ireland kept unarmed black pioneers on the rolls. Others such as Butler's Rangers and the King's Royal Regiment of New York managed to retain black soldiers in the ranks. Denied official sanction as soldiers of the official Provincial Corps, blacks served in irregular and militia units, including the King's Militia Volunteers and the Loyal Refugees and Associated Refugees (later renamed the King's American Regiment). German Hessian and Brunswick regiments also recruited blacks, not only as musicians but also as artillerists and infantrymen.

The most common service for blacks was the Civil Branch of the Army and the Ordnance Department. Thousands served in that capacity. The most notable use of blacks came at Yorktown, where members of the Civil Branch constructed much of the British defensive works throughout the summer of 1781. Although some southern blacks evacuated along with the refugee white Loyalists from Charleston when Crown forces departed in 1782, most were forced back into slavery. For the thousands of men who served in various Crown formations, the inducement was the promise of freedom from slavery for all those who enlisted as declared by Clinton in the Philipsburg Proclamation of 30 June 1779. Unhappily for most, especially those who served in the South, once the Patriots won the struggle, they returned to bondage. Yet they did provide exemplary service to Crown forces. Captain George Smith published in 1779 an excellent description of the regimental pioneer that captures the role played by many black Loyalist volunteers: "Pioneers, in war-time, are such as are commanded from the country, to march with an army, for mending the ways, for working on intrenchments, and fortifications, and for making mines and approaches. . . . Our regiments of infantry and cavalry have 3 or 4 pioneers each, provided with aprons, hatchets, saws, spades, and pick-axes."[30] While blacks served in many capacities in the effort to pacify the colonies, as with the American Indians, their services did not compensate for the ultimate failure of the Loyalist strategy and the disappointing turnout of whites in support of the royal cause.

## "King George and Broadswords!": Moore's Creek Bridge, 27 February 1776

Expectations for southern Loyalist turnout and support did have some validity. The early rising of North Carolina Loyalists indicated a potential for significant numbers. Royal Governor Josiah Martin advised Lord Dartmouth that he could raise 3,000 Highlanders from the Cross Creek area (modern Fayetteville, North Carolina) if General Gage in Boston sent sufficient arms and supplies. Martin forecast raising a 20,000-man force that would restore royal government in the Carolinas and Virginia.[31] Since the total North Carolina population in 1775 stood at roughly 200,000 and excluding nonadult males of military age, Governor Martin's estimate seems wildly extravagant. Nonetheless, such entreaties played into the perception in London that a huge wellspring of support would appear once regular troops arrived and if the Loyalists received arms, ammunition, and supplies. Martin's proposal exemplified a notion that persisted in the British official mind (regardless of the officeholder) until literally the final weeks of the later Southern Campaign. When Dartmouth handed over the office to Germain, the concept remained and resulted in the abortive Charleston expedition of 1776.

Dartmouth's plan called for employing troops drawn from Ireland, to be commanded by Cornwallis and supported at sea by a Royal Navy squadron under Rear Admiral Sir Peter Parker, along with reinforcements from the Boston garrison. The expedition carried with it 10,000 muskets to arm the Loyalists. The squadron would sail up the Cape Fear River and land the army, which would then rendezvous with Martin's Highlanders. Together, the Crown forces would overwhelm any Patriot resistance in North Carolina before moving on to South Carolina. Reliance on Loyalist turnout was fundamentally important and anticipated based on Martin's reports. Dartmouth's orders indicated that "the whole success of the measure . . . depends so much upon a considerable number of the inhabitants taking up arms in support of government." Yet a hint of doubt clouded the issue of Loyalist turnout, a doubt that haunted British strategic planning for the entire southern adventure of 1778 and through to the war's end. The American secretary stated, "I hope we are not deceived in the assurances that have been given, for if we are, and there should be no appearance of a disposition in the inhabitants of the southern colonies to join the King's Army, I fear little more will be effected than the gaining possession of some respectable post to the southward."[32] These words from 1775 eerily captured the strategic and operational conundrum faced by Clinton and Cornwallis in the last year of the struggle.

In January 1776 Martin received word of the plan's approval and set about recruiting his army, primarily among the Cross Creek Highlanders. Indications that royal support ran high came from the efforts of two regular officers, Lieutenant Colonel Donald MacDonald and Captain Alexander MacLeod, brought back on active duty to raise men for the Provincial Corps. Many of their recruits were veterans of the Scottish Highland regiments that had served in North America during the French and Indian War who, upon demobilization of their units, had opted to settle in North America. This corps eventually came onto the regular establishment as the 84th Regiment of Foot (Royal Highland Emigrants). Additionally, Allan MacDonald of Kingsburgh, husband of Flora MacDonald of Bonnie Prince Charlie and "The '45" fame, encouraged these men to join. Governor Martin issued proclamations encouraging enlistment and announced a rendezvous by mid-February. He commissioned MacDonald as brigadier general of militia and MacLeod as lieutenant colonel, with their 300 or so recruits already enlisted serving as the militia force's foundation. Martin also counted on the participation of the Regulators, who had rebelled against Royal Governor William Tryon and the overbearing domination of the eastern coastal planter elite in the late 1760s and early 1770s. Many Regulators still seethed from their crushing defeat five years earlier by troops associated with the planters. Additional incentives included a promise of twenty acres and a long-term tax exemption. Loyalist leaders assembled at Cross Creek on 5 February and made a tragic decision to march to Wilmington without waiting for Cornwallis's arrival. Within days some 1,200 to 1,400 Loyalists, predominantly Highlanders, gathered at Cross Creek, many unarmed. Former Regulators failed to show up, and only a hundred other backcountry Loyalists arrived. In the hinterland many others gathered to march to Cross Creek but were attacked or dispersed by Patriot militia, indicating a vibrant anti-Crown sentiment throughout North Carolina. This factor ought to have been an early sign that counting on vast Loyalist support, a significant component underpinning the eventual Southern Strategy, would be problematic at best. Royal authorities either dismissed or ignored the warning. Thus, Crown authorities and strategic decision makers failed to recognize that the nature of the coming struggle in the South would not be as they conceived.

Hearing of the Loyalist gathering and their intent to march down the Cape Fear River toward Wilmington, the 1st North Carolina Regiment of the Continental Line under Col. James Moore, with a strength of 650 troops, erected a defensive position several miles from Cross Creek. Soon 450 militiamen under Cols. John Lillington, James Kenan, and James Ashe reinforced the Continentals. The Loyalists started their march on 18 February only to find their way blocked by Moore's Patriots. MacDonald deftly crossed the river, burned his boats, and bypassed the colonel's forces. In response, Moore ordered Richard Caswell and 600 militia to take station at Corbett's Ferry on the Black River, with Ashe and Lillington soon to reinforce him. Meantime, the 1st North Carolina Regiment gave chase. As before, MacDonald outwitted the Patriots when he reached Corbett's Ferry on the twenty-third. Keeping several men close to the enemy position to simulate an attack by a much larger force, the Loyalists skirted around Caswell's position, crossed the Black River using a temporary bridge on the twenty-sixth, and continued toward Wilmington.

Moore ordered Caswell to a third blocking position, this time at the bridge on Widow Moore's Creek eighteen miles north of Wilmington and directly in the Highlanders' path. Lillington and Caswell reached the bridge on the twenty-sixth ahead of MacDonald. Moore's Creek runs into the Black River, which courses through swampy ground and empties into the Cape Fear River. The Patriots threw up a breastwork, removed the bridge planking, and greased the log stringers running from bank to bank with soap and tallow. Two small-caliber artillery pieces enhanced the defensive position. Arriving at the creek on the night of the twenty-sixth, the Loyalists held a council of war and determined that a broadsword charge in the age-old Highland tradition would unnerve the Patriots positioned across the sluggish, mossy creek. Despite the fact that many Jacobite Rebellion veterans had witnessed the destruction of their forces in a similar attack in April 1746 at Culloden Moor, the impatient Scots implemented the disastrous plan. With MacDonald ill, MacLeod took command. After a night march through rough terrain, the Loyalist force reached the creek just at dawn on the twenty-seventh.

Led by MacLeod and Farquard Campbell, the broadsword-wielding clansmen raced toward the bridge shouting, "King George and Broadswords!" At thirty yards the rebels loosed their first volley. Staggered but not deterred, the survivors pressed forward only to be shot off the greased logs. Reports vary as to who and how many Highlanders reached the opposite bank as men slipped into the murky stream and drowned; one account claims that both MacLeod and Campbell made the crossing but died before reaching the breastworks. With their opponents milling about on the opposite bank after their charge and unable to reach the Patriot position, the rebels replaced the bridge planks, counterattacked, and captured 850 Loyalists, including Brigadier MacDonald, and their entire stand of arms, ammunition, and baggage. Thirty Loyalists died outright while many more suffered wounds; only one Patriot was killed and one wounded. A few weeks later Clinton landed at Wilmington; the force under Cornwallis, transported by Parker from Ireland, arrived in April. News of the Moore's Creek Bridge disaster led the generals to reembark the troops. The expedition then proceeded against Charleston, the secondary objective. That adventure failed as well. The cause of Loyalist participation in North Carolina never recovered from the blow.[33]

## "The Fullest of Peril and Delusion": The Loyalist Strategy

The fundamental underpinning of the Southern Strategy derived from the assumption that once offensive operations commenced, the heretofore-suppressed Loyalists would turn out in great numbers. With French entry into the fight in March 1778 and the consequent threat to the British West Indies, Ireland, India, and the home islands themselves, a new strategy had to be devised that accounted for both suppression of the rebellion and defense of vital imperial possessions. This dynamic prompted the immediate detachment of 5,000 troops from Philadelphia for West Indies defense and the abandonment of that hard-won city for the relative safety of New York. Faced with the need to overturn the rebellion on the cheap, strategic decision makers in both London and the colonies focused on the Loyalist factor, largely dormant since the disappointments in the South of the early years. Owing to the efforts of Lieutenant Colonel Allan MacLean, many French and Indian War veterans of various Scottish Highland regiments, who had settled in Canada, New York, and the Carolinas, had enlisted in what became the 84th Regiment of Foot (Royal Highland Emigrants). Further, the actions of the North Carolina Highlanders in early February 1776, while resulting in the disaster at Moore's Creek Bridge, had indicated a great deal of latent Loyalist support, especially in the settlements around Cross Creek. Though ultimately a catastrophic disaster, this had reinforced in British strategic minds the concept that thousands of Carolina Loyalists awaited only the arrival of regular troops to rise up and crush the rebellion in the South.[34] Indeed, the underlying strategic assumption for the Southern Campaign rested on a massive Loyalist turnout. The concept received encouragement and credibility from various notable sources, including the exiled royal governors of South Carolina and Georgia, William Campbell and James Wright. In a statement to Germain, the governors captured the essence of the desired strategic effect of regular troops in the South: "From our particular knowledge of those Provinces [South Carolina and Georgia], it appears very clear to us, that if a proper number of troops were in possession of Charleston . . . or if they were to possess themselves of the back country thro' Georgia, and to leave a garrison in the town of Savannah, the whole inhabitants of both Provinces would soon come in and submit."[35]

Other reports from the South reinforced the perception that Loyalists only awaited the arrival of the army to rise in great numbers. For example, the ministry tasked James Simpson, a prominent landowner and royal attorney general for South Carolina, to assess the potential level of support. Simpson sent highly optimistic reports to London. His assertions that "whenever the King's troops move to Carolina they will be assisted by a very considerable number of the inhabitants" proved persuasive.[36] Joseph Galloway, another prominent Loyalist, sent a stream of letters to the American secretary assuring him that the colonies abounded with royalists anxious to turn out in support. North Carolinian Jonathan Boucher painted an image of the numerous invisible Loyalists who dared not declare for the king for fear of retribution: "North Carolina was the poorest country in the revolted colonies, . . . of its people even the most loyal could hardly declare themselves, for they live so dispersed that they would be an easy prey [to Patriot reprisal]."[37] From Maryland, well before Lexington and Concord, word came that only a few "particular men" had swayed the majority of the population despite their actual loyalties: "In popular assemblies particular men generally govern the rest, and the proceedings take their colour from the temper and views of a few leaders. The moderate and diffident are carried with the stream; and their silence and acquiescence by swelling the apparent majority indicate an approbation of violences they really condemn."[38]

By 1778, experience should have convinced Germain and the American Department that Loyalist support represented a thin reed upon which to base the Southern Strategy. One need only look at the poor turnout in support of Burgoyne as he plodded through the New York wilderness. In Canada, though a goodly number of Scottish Highland veterans did volunteer, Carleton experienced disappointment in his recruitment efforts at the rebellion's start. Nonetheless, the testimonials flowed to London. In fairness, late 1776 and early 1777 did represent the high point of Loyalist recruitment in the middle colonies, attributable to British military successes in the New York and New Jersey operations. But this temporary rush of enthusiasm did not last; authorities in London, most notably Lord Germain, took the wrong lesson from the momentary dynamic.[39]

Swayed by such testimonials, a strategy based on the assumption of a massive Loyalist turnout evolved by early 1778. Despite warnings from the field by Clinton and later from Lieutenant Colonel Francis, Lord Rawdon in South Carolina that the Loyalists did not turn out in the expected numbers or with the anticipated enthusiasm, Germain preferred the intelligence from Lieutenant Colonel Nisbet Balfour, military commander in Charleston once Cornwallis departed into the backcountry. Balfour assured the secretary on the eve of the earl's second invasion of North Carolina in January 1781 that many prominent men of that colony had already declared for the king and that many more would do so.[40] But in an occupied city, what of the human tendency to profess loyalty to the existing authority? How might that dynamic have swayed Balfour's perception?

Other factors that might have played into these calculations were religion, economy, and ethnicity. British authorities and strategic decision makers had far more in common with southerners than northerners. The landed gentry in South Carolina's Low Country, centered around Charleston, dominated as in Britain. The backcountry folk, predominantly Scots and Scotch Irish (those who had emigrated from Scotland to Northern Ireland in the seventeenth century, then on to the colonies in the eighteenth century), brought their Presbyterianism with them. They tended to be independent minded but did follow respected local leaders, a legacy of the old Highland clan system. Anglicanism (Episcopalian) predominated in the Low Country and coastal plains. In the northern and middle colonies, dissenters such as the Puritans and Quakers dominated who had a longstanding dispute with the establishment Church of England. Overall, one might say the South replicated more closely the home islands. A largely subsistence-farming economy, similar in character to Ireland, Scotland, and rural parts of western and northern England, characterized the backcountry. Based on the similarities with rural Britain, where local aristocrats set public attitudes and opinion more so than in the urban areas—London, Edinburgh, Dublin, Liverpool, Boston, Philadelphia—where merchants, tradesmen, and laborers dominated, one can see why Crown authorities assumed loyalism more than rebellion dominated.

In reality, the number of Loyalists who fought or provided logistical support proved disappointing when compared to the grossly inflated expectations of 1778. For Crown fortunes, the faulty assessments encompassed by the Loyalist component of the Southern Strategy were the first in a long line of erroneous and ultimately devastating elements of a flawed theory of victory and a woeful misunderstanding of the nature of the war in the southern colonies.

Cornwallis's concept of honor and ethics in warfare further complicated the loyalty issue and adversely affected southerners' willingness to support the cause. The earl proved reluctant to take dramatic and radical steps to destroy the rebellion, among them executing former Crown soldiers captured while serving as rebel combatants. Only a few such men were actually executed for treason when caught, though all could have been by rights. British officers preferred to grant a parole to captured Patriots on a promise of good behavior and no further participation in rebellious activity. Many captured rebels thus returned to action a few days or weeks later. Frustrated with the unwillingness or inability of British authorities to stamp out the rebellion with harsh measures even when the revolt tottered on the edge of collapse, many Loyalists turned inward to wait out the conflict and refused to participate further, looking instead to the safety of their own families and property. Whereas Cornwallis initially chafed at harsh measures except for the most notorious (or effective) rebel leaders, he gradually realized the strategic need for assaulting their property, which occurred in the Virginia Campaign of 1781.

The prominent British Army historian Sir John Fortescue succinctly sums up the Loyalist problem, the misunderstanding of the nature of the war, and its debilitating strategic consequences: "At the bottom of the whole design lay the fundamental error of reliance on the help of the royalists."[41] In his analysis of the Loyalist strategy, he declares: "Of all the foundations whereon to build the conduct of a campaign this is the loosest, the most treacherous, the fullest of peril and delusion; yet as shall be seen in the years before us, there is none that has been in more favour with British ministers, with the invariable consequence of failure and disaster."[42]

Paul H. Smith points out a fundamental flaw in this strategy, asserting that British authorities never quite had a firm grasp on how to best utilize Loyalists: "Perhaps the most accurate general statement that can be made on the subject is that Loyalists never occupied a fixed, well-understood place in British strategy. Plans to use them were in the main *ad hoc* responses to constantly changing conditions, and, like British strategy throughout the war, were developed to meet various particular situations."[43] In the case of the South, that particular situation was the injection of France and later Spain into the war, necessitating a dramatic reapportionment of British military and naval resources.

## "Mandatory Pressures": Strategy Adrift, 1778

With the authorities in London fully embracing the promise of a heavy turnout, Loyalist support as the centerpiece of the Southern Strategy came to life. Lord Germain stated to Clinton in March 1778 in a "Most Secret" correspondence that "the generality of the people desire nothing more than a full security for the enjoyment of all their rights and liberties under the British Constitution."[44] The American secretary informed his North American CinC of "his Majesty's firm purpose to prosecute it [a war to pacify the colonies and return them to allegiance] with the utmost vigor. . . . It is therefore proper that I should now acquaint you with his Majesty's intentions respecting the operation of the next campaign." Germain then added the promise of ten to twelve thousand additional troops, including a regiment or two of German infantry. He pointed out that George III had made his position clear from well before the first shots at Lexington and Concord, saying, "I am not sorry that the line of conduct seems now . . . chalked out . . . ; the New England governments are in a state of rebellion, blows must decide whether they are to be subject to this country or independent."[45] Where Germain planned to obtain these reinforcements seems indicative of his typically unrealistic and problematic assessment of the nature and complexity of the rebellion.[46]

Despite the French intervention, Germain still advocated aggressive offensive operations in conjunction with the Carlisle Peace Commission. Should the peace negotiations fail to end the rebellion, the American secretary proposed some elaborate and mostly unrealistic campaign plans in addition to his promise of additional troops. The plans included raiding along the New England coast; strengthening defensive positions in Florida, Canada, Nova Scotia, and Newfoundland; and executing an autumn attack on the South coupled with a diversionary operation in the Chesapeake Bay region. Clinton in Philadelphia chafed when he received the letter detailing the 18 March cabinet-meeting decisions ordering him to assume a defensive posture, abandon Philadelphia, retreat to New York, and send 5,000 troops for an attack on Saint Lucia, with an additional 3,000 men sent to East Florida. In that order came the initiation of the Southern Strategy. The American secretary instructed the CinC in America to "give up every idea of offensive operations [in the North]" and transfer the major effort to the southern colonies.[47] On the withdrawal back to New York, Washington attacked the rear of Clinton's column at Monmouth Court House in New Jersey. While the battle resulted in a tactical draw, the much-improved Continental Army's performance and stoutness ought to have been a harbinger of the increased difficulty in defeating the Patriots in conventional warfare. With the inability to crush Washington in a decisive battle, and based on the instructions of 21 March, Clinton thus initiated the Southern Campaign, which ultimately led to defeat and the loss of thirteen American colonies.

A frustrating series of letters went back and forth between New York and Whitehall for the remainder of the year. Germain saw the Loyalists as the key to victory. But with the global maritime war against France, the secretary's attention to America dissipated, thus injecting a further element of strategic incoherence as his suggestions drifted from one plan to the next. Germain went back and forth on the need to hold Rhode Island, with its excellent port at Newport, and other raids in the Chesapeake and against the New England coast. He also counted the number of troops in America as a whole, including those unfit for duty due to sickness or wounds, rather than the number of actual effectives. Frustrated by such strategic drift and inattention from London, within months both Clinton and Cornwallis requested to be relieved of command. Germain refused. The king and the War Office both supported Sir Henry remaining in command, and the secretary could not afford the political aftershock of allowing the general to resign. Alan Valentine captures the CinC in America's dilemma: "Lord George's wishes developed into almost mandatory pressures, and not to follow them was to court the displeasure of one of the most powerful and unforgiving men in

England."[48] A frustrated Clinton could only endure and plead for more troops and supplies.

Clinton's reticence in undertaking a southern operation created a dynamic that increasingly undercut his command and control over the North American theater and complicated the already shaky strategic coherence. At this point Germain began corresponding directly with Cornwallis, violating the military imperative of maintaining the chain of command. The situation worsened in 1781 as the earl invaded Virginia, but the seeds of this foul weed were seen in early 1779, soon after the initial operations against Georgia got underway.

Germain encouraged Clinton to detach troops to subdue Georgia and the two Carolinas in his letter of 8 March 1778. The general despaired. To his mind, London's management of the war effort showed no appreciation for the logistical and command-and-control problems inherent in such an operation. More importantly, the drain on his New York garrison chronically worried the CinC. Demands from Germain to detach troops to the West Indies to counter any French threat and to Canada to reinforce General Sir Frederick Haldimand left him precious few to guard the main base of North American operations from not only Washington but also potential French actions. In April 1779 Clinton informed Germain: "I have as yet received no assurances of any favourable temper in the province of South Carolina to encourage me to an undertaking where we must expect so much difficulty. . . . The small force which the present weakness of General Washington's army would enable me to detach might possibly get possession of Charleston . . . , but I doubt whether they could keep it . . . [while the detachment] would reduce me to the strictest defensive in this country."[49]

In July the general informed the secretary that the 12,000 troops remaining after all the detachments provided only "a very inadequate number for the defense of the place [New York], which alone would require at least 15,000 men even if we had exclusive command of the Sea."[50] Nonetheless, London insisted on a southern campaign. In early August the secretary informed Clinton that the instructions of 8 March called for a winter offensive in the South. Though superseded by the 21 March change in direction, Germain instructed him to adopt the earlier directives as far as circumstances allowed.[51] Accordingly, the CinC laid out courses of action. Clinton's eventual operational plan called for three specific phases. The first phase amounted to a series of coastal raids designed to disrupt Continental recruiting. The second phase hoped to lure Washington into the Hudson Highlands, where Clinton could destroy the main Patriot force in a conventional battle. Once these two antecedents had been accomplished, the southern operation would commence. As it happened, coastal raids did occur, but Washington refused to accommodate Clinton's phase two. In this regard, while the third phase went forward, the existential threat to New York, a dynamic

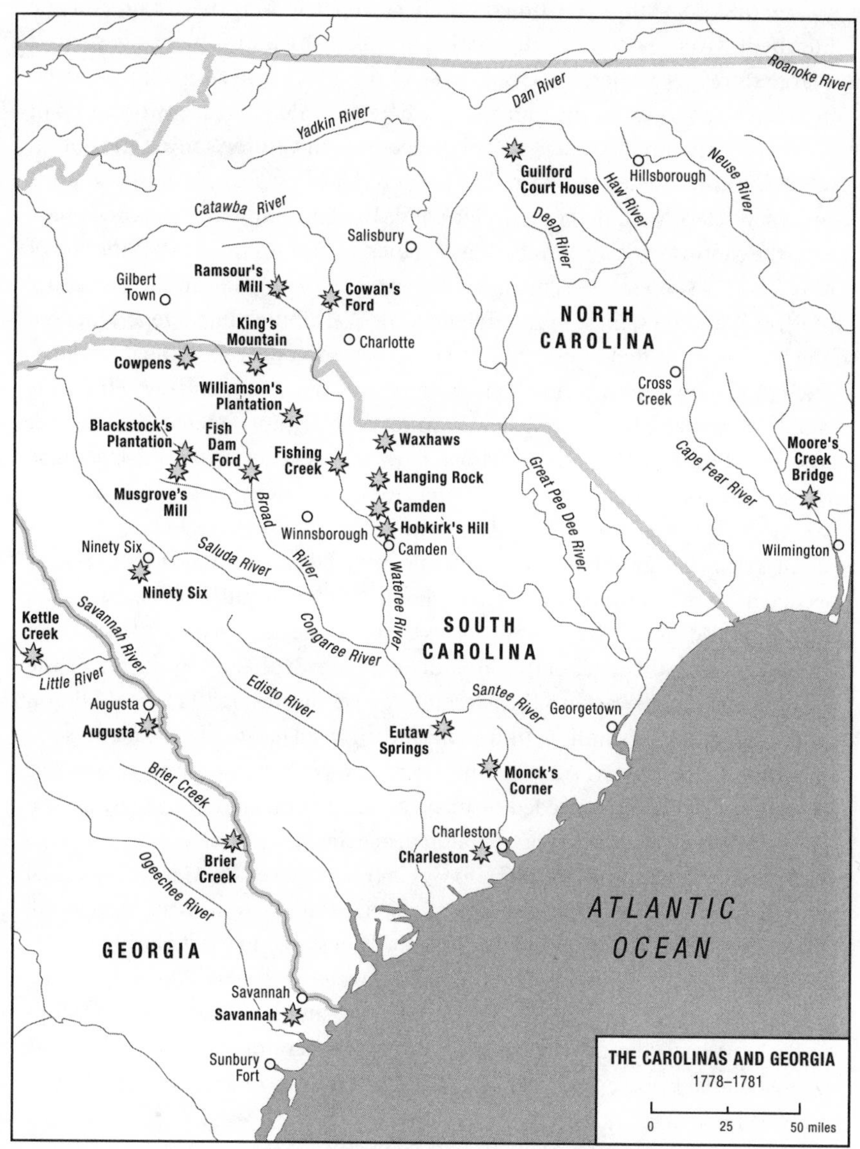


The Carolinas and Georgia, 1778–1781. Map by Erin Greb Cartography.

that adversely affected the Southern Campaign from the beginning, hung over every strategic and operational move by Crown commanders.

The first coastal operation commenced in early May, with raids on the Elizabeth River region at Portsmouth, Virginia, which captured or destroyed a large store of supplies. This first strike of the Southern Campaign occurred in Tidewater Virginia, only miles from where it would conclude two and a half years later. The raid's success must have planted in Clinton's mind the notion of establishing a defended operating post on the Chesapeake at Portsmouth, a concept he clung to until the campaign's end. The CinC initiated his second phase with the capture of Stony Point and Verplanck's Point in New York at the end of May. Though successful in cutting off the Patriots' main Hudson River crossing south of West Point, these moves did not draw Washington into a general action. The Virginian shifted to cover West Point, but no other engagement resulted. Though Clinton had drawn Washington out of New Jersey and away from his supply source, the late arrival of Arbuthnot with reinforcements from Britain scotched any further main-force actions. Crown forces afterward conducted some raids along the Connecticut coast, but a counterattack by Brig. Gen. Anthony Wayne recaptured Stony Point, stalemating this second phase.

On 21 July Cornwallis arrived back from England and resumed his position as second in command and heir apparent should Clinton be killed or incapacitated; he also carried an inactive commission as CinC. While the two men ostensibly got on well enough, the seeds of the bitter disputes of 1781 already lay dormant. The earl arrived with news that a French squadron was headed for America. Clinton determined that the southern (third) phase of his plan had to be executed as soon as Arbuthnot tardily arrived with reinforcements. Washington's army would have to wait; South Carolina needed securing before a combined Franco-American move choked off that possibility. Clinton dispatched the initial operation toward Savannah in late October 1778. On 10 October he received the Germain letter of 5 August, authorizing him to make corrections as the local situation warranted, and consequently redirected a force previously destined for East Florida against the Georgia port. In so doing, though, he warned that once Washington, not far away from New York, learned of the detachment of several thousand troops to the southern colonies, he could launch a counterattack and take back any Crown gains. Prescience is helpful. Clinton was correct, only his timing was off by three years.

Clinton's concerns for New York's safety as he embarked on the Southern Campaign might explain his continual reluctance to fully support Cornwallis with reinforcements or conduct a robust Chesapeake diversionary operation as the earl thrashed about in the southern hinterland. Above all, the two generals' strategic concepts diverged widely following Cornwallis's victory over Gates at

Camden, South Carolina, in August 1780. While the CinC advocated minimal operations north of South Carolina, especially until Georgia and South Carolina were fully pacified, his second in command argued that the key lay farther north. The earl saw North Carolina and ultimately Virginia as the essential focus for operations. In attacking the Patriots there, supplies and reinforcements would be choked off and rebel forces farther south finally subdued. This divergence created tremendous strategic incoherence as 1781 progressed and further eroded the already shaky British command-and-control relationship. From literally the start of the Southern Campaign, command indecisiveness and strategic incoherence crept into the British plan for recovery of at least a portion of the rebelling colonies.

CHAPTER 2

# "They Are Not Prepared for a Scene of War"

## *The Southern Campaign Begins*

While the Charleston operation in early 1780 represented the implementation of the main southern thrust, precursor operations prepared the battlespace. In accordance with the overall strategic concept of rolling up the southern colonies one at a time, two sites in northeastern Georgia were obvious initial targets—Savannah on the coast and Augusta farther inland up the Savannah River. These two towns represented endpoints in a critical line of demarcation that once controlled would isolate Georgia from South Carolina. Beyond Augusta to the north and west lay frontier lands with little colonial settlement. Savannah, located where the Savannah River empties into the Atlantic, provided an excellent port for seaborne operations. Control of these two endpoints would permit Crown forces to dominate the border, inhibiting any Patriot resupply or reinforcements into Georgia. Savannah could receive logistical support from the ocean, while Augusta could rely on support by river transportation. The geography combined with the relatively small population provided Clinton an ideal starting point for his third phase of operations.

Another element played into the desirability of Savannah and Augusta as the first Crown targets—their proximity to the Floridas. Two colonies had been formed along the Gulf Coast from territory obtained from Spain under the terms of the 1763 Treaty of Paris—East and West Florida. With the capitals at the old Spanish settlement of Saint Augustine for East Florida and Pensacola for West Florida, the thinly populated regions represented a safe haven for northern Loyalists displaced by Patriots, particularly those from the Carolinas. As a result, neither colony rebelled. The Floridas remained almost entirely Loyalist and provided many troops for the Crown cause, including the East Florida Rangers and volunteers for the 60th Regiment of Foot (Royal American Regiment), a regular infantry unit heavily engaged in combat and garrison operations in the

Floridas, Georgia, and South Carolina.[1] With both colonies firmly under Crown control and populated by an overwhelmingly Loyalist citizenry, royal forces stationed in Saint Augustine and Pensacola stood well positioned to impede any French or Spanish interference from New Orleans as well as any attempt to land forces along the Georgia coast. To bolster the strategic thinking toward an assault on Savannah and Augusta, Patrick Tonyn, royal governor of East Florida, and his military commander, Major General Augustine Prevost, both forecast that the South would not be difficult to conquer: "I am certain the four southern provinces are incapable of making any formidable resistance; they are not prepared for a scene of war."[2]

## The Strategy Unfolds: December 1778–June 1780

Under the command of Lieutenant Colonel Archibald Campbell and Commodore Hyde Parker, an assault force of 3,500 troops, composed of British regulars, German auxiliaries, and four battalions of Provincial troops anchored by the 71st Regiment of Foot (Fraser's Highlanders) and the Regiment von Wissenbach (Hessian) and Regiment von Wöllwarth (Hessian), departed for Georgia from New York on 27 November 1778. The plan anticipated a large outpouring of Georgia, Florida, and South Carolina Loyalists as well as local Indian allies in support of the operation. On the surface this seemed sound. Based on the reports of the two deposed royal governors, Wright and Campbell, large numbers of ardent Loyalists could be anticipated. If events unfolded according to the strategic concept of "clear and hold," these Loyalists would restore and maintain Crown security and government, thus freeing the regulars for operations farther north into South Carolina.

Indian allies might prevent Patriot reinforcement down the eastern slope of the Appalachian Mountains, along a route called the "Cherokee Trail," over which thousands of settlers had moved down from the mid-Atlantic colonies into western Virginia, the Carolinas, and Georgia. If not preventing the flow of reinforcements, at a minimum the Indians might impede any resupply. The Indian boundary lines established in 1768 and 1773 delineated the Creek and Cherokee Nations' areas north, west, and south of the Georgia settlements and in theory provided a bulwark against a Patriot approach from those quarters.[3] Yet two fatal flaws existed in the concept, both of which severely undercut the entire strategy: Loyalist turnout and Indian association with the Crown. Reliance on Loyalist support would prove a weak foundation upon which to base the strategy and resultant operations. Colonial concerns with Indian participation should have been obvious to British authorities. Simply analyzing recent events in the

Carolinas made it plain that, at least for many frontier settlers, the Indian threat far outdistanced any concern over Crown authority or perceived oppression. The two Cherokee wars (1761 and 1776) in the Carolinas demonstrated that faulty assumption. A look at the 1776 affair, when Loyalists joined with Patriots and neutrals to counter the Cherokee threat and, so to speak, bury hatchets into Indian heads rather than each other's, starkly illustrates this.

Tryon County, roughly thirty miles west of the small hamlet of Charlotte (Charlottetown), lay at the frontier between Indian territory and the growing western North Carolina settlements. Its inhabitants played a major role in the Cherokee War of 1776, illustrating the dynamic of Loyalists and Patriots coming together for a mutual cause. The county is of even more importance in the role it would play in the destruction of western North Carolina loyalism in 1780 and in the start of the second North Carolina Campaign, initiated by Cornwallis in January 1781.

During the first week of July 1776, Cherokee war parties raided settlements in South Carolina and at Holstein and Watauga farther north, killing about twenty colonists, mainly women and children. But since advance warning had alerted the settlers, most escaped. Failing to capture the forts at Holstein and Watauga, the war parties attacked settlements at Crooked Creek near Rutherfordton and crossed into Rowan County, North Carolina. The incursion caused militia general Griffith Rutherford to send a desperate plea to the North Carolina Provincial Council, then in session at Halifax, requesting supplies, troops, and 1,000 pounds of powder to repulse the Indians.[4] Within a week of his report, Rutherford gathered 2,500 men and marched west with forty days of rations carried by 1,400 pack animals and eighty horses. By early September, this force reached Swannanoa Gap in the Appalachians. In the few weeks of his campaign, Rutherford destroyed several Indian towns, damaged or destroyed crops, and scattered the Cherokees, most of whom retreated into the mountains. Forced by circumstances to cede territory by subsequent treaties, the Middle Cherokees of western North Carolina gave up all their traditional tribal lands east of the Blue Ridge Mountains as well as along the Nolachucky, Watauga, and New Rivers. The Tryon County contribution to the expedition proved substantial. For example, after arriving at Old Fort near Salisbury, Rutherford detached Captains William Moore and Joseph Hardin with a hundred Tryon County Light Horse to attack previously untouched Cherokee villages.[5] In addition, Captain Peter Carpenter's company formed part of Rutherford's infantry force. Later in June 1780, long after the Cherokee threat had been neutralized, Carpenter would lead these men at the Battle of Ramsour's Mill, where he would suffer an abdominal wound and be the lone survivor among the six Loyalist company commanders there. Carpenter illustrates the shifting nature of loyalism and the dynamic of

Patriots and Loyalists joining in common cause against Indians, yet facing each other in combat as the main seat of the war came to their county.

## Savannah, December 1778

The Savannah operation illustrated the dominant strategic culture of Britain since the rise of the Royal Navy during Henry VIII's reign (1509–47). It and the actions against Charleston in 1780 are prime examples of a successful seaborne expeditionary strategy. Britain had used its amphibious capability in the assault on New York in 1776 and would again employ it at the start of the Southern Campaign. Maj. Gen. Robert Howe, with less than a thousand Continentals and roughly a hundred Georgia militiamen, commanded at Savannah. He maintained only poor relations with local Patriot authorities, a situation always fraught with peril when an invading force neared. Howe, a planter from New Hanover County, North Carolina (near Wilmington), had significant military experience, having served as a militia company commander during the French and Indian War as well as against the Regulators in his home colony just prior to the American Revolution. While the causes of the civil-military tension in Savannah are not well known, Howe's role in defeating the Regulator cause at the Battle of Alamance in central-western North Carolina in May 1771 may have played a role in the lack of cooperation and a unified defense.

As a member of a Committee of Safety, a prominent Patriot, and a North Carolina militia officer, Howe had led the forces that captured Fort Johnston on 15 July 1775, which precipitated the flight of Royal Governor Martin from the colony. Promoted to colonel and placed in command of the 2nd North Carolina Continental Regiment, he participated in the Norfolk Campaign against Virginia royal governor Lord Dunmore. Promoted to brigadier general in March 1776, Howe then took part in the June defense of Charleston under Maj. Gen. Charles Lee. Appointed commander of the Southern Department in 1778, the North Carolinian soon after attempted a failed assault against Saint Augustine. Based on this extensive command experience, Howe cannot be seen as a military neophyte by the time Campbell and Parker approached Savannah.[6] To be fair to the general, constant disputes and poor relations with Georgia authorities compromised his military situation and ability to defend the colony. To add to his difficulties, the constant drain of troops and resources for operations into East Florida, the repulse of multiple incursions from Saint Augustine, and dealing with Indian raids from the west, not to mention the usual strain of disease and desertion, diminished his available manpower. Under such conditions, Howe now faced a much larger and highly experienced invasion force.

The Savannah defense unraveled from the start. In a weakly opposed landing on 28 December, Campbell captured a small militia band and moved his force ashore just below the city. Howe had conceived a plan to defend Savannah along the approach road flanked by swamps, rice fields, and a river. But at this point his lack of military skill unhinged his plans. Despite warnings from subordinates that the position lay vulnerable to flank attack, Howe declined to flood the rice fields or post blocking forces at the trails and approaches to his main position, particularly on his right flank at Fair Lawn plantation, just south of the city.

Recognizing the vulnerability in these defensive arrangements, Campbell used a clever deception of drawing into battle line, apparently for a frontal assault, when in reality the main attack came in the American rear and right flank, an excellent example of convergent assault whereby the successful commander attacks the opponent from several directions simultaneously.[7] Aided by a slave with knowledge of the area, Campbell discovered an unguarded path through the swamps. His light infantry, composed of some 200 regulars and Loyalist volunteers, careened into Howe's flank while the main force pressed the front. The Patriots dissolved into chaos and retreated across a causeway at Purysburg into South Carolina. Although Howe escaped with much of his disheveled force, the Georgia Continentals under Samuel Elbert remained, trapped as in a vise. Elbert and some others escaped by swimming across the river, but most surrendered and spent the remainder of the conflict as prisoners of war. According to Campbell in his after-action report, Crown forces lost only a single officer and two privates killed, with a further ten wounded. He reported recovering eighty-three enemy dead from the battlefield. More critically for the Patriot cause in addition to the loss of Savannah was the capture of almost five hundred Continentals and militia, sixty-three field pieces and mortars, massive amounts of gunpowder, and all the shipping at the city wharfs.[8]

In short, Howe's defeat and Savannah's loss ripped open and laid bare the entire Patriot southern flank. The remaining defenders still capable of resistance later surrendered at Sunbury Fort, south of the city. Major General Prevost, advancing from East Florida, captured the post on 16 January 1779, thereby eliminating the last organized Patriot opposition on the Georgia coast. As the senior officer, Prevost assumed command of all Crown forces in the South. From an operational and tactical viewpoint, the capture of Savannah signaled the initial success of British arms in the southern colonies. From the strategic perspective, the campaign started with a stunning victory; the results at Savannah ostensibly validated the strategic concept.

Campbell and Prevost now faced a conundrum—what next? Their orders to establish control over Savannah only tangentially referred to conducting "prudent" operations.[9] With the successful capture of Saint Lucia in the West Indies earlier in the year, Clinton anticipated the return of Major General James Grant's expeditionary force to New York, which would give him the additional troops necessary to pacify South Carolina. Yet neither a firm plan to reinforce Georgia nor specific intentions from Clinton materialized, thus leaving the local field commanders to their own initiative—the Southern Strategy started to unravel immediately after its successful opening moves. Faced with no organized opposition, Campbell and Prevost initiated operations that ultimately undid their success at Savannah. From almost the start of the Southern Campaign, strategic incoherence between the political authorities in London, the CinC in New York, and the field commanders set in. Crown efforts suffered from poor planning, particularly in terms of any follow up to Savannah, and a lack of clear operational direction from the key decision makers in both New York and London. Well before Cornwallis ever arrived in the field, this pattern of incoherence emerged, characterized by operations and engagements that, while successful in destroying enemy force after enemy force in battle, failed to completely undo Patriot opposition or pacify territory. The "clear and hold" strategy was failing from the start.

With Howe's defeat, Congress required a new commander for the Southern Department and turned to a New Englander, Maj. Gen. Benjamin Lincoln, a prominent former Massachusetts militia leader who had prospered in the Continental Army and won the trust of Congress as well as General Washington. Congress appointed Lincoln on 26 September 1778, but it took him several weeks to arrive in theater and relieve Howe at Purysburg, South Carolina, on 3 January 1779.

Highly regarded by Congress and Washington as expert in such key military areas as supply and logistics, recruitment, and training, Lincoln had extensive military experience from the French and Indian War, when he served as adjutant with the 3rd Suffolk Regiment. As a major general of militia, he commanded the Massachusetts Militia in the 1776 New York Campaign before obtaining a Continental Army commission as major general in February 1777. Lincoln further proved his military talent during the Saratoga Campaign, sustaining a leg wound that afflicted him for the remainder of his life. Noted as a patient, diplomatic, and meticulous man who could organize and rationalize a deteriorating military situation, he seemed the perfect fit to master the evolving whirlwind of chaos and disaster created by Crown southern operations. As with the appointment of the Virginian Washington to command the army in New England, sending the northerner Lincoln to command the Southern Department fostered a sense of unity but also brought recent operational experience to aid southern forces, which had not seen significant action since 1776. The coming months greatly tested his talent and abilities as Crown victory followed Crown victory.[10]

## Augusta, January 1779

In late January Lieutenant Colonel Campbell initiated the next sequential operation—the assault on Augusta.[11] This made sense from both a strategic and an operational standpoint. Control of the two populated endpoints—Savannah and Augusta—and the navigable portion of the Savannah River created a barrier to Patriot movement of forces and supplies from South Carolina. A good argument could be made for capturing Augusta, but with the failed British attempt to foment Indian risings against Georgia backcountry settlements, the chances of holding the city in the face of local resistance appeared in retrospect dicey at best. The main threat faced by the backcountry settlers came from Native Americans, most notably the Cherokee and Creek tribes. To address this problem, Royal Governor Sir James Wright and Indian Superintendent John Stuart secured in 1773 a treaty ceding over two million acres of Indian land to Georgia in exchange for the cancellation of debt to Augusta-based merchants. But land meant more to the tribes than the debt cancellation. The Creeks reacted in the winter of 1773–74, resulting in the banning of all Indian trade with Augusta, a migration of backcountry settlers into Augusta, and the signing of Creek loyalty oaths. A treaty executed in October 1774 restored trade but brought no further land concessions. With this disappointment, backcountry settlers trended toward a nascent anti-Crown attitude already appearing in Savannah. As tensions grew, Crown opponents created the Georgia Provincial Congress and raised Sons of Liberty–style Patriot associations. Among other activities, these groups spread word of an Indian uprising instigated by British agents. Though false, the rumors roiled the backcountry.

A critical incident occurred that hardened Loyalist and Patriot opposition—the Thomas "Burntfoot" Brown affair. Having arrived from Yorkshire in 1774 with over seventy indentured servants, Brown established a substantial plantation north of Augusta along with the town of Brownsborough. He became highly critical of the new Georgia Provincial Congress. In response, the Liberty Boys, one of the new Patriot associations, determined to make an example of the planter. They gathered at his home and demanded that he join their association. When he quite naturally refused, the Liberty Boys fractured his skull, scalped him, burned his feet (hence the nickname), and paraded the semiconscious man about Augusta as an example. Once healed, Brown fled first to South Carolina and then to East Florida. As a result of his own suggestion to Governor Tonyn, the planter received a lieutenant colonelcy and permission to raise a Loyalist ranger regiment (later the East Florida Rangers) and recruit Indian allies. Operating mainly out of northern Florida, Brown embarked on a series of raids along the South Carolina–Georgia border. In November 1778 his rangers advanced into

Georgia, where they eventually joined Campbell's Augusta expedition. Brown became the chief administrator of Indian affairs for the Atlantic District, one of two sections in the Southern Indian Department. Augusta, however, remained in Patriot hands and a threat to the South Carolina backcountry, particularly the Loyalist region around Ninety Six, as well as to British-held Savannah. In May 1780 Brown captured Augusta, a linchpin in Crown efforts to control the backcountry and promote Indian support, but he could not hold it. Despite a successful defense under Colonel John Harris Cruger in September, in June 1781 Augusta again fell to Patriot forces led by Continental Army dragoon commander Col. Henry "Light Horse Harry" Lee and South Carolina partisan leader Brig. Gen. Andrew Pickens. Despite the setback, Brown's presence and the actions of the East Florida Rangers and other less-formal Loyalist groups no doubt furthered the perception that substantial Loyalist support would be had once British and Provincial regular troops arrived.

From a strategic position, Augusta was critical. Control of the Savannah River region both encouraged Georgia Loyalists and discouraged Patriots. From an operational aspect, holding Augusta added to the security of Loyalist enclaves and Crown outposts in the South Carolina backcountry by inhibiting Patriot movement between that colony and Georgia. In the summer of 1781, Cornwallis and Rawdon would learn just how critical the city was to Crown operations. But for now, with the importance of Augusta in mind and with the support of the Loyalist rangers, Campbell and Prevost set out from Savannah in January 1779.[12]

From the start, the Augusta expedition broke down. Campbell expected an outpouring of Indian and Loyalist support, neither of which materialized. Recent history should have demonstrated to him the folly of relying on Indian allies; Burgoyne already had learned this harsh lesson in New York. With an entirely different strategic and social culture than white Europeans, those Indian allies who did join Crown expeditions tended to become restless and simply walked away in frustration. Campbell and Prevost should also have noted the experience of the most-recent Cherokee war—few things were more likely to unite the backcountry frontier population, Patriot and Loyalist, than the threat of Indians rampaging through the countryside. In a backhanded turn of fortune for Campbell, few Indian allies actually joined his force moving up the Savannah River.

More problematic for the expedition was Loyalist turnout. Initially, support appeared promising, the likelihood of British arms prevailing encouraging many Loyalists previously intimidated by the Liberty Boys and other Patriot groups. Occupying Augusta took little effort and cost few casualties; holding it became a different matter. Two seminal events turned against Campbell: the Battle of Kettle Creek and the arrival of a large Patriot militia force under John Ashe on the Savannah, which culminated in the Battle of Brier Creek.

## Kettle Creek, 14 February 1779

John Boyd, a prominent South Carolina Loyalist introduced to Campbell earlier by Clinton, accompanied the expedition to Georgia; he departed Savannah in mid-January 1779 to recruit South Carolina Loyalists. Promoted to colonel on the Provincial establishment based on the British scheme of commission and rank for recruitment numbers, a process that did not always guarantee effective military leadership, Boyd was optimistic of success. Having embodied a strong force of 350 Loyalists, he made camp near present-day Spartanburg, South Carolina, on 29 January as his base for gathering in more recruits. Departing camp on 5 February and skirting along the Indian frontier, Boyd's men marched for Augusta to join the occupation force. Along the route, they rendezvoused with Colonel John Moore, who brought in 250 North Carolina Loyalists. Despite shadowing by numerous Patriot militiamen, Boyd advanced relatively unimpeded, the Patriots lacking sufficient numbers to confront the larger Loyalist force. Boyd and Moore engaged garrisons at Fort Independence and Broadmouth Creek before successfully crossing the Savannah River on 11 February at Vann's Creek. By the fourteenth, the Loyalists reached Kettle Creek and established an encampment atop a hill. At this point a crucial flaw emerged that repeatedly flummoxed Cornwallis and practically every Crown commander throughout the Southern Campaign—lack of intelligence, known in the modern era as situational awareness. Boyd and Moore did not realize that the bulk of royal forces occupying Augusta had already departed for Savannah. Campbell had never received word of Boyd's approach, leaving the Loyalists isolated and unsupported as they stopped at Kettle Creek.

Meanwhile, Pickens and Georgians Col. John Dooly and Lt. Col. Elijah Clarke, with 350 South Carolina and Georgia Patriot militia, prepared to attack the unsuspecting Loyalist camp. Pickens's plan appeared sound from a tactical viewpoint. In linear warfare, if one can assault the opponent in the front while simultaneously attacking his flanks or rear, chances for success greatly increase. If the opponent has the discipline and training to execute a "refuse the flank" maneuver, he can probably repulse the attack.[13] In the Georgia backwoods of 1779, few militiamen on either side had the experience or training to mount a simultaneous front or flanking assault. As might be expected, the action soon degenerated into a chaotic melee. Pickens led two hundred troops in the frontal assault, while Dooly and Clarke crossed the creek and attempted attacks on both the Loyalists' right and left flanks. The plan deteriorated immediately. Patriot advance guards fired on Loyalist pickets, thus giving alarm to the encampment. With Dooly and Clarke caught in a swamp and unable to close up on Boyd's flanks, the Loyalist commander sprang an ambush on Pickens's advancing main body. As often happened in the clash of irregular militiamen and volunteers that characterized much of the war in the South, a key leader went down and the troops panicked. Wounded by a Georgia Patriot who had made his way into the camp, Boyd collapsed and soon perished. Not surprisingly, the undisciplined and untrained Loyalists panicked and fled as the battle disintegrated into chaos. Boyd and nineteen men died; the Patriots captured an additional twenty-two. While the number of prisoners appears small, by the time many of the refugees reached home and eventually surrendered to local Patriot authorities, Crown losses represented over 150 men. Comparatively, Pickens lost seven killed in action and fifteen wounded. Roughly 270 of the Loyalists eventually reached British forces. Campbell formed the men into two Provincial regiments, the North Carolina Royal Volunteers, under Colonel Moore, and the South Carolina Royal Volunteers, which later formed the 2nd Battalion of the South Carolina Royalists Regiment. While impressive sounding in their names, both units proved ineffective as military bodies. Desertions proved devastating, and within a few months neither formation existed in practical terms.[14]

Kettle Creek was representative of the struggle at the local level between American colonists on both sides. Often, no Continental or British regulars participated in these engagements except for a few senior officers, so they tended to be disorganized melees that typically turned into routs once one side or the other broke and ran. While militarily insignificant in terms of the greater conventional battles at Charleston, Camden, Guilford Court House, and Cowpens, these small actions effectively tamped down Loyalist enthusiasm and simultaneously inspired Patriot hopes; most of the victories belonged to the Patriots. While insignificant in terms of casualties and numbers engaged, Kettle Creek set a trend that should have been recognized at some point by Crown authorities in New York and London, who placed such high hopes in both the willingness of Loyalists to turn out for service and their fighting ability once in the field. The fact that Boyd and Moore could raise only 600 volunteers, despite the relative ease with which Savannah and Augusta were captured, should have given British strategists pause. Kettle Creek established a pattern of Loyalist failure that plagued Cornwallis and all other Crown commanders throughout the campaign and ultimately destroyed the Southern Strategy. In short, this type of hybrid warfare doomed any Crown efforts to achieve the policy objective of restoring the South to allegiance by pacification through a "clear and hold" strategy.

## Brier Creek, 3 March 1779

The second significant event along the Savannah River resulted in a Crown victory—the Battle of Brier Creek on 3 March 1779. Faced with growing enemy activity and the understanding that his plan to attack the rebels gathered across the river had been compromised, Campbell evacuated Augusta on 14 February, the same day as the Kettle Creek action; he retired to a post at Hudson's Ferry downriver. Brig. Gen. John Ashe, a prominent North Carolina planter, politician, and militia officer who had led a Patriot contingent in the Battle of Moore's Creek Bridge, took command of a force consisting of 200 Georgia Continental regulars and over 1,000 North Carolina militia, raised and organized to defend South Carolina or to operate against East Florida. The force—raw, inexperienced, and untrained—arrived at General Lincoln's camp outside Charleston on New Year's Day 1779. To prevent British incursions across the Savannah into South Carolina, Ashe advanced to Purysburg, South Carolina, then to Fort Moore Bluff across from Augusta, overlooking the river. As Campbell withdrew, Ashe received orders to follow and engage. This led to disaster. Having arrived at the bluff with desertions already running high and enlistments expiring, Ashe knew that attacking an experienced, well-trained, and disciplined British force represented folly of the highest order. Nonetheless, he persisted to carry out his instructions.

Advancing along the riverbank, Ashe's command arrived at the junction of Brier Creek with the Savannah. Crown troops under the command of Lieutenant Colonel Jacques Marcus (or James Mark) Prevost, brother of Augustine Prevost, previously had destroyed the bridge across the creek. Ashe did not realize his danger and ordered the men to rebuild the span and await reinforcements. Prevost, in a daring forced march with 900 of Campbell's regular troops up the west side of Brier Creek on 3 March, attacked Ashe's command from the rear. The movement carried off so quickly that the Patriots never realized that the enemy was in their rear until the advancing British line appeared only 150 yards away. Given the period weapons and tactics, this distance represented almost first-volley firing distance. The battle, or rout more accurately, lasted a brief five minutes. Surprised, unready, unsteady, ill-disciplined, and lacking experience and training, the North Carolina militia fled, carrying General Ashe along with them. British "cold steel" quickly prevailed, resulting in stunning casualties. An estimated 150–200 Patriots died in action, with 173 others captured. Col. Samuel Elbert, commanding the Georgia Continentals, stood his ground against the advancing red tide, but to little avail. Despite the Continentals' training, unit cohesion, and discipline, the superior British force quickly overwhelmed the Georgians, losing only five men killed and eleven wounded.[15]

The affair at Brier Creek illustrated several essential dynamics of the coming campaign in Georgia, the Carolinas, and Virginia. When British regulars came up against Patriot militia, the results were often devastating. Continentals, by this late stage in the war, generally could stand toe to toe with their British and Provincial counterparts, but with the destruction of large Continental forces at Charleston and Camden, regular-army commanders never had enough seasoned troops to seriously challenge Cornwallis and other Crown commanders in the field until the British defeat at Cowpens in January 1781. Yet as the campaign progressed, engagements between regular forces did not ultimately win the war in the South. While a conventional engagement—a traditional siege—characterized the Franco-American Yorktown victory, the antecedents for the British disaster lay in the many small actions throughout the southern colonies in the months leading up to October 1781. Despite a few victories, the British strategy foundered on the Loyalists' continuous defeats at Patriot hands in one small engagement after another. These irregular-force actions ultimately undercut an essential leg of the Southern Strategy—active Loyalist support. Thus, British planners and decision makers in London, New York, and in the field suffered not only from a profound strategic incoherence and a breakdown of command and control in the field but also from a devastating misunderstanding of the nature of the war in the South, especially the enthusiasm and willingness of local Loyalists to volunteer for military service and to provide the political and logistical aid necessary to achieve the Crown's "clear and hold" ambitions.

## Prevost's Invasion of South Carolina, April 1779

Despite the Brier Creek debacle, Patriot enthusiasm in Georgia and South Carolina swelled; volunteers poured into camp at Purysburg. By early April, nearly 5,000 Patriots, mostly local militia, had embodied in South Carolina, giving Lincoln a numerical if not a qualitative advantage. He decided to go on the offensive. His operational plan called for a march along the Savannah River's northern bank, crossing at Augusta, to threaten the Georgia backcountry. Leaving 200 men under Brig. Gen. William Moultrie at Black Swamp and Purysburg to counter any Crown moves into South Carolina, Lincoln arrived at Augusta on 22 April. Prevost, however, illustrating the dictum that in war, the enemy always has a vote at your strategic table, flummoxed the Continental commander. Rather than stay to defend Georgia, he launched an offensive of his own aimed at Charleston. If boldness and aggressiveness are traits of an effective field commander, Prevost certainly displayed such characteristics, much to Lincoln's chagrin.

Crossing the Savannah River on 29 April with just over 3,000 effectives, Prevost bypassed the weak defenders at Purysburg and marched for Charleston. His operational intent lay in drawing Lincoln away from Georgia, thus defending Crown gains there by default. Whether or not he believed that he could hold Charleston is not clear. Prevost did understand that Lincoln would have to react and thus draw away from Georgia, the desired strategic effect of the advance on Charleston. A chase ensued as Moultrie desperately raced ahead toward the city while destroying bridges along his march. Despite these delaying efforts, he arrived in Charleston less than five miles ahead of his adversary. From time immemorial, in warfare swiftness and rapidity of movement have always given an advantage to the offensive force. So it was with Prevost.

As Moultrie entered Charleston, one can only imagine the psychological terror gripping the civilian community. Other than the failed threat in 1776, the war had been a distant event to Charlestonians. Now a Crown force, coming not from the sea, but by land, threatened the capital as it arrived at the Ashley River by 10 May. Despite the city's formidable defensive works, the moral factor had to be considered. Symptomatic of the fear, Gov. John Rutledge, having heard accounts that over 7,000 British troops lay southwest of the city, proposed a flag of truce and a parley with Prevost. The proposal assumed that in accordance with the Articles of War typical of the period, soldiers paroled and disarmed could return to their homes; civilians and property would be unmolested. Despite such hopes, Prevost reacted coolly and insisted that all inhabitants must declare their allegiance to the Crown; all who did not would not be granted parole, rather they would be regarded as prisoners of war. He gave the governor's Privy Council four hours to consider his counteroffer. Although Moultrie and his subordinate officers, such as Lt. Col. John Laurens and Brig. Gen. Kasimir Pulaski, attempted to convince the council and the governor that their forces roughly equaled Prevost's and that the Patriots held the defensive advantage, the civilians buckled. Despite the fact that Lincoln had finally reacted and stood only a few days' march distant, the council voted to declare South Carolina essentially neutral, its future status to be based on a peace treaty between South Carolina and Britain. One can only imagine the Patriot officers' fury. Laurens refused to deliver the message to Prevost, and eventually two junior officers had to deliver the document.

Lieutenant Colonel Prevost represented his older brother but refused to convey the council's proposal, arguing that surrender was an entirely military matter. With the British refusal, Moultrie asserted his authority by declaring that the garrison would defend the city. Fortunately for him, the episode had caused a delay in action, allowing Lincoln to close the distance. As a bold and aggressive but ultimately rational and prudent commander, Prevost understood the danger of entrapment between two enemy forces, with Moultrie inside the city and a larger contingent under Lincoln approaching in the field. Julius Caesar had faced a similar situation in his siege of Alesia in 52 B.C.E. and won. But he had had the advantage of time and Roman military engineering in building fortifications that not only enclosed the besieged town but also protected his outer flank from Gallic relief forces. Prevost had neither the time nor the engineering capability. In advancing into South Carolina in hopes of drawing off Lincoln, he had gambled and won strategically. The same bold risk-taking tactically might have worked at Charleston had Moultrie been of a different temperament.

Prevost's offensive in the spring of 1779, despite its eventual failure to take Charleston, had tremendous strategic and operational implications. Not only did it ensure the Crown hold over Georgia, but it also established Charleston as a prime target for the next major British assault. Like a row of dominoes, the events of the first few months of 1779 set in motion a chain of events that would culminate at the tiny village of Yorktown over two years distant.

## The French Counterattack: Second Battle of Savannah, 9 October 1779

By mid-1779, from the strategic viewpoint, the British had achieved the initial objective of obtaining a critical southern port and securing the southern flank from attacks from Georgia at the cost of relatively few casualties. Realizing the danger in the loss of Savannah, French admiral Charles-Henri-Theodat, comte d'Estaing, sending an envoy to Lincoln, proposed a combined operation against Prevost at Savannah. The troops available to Lincoln included Continental forces and regional irregulars, such as those under Col. Francis Marion, soon to be famous as the "Swamp Fox." With a force of nearly four thousand French regulars and colonial troops, including West Indian volunteers, d'Estaing sailed from Haiti on 16 August. The French commander initiated an assault against Savannah on 9 October 1779 by landing troops on Tybee Island. This force consisted of a small landing party, however, and not the main body. The landing alerted British defenders of the pending attack, a factor that weighed heavily in the ultimate outcome. The old maxim of "he who hesitates is lost" applies in great measure to d'Estaing at Savannah.

The comte held rank as both a vice admiral and a lieutenant general, therefore he served as the overall joint commander of both land and sea forces. In the modern military sense, a joint commander is the normal arrangement in such operations, providing unity of command and effort. Militaries over the ages have learned the harsh lesson of a lack of unified command. For the British, the assault on New York in the summer of 1776 benefited from the close cooperation of the Howe brothers in the highly successful amphibious attack. That situation represented an anomaly rarely repeated. The following year Crown forces in the Saratoga Campaign suffered from the lack of strategic coherence caused by the uncoordinated simultaneous operations in New York and against Philadelphia. A unified command with a CinC well versed in the dynamics of both land and sea warfare and supported by a subordinate council of war, composed of experienced naval and military officers, might have avoided the deleterious effect of a lack of unity of command and effort. Indeed, in 1781 the same dynamic would handicap any chance of rescuing or reinforcing Cornwallis at Yorktown due to disputes between senior army and navy leaders in New York, all complicated by the lack of strategic coherence between the North government and the North American commanders.

While speculative, d'Estaing, a veteran seagoing officer, may have lacked the requisite comprehension of the vital importance of speed and surprise in a land campaign despite having commanded several successful West Indies expeditions. He had captured Saint Vincent, Grenada, and several other British Caribbean islands. But a fundamental difference existed as he prepared to land his force in Georgia—Savannah was not an island on which the defenders are essentially frozen in place with little hope of reinforcement or relief against as well-orchestrated siege. As will be seen, Prevost took advantage of that factor to upend all Franco-American hopes of retaking the strategically critical city. Despite having been promoted to brigadier general at age twenty-seven, d'Estaing was first a seaman. He might well have viewed Savannah as he had a West Indian target; if that is true, then the effort proved flawed from the start, with an attendant loss of the critically important surprise factor. Perhaps also, subordinate commanders in the operation failed to make the point that a leisurely landing and advance on Savannah would allow Prevost time to react.

The small force on Tybee Island essentially sat in place, their presence alerting the defenders and allowing Prevost time to prepare his defenses for an impending siege. From a tactical and operational viewpoint, d'Estaing committed a blunder that would undercut any chance of retaking Savannah. Speed of movement and mass/concentration are two principles of war that no commander should ever ignore—to do so risks a poor outcome. In eighteenth-century warfare, with a lack of modern detection and means of gathering tactical intelligence, an amphibious or expeditionary capability gives the aggressor the chance for strategic surprise and the opportunity to catch the opponent unawares and unprepared. In landing what was essentially a scouting force at Tybee Island, the French squandered this critical advantage.

Between 12 and 14 September, d'Estaing landed the bulk of the army at Beaulieu Plantation, twelve miles south of Savannah. As is so often the case in early modern warfare, the troops embarked upon a campaign of pillage and looting, confiscating farm animals, horses, cattle, wagons, and alcohol stores. Local residents predictably responded as had colonists in the northern and middle colonies against earlier depredations, particularly by the German troops in New Jersey. While a diminution of local support in this expedition did not prove crucial in a direct military sense, it nonetheless amplified a pattern of anger, mistrust, and a desire for retribution that increasingly characterized the war in the southern colonies.[16]

As is normal with traditional European siege warfare, d'Estaing called on Prevost on the sixteenth to surrender the city based on the overwhelming array of land and naval forces against him. Such a gentlemanly act, however, further undercut d'Estaing's position. Prevost requested a temporary truce to consider the proposition, to which the comte agreed, a second critical error that further ensured the expedition's defeat. To be fair to d'Estaing, he simply followed the prevailing European conventions. Under this rubric, once a siege commenced and there appeared little hope for imminent relief, if the garrison surrendered after initially offering some form of resistance, particularly if the defenses had been breached, the besiegers were obligated to afford the "Honors of War." The surrendering forces could then march out of the castle or town under arms with music and colors. During the British Civil Wars of the previous century, in such instances weapons had to be unloaded, but the soldiers could carry several musket balls in their mouths. While the practice of "Honors of War" might seem comical to post–World War II sensibilities, the positive effect on the loss of life represented a practical reason for such mercy. If the doomed garrison resisted beyond the degree deemed reasonable to satisfy honor, however, then all civilities vanished. Once the garrison had fallen, rape, pillage, burning, looting, and the murdering of survivors inevitably followed. The horrors of the Thirty Years' War during the seventeenth century, whereby an estimated one-third of the Holy Roman Empire's population perished primarily from starvation and the depredations of war, no doubt weighed heavily on the minds of eighteenth-century military officers. Nevertheless, from a purely military standpoint, d'Estaing's noble action merely gave Prevost the opportunity to gather reinforcements. Despite such gestures intended to ameliorate excessive bloodshed, the war in the South soon turned to barbarism, cruelty, and a complete breakdown of civility that shocked Europeans and most American colonists.

While Prevost considered and d'Estaing waited, troops under Lieutenant Colonel John Maitland arrived by way of Beaufort and Port Royal, South Carolina, having made their way through the swamps and woods into Savannah without opposition from the French besiegers. These 800 reinforcements gave Prevost roughly 3,200 effectives. Almost as importantly, Captain James Moncrief of the Royal Engineers set about constructing stout fortifications and moving artillery into position to repel any landward assault. The defensive line, anchored on the northwest by the Savannah River, extended from the Sailor's Battery and wound around southward to the Spring Hill Redoubt. The line then wrapped around the city and anchored its opposite end on the south bank of the river east of Savannah.

By the twenty-first, the balance of d'Estaing's troops had landed and Lincoln's reinforcements had joined the combined force. Lincoln brought into the fight 600 Continentals and the mounted dragoons and 200 infantrymen of the Pulaski

Legion.[17] In accordance with the overall plan, Lincoln assembled his forces at Ebenezer, north of Savannah. Almost immediately the plan went awry. Prussian general and military theorist Carl von Clausewitz cautions that war is fraught with chaos and probability. Few examples in the War of American Independence better illustrate this dynamic than the badly mismanaged Savannah Campaign. With Lincoln covering the northern approaches and the French to the south, Prevost should have been isolated and helpless; no one accounted for Maitland's force finding its way through the swamps, woods, and backcountry into Savannah unmolested. Faulty intelligence compared to what Prevost received further disjointed the Franco-American effort. Lincoln badly underappreciated the strength of the British defensive works and the state of Prevost's troops. Coordination suffered. Delays plagued Lincoln in assembling his forces, giving Moncrief added time to build and fortify. Relations between Lincoln and d'Estaing soon became frosty and uncooperative.

It is impossible to estimate the number of local militia who turned out for the siege since their numbers changed daily as men came and went. What is clear is that the French landing signaled Georgia and South Carolina militia to turn out in large numbers. As always, their military value remained questionable. Regardless, frustration reigned in the Allied camp with the siege's slow progress. By 23 September, Lincoln and d'Estaing had all preparations completed, but the actual bombardment of British positions did not commence until 4 October. The artillery barrage produced little damage to Moncrief's stout defenses and inflicted few casualties. The comte, distressed at the lack of progress, ordered an all-out assault. While the attack plan had merit, thanks to a deserter, Prevost knew the particulars and arranged his strongpoints accordingly. To the south, over 3,000 French troops supported by Brig. Gen. Isaac Huger's Continentals assaulted the British line. To the north, Lincoln's Continentals, supported on their left flank by Frenchman Theobald Dillon's regiment, struck the Spring Hill Redoubt. Pulaski commanded the Allied cavalry and advanced ahead of the Patriot infantry. The attack came unglued almost from the start. Dillon's regiment aimed for the Sailor's Battery but failed to ford the creek running south from the Savannah, turning away under heavy fire. The comte, who personally led the assault, was wounded twice and left for dead until a French officer managed to drag him to safety. In a sign of respect, the opposing British troops held their fire until the comte could be evacuated from the field. Seeing d'Estaing down, Pulaski assumed that command devolved to himself, turning over the cavalry to a Continental subordinate and making for the headquarters area, accompanied by his aide-de-camp. Within moments both officers suffered grievous wounds. Pulaski, hit by grapeshot in the groin, collapsed.[18] With the loss of these key commanders, the attack faltered. Repulsed at all points, the Franco-American forces retreated. Savannah held. French forces suffered over 600 casualties, while Lincoln's Patriot troops lost roughly 200 men. Prevost, meanwhile, lost around 150 men.

Poorly executed, badly coordinated, and failing to concentrate against the critical British defensive fortification, the attack faltered despite its considerable numerical advantage. Its timing proved to be disastrous. Had Lincoln moved more quickly in assembling his forces and cutting off the northern approaches, including the routes from Port Royal, Prevost would have been placed in a precarious position vis-à-vis the balance of forces. Once the Allies realized that the defenses could not be quickly breached with artillery, the impatient d'Estaing pressed an assault destined to fail. Had he been this keen to land his forces quickly and go on the attack at once, he would have caught Prevost with inadequate defensive fortifications, especially artillery positions, and short of manpower. Once the advantage of celerity had been lost, the advantages of time that a besieger enjoys—starving out the garrison, etc.—were squandered. Disregarding the entreaties of a frustrated Lincoln and displaying the timidity and unwillingness to take bold risks that unfortunately characterized so many French naval commanders of the period, d'Estaing settled for a slow-developing siege. The French soon abandoned the operation, reembarked on their vessels, and sailed to Newport, Rhode Island. Lincoln could only retreat to Charleston to await his turn as besieged.

The outcome at Savannah guaranteed that conditions for Clinton's subsequent operations remained positive. In terms of the strategic effects of the operation, the capture and follow-on defense of the city seemingly validated the Southern Strategy. Events in Georgia created the illusion that battlefield victories through conventional operations represented the key to success and the ultimate restoration of southern allegiance. They also negated French seapower and in no way compromised the use of traditional British expeditionary actions. The French naval presence in theater did not undercut the Royal Navy's ability to transport land forces across great swaths of ocean, land them successfully on the periphery of a defended site, and sustain and reinforce those troops logistically from the sea. The king's troops now firmly held Savannah, the key to defending the southern flank of Crown operations in South Carolina. But had British military officials been more reflective, they would have noticed the disappointing Loyalist turnout around Augusta in the spring. Instead, flush with victory fever, Sir Henry laid plans to press ahead with the next target of the Southern Campaign—Charleston.[19]

Clinton in New York and Germain in London did not fail to see the strategic possibilities. Charleston would be stoutly defended by the Patriots. Nevertheless, it presented a magnificent target for the next step in the southern gambit. With

Charleston situated on a narrow peninsula surrounded on three sides by water, whoever commanded the sea, commanded the city. Clinton and Commodore Parker had failed to take local command of the sea in 1776. In 1780 a different operational plan should mean a better operational result. Despite his wishes to resign the North American command to Cornwallis and return to Britain, Clinton had to be optimistic and buoyed after the string of victories in Georgia. Of the repulse of d'Estaing and the Allied force at Savannah, the CinC commented: "I think this is the greatest event that has happened [in] the whole war. . . . I need not say what will be our operations in consequence."[20]

The string of Crown battlefield victories continued into 1780. Beneath the surface, however, the seeds of destruction lay germinating in the South Carolina backcountry. At this juncture—victorious, encouraged, and emboldened—British authorities failed to understand the ultimate nature of the war in the South and the fatal strategic and operational flaw in the Southern Strategy—Loyalist support and turnout. The lessons learned from the Georgia undertaking that launched the southern gambit proved simply the wrong ones.

## The Siege of Charleston, April–May 1780

Based on the success at Savannah, Clinton saw the capture of Charleston as the tipping point that would destroy the rebellion, or at least recover the more valuable southern colonies. He proposed several possible courses of action for the 1779 operations.[21] If British forces held superiority at sea and by land, they could either force Washington into a decisive battle in New York or attack in the South, defeat any opposing forces, and then use local Loyalists to restore and maintain royal government. This course of action essentially describes the ultimate concept of "clear and hold." If Crown forces held a land superiority but not at sea, the danger of posts being defeated in detail existed, though with a concentration of a large-enough force, they could draw out and finally destroy Washington's army. If Britain had command of the sea but not land superiority, only coastal raiding remained as an option. Clearly, without sea control, no concentration of force against Washington could occur. Coastal raiding accomplished little. And Crown forces had not managed to destroy the Continental Army in several northern battles. The best option, then, appeared to be the Southern Campaign and its reliance on southern Loyalists, the critical vulnerability in the entire scheme. In August Clinton made his fateful decision to shift the main action to the South. He learned that the troops sent the previous year to Saint Lucia would not be returning and that he might receive orders to dispatch two thousand men to reinforce Canada. His attempts to lure Washington into a major battle had come to naught. Patriot threats to the gains made in northern Georgia also factored into his decision to focus south. It could be said that Clinton decided to abandon the war in the North and focus on Charleston primarily to defend Georgia. He advised the American secretary of the decision.[22] In splitting his forces by leaving a defensive garrison in New York and mounting a southern offensive against Charleston, Clinton took a great gamble that violated one of the most fundamental principles of war—concentration. It was a risky gambit; success or disaster relied on the Royal Navy maintaining command of the sea.

On 9 February the first troops touched ground at Simmons (now known as Seabrook) Island, initiating the longest and largest British siege operation of the war in North America. Charleston, the economic dynamo of the South, had long been a target. Clinton's 1776 expedition failed to overcome both the defenses and the sandbars outside the harbor. The British would not repeat those mistakes. The invasion force of nearly 9,000 troops and 400 horses sailed from New York on Boxing Day (26 December) 1779. Vice Admiral Arbuthnot commanded Royal Navy forces in the North American theater and accompanied the invasion fleet. Clinton, as CinC of the land forces, personally embarked to lead the invasion army for the next crucial step in the Southern Campaign. As stated earlier, no joint-command system in the modern sense existed in the eighteenth century; rather, expeditionary operations relied upon cooperation between army and navy authorities on the scene. Under the Howe brothers, General Sir William and Vice Admiral Lord Richard, army-navy coordination occurred almost frictionless during combined operations such as the New York Campaign. This was not the case by 1780. Arbuthnot—known as crotchety, frequently obstreperous, and prone to vacillation and to changing decisions willy nilly once made—and Clinton—prickly, overly concerned with other's opinion of his generalship, and often personally unsociable—simply did not get on with each other. While the admiral spent the campaign in his sea cabin aboard the flagship and the general remained ashore, very little coordination occurred. In truth, the lack of cordiality and more importantly joint army-navy cooperation did not seriously affect operations once the army landed; however, it was symptomatic of the strategic incoherence that plagued British efforts in the final years of the war. Clinton and Arbuthnot's antipathy, unwillingness to cooperate for the common objective, and downright obstreperousness created a breakdown in joint cooperation that paid onerous dividends the following year. When Clinton returned to New York following the capture of Charleston, he made plans to attack the French, who had occupied Newport, Rhode Island, and Narragansett Bay. Even then the CinC and the admiral failed to cooperate for such an expedition, even though Crown forces possessed a temporary two-to-one naval superiority and a significant numerical troop advantage. As the autumn waned and Sir Henry became more and more fixated on a Chesapeake Bay operation, the Rhode Island opportunity faded, to the detriment of British arms. It would be from Newport that the French forces under the comte de Rochambeau and the siege-artillery train sallied forth to Virginia, joining Washington's troops in the final great drama at Yorktown. In the "friction" of war, personality often plays a devilish role.[23]

More important in the end, the frostiness between Clinton and senior subordinates, most critically Lord Cornwallis, second in command of the expeditionary force, plagued command unity. Though each officer respected the other, their relations had been curt and strained due to an incident in 1776 when Clinton, on a rant against Howe, made indiscreet remarks that Cornwallis passed on to their commander. Paranoid about personal criticism, Clinton regarded the incident as a personal betrayal; the two senior officers never fully reconciled. Due to the illness of his wife, Jemima, Cornwallis took leave in the autumn of 1778 and returned to Culford, his Surrey estate. Following her death in 1779, the earl wrote to Clinton that he would happily serve anywhere, indifferent as to where in the world the army sent him. He further revealed to Clinton: "If you should think that you can have any material employment for me, send for me and I will most readily come to you; I really come with pleasure." In a follow-on letter he stated, "I come to share fortunes with you but I will not let you desert me."[24] As time passed, however, Cornwallis, who held a dormant commission as the North American CinC, warmed to the notion of taking over Clinton's position. Writing to his brother William, the earl clearly had become more enthusiastic about American service: "I have many friends in the [British] American army. I love that army, and flatter myself that I am not quite indifferent to them. I hope Sir H. Clinton will stay. . . . If he insists on coming away, of course I cannot decline taking the command and must make the best of it. And I trust that good intentions and plain dealing will carry me through."[25]

Despite the personal animosity, Clinton understood the earl's tremendous military talent and, in his bid to resign the frustrating command, recommended Cornwallis as his successor. Germain's letter of 4 November, cleverly worded to imply the king's great disappointment should the general chose to resign after such a magnificent run of victories, especially when the kingdom was most threatened, must have encouraged Clinton. The American secretary assured him that George III was "too well satisfied with your conduct to wish to see the command of his forces in any other hands."[26] Having anticipated that the king would accept his resignation, however, Clinton had included Cornwallis in the campaign planning. When Germain's letter arrived on 19 March 1780, Cornwallis in a pique requested to be relieved of any further participation in strategic and operational planning and that he receive an independent and separate command. He also ceased providing advice to Clinton and participating in staff meetings, a sign of their growing frostiness and a looming shattering of British command-and-control relationships. In late April Clinton detached Cornwallis to take command of the forces north of the Cooper River, essentially the desired independent command.[27]

From a personal level, Clinton resented the respect and admiration garnered from the subordinate officers and headquarters staff by the far more sociable and popular nobleman, perhaps never realizing that his own difficult personality contributed heavily to his own unpopularity. That Cornwallis generated such loyalty and devotion not only from subordinates but down to the common soldier must have further heightened the enmity. While Clinton tended toward insularity, sensitivity to criticism, and a lack of charm and warmth, the earl exuded an air of both humility and authority at the same time. Captain John Peebles of the 42nd Regiment of Foot (The Black Watch) captured Cornwallis's persona when writing that the earl exuded "ease, elegance & temperance."[28] More serious than the disconnect between army and navy in terms of cooperation and coordination, the increasing ill will between Cornwallis, the eventual field commander in the southern colonies, and Clinton, the soon-to-be distant senior commander, roiled command-and-control relations, degenerating into a disastrous series of miscommunications, muddled orders, and confused strategic intent that culminated eighteen months later on Surrender Field near Yorktown.

Relations between the CinC and Whitehall roiled command and control as well. Clinton felt that Germain (to use a modern term) "micromanaged" him unnecessarily. He resented the interference by the civil authorities in his war management and strategic decision-making. Moreover, he chaffed at the reduction of forces based in New York for what he viewed as ill-conceived peripheral operations in the West Indies. As Piers Mackesy has observed, Clinton "continued to bathe in self-pity over the reduction of his force."[29] The general feared that any strategic failure would be blamed on him when he had little input into the actual strategic decisions. He was well to think that in light of the controversy that raged in Britain in the years following Yorktown. In a back-and-forth pamphlet war with Cornwallis over who was to blame for the collapse of the Southern Campaign and the Yorktown debacle, the earl emerged victorious.[30] Indeed, the weight of history over the centuries still tilts in Cornwallis's favor. Once again, Clinton showed his prescience on future catastrophes, though with little ability to avoid them. Expressing his frustration over his lack of control over strategy and operations, he fairly shouted to Germain: "For God's sake . . . if you wish that I should do anything leave me to myself, and let me adapt my efforts to the hourly change of circumstance. If not tie me down and take the risk of my want of success."[31]

Despite the hidden trouble brewing in the British high command, the army that embarked on the cold day after Christmas 1779 boasted several of the most experienced and veteran regiments in the North American theater. The force included a number of regular infantry regiments that would be tested in continuous and arduous combat and campaigning for months to come, including the 7th, 23rd, 33rd, 63rd, and 64th Regiments of Foot. The light companies drawn from these line regiments formed the Corps of Light Infantry. Grenadier companies from the line regiments were typically formed into grenadier battalions. German troops, mainly hired from the principalities of Hesse-Cassel, Anspach, Bayreuth, and Brunswick, formed into four battalions. A battalion of New York Volunteers rounded out the assault force. A further 1,500 troops departed in a later wave from the British Legion, formed mainly from New York, New Jersey, and Pennsylvania Loyalists under the command of Major Banastre Tarleton, an officer whose reputation for cruel but effective operational artistry became a mythic feature of the popular perception of the campaign. Foul weather resulted in a difficult passage, but by February 1780 Clinton had arrived off Charleston, garrisoned by several thousand Continental troops under Lincoln's command.

British commanders had a good concept of the geography of the Charleston region. Captain George Elphinstone (later Admiral Lord Keith), commanding HMS *Pegasus*, a fast 20-gun frigate, conducted extensive surveillance and reconnaissance particularly of potential landing sites along the South Carolina coast. The North Edisto River, some twenty-five miles south of Charleston, seemed the ideal location for putting forces ashore. Additionally, Prevost's earlier foray had operated in that area, all providing Clinton with the advantage in geographic intelligence . The previous 1776 expedition had showed the folly of a direct attack on the city, even if the troop transports could make it safely past Fort Moultrie's guns. The British plan now called for approaching the city by land and initiating a classic siege. Charleston's position at the end of a peninsula made an indirect approach possible by land, which would also avoid the defenses set to repel a seaborne attack. Therefore, the plan called for cutting off the city by building siege works on the narrow Charleston Neck and controlling the waterways on the north, east, and south sides of the peninsula.

The city's defenses had deteriorated since the 1776 attack. Lincoln frequently encountered interference from local and state political authorities, including Governor Rutledge and Lt. Gov. Christopher Gadsden. This meddling ultimately doomed the beleaguered command and led to the most grievous surrender of U.S. forces until the Bataan debacle in 1942. The siege of Charleston represented a profound breakdown in Patriot civil-military relations that led to Lincoln's surrender and the loss of the city. Civil authorities defied sound military recommendations, insisting on defending the city in the face of an unwinnable situation and refusing to allow Continental forces to escape their otherwise inevitable destruction. The "fog and friction" of war applies to all parties; how

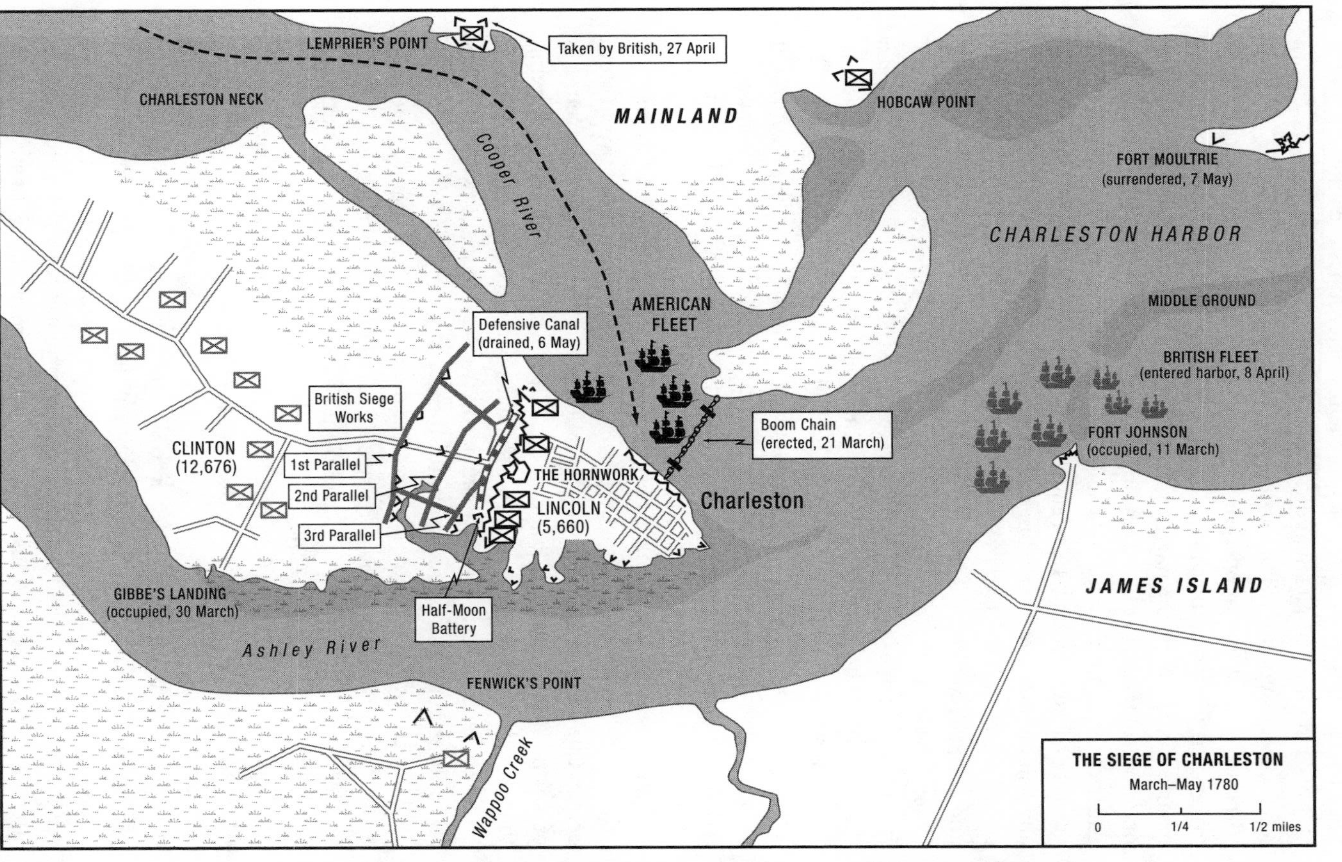


The Siege of Charleston, March–May 1780. Map by Erin Greb Cartography.

one manages the chaos of conflict frequently determines the outcome. In the case of Charleston, despite their own command-and-control difficulties, Crown forces proved superior to the Patriots in that management.

From a standpoint of operational planning, Charleston presented an easy target. Surrounded on three sides by water (the Ashley and Cooper Rivers and Charleston Harbor), the narrow isthmus meant that a besieging force need only control the strip of land leading inland from the city. The French North American squadron's retreat to Rhode Island made British naval control a foregone conclusion. Clinton, then, enjoyed mobility and the flexibility to strike at any point and at any time, a huge advantage over the stationary defenders. In eighteenth-century warfare, so long as the besieger had superior or equal numbers and adequate artillery, particularly heavy siege mortars, the result generally favored the attacker unless the beleaguered garrison received reinforcements. With Crown forces controlling the waterways and the strip of land between the two rivers, Lincoln and the Charleston defenders had little hope of success. Thus, Clinton's simple plan called for cutting off retreat and taking the city by a traditional siege, all keyed to the mobility provided by local sea control; if competently executed, it assured victory. In pursuance of this operational plan, Arbuthnot eventually forced his way up the Cooper River north of the city, his ships furthering hampering any line of retreat.

Lincoln realized his dilemma, but pressure from the civil authorities nullified any escape plan. By late March, the Governor's Council demanded that Lincoln defend Charleston and the civil population. Even with some reinforcements of North Carolina and Virginia Continentals and substantial improvement in the fortified semicircular line across the narrow neck, consisting of redoubts, breastworks, trenches, a swampy canal, and two lines of abatis (wooden stakes set in the ground and pointing toward the enemy), the situation worsened as each day passed. A masonry hornwork and an advanced redoubt called Half Moon Battery anchored the defensive line. The outer trench, designed to be flooded and act as a moat, stretched from river to river across the Charleston Neck. Three 28-gun frigates and a sloop of the Continental Navy as well as some smaller vessels of the South Carolina state navy, all commanded by Commodore Abraham Whipple, arrived to bolster the defenses.

From his base on James Island, on 29 March Clinton struck. Moving his troops by flatboats across the Ashley River to the southern side of the peninsula the previous night, he conducted an amphibious landing several miles northwest of the city. Meanwhile, Arbuthnot's warships blockaded the harbor, prevented reinforcement by sea, and perhaps most importantly attracted the defenders' attention toward the sea, thus masking Clinton's movements. In an operation reminiscent of the 1759 attack on Quebec, where British troops in boats crossed under the guns of the fortress by night unseen, the flatboats passed up the Ashley undetected. By the end of the day, Crown forces controlled all landward and seaward access to Charleston. On 1 April the first parallel trench had been completed 800 yards from the Continental front lines, initiating the siege. Simultaneously, as the British parties toiled by night in their diggings, the last of the Continental reinforcements sent by Washington sailed down the Cooper River. Inside the city, church bells rang out in celebration and troops fired a *feu de joie*, an ultimately useless gesture and waste of vital gunpowder. These reinforcements only added to the tally of prisoners of war weeks later. Lincoln would have no more help as the siege progressed.

By April 8, the stranglehold had tightened with the completion of the first British parallel of two miles stretching across the neck. Fortified artillery batteries capable of bombarding Patriot lines came into action two days later. The defending guns fired back, and at one point almost killed Clinton on a walkabout of the lines, but ultimately to little effect. Work progressed inexorably. With the bombardment batteries fully operational, Clinton sent in a surrender summons, the age-old call for an honorable capitulation by a fortress or city under siege. Lincoln demurred, thus sealing the fate of Charleston and the over 5,000 defenders. Arbuthnot, after a polite prod from Clinton, finally sent his frigates past Fort Moultrie, on Sullivan's Island, in a dash for the inner harbor. Only a single ship, which ran aground, suffered any damage. Arbuthnot thus rendered the harbor unavailable to Lincoln for either escape or reinforcement. Moultrie had been a main impediment to the unsuccessful 1776 operation; Clinton thus understood the vital imperative of nullifying its presence and controlling the inner harbor. Now only the Cooper River remained available as Lincoln's window for escape gradually closed.

## The "Green Dragoon" Emerges: Moncks Corner and Lenud's Ferry

For Clinton, the operational imperative lay in cutting off Lincoln's remaining line of retreat and in intercepting any incoming reinforcements. Accordingly, he detached Lieutenant Colonel James Webster of the 3rd Foot Guards (and acting commander of the 33rd Regiment of Foot) with two regiments and the advance guard under the command of two of the most notable and controversial officers of the campaign, Major Tarleton and Major Patrick Ferguson of the 71st Regiment.[32] Tarleton had earlier shown his command talent at two minor skirmishes in late March, at Pon Pon on the Edisto River and at Rantowles south of the city. In both actions the twenty-six-year-old dragoon officer demonstrated the skills and leadership that soon made him feared and respected but also hated by Carolina Patriots. Earlier in the war, he had exhibited the bold, aggressive, sometimes impetuous, and supremely confident air and attitude that had won him the loyalty and admiration of his troopers and eventually gained him field promotion to a lieutenant colonelcy on the Provincial Establishment. Clinton had the perfect officer for the rapid movements and bold action needed to slam shut any hope of escape from the city or succor from places north.

On 14 April Brigadier General Huger and several hundred Continentals occupied and maintained a critical supply depot for Charleston a few miles away at the Moncks Corner crossroads near the Biggin Bridge across the Cooper River. Any incoming reinforcements would likely have to cross the span. Tarleton intercepted a message from Huger to Lincoln carried by a slave that described in detail the defensive dispositions at Moncks Corner. Approaching in the darkness before dawn, Tarleton and Ferguson overran the ill-prepared and poorly guarded positions. Huger's contingent of dragoons and infantry, among the best troops in the Continental Army, could not withstand the sudden assault; the defense collapsed. To follow this success, Ferguson's infantry stormed across the bridge while Tarleton's British Legion guarded the approaches. Within days more troops arrived to consolidate the British blocking position north of the city. More than a bridge had been lost at Moncks Corner, though, as Crown forces captured over four hundred horses, supplies intended for the Charleston garrison, and a hundred prisoners. Several hundred Continentals escaped into the surrounding swamps, but as a cohesive military unit, Huger's command ceased to exist. Not only had the defenders in Charleston lost a vital logistical center but also one of their few remaining lines of retreat and supply.

By early May, some 200 of the Moncks Corner refugees had reassembled, joining some local militia under Lt. Col. Anthony White on the north bank of the Santee River. With this scratch force, White determined to attack British foraging parties. In many regards his decision to engage in the irregular warfare of ambush and hit-and-run attacks presaged the partisan fighting that emerged later that summer as regular Patriot forces crumbled under relentless assault. Attacking and capturing a twenty-man foraging party, White's actions attracted Tarleton's attention. To engage the enemy, White had moved south of the Santee to Lenud's Ferry, where he intended to cross back during the afternoon of 6 May. In characteristic fashion, Tarleton, privy to the Patriots' movement, charged through and past the picket guard and smashed into the main body. Ill prepared for battle and surprised, White's men had no chance. Forty of them became casualties; Tarleton recovered the forager prisoners and captured sixty Continentals as well. White and some others swam the river and escaped, but once again Tarleton, soon dubbed "The Green Dragoon" for the forest green uniforms worn by his British Legion, had prevailed.[33] With the destruction of

White's force, any effective Continental combat presence on the Charleston periphery all but ceased. Now only the Wando River and Hobcaw Point remained as escape or resupply routes. However, Royal Navy landing parties, assisted by freed black slaves, carried galleys and other small vessels across the Charleston Neck to the Cooper River. Cornwallis then attacked and took Hobcaw Point and moved up the Wando River, finally closing off all routes in or out of Charleston.

The actions at Moncks Corner and Lenud's Ferry represent a characteristic of British commanders seen in the many struggles over the next several months—bold, aggressive, offensive-minded action, though often accompanied by injudicious and imprudent risk taking and a willingness to attack without proper situational awareness. Clausewitz admonishes that understanding the nature of a conflict is the "first, the supreme, the most far-reaching act of judgment that the statesman and commander have to make." While the august Prussian referred to overall national policy and strategy, at the operational and tactical level of war, the admonition to establish awareness of the nature of the fight one is about to engage in is critical to success. Unfortunately for Crown arms, the otherwise supremely talented officers engaged in the Southern Campaign typically dismissed or ignored this imperative at all levels of consideration.[34]

Tarleton and Ferguson certainly exemplified boldness, aggressiveness, and an offensive mindset, but so too did their senior officer, Lord Cornwallis, appointed by Clinton as the independent commander for all Crown forces north of the city and east of the Cooper River.[35] In this regard both Tarleton and Ferguson fit into the Cornwallis mold, a commander noted for bold, aggressive, swift strikes against an unprepared or vulnerable opponent, but also an officer who commanded incredible loyalty and sacrifice from his soldiers, a sign of the immense moral authority of each man. Another officer emerged in the early weeks of the Southern struggle—Lieutenant Colonel Francis, Lord Rawdon, commander of the Loyalist Volunteers of Ireland—who played a pivotal role in British attempts to hold South Carolina once Cornwallis advanced into North Carolina and Virginia. (More will be heard from Rawdon in due course.) So as the fall of Charleston unfolded, the British command team that would drive the Southern Campaign evolved and emerged. In granting Cornwallis a free hand—"In all this, however, I rely on your Lordship's zeal and knowledge to act in every respect in the manner most beneficial to the King's service"—Clinton opened a Pandora's box of evils from which British strategic coherence and command and control never recovered. Perhaps those words came to haunt the CinC as the campaign unfolded into 1781. Cornwallis—determined, aggressive, and often headstrong, with specific strategic conceptions often at odds with his superior's ideas—increasingly chafed at any direction from Clinton. But in 1780 these orders allowed the aggressive Cornwallis free rein, and he took full advantage.[36]

In an ironic way, the ease of victory at both Moncks Corner and Lenud's Ferry ultimately became a strategic disaster for the Crown. If one examines the "lessons" from the affair as they appeared on the surface, one can easily see how the events validated Cornwallis's operational concept that bold, aggressive, offensive action would win the day and crush the rebellion. Afterward, the "clear and hold" strategy could take hold and restore Crown authority. Less apparent was that in destroying conventional enemy forces in these actions, enemy interaction and adaptation would inevitably occur. Faced with few strategic alternatives, South Carolina Patriots turned to irregular tactics in the following months. Despite their best efforts to rouse Loyalists and to tamp down the Patriots using regular forces, Cornwallis and his subordinate officers never implemented an effective counterstrategy to address the emerging nature of the war in the South that summer. Thus, guided by his natural strategic and operational inclinations, Cornwallis plowed ahead with the "clear and hold" strategy once he assumed overall Crown command in the South in June. Sun Tzu advocated attacking the enemy's strategy and alliances above all else.[37] For the next several months, Cornwallis stuck to the lessons of Moncks Corner and Lenud's Ferry, while the Patriots adopted a Sun Tzu–like strategy of attacking the Crown alliance of Loyalists and regulars, frustrating British offensives with attrition by strategic defensive (more commonly known as a Fabian strategy) as carried out magnificently by Nathanael Greene throughout 1781. As Cornwallis marched inland in pursuit of the conventional victory, his task became harder and harder as British strategic cohesion and command and control deteriorated. Indicative of this breakdown between Cornwallis and his commander are Clinton's words of 26 April: "He will play me false, I fear."[38]

## The Fall of Charleston, May 1780

Using classic siege techniques, British diggers advanced the trenches forward. Constructing a second parallel that reached from river to river at 450 yards from the Patriot front line, the batteries moved forward. By 25 April, a third parallel became active. This line almost reached the canal that formed the outermost defensive works. Now within sniper range, casualties among the diggers and the infantry manning the trenches increased. Although the parallels zigzagged across the line to complicate oblique firing from the enemy, great care still had to be taken to not expose oneself to enemy fire. Since much of the digging occurred at night, the Patriots set fire to the tangle of branches and trees forming the abatis in front of their first line to illuminate the British workers and provide light for sniping.

To counter this threat, Clinton posted the German Jägers in the front positions. Armed with rifles, many were foresters and huntsmen from the Black Forest region of the southern Germanic states, now serving as skirmishers, scouts, and snipers. These expert marksmen severely limited the enemy sniping and confounded Patriot attempts to destroy the British works with artillery.[39] With the canal breached by the thirtieth, engineers drained the last great barrier between the lines in preparation for the inevitable infantry assault.

As the entrenchments moved forward throughout April and into early May, it took several days to move the 24-pounders into their new positions and to reestablish the logistics tail from the batteries to the rear magazines. By 8 May, the British works had advanced to within a few yards of the Patriot breastworks, placing Charleston within range of mortar fire. To add to Lincoln's woes, the Fort Moultrie garrison surrendered on the sixth to a Royal Navy landing party, allowing unmolested passage for any naval transits in or out of the harbor. With recent reinforcements, Clinton now had over 10,000 troops poised to invest Charleston. Once the Royal Artillery commander reported that his guns and logistics were in place, they could commence bombardment at any time. Clinton wanted to avoid the bloodshed that characterized any infantry assault on a defended city and the inevitable civilian slaughter that followed. In a visit ashore to meet with the general, a habit he did not normally engage in, Arbuthnot again waffled as to when his frigates sitting in the inner harbor would close the distance and bombard the city. Even with Fort Moultrie neutralized, the city's defenses against seaborne attack promised considerable damage to the warships. The admiral did agree to conduct desultory attacks on specific targets, after which his vessels periodically closed the range and opened fire. Whipple's few ships remained powerless to oppose these pinprick attacks. Before Arbuthnot returned to his flagship, he and Clinton composed a final surrender demand.

Despite the threat of utter destruction and the lack of any hope of relief or reinforcement, the characteristic Patriot stubbornness, witnessed in so many incidences in the northern and middle-colony campaigns, caused Clinton consternation and distress. Lincoln hoped for an honorable surrender in accordance with the Honors of War, which would allow his men to evacuate the city. But civilian leaders, notably Lieutenant Governor Gadsden, would have none of it. As expressed in a letter to Cornwallis, a frustrated Clinton remarked, "I begin to think these people will be blockheads enough to await the assault."[40]

In response, Lincoln, now desperate to mitigate bloodshed, proposed that all militia should be demobilized and sent home rather than sharing the fate of the Continental regulars and becoming prisoners of war. Further, in accordance with the traditional "Honors of War," he insisted that the Continentals be allowed to march out of the city with regimental colors and martial music. But a key condition remained unaddressed—the fate of Charleston itself. In the absence of such, Clinton and Arbuthnot refused Lincoln's truce request. The next morning the bombardment of Charleston commenced. Captain Johann Ewald described the action thusly: "Orders were given to fire on the city with red-hot shot, which set fire to several houses and made the sight more terrible and melancholy, whereupon the enemy fire weakened somewhat. The Commander in Chief, who pitied the city being reduced to ashes, issued orders about ten o'clock to stop the firing of red-hot shot, and granted the besieged time to reconsider."[41]

The threat of British "hot shot" so unnerved civil authorities that on 11 May the council advised Lincoln to seek the best possible terms.[42] Lincoln's rage at this tardy decision to capitulate must have been sublime. Indeed, from an operational viewpoint, he still had alternatives. Had he moved his forces northwest of Charleston, thus allowing Clinton to enter and occupy the city, he might have become the besieger; at the least, Lincoln could have preserved the largest Continental force south of New York. With the British in Charleston, what if the French could be induced to land troops north of the city to initiate a siege while their navy challenged Arbuthnot's command of the sea? Many possibilities lay before Lincoln if only he could have escaped when he had a reasonable chance. By 11 May, that chance had disappeared. Early that afternoon a white flag appeared above the Patriot defenses.

On 12 May Lincoln surrendered Charleston and his army unconditionally. Clinton and Arbuthnot, accompanied by two grenadier companies, rode toward the city, where Lincoln waited at the hornwork gates. By the terms of the surrender, militiamen received a parole and could return home, though without arms and ammunition. The Continentals marched out, with their regimental bands playing "The Turk's March," to stack arms but with colors cased. The men of these ten regiments from North and South Carolina and Virginia became prisoners of war. Based on official British tallies, the final accounting came to 5,500 Continental regulars, 500 or so militia, 33,000 cartridges, 400 guns, over 8,000 artillery round shot, four frigates, and great quantities of other supplies captured. With the loss of only seventy-six killed and fewer than three hundred wounded, Clinton had inflicted the worst defeat of the war on the American Patriots.

With the primary southern city again under the royal standard, a twenty-two-gun salute celebrated the victory. Unbeknown to the celebrating British, German, and Loyalist troops and supporters, the conquest of Charleston represented the high-water mark of the fight to regain the South and restore at least the most economically important colonies to allegiance. For the moment, however, the Charleston victory validated the "clear and hold" strategy. British arms had crushed Continental Army resistance by conventional operations and had conquered a key geographic position. Charleston would serve as the linchpin for the pacification efforts in the hinterland by force of arms, allowing the Loyalists to turn out and reestablish royal government and security. Ironically, the circumstances of the city's fall—a classic siege, land-and-sea operational cooperation, trapping the opponent in a fixed and vulnerable site, where the loss of command of the sea negated reinforcement or escape—mirrored precisely the situation seventeen months later at Yorktown. As Clinton thanked his principal subordinates in his after-action report of 13 May to Lord Germain, he also cited the "Courage and Toil" exhibited by the troops and sailors engaged in the operation.[43]

## Dissolution of a Strategy, May–June 1780

Despite the astounding victory at Charleston, within weeks British hopes for restoring the South to allegiance began to unravel. Based upon the self-serving reports of prominent southerners such as James Simpson—and perhaps the hopes of an increasingly frustrated military command and ministry—the Southern Strategy offered the possibility of a quick campaign to end the rebellion in Georgia, the Carolinas, and Virginia. But that plan relied foremost on one central, pivotal dynamic—"winning the hearts and minds" of the people. Perhaps overused in the popular vernacular when describing irregular, civil, or guerrilla war, the phrase is still nonetheless valid in terms of capturing the essence of the social dimension of warfare. Popular support is indeed the keystone to victory. With it, even a weak irregular force has at least a chance at victory. Without it, even the most capable, resolute, and powerful conventional force might well lose in the end. British strategy relied on not only the goodwill of southern Loyalists but also their active military and logistic support. Loyalists would not only reinforce and support regular forces but also provide security, maintain royal control once the regular army had moved on, suppress rebel activity, and encourage and protect Loyalists and neutrals.

Three separate events occurred that undermined the Southern Strategy and proved it ephemeral, hollow, and brittle. One can also rightly argue that other events might have been critical in its unraveling, including its reliance on the transitory and fickle nature of public opinion and popular will. But the three events—the loyalty proclamations of 22 May–3 June 1780, the Waxhaws Massacre of 29 May, and the Battle of Ramsour's Mill in Tryon County, North Carolina, on 20 June—certainly had the compounding effect of exacerbating the rapid deconstruction of "clear and hold." Clausewitz advocates the concept of the "culminating point," whereby the maximum value or the zenith of military success is reached. On a broader scale, once one reaches the culminating point of victory, one has achieved the maximum possible advantage militarily or politically. He cautions that to go beyond such definitive bounds, the attacker or the state in general will see the correlation of forces turn to the defender's advantage. If one looks at the Charleston victory in light of Clausewitz' culminating-point concept, an argument can be made that as of 11 May 1780, the British culminating point of victory for the restoration of American allegiance had been reached. Such realizations usually only become apparent in hindsight.[44]

## "A Want of Discrimination": The Charleston Proclamations of May and June 1780

At the Southern Campaign's outset, British forces appeared on the verge of ultimate strategic and political success. After the fall of Charleston, Clinton departed for New York on 5 June, leaving Cornwallis in overall command for what appeared to be a seemingly simple mopping-up operation combined with embodying, training, and equipping the vast numbers of expected Loyalists. In hindsight, one can generally identify a point at which the momentum shifts from one side to the other in any contest. Although neither officer nor any other senior decision maker in the Crown camp recognized it at the time, Clinton's issuance of the proclamation of 3 June 1780 became that tipping point. While the series of proclamations issued on 22 May and 1 and 3 June generally granted lenient paroles to captured soldiers and promised harsh treatment for anyone guilty of harassing or attacking Loyalists, a provision of the 3 June decree stipulated that all citizens who failed to take the oath of allegiance to the Crown would be considered in rebellion. Additionally, a captured and released Continental Army or Patriot militia soldier could not be on parole and remain neutral. While many neutrals might have simply ignored events in hopes of staying above the fray, this declaration ensured that all must be involved.[45]

The 1 June proclamation, issued by Clinton and Admiral Arbuthnot serving as joint peace commissioners charged with civil government and the restoration of tranquility in the South, seemed reasonable enough. It promised that former rebels would have all of their property restored, guaranteed, protected, and not subject to parliamentary taxation. Additionally, it offered a full pardon to all Patriot prisoners of war as well as any other rebels still fighting if they simply laid down their arms and swore the oath of allegiance. With a simple oath, these colonists had their full rights as Britons restored. Those still in rebellion faced two starkly opposing alternatives—either take the loyalty oath, return home peaceably, and engage in no further rebellious activity or face imprisonment, most likely in one of the infamous prison hulks. Faced with such a choice, one wonders how sincerely Patriots swore the oath of allegiance.

The 1 June proclamation stunned and alarmed Loyalists. Expecting the appropriate punishment for treason and rebellion, which included steps ranging from simple property sequestration to death by hanging, they expected Crown authorities to exact harsh punishment and retribution for the oppression suffered at Patriot hands over previous years. Instead, the proclamation granted rebels all the rights and protections for which Loyalists had fought, suffered, and died. Why Clinton and Arbuthnot included terms bound to infuriate their Loyalist allies and "Friends" is a legitimate question. From a practical standpoint, Clinton opposed the premature restoration of civil government in the colonies and questioned the "hold" aspect of the overall pacification strategy. He had qualms about relying upon good faith and willing Loyalist support; additionally, he doubted that pure military force could restore ultimate peace and allegiance. In addition, he wanted a firm military basis for imposing a peace with conditions on America. Arbuthnot challenged Clinton to define their future intentions for restoring government, which spurred the issuance of the proclamations hard on the heels of the resounding Charleston victory. To Clinton, they seemed a legitimate measure to restore tranquility and assure a gradual, stable transition to royal governance. Instead of tranquility, though, his unilateral 3 June measure further divided the Americans into two distinct camps by warning them that they must actively support the British effort to restore the king's rule or be identified and treated as rebels—it polarized the issue. In essence, the proclamation provoked opposition and solidified the Patriots in their cause. Ultimately, neutrals went over to the independence side in great numbers, not that many actively participated in a military way, but in terms of not supporting the Crown, their actions or lack of action became a crucial aspect of keeping the war going. Additionally, many paroled rebel militia and Continentals, faced with a hard choice of swearing a false allegiance or breaking parole, chose the latter.

What did Clinton hope to achieve by these proclamations? If he could pacify the Patriots, it would permit Loyalists the maximum opportunity to demonstrate their commitment. While the edicts demanded that rebels declare their loyalty, it offered no mechanism for enforcing good faith except by brute military force. It also compelled Loyalists to openly declare their fealty but left them unprotected from any backlash. The proclamations created uncertainty and disillusionment. While forcing southerners to affirm their allegiance—without enforceable credibility—they undercut the ability to protect, nurture, or exploit Loyalists who openly embraced the royal cause. In fact, Clinton's acts may have diffused the British powerbase rather than consolidate it. These measures created a drain on British military strength when resources had to be dispersed to protect Loyalist enclaves such as Ninety Six once the regular army had moved out in the pursuit of Continental Army forces.[46]

Clinton and Arbuthnot perhaps felt that the proclamations would be successful based on the New York–New Jersey precedent. Following the victories in the

New York and New Jersey Campaigns of July–December 1776, more especially after they drove Washington and the Continental Army out of New York City by late summer, the Howes issued a similar joint proclamation, leading to an immense Loyalist turnout, many likely having been previously neutral or trending Patriot. Provincial regiments that later campaigned in the South, such as De Lancey's Brigade, the Volunteers of Ireland, the Queen's Rangers, and the British Legion, experienced massive enlistments. These Loyalist troops in many respects became as good as the British Army regulars. Based on that experience, why not expect the same result in the South? Would the fact that so many Low Country (Charleston-area) citizens signed the loyalty oath have caused British authorities to believe that the backcountry people would do likewise? A look at the page after page of Charlestonians who signed the oath just after their city's surrender starkly illustrates the impression that Clinton and Arbuthnot must have had of the prospects for the countryside.[47]

There existed another deadly trap for the strategic assumptions made by British commanders and civil administrators. Is it reasonable to assume that most of the Loyalists likely to turn out for actual military service had done so by 1780, with many Provincial regiments already having been raised and fully trained, disciplined, and equipped since 1776 and 1777. In the South, units included the Royal North Carolina Regiment, South Carolina Royalists, and East Florida Rangers. And as noted earlier, many veterans of the French and Indian War who had demobilized in the colonies, especially from the various Scottish Highland regiments such as the 77th Regiment of Foot (Montgomery's Highlanders), the 78th Regiment of Foot (Fraser's Highlanders), and the 42nd Regiment of Foot (The Black Watch), joined Provincial units, including the future 84th Royal Highland Emigrants.[48] Recruitment proved especially heavy among recent Highland settlers in the Cross Creek region, many of whom fought in the Moore's Creek debacle. While pure speculation, could this dynamic—that those most inclined to serve had already taken the king's shilling—be an explanation for the paltry numbers who turned out in 1780–81?

Cornwallis found the proclamations a hindrance and an embarrassment; eventually he repudiated most of his commander's edicts. They galvanized opposition, which gained strength and momentum through the summer of 1780, just as Cornwallis moved inland to complete the South Carolina pacification. Clinton's declarations created a perspective that the British acted in bad faith. They alienated Loyalists who expected to be treated better than former rebels and proved that the British could offer no genuine guarantees or protections. Crown forces simply could not crush the rebellion when they ostracized their allies and provoked their enemies to resist. Ultimately, Cornwallis lost control of the political forum in the South as Patriots reacted to fill the power vacuum left in his army's wake. Patriots and Loyalists soon engaged in a violent, irregular vendetta struggle that escalated into a terrible civil war. This struggle degenerated into political disorder, wrecking efforts at political pacification. While the "clear" strategy seemed to be working after Charleston, the "hold" aspect came to ruin literally within weeks of that triumph.

Rawdon wrote with discouragement on the almost immediate detrimental effect of the pronouncements: "That unfortunate Proclamation of the 3d of June has had very unfavorable consequences. The majority of the Inhabitants in the Frontier Districts, tho' ill disposed to us, from the circumstances were not actually in arms against us . . . , and nine out of ten of them are now embodied on the part of the Rebels."[49] Cornwallis also realized their devastating effect. In a letter to Arbuthnot he stated succinctly:

> I hope you will not be offended when I assure you that the Proclamation of the Commissioners, of the 1st [June], and that of the General [Clinton] of the 3rd, did not at all contribute to the success of my operations. Nothing can in my opinion be so prejudicial to the affairs of Great Britain as a want of discrimination. You will certainly lose your friends by it, and as certainly not gain over your enemies. There is but one way of inducing the violent rebels to become our friends, and that is by convincing them it is in their interest to be so.[50]

In terms of strategic communication and winning the "hearts and minds" of the public, Clinton and Arbuthnot's proclamations accelerated the long downward spiral of British misfortunes on the road to Yorktown.

## "Tarleton's Quarter": The Waxhaws Incident, 29 May 1780

Within days of the first proclamation's issuance and Cornwallis's opening moves, an incident occurred that epitomized the struggle's coming brutality. Col. Abraham Buford's 3rd Virginia Regiment of the Continental Line along with some troopers of Col. William Washington's Continental Dragoons (Virginians) and local militia that had escaped from the Moncks Corner disaster earlier had been on the march to reinforce Charleston. Barely forty miles distant when they arrived at Lenud's Ferry on the Santee River, they heard of Charleston's surrender. General Huger ordered Buford to retreat to Hillsborough, North Carolina, that colony's capital. Retreating northward toward safety, Buford's command arrived at the Waxhaws settlement just south of the North Carolina line. With approximately 350 Virginia Continentals, two 6-pounder field pieces, and a scattering of the Moncks Corner and Lenud's Ferry refugees, Buford's command then represented the only organized Patriot military force in South Carolina.

Clinton, still headquartered in Charleston, saw an opportunity to catch the refugees with a fast moving "flying column" and dispatched Cornwallis with 2,500 troops accompanied by Tarleton's British Legion and several field pieces. The

CinC's orders mandated three distinct missions: (1) capture Governor Rutledge, who had escaped from the Charleston noose and joined Buford; (2) neutralize Buford's Continentals; and (3) begin the work of pacifying the Carolina backcountry.[51] The third task appeared imminently accomplishable. After all, Rutledge's pleas to the upcountry Patriot militias to come to Charleston's aid had fallen flat, further enhancing the impression that cowing the colony into submission would not be difficult.

By the twenty-sixth, Cornwallis had only reached Nelson's Ferry on the upper Santee. Meanwhile, Buford moved steadily north, confident of his escape. At this juncture Cornwallis, in an action that characterized his modus operandi throughout the Southern Campaign, defied the normal doctrinal commandment to concentrate forces and detached Tarleton on 27 May with elements of the 17th Light Dragoons, British Legion, and 100 mounted infantry accompanied by a single 3-pounder field gun—approximately 270 mounted men— to give chase. The eager Tarleton moved swiftly to intercept Buford's bedraggled command in a two-day forced march in the intensely humid early summer air. In typical Tarleton fashion, the men traveled by day and night with few rest stops, eating rations in the saddle and enjoying little sleep. (This last factor must be borne in mind in terms of the effect of physical stress and exhaustion on the soldiers, especially their psychological state of mind, in their subsequent actions.) Racing through swampy terrain and sandy pine barrens, the force covered 105 miles in fifty-fours hours, a movement rarely equaled in military history. Arriving at Camden the following day, he rested his men for a few hours before continuing the chase in the early morning of the twenty-ninth. At Colonel Rugeley's Mill north of Camden (the site of another engagement in the upcoming partisan war), Tarleton realized that his intended quarry there had escaped; Governor Rutledge and his staff, on hearing of the rapid British movement, had departed in another direction. He then pressed ahead after Buford and, on the early afternoon of the twenty-ninth, came upon the Continentals at the Waxhaws.[52]

With Buford's men strung out in a ragged line along the road and the accompanying artillery too far ahead to provide effective support, Tarleton seized the tactical advantage and struck the Continental rear guard. But he faced the same disadvantage as Buford in that those troopers unable to maintain the headlong pace remained strung out over several miles. Tarleton needed a deception and decided to send out an officer with an offer to accept Buford's surrender on the same terms as accepted by Lincoln. The envoy also claimed that the British had over 700 men ready to attack, with Lord Cornwallis and his main force just behind and in hot pursuit.

The ruse gave Tarleton time to pull in stragglers and organize his cavalry for an assault. Buford, observing the developing attack, arranged his defense by forming a single line through a lightly wooded and essentially flat area, ideal terrain for cavalry deployment. In this regard the colonel committed a critical tactical error. Before the Industrial Age, the only effective defense against a stout cavalry charge lay in concentration. British infantry had mastered the square, essentially a two-row-deep square or diamond formation with the front row kneeling, bayonets out, and the second row with arms at the shoulder or poise position, ready to fill any gaps on the front row caused by casualties. Not surprisingly, horses are not terribly keen on jumping into or over a solid row of bayonets. The worst possible formation to receive charging cavalry is an extended line; why Buford chose this deployment remains a mystery. Meanwhile, the Continental baggage wagons and artillery pressed on in flight, another grave tactical error. The second-most-effective defense against charging cavalry is artillery firing canister or grapeshot; it not only causes heinous damage to riders and horses but also creates chaos and disrupts the charging unit's cohesion. Again, why Buford elected to dispense with his artillery advantage is surprising and mystifying from a tactical and doctrinal perspective.

Tarleton launched a three-pronged attack on the Continental's left, center, and rear. Shortly past 3:00 P.M. the attack commenced, with sixty dragoons, supported by volleys from another sixty dismounted legionnaires, charging against the Continental left. Meanwhile, forty horsemen of the 17th Light Dragoons, one of only two regular-army cavalry regiments in the Southern Campaign to that point, struck the Patriot center. Tarleton, leading thirty or so men, circled around the enemy right and struck from the rear. Given Buford's situation and his tactical deployment, the only defense against this triple envelopment was to right-left about turn, where every other man does an about face, thus fronting the enemy on both sides. The disadvantage, of course, is that this effectively reduces firepower by half. Meanwhile, British stragglers and the single artillery piece arrived on a slight hill near the center of the line, providing a reserve of sorts. Once again Buford made a critical tactical error by allowing Tarleton's stragglers to occupy the high ground. While the ultimate result was in no way influenced by this last mistake, had the engagement gone on for an extended time, this terrain issue might have been decisive.

According to Tarleton's account, he heard Buford order the line to hold fire until the approaching enemy reached ten paces.[53] It is most unlikely that in the noise and chaos of combat he could have overheard such an order and probably invented this particular item in his account. Nevertheless, the Continentals did hold their fire until the British came practically upon them—yet another grievous tactical error. The resulting volley did little damage to the charging dragoons, who in seconds reached Buford's line. As the Continentals started to prime and load after the initial volley, the charging troopers caught them fumbling with cartridge boxes. (Alternately, the command "Charge Bayonet" might have been given. Regardless, a horse at full gallop would cover the ten paces, or about thirty feet, in literally a few seconds.) With men trying to bite off the ends of cartridges to prime and load or, even still, removing them from the box (or for that matter attempting to bring the musket to the "Charge Bayonet" position), they were defenseless when the horsemen struck. Inevitably, carnage ensued as troopers slashed with their heavy cavalry sabers and broadswords at the hapless infantrymen. The sudden, violent charge broke apart the Patriot formation and collapsed the line in a classic demonstration of the convergent assault. Chaos reigned as Buford lost tactical control of the battlefield. In an excellent demonstration of what Clausewitz calls the chaos and probabilistic nature of warfare, communications between the various segments of the Continental formation broke down.[54] A junior officer, supposedly Ensign John Cruit, on the Continental right flank attempted to parley by mounting a white cloth on his sword and walking forward. But Continentals on the far side of the line, either refusing to surrender or not understanding the parley attempt, kept on fighting. At roughly the same time Tarleton's horse went down, trapping the commander under the saddle. Thus, on both sides command and control collapsed for a crucial few minutes as troopers freed Tarleton from under his wounded mount. Other dragoons, enraged and believing that their commander had been killed or wounded, made no distinction between surrendering troops and those still resisting. A slaughter ensued as individuals and groups of soldiers attempted to surrender. Legion troopers slashed with heavy sabers and thrust with bayonets at stunned victims in the blistering late-afternoon sun.

American accounts of the engagement claim that Buford had raised a surrender flag, yet Tarleton drove his men on to the attack. According to these reports, Crown troops kept up their assault for a full quarter hour as the Virginians attempted to defend themselves. Tarleton reported that when his horse was killed, word spread among his men that he had been slain as well. By the time he remounted and took positive control of events, the massacre had already happened. The entire engagement lasted for only a half hour, but the damage to the Crown cause proved immense in the coming months. Historian Jim Piecuch explodes the Waxhaws mythology through a systemic evaluation of the contemporary and later accounts from participants and commentators. He concludes: "The evidence does indicate that some British troops killed Americans who tried to surrender because the British believed these men had killed their commander. These killings clearly occurred on a small scale, both in absolute numbers and relative to similar incidents perpetrated later in the war. An objective analysis shatters the myth of the Waxhaws 'Massacre,' although it comes far too late for the hundreds of British and Loyalists soldiers who died needlessly at the hands of Americans shouting 'Tarleton's Quarter.'"[55]

Whatever the truth of the matter, it became irrelevant in terms of strategic communication and public perception. As word of the catastrophe spread, no doubt greatly exaggerated with each retelling, the event came to be called the "Waxhaws Massacre," and the rallying cry of "Tarleton's Quarter" as a symbol of resistance to royal tyranny struck a profound blow to British chances of achieving strategic victory in the South. In the final reckoning, Crown forces inflicted horrendous casualties on Buford's command: 113 killed in action, 150 wounded, and 53 captured; Tarleton lost only 5 killed and 14 wounded. While British commanders viewed the event at Waxhaws as a stunning victory, to a populace imbued with the concepts of honor in war and the avoidance of barbarity, the incident started the accelerating slide of otherwise neutral southerners toward the cause of independence. Thus, in the battle for the allegiance—and perhaps more importantly the necessary physical support—of the southern Loyalists, British commanders squandered public good will through actual or perceived egregious actions that, while perhaps militarily necessary, violated popularly held concepts of the civilized conduct of war. In terms of British strategic communication, the Waxhaws affair proved a devastating setback. Ironically, Lord Germain wrote to Clinton on 5 July of the king's pleasure with Tarleton's victory and instructed the CinC to "Convey to Major Tarleton His Majesty's Approbation of His Conduct, and of the Behaviour of the Corps he commanded in the affair at Wacsaw, The celerity of the March, and the Vigor of the Attack, do them equal Honor, and merited the complete Victory with which they were crowned."[56]

Whereas Tarleton accomplished a brilliant tactical and operational success, this incident underscores a key Crown weakness throughout the conflict—the failure to fully understand the war's nature, with public opinion representing the actual center of gravity in the South. Cornwallis eventually understood that critical dynamic as his campaign progressed, but as he marched into the South Carolina interior, the reality, clouded by the ease of success in conventional engagements such as Charleston, Moncks Corner, Waxhaws, and others had not yet become apparent. While Continental forces might have appeared to Cornwallis, his subordinate officers, and independent commanders in the field to be the Patriot power opposing them, in reality, negative public opinion proved far more important and ultimately dangerous to the "clear and hold" strategy. Crown forces showed repeatedly the ability to accomplish the "clear" portion, but the "hold" aspect remained difficult and ultimately an illusion. The consequences of this blind eye to effective strategic communication became starkly clear in the coming months. Yet with the glow of victory at Charleston and apparently at

Waxhaws, British arms advanced along with the reputation of key officers, notably Tarleton. In his after-action report of 13 May, Clinton recommended breveting the young officer to lieutenant colonel. General Amherst, the CinC of the British Army, concurred. While Tarleton basked in adulation and congratulation, the Patriot propaganda effort forged full speed ahead. The battle for "hearts and minds" was joined.[57]

## "This Unlucky Business": Ramsour's Mill, 20 June 1780

By late June, events in North Carolina spiraled out of Cornwallis's control. Despite his admonitions to tend to their harvest and to await his arrival in the fall, western North Carolina Loyalists embodied and prepared for the upcoming campaign. John Moore arrived from Charleston on 7 June determined to raise the western North Carolina Loyalist militia. Moore, a Tryon County native, had served with Crown forces through the South Carolina operations; he wore a uniform with colonel's rank, thus giving some credibility to his quest. Arriving back in Tryon County, Moore called a meeting at his father's home at Indian Creek for 10 June and presented his plan to muster the Loyalist forces at Ramsour's Mill on Clark Creek near the Little Catawba River, thirty miles west of Charlotte.[58] Many prominent Loyalists attended the meeting at Moses Moore's house, only six miles from the battle site that would end their dreams of restoring North Carolina to allegiance. The colonel announced Cornwallis's intent to invade North Carolina and free the Loyalists from the oppression of their Patriot neighbors. His enthusiasm and apparent authority had the necessary effect. Among the first volunteers came Major Nicholas Welsh, an officer in the Royal North Carolina Regiment, a veteran Provincial unit raised mainly from French and Indian War veterans.[59] Arriving in full field-officer uniform, Welsh also gave the aura of official military sanction. Within days, nearly 200 men flocked to the royal cause at Ramsour's. By the twentieth, 1,300 Loyalists had gathered at the mill. Although nearly a quarter of them lacked proper weapons, many were veterans of the 1776 Cherokee War and had served for years in the North Carolina militia. Organized into six companies, the Loyalists ground corn at the mill, organized, and prepared to join Cornwallis in South Carolina.

Patriots quickly responded. The actions in South Carolina so alarmed these North Carolinians that they had already initiated action. Brigadier General Rutherford, hero of the 1776 Cherokee War, called out the North Carolina militia on 3 June. Within two weeks, the rebel forces in the state included nearly a thousand militia infantry under Rutherford, several troops of horse under Maj. William Richardson Davie, and roughly 300 Continental light infantry of the 1st North

Carolina Continental Line commanded by Col. William Davidson. Maj. Joseph McDowell commanded an additional body. A further 400 militiamen drawn from Rowan, Mecklenburg, and Tryon Counties came together under Col. Francis Locke at nearby Mountain Creek, some sixteen miles from the mill. Rutherford initially decided to stay at Charlotte but eventually marched west to rendezvous with Locke at Colonel Dickson's plantation near the present town of Mount Holly. At this point the general committed what might have been a disastrous tactical error by dividing his forces in the face of the enemy, ordering Locke to attack and disperse the Loyalists mustered at the mill. The colonel advanced on Ramsour's Mill on the nineteenth. Adam Reep, a local Patriot, briefed Locke on the enemy's position and the approaches to the defensive post atop the hill. A clash of North Carolinians, the first time since Moore's Creek Bridge, would occur at Ramsour's Mill, one that on the surface seemed minor, but in terms of the unraveling Southern Strategy, particularly the Loyalist component, had significant and woefully detrimental consequences.

The terrain gave the Loyalists a tactical advantage. Encamped on the hilltop some 300 yards from the river, the mill, and a millpond, they enjoyed the advantage of a 200-yard, gently sloping field of fire. In the early morning of the twentieth, guided by Reep, the Patriot force advanced though a heavy fog undetected. Anticipating an enemy assault, Moore had stationed pickets at several hundred yards' distance from his camps. Unfortunately for the Loyalists, these men proved anything but reliable. Surprised by the approaching Patriots, who expertly used concealment and cover to approach the unwary men, the sentries loosed several random and ineffective shots. Although alerted to the enemy presence, the random firing and the subsequent race back to camp by the panicked pickets undermined any attempts to organize an effective defense as chaos spread through the gathered Loyalists. Several men fled without taking any part in the ensuing action. The appearance of Locke's mounted troopers, though few in number, only increased the panic. As the fighting unfolded, Locke's horsemen succeeded in enfilading Moore's flank, which caused the Loyalists to retire down the ridge to the millpond. In so doing, they surrendered the tactical advantage of elevation.

Once Moore and his company commanders restored order with the remaining troops, a counterattack drove the horsemen back but ultimately failed to drive off the Patriots. The colonel ordered a retrograde movement back to the hilltop. But by this time Patriot infantry had arrived and essentially surrounded the Loyalist encampment. With the exception of some senior officers, few men wore formal uniforms. Loyalists attached green-leaf twigs to their hats, while Patriots pinned on white paper. Inevitably, theses signifiers fell off; enemy identification became practically impossible, particularly as hand-to-hand combat erupted. With a mishmash of weapons and no bayonets, muskets and rifles became cudgels. Unarmed men fought with rocks and branches or simply their fists, often neighbor against neighbor.

Still, Moore had the advantage of numbers, but a critical factor changed the dynamic—leadership. In a trained military force, when one level of command is removed by casualty, the next level takes charge. With a thrown-together militia force characterized by little formal training and even less unit discipline, the loss of the senior leadership generally heralded bad results. Many of the Loyalists as well as the opposing Patriots had served under Rutherford during the Cherokee War and thus had some rudimentary military experience. Even then, some combat experience cannot overcome the lack of consistent training and regular military discipline as experienced by professional troops. While the six Loyalist company commanders, especially Captain Nicholas Warlick, initially maintained some order and cohesion, one by one they went down. Of the six officers, only Captain Peter Carpenter, though grievously wounded by a musket ball through the abdomen, remained. While he survived the battle, Loyalist leadership at the company level did not.[60]

Despite facing superior numbers, tactical deception and simple boldness determined the outcome for the Patriots. As the battle disintegrated into a melee, and with his troops pushed down toward the millpond and creek, where several drowned in the confused fight, Moore requested a truce to recover the dead and wounded. Knowing of Rutherford's advance to the site with reinforcements (which actually arrived two hours later), Locke acted as if he had superior forces and demanded an immediate surrender. Sensing a hopeless situation, Moore ordered as many of his men as could to slip away. Only fifty Loyalists remained once Locke had reformed his line for a second assault. The remaining Loyalists rapidly dispersed. Despite a one-to-three disadvantage in numbers, Locke, through bold deception and good fortune, achieved a stunning victory. Moore and about thirty refugees eventually joined Cornwallis at Camden. Casualties on each side appear equal, with thirty-five killed, a hundred wounded, and fifty Loyalists captured. Loyalist senior leadership, however, had been decimated. In the absence of an effective organizing cadre, western North Carolina Loyalists became a nonfactor for the remainder of the war.[61]

A significant feature of Ramsour's Mill previously missing in the Southern Campaign was the exclusive participation of irregular forces on both sides. Hitherto, actions in South Carolina and Georgia had been generally between regular troops or a mixture of regulars and militia. At Ramsour's Mill neighbor fought neighbor. Due to the lack of ammunition, men used muskets and the occasional rifle as clubs, a particularly brutal form of hand-to-hand combat. In such actions harsh feelings were bound to emerge and fester. Crown authorities in South Carolina regarded the engagement as "this unlucky business [that] will not materially affect the general Plan, or occasion any commotions on the frontiers of this Province."[62] In reality, the seemingly little affair in western North Carolina heralded a disaster for British plans.

The three events of 22 May–20 June 1780—the proclamations, Waxhaws, and Ramsour's Mill—set in motion a pattern of incidents and events that ultimately doomed any hope of restoring the South to the royal fold. The proclamations placed citizens on "death ground" by forcing them either to swear an allegiance that violated their conscience or to be regarded as treasonous; most chose treason and rebellion. The proclamations removed the neutrality option that many sought. The Waxhaws incident created a firestorm of bad public perception that not only caused neutrals to lean away from the Crown but also further alienated committed rebels. Moreover, whereas little empirical evidence exists to support the notion, it might well have caused many Loyalists to question their commitment to the royal cause. Finally, Ramsour's Mill removed a potentially substantial Loyalist irregular body from the playing field, a force that would have been useful in light infantry operations such as foraging, scouting and reconnaissance, intelligence gathering, and suppression of enemy irregular forces. Additionally, this Loyalist defeat set in motion the cycle of violence that roiled the Carolinas for months. It led to the inhibition of North Carolina Loyalists to actively either join Cornwallis for his North Carolina operations or provide the necessary logistical support to maintain his fast-moving offensive in a lightly populated and rugged frontier environment. While no one in the British high command fully understood the implications of these three events in the early summer of 1780, clearly a pattern had been established that, when combined with other factors, including the lack of strategic coherence and breakdown in unity of command and control, made Cornwallis's quest in the South simply unachievable.

## "In Arms against Us": The Strategic Situation, Summer 1780

By the mid-summer of 1780, British authorities in Charleston and the various posts looked out over a seemingly tranquil South Carolina. With Charleston in hand, Lincoln defeated and captured, and posts being established throughout the backcountry, the "clear and hold" strategy appeared to be working. Clinton reported the status of forces under his command as of 1 May as present in South Carolina, 11,569; New York and posts, 15,549; Nova Scotia (Canada), 3,145; East Florida, 457; West Florida, 1,308; Georgia, 1,695; Bermuda, 304; and the Bahamas, 118—a total of just over 34,000 troops. The Ramsour's Mill action, while troubling, had not yet produced the eventual devastating effect of suppressing

North Carolina Loyalist enthusiasm. No regular Continental force operated in the South except for a small contingent moving down from the north under Maj. Gen. Johann de Kalb; only scattered Patriot militia groups represented any armed opposition. Georgia had been pacified, the Floridas secured, and South Carolina seemingly so. But this was an illusion. As summer passed, Loyalists became increasingly edgy, anxious, and angry over the paroles offered by Clinton's proclamations. Meanwhile, put on "death ground," parolees and neutrals flocked to the Patriot side as their partisan bands formed throughout June and July. Accounts of the Waxhaws Massacre reverberated through the backcountry with talk of "Bloody Ban" Tarleton and British barbarism. In terms of strategic communications and the loss of the "hearts and minds" of the populace, the Waxhaws affair's ramifications had not been recognized by Crown authorities. Based on the approval and credit lavished on Tarleton and his legion, in British minds the event represented a significant victory for the "clear" aspect of the campaign's strategy.

On the eve of the victory at Camden in mid-August, the Southern Strategy seemed to be working as anticipated. But the grave misunderstanding on the part of Cornwallis, Clinton, and authorities in London underscores a central failing in that they did not recognize the true nature of the southern struggle until far too late. As a result, Cornwallis in the field, Clinton in New York, and Germain in London never crafted a coherent strategy that addressed the true southern centers of gravity—Loyalist support along with the general public attitude. The observation of Major James Wemyss of the 63rd Regiment of Foot in late September should have added to Cornwallis's increasing worries over backcountry opposition. Wemyss reported: "It is impossible for me to give your Lordship an idea of the disaffection of this country. Every inhabitant has been or is concerned in the rebellion and most of them very deeply." Some introspection on the major's part might have been helpful. As one of the worst abusers of the local population in his efforts to root out the rebels, Wemyss garnered a reputation for cruelty and destruction. Almost too cavalierly, he added in a postscript to his letter of 20 September: "I forgot to tell your Lordship that I have burnt and laid waste about 50 houses and plantations mostly belonging to people who have either broke their paroles or oath of allegiance and are now in arms against us."[63] Like a row of dominoes, the events of the first few months of 1779 followed by the success at Charleston the following spring set in motion a chain of events that culminated on a Virginia Peninsula over two years distant.

CHAPTER 3

# "Everywhere and Nowhere"

## *Partisan Warfare in the Carolinas*

They seek him here, they seek him there, those Frenchies seek him everywhere.
Is he in heaven? Or is he in hell? That damned elusive Pimpernel!

—Emma Orczy, *The Scarlet Pimpernel*

Like the elusive Scarlet Pimpernel in Baroness Orczy's famous play and novel, the rise of the Carolina partisan bands led by officers such as Francis Marion, Thomas Pinckney, and Thomas Sumter totally flummoxed British efforts to control the South Carolina backcountry following the fall of Charleston. As Sir Percy Blakeney befuddled and confounded the French revolutionaries while rescuing otherwise doomed aristocrats from execution, the elusive Patriot partisan bands prevented the execution of the "hold" aspect of the Crown's strategic plan. For months beginning in the summer of 1780, these forces conducted raids and ambushes on British logistics and communications while inhibiting Loyalists from turning out in the expected numbers to implement their role in the restoration of royal authority. Occasionally, the Patriots engaged in larger-scale actions that undercut British troop strength. Not only did these actions inflict casualties on an already woefully undermanned force, but they also caused Cornwallis to detach troops to chase down the rebel bands and to garrison or defend vital posts to his rear. Sun Tzu advocates that the most successful strategy is to attack an opponent's strategy and his alliances.[1] Through their actions and activities as Cornwallis attempted to execute the "clear" part of the overall plan, the partisans not only successfully attacked both that aspect of the British strategy but also, by intimidation, the "hold" component—the Loyalist alliance.

## Rise of the Partisans, Summer 1780

Despite several battlefield victories against irregular and Continental Army forces, Cornwallis never pacified the backcountry, a clear strategic imperative and the anticipated effect of his "clear" operations. The partisans forced him to play something like the popular modern arcade game Whac-a-Mole—whenever Crown forces defeated or drove off an irregular force, it simply popped up elsewhere or in another area. Combined with his losses at King's Mountain in October 1780 and Cowpens in January 1781, Cornwallis never successfully cleared or held South Carolina, with the exception of the more strongly defended posts such as Charleston, Georgetown, Camden, and Ninety Six. Frustrated with the inability to control South Carolina, he launched two invasions into North Carolina, first in the autumn that ended in disaster at King's Mountain, and later in January 1781 in a futile attempt to destroy yet another Continental force under Maj. Gen. Nathanael Greene. British and Loyalist forces garrisoned key sites such as the hamlet of Camden, where they established a forward operating base and a fortified post to protect an extensive magazine. At Ninety Six, west of Charleston near the Georgia border, another significant post guarded the main trading routes leading from the north toward Georgia. While on the surface these posts represented a natural extension of "clear and hold," as the partisan war unfolded, they represented "targets of opportunity" for the various Patriot bands and militia forces. Thus, as the summer and autumn unfolded in the backcountry, Cornwallis and his subordinate commanders sought to ferret out and destroy these shadowy enemies to help establish Loyalist control as the main regular forces moved north in search of a conventional battlefield victory. In this endeavor they failed.

Frankly, the chances of cowing the backcountry by proclamations, Crown battlefield victories, or fire-and-sword declarations were minimal. Such actions were far more likely to stir the frontiersmen and backcountry residents to greater resistance. These settlers, scrapping out an existence on the frontier or in small, subsistence upland farms, exhibited a fierce independence and willingness to do violence when wronged. Such hardy people were typically far less likely to break or bend under strain. It should not have surprised Crown officials that they took up Patriot arms in great numbers despite (or perhaps due to) the threats and proclamations. Loyalty oaths and charges of treason bore no more weight with them than did Major Ferguson's threat of death and destruction issued in October 1780. John Buchanan nicely captures the tenor of the backcountry folk, stating: "These were the people who buried Buford's dead soldiers where they died, nursed the wounded at the Waxhaws Presbyterian Church, and plotted dark deeds of revenge. These were the people who in the blackest time for the cause would bend but never break. They were hard men and women, accustomed to privation, travail their normal lot, mercy to an enemy never uppermost in their thoughts."[2]

Largely Scotch-Irish in origin and Presbyterian in theology, their Calvinist outlook held that government, whether monarchy or republican, had the duty to enforce the law rather than being the source of law—that remained only God's prerogative. These religious beliefs produced political views that naturally led to opposition and an unwillingness to be dictated to by a faraway regime. The Fincastle Resolves from Virginia of early 1775 express a common sentiment held throughout the rural South:

> Many of us and our forefathers left our native land, considering it as a Kingdom subjected to inordinate power, and greatly abridged of its liberties; we crossed the *Atlantic*, and explored this then uncultivated wilderness, bordering on many nations of Savages, and surrounded by Mountains almost inaccessible to any but those very Savages, who have incessantly been committing barbarities and depredations on us since our first seating the country. These fatigues and dangers we patiently encountered, supported by the pleasing hope of enjoying those rights and liberties which had been granted to *Virginians*, and were denied us in our native country, and of transmitting them inviolate to our posterity; but even to these remote regions the hand of unlimited and unconstitutional power hath pursued us, to strip us of that liberty and property with which *God*, nature, and the rights of humanity have vested us. We are ready and willing to contribute all in our power for the support of his Majesty's Government, if applied to constitutionally, and when the grants are made by our own Representatives, but cannot think of submitting our liberty or property to the power of a venal *British* Parliament, or to the will of a corrupt Ministry.[3]

Little wonder then that as Cornwallis embarked on his quest to restore the Carolinas to allegiance, he ran into a backcountry buzz saw powered by the hardy people that populated the region.

## "Huck's Defeat": Williamson's Plantation and Cedar Springs, 12 July 1780

Despite the apparent operational success of Crown arms in South Carolina, by early summer, hopes of pacifying the backcountry collapsed. Through a series of small actions typically fought between the rising partisan bands and Loyalist units, though often augmented by Continental, British, and Provincial regulars, the war continued there. At James Williamson's plantation in York County, a significant milestone occurred that further hampered Cornwallis's efforts to subdue the interior and promote Loyalist domination. Captain Christian Huck of the British Legion had been given an independent command composed primarily of British and Provincial regulars (dragoons and mounted infantry) to suppress rebel activity along the North Carolina border. His mission was simple—intimidate the local population into either signing the loyalty oath or at least noninterference with the restoration of Crown authority. Noted for his cruelty and rapaciousness, Huck, a Philadelphia Loyalist officer and lawyer, became widely despised and a target of local Patriots. Despite Cornwallis's explicit instructions to avoid plunder and other depredations, Huck's troops committed acts designed to instill physical terror and pillaged the local population.[4] Throughout June and early July, Huck charged about the South Carolina uplands disrupting Patriot attempts to muster forces. In late June he destroyed an ironworks belonging to a significant Patriot officer, which further aggravated area rebels. The captain's determination to hang two prisoners for treason and rebellion brought on the attack that would be his downfall.

On 12 July at Williamson's Plantation, Huck's luck ran out as a large Patriot force assaulted his encampment at dawn. Commanded by local Patriot militia officers, approximately three hundred men approached the plantation house at dawn and struck the unwary enemy camp surrounding it. Huck, roused from his sleep, rode out to rally his men only to be shot out of the saddle in the first musket volley. He and perhaps as many as thirty-five officers and men died; many of the wounded did not survive. Barely fifty men escaped, mounted infantry of the Provincial New York Volunteers and dragoons of the British Legion who could saddle up and flee quickly. Most of the attached Loyalist militia fared badly. While not British regulars like the dragoons, the Provincial regiments proved to be excellent, aggressive, well trained, and disciplined throughout the Southern Campaign. Had the force surprised at Williamson's been made up entirely of Loyalist militia, Huck's defeat might have been less worrisome—an insignificant militia-on-militia clash. Given the British and Provincial players involved, however, the portents for reestablishing Crown authority boded ill. Cornwallis's initial report to Clinton indicated that Huck had been careless in being "encamped in an unguarded manner," resulting in his being "totally surprised and routed."[5]

With the "fog of war" in full throat, Cornwallis suffered constantly from bad intelligence and a poor situational awareness of the backcountry conditions, indicated by the fluctuation in Williamson's Plantation casualty figures. Initially, he reported that only a dozen men escaped. In a later letter the earl modified his casualty calculation, stating that the surprise attack and the loss of Huck "turn'd out of less consequence than it appear'd at first. The captain and three men of the Legion were kill'd and 7 men of the New York Volunteers taken."[6] With sketchy records from the period, it is difficult to say which figures lie closer to the truth. What is certain is that the loss of Huck represented a further breakdown of any chance for Crown control of the South Carolina backcountry. Cornwallis sensed it as well, saying initially of the defeat: "This little blow will, I fear, much encourage the enemy and greatly increase the difficulty of protecting our borders. I see no safety for this province but in moving forward as soon as possible."[7]

On the same day as Williamson's Plantation, Patriots routed a Loyalist militia force at Cedar Springs near present-day Spartanburg. A local woman, whose son served with a Patriot militia formation known as the Spartan Regiment, heard of plans to assault the unit while she visited the Loyalist post at Ninety Six. Rushing home, she warned the Patriots, who ambushed the advancing Provincials, inflicting significant losses. As with Ramsour's Mill, the numbers involved and the outcome at Cedar Springs seem inconsequential at first blush; in terms of public perception, however, the results of this small engagement (and others) proved significant. For the first time, rebel militia had defeated British regular troops, albeit Provincials, in open, linear battle, a situation that boded badly for Cornwallis as he contemplated an advance into North Carolina with less than the numbers he required against an increasingly confident opponent while South Carolina became increasingly unsettled.

## "An Absolute State of Rebellion": The Carolina Summer of 1780

Throughout the summer, rebel forces under partisan leaders such as Thomas Sumter (sometimes seen as Sumpter) operated along the Santee River while other small bands made significant inroads in British control over the backcountry. Sumter, a former Continental Army officer and plantation owner whose home had been looted and burned by Tarleton's dragoons, emerged as one of the primary insurgents. Earlier in the struggle, he had commanded the 6th South Carolina Rifle Regiment at Haddrell's Point in the abortive British attempt to take Charleston in 1776. Eventually known as "The Gamecock," Sumter proved especially effective at overwhelming Loyalist opposition and interdicting British supply and logistics lines from Charleston to the interior posts. As such, his activities would play a large role in the breakdown of British command and control.

On 1 August Sumter struck. Rocky Mount, at the confluence of the Catawba River and Rocky Creek, served as an outlying advance post for the newly established magazine at Camden. A wooden palisade and abatis surrounded several buildings. Held by 150 men of the New York Volunteers and commanded by Lieutenant Colonel George Turnbull, the post provided a tempting target for Brigadier General Sumter, who rode at the head of between 500 and 600 Patriot militia, mostly mounted, some armed with rifles. Despite having no artillery to batter the fortified walls, Sumter demanded the post's surrender. He possessed two advantages—mobility and firepower. With most of his troops mounted and outnumbering the defenders by a more than three to one, he could strike them at any point. This forced the Loyalists to defend at all points, which diluted their volley-fire potential. Additionally, many of the upcountry Patriots possessed rifled weapons, more common along the frontier than in the lowlands. The riflemen, if well placed, could pick off defenders on the walls from a safe distance well beyond musket range. While not used to full advantage at Rocky Mount, increasingly, these frontiersmen from the Piedmont and Appalachian regions of the Carolinas and Virginia played an important role in such actions as King's Mountain, Cowpens, and Guilford Court House. Therefore, a few words about the use of rifled weapons are necessary.

Three problems with the rifle in the late eighteenth century limited its utility except in small-scale, irregular actions such as Rocky Mount. The prohibitive cost made them rare and valuable. For a frontiersman, who relied on his hunting skills to feed his family, a well-made rifle might be his most valuable possession. Their rarity meant that militia units raised in frontier regions typically came armed with more rifles than those from the coastal Low Country or Carolina Piedmont. As the civil struggle evolved and intensified through the summer, largely resulting from the disastrous proclamations and depredations by Loyalists such as Huck, rifle-equipped frontiersmen increasingly came out in support of the Patriots, with the ultimate expression of that sentiment at King's Mountain in October.

Loading time created a second factor making rifle use limited. One simply could not just jam things down the barrel as with a smoothbore musket. After pouring in the powder charge, the rifleman first placed a greased or wet (saliva worked well) patch over the muzzle for lubrication, carefully seated the ball, tapped it down slightly with a small hammer or similar instrument, and then slowly rammed the charge down the barrel. Failure to carry out any of these steps usually meant damaging the rifling. (Eighteenth-century metallurgy had not reached a point where the barrel could withstand too much stress without destroying the grooves carefully cut into the metal.) It took a full minute to prime and load a rifle, but British regulars could get off three or sometimes four musket volleys per minute. While the rifleman might get in a shot or two earlier from a greater range, with the close distances of conventional battles, the musket-equipped opponent threw a lot more lead in the rifleman's direction than he could return.

A third problem with rifles was that they were not configured to hold a bayonet. The typical British tactic was firing one to three volleys, followed by the bayonet charge, at which they were expert. With no bayonet to use defensively, the riflemen stood a good chance at getting slaughtered. Thus, the rifle proved problematic in linear battle. But it did have utility in irregular wilderness actions, such as at Rocky Mount, and other such skirmishes in the South Carolina setting. Riflemen often could be posted in front of a main line as skirmishers to inflict early casualties at range, then scatter when the enemy line reached the optimum firing position for musketry, typically between forty and one hundred yards. If sniping from a concealed position at a marching formation, then one might get off a shot or two before revealing his position. In these instances British light infantry, troops specifically tasked to flank the formation on the march and perform skirmishing duty in battle, would be on the rifleman with the bayonet or tomahawk, which each soldier carried in the wilderness. Thus, in eighteenth-century warfare, the rifle proved of limited utility. In a conventional linear battle, such as at Camden or Guilford Court House, rifled weapons were of little use except for initial sniping at an advancing enemy line. But in the small, irregular actions in the rural South during 1780–82, riflemen held a keen advantage.

At Rocky Mount, however, stout walls and well-delivered musket volleys overcame numbers, mobility, and rifle firepower. Unable to break through the stockade, Sumter's men attempted to set fire to the internal buildings. But then the probabilistic nature of war reared its head. A thunderstorm, so typical in the South in summer, opened up and doused the flames. Having already suffered several casualties and with no luck in forcing the palisades due to the intense and effective volley fire, the Patriots withdrew back toward the Catawba. Cornwallis reported that Turnbull lost one officer killed and another wounded along with "ten or twelve men kill'd and wounded."[8] After abandoning their assault, the Patriots ran into a party of British reinforcements sent to relieve the besieged garrison. Sumter's luck changed. Although he lost an additional twenty casualties, his men killed or captured some sixty British and Loyalist troops along with their horses and weapons. Overall, Rocky Mount continued the string of small Patriot victories in the backcountry.

An even more devastating event for Cornwallis and the "clear and hold" strategy had occurred two days earlier. At Thicketty Fort on 30 July, Col. Isaac Shelby's rebels captured a Loyalist party of nearly a hundred men without firing a shot. Lieutenant Colonel John Cruger, commanding officer at Ninety Six, reported that he had received news from Ferguson: "The rebels being in considerable force from 12 to 1500 advancing towards him at his post near the Tyger [River], that no man with him doubts but that there are two very considerable rebel partys [*sic*] within ten miles of the Broad River amounting by all conjecture to thrice his numbers, that some of our militia had surrender'd to the rebels a stockade fort on Thicketty."[9] With the backcountry aflame, chances for strategic success diminished day by day.

## Hanging Rock, 1 and 6 August 1780

At Hanging Rock on 1 August, Major Davie from North Carolina assaulted an encampment near the fortifications there with only eighty mounted riflemen and dragoons, routing three mounted infantry companies from Colonel Samuel Bryan's North Carolina Volunteers. Chastened by the defeat, the British reinforced Hanging Rock with elements of Tarleton's British Legion, the Prince of Wales American Regiment, and the remnants of the North Carolina Volunteers. With upward of 500 effectives and heavily fortified, the post presented a challenge to Sumter, who nevertheless mounted a renewed effort on the sixth. Formed into three assault columns, the North and South Carolina militia moved to the attack. All three assaulted Bryan's North Carolinians simultaneously, devastating them but subjecting themselves to enfilade fire from the remaining defenders. Despite these effective volleys, the Patriots continued their assault and captured the post. The attack might have been more complete except that Sumter's men fell into looting the British camp, with the rum ration as the primary booty, though more arms, ammunition, and horses also fell into Patriot hands. Another significant Loyalist force, in this case well-trained and equipped Provincial units, had been defeated, suffering over 200 casualties and losing another significant strongpoint.

The effect on British and Loyalist confidence and Patriot aspirations had be to profound. Cornwallis wrote to Clinton days later on the Hanging Rock debacle, indicating his growing disenchantment with the local Loyalist militia. He reported losing five officers killed and five wounded in the engagement. More importantly for the overall British strategy, he declared: "These accounts, added to the infidelity which we have experienced of our militia are not pleasing. I am just going to set out to join the army and hope to get there before anything of consequence happens." So as to strike home again his strategic concept of a North Carolina invasion supported by a Chesapeake Bay diversionary expedition, he reminded his senior: "If we succeed at present and are able to penetrate into North Carolina, without which it is impossible to hold this province, your Excellency will see the absolute necessity of a diversion in the Chesapeake, and that it must be made early."[10] But Clinton dithered. Not only did Sir Henry worry about New York's safety, but French activities, or rather potential activities, also roiled plans for a two-pronged campaign in the South. Referring to French forces available in North American waters, he could confirm only seven ships and 6,000 troops. But in a growing pattern of caution and resistance to taking bold, aggressive action, unlike his subordinate in South Carolina, Clinton hinted at possible French action that might threaten New York, stating that "a second [possible French move] is talked of to Chesapeak [*sic*], which may possibly frustrate our views in that quarter. Indeed, without I am reinforced considerably, I dare not go there in force, and, without I do, nothing can be expected."[11] One can imagine Cornwallis's reaction to those words. The pattern of strategic disintegration between the CinC and his main field commander marched steadily toward disaster.

Other troublesome Patriots soon emerged in South Carolina to play a prominent role in the British strategic conundrum, notably Col. Francis Marion, a prominent planter and Continental Army officer whose irregular, guerrilla-type operations along the Santee and Pee Dee Rivers continually frustrated and complicated Crown operations. Marion's first significant action occurred on 12 August as he crossed the Pee Dee at Port's Ferry and defeated a Loyalist detachment. It proved to be the first of many successes in the Low Country, victories that not only fired up the spirit and enthusiasm of local Patriots but also further inhibited and suppressed Loyalist recruitment and military activity.

By summer's end, Cornwallis realized the strategic importance of the irregular war in terms of the fragility of Crown control over South Carolina and the debilitating effects on the overall British strategy, particularly the Loyalist aspect. From Ramsour's Mill, through the demise of Huck at Williamson's Plantation, through Marion's raid at Port's Ferry, Loyalist and regular British forces suffered over 500 casualties. More importantly, as Cornwallis contemplated an advance into North Carolina, he faced leaving behind him an unsettled backcountry in which Patriot militia and bands of irregulars dominated. The earl had enthusiastically reported to Clinton at the end of June that he viewed South Carolina as under control, therefore the next logical operational move should be against North Carolina to establish a security barrier for South Carolina and Georgia. He proposed an operation, with the troops currently available, commencing in August or September.[12] Yet given the events of the Carolina summer, by early August, a frustrated and perplexed Cornwallis appeared not so sanguine as to the security situation. He reported to Clinton that "the Whole Country between Pedee [*sic*] and Santee has ever since been in an absolute State of Rebellion; every friend of Government has been carried off, and his Plantation destroyed; & detachments of the enemy have appeared on the Santee, and threatened our stores and Convoys on that river."[13]

In terms of the effect on the Loyalists and ultimately the success of the Southern Strategy, Cornwallis commented that the "unfortunate business, if it should have no worse consequences, will shake the confidence of our friends in this Province and make our situation very uneasy until we can advance."[14] This last phrase is particularly critical in assessing Cornwallis and his concept of how to overcome the rebellion. Those few words—"until we can advance"—capture the essence of the man as a commander and his understanding of war. More importantly, they underline a dominant problem inherent in the British theory of victory and the inability to assess the true nature of the conflict. Cornwallis's entire being and personality drove him to bold, risky, aggressive, and offensive-oriented warfare, at which he proved a master, both tactically and operationally. Unfortunately for the royal cause, these actions proved to be completely counter to a war-winning strategy in the rebellious colonies. The desired strategic effect of crushing the Patriots' political will by destruction of their war-making ability and the elimination of regular, conventional forces, while seemingly the correct outcome, in actuality proved a false concept. In pursuit of this outcome, Cornwallis committed his forces to a campaign of attrition by a strategic offensive that would carry him eventually to the final calamity at Yorktown. But by August 1780, Patriots handed to the earl the very justification for launching his offensive—the arrival of a new southern Continental force under the command of the Saratoga victor, Maj. Gen. Horatio Gates. Even at this stage of the campaign, the seeds of the strategic dispute between the CinC and his field commander can be seen. From Charleston, Cornwallis commented to Clinton in New York: "An early diversion in my favour in Chesapeak [*sic*] Bay will be of the greatest and most important advantage to my operations. I most earnestly hope that the Admiral [Arbuthnot] will be able to spare a convoy for that purpose."[15] This debate over a Chesapeake operation roiled command relations between Cornwallis and his superior and flummoxed any attempt at a cohesive British strategy, eventually contributing to the British march to Yorktown. First, though, came the challenge of a newly reconstituted Continental force marching south and leading to the clash at Camden, South Carolina. For the earl, the outcome of that battle validated his strategic concept.

## "Cool Intrepidity": The Battle of Camden, 16 August 1780

In an attempt to reinforce Charleston—or to provide a hedge against British activities once the city fell—Washington detached units of the Maryland and Delaware Continental Line under Maj. Gen. Johann de Kalb, a German who had reached the rank of brigadier in the French service before coming to America to fight for the Patriot cause. Qualitatively, these units were some of the best troops in the Continental Army. With 1,400 men, de Kalb departed Philadelphia on 13 May and arrived in Petersburg, Virginia, on the twenty-third, too late to relieve Charleston but certainly in time to complicate the reestablishment of royal authority in the Carolinas. At Hillsborough he found little support in terms of expected supplies and reinforcements. Eventually, however, de Kalb's army obtained more troops as it advanced toward Camden in the form of two brigades of North Carolina militia commanded by Maj. Gen. Richard Caswell, a hero of Moore's Creek Bridge and the new state's first governor. While numerous, Caswell's militia, which had gathered at the Yadkin River, represented an asset of unknown quality compared to Cornwallis's skilled, disciplined, and victorious veterans, both British regulars and Loyalist Provincials. Additionally, a body of Virginia militia under Brig. Gen. Edward Stevens soon rendezvoused with the Patriot force. These Virginians benefited from a higher level of training and drill compared to the typical militia body, especially the inexperienced North Carolinians. While more than doubling de Kalb's numbers, the militia's dubious fighting quality would play a major role in the outcome at Camden. Armand's Legion (formerly Pulaski's Legion), commanded by Col. Charles Armand, provided cavalry support as well as some additional infantry.

Another qualitative factor that loomed large at Camden was leadership. Negative effects emerged with the appointment of Gates as commander of the Southern Department to replace the captured Benjamin Lincoln. Appointed on 13 June not by Washington, who doubted his leadership qualities, but by Congress, Gates arrived to assume his command on 25 July at the Quaker Meeting House on the Deep River near Hillsborough, North Carolina. What he found could not have heartened the hero of Saratoga. Roughly 1,400 men, ragged, ill nourished, and destitute, formed the southern Continental command. Nonetheless, he supplied the force with a heroic name—"Grand Army." He ordered an immediate march toward Camden, a stunning and ill-considered move given his troops' physical state. On the twenty-seventh the Grand Army departed Hillsborough for an unknown destiny. Basing his decision on the erroneous report that Cornwallis had departed for Savannah, Gates hoped for a quick strike before the earl could return to South Carolina. Even had the report been accurate, he must surely have known of the quality of Lieutenant Colonel Rawdon's forces based at Camden and nearby posts. In another show of hubris, Gates appeared to have discounted enemy reinforcements coming up from Charleston once his movement commenced. His operational decisions demonstrate a high degree of aggressiveness and risk taking, but what seems missing is the critical element of boldness guided by prudence.

From Cornwallis's perspective, the time to press north neared. Intelligence from the Carolina upcountry reported parolees joining Sumter. From North Carolina came estimates of de Kalb as having over 2,000 Continentals. Unconfirmed reports from Virginia alluded to 2,500 Virginia militia joining de Kalb. Though exaggerated as such reports tended to be, Cornwallis concluded that the enemy intended not only to defend the Carolinas vigorously but also to initiate offensive operations. Accordingly, he moved large amounts of provisions, ammunition, and arms to the post at Camden, some one hundred miles northwest of Charleston, then under the command of Lord Rawdon and the major forward operating base in the northern South Carolina interior. On 3 August Rawdon reported that he had no intelligence of Gates's movements even though he had many "emissaries abroad."[16] Throughout the first days of the month, he attempted to ascertain Gates's whereabouts with little luck. On the eleventh the lieutenant colonel reported that some advance troops from the Patriot force lay at Rugeley's Mill, north of Camden, and that Gates might have arrived there as well, adding that he was not positive as he could "procure but miserable intelligence." But Rawdon felt confident that the general meant to assault his garrison and perhaps get between himself and Charleston. Nevertheless, the young Irish lord remained supremely confident in his men's ability to withstand any assault. While rumors put Gates's forces at over 5,000 troops, Rawdon believed it to be more like 3,500—still a considerable threat. While a preventive assault against the advancing army might have accrued some advantage, at least in strategic surprise, Rawdon demurred: "No opportunity offered of attacking him consistent with the safety of our magazines, tho' I thought my force fully equal to the attempt."[17]

As the enemy moved inexorably toward the hamlet with its priceless magazines, Rawdon awaited events with a determination and sense of confidence buoyed by the quality and demeanor of his men. Returns of the thirteenth show 885 men (sergeants, drummers, and rank and file) of the 23rd, 33rd, and 71st Regiments of Foot present and fit for duty. To bolster these British regulars, three of the most experienced and reliable of the Provincial regiments—the Prince of Wales American Regiment, Rawdon's own Volunteers of Ireland, and Tarleton's British Legion—added a further 724 effectives. Fleshing out the command, various units of Loyalist militia, totaling 662 fit for duty, gave the post commander 2,271 total infantry and cavalry. The garrison also included the field guns under Lieutenant John MacLeod of the Royal Artillery, with twenty-eight artillerists manning five 6-pounders, three 3-pounders, and two cohorns (small bronze mortars). Fourteen pioneers rounded out the force. Rawdon fretted over the number of "sick present," particularly in the 71st Regiment (Fraser's Highlanders), hardest hit by malaria and other illnesses. As Cornwallis and other British commanders soon discovered, campaigning in the South in the summer months brought the threat and reality of disease and illness, especially dysentery and malaria, which often debilitated Crown forces.[18] By the return just prior to the Camden battle, which Cornwallis received upon his arrival on the night of the thirteenth, Rawdon reported 711 "sick present."[19] The earl still considered the Loyalist militia as a force multiplier, despite his earlier letter to Clinton containing hints of doubt about their military utility and stressing that a regular force always had to prop them up. Thus, the British suffered the same qualms and doubts about their irregulars as did Continental commanders, an attitude soon to be borne out on both sides—and for the Patriots and General Gates, particularly in the coming engagement.[20]

Gates did not wait for Rawdon to initiate the action and made two ultimately fateful command decisions. Clausewitz stresses the importance of concentration, stating that " there is no higher and simpler law of strategy than that of keeping one's forces concentrated, . . . to be strong; first in general, and then at the decisive point."[21] The Patriot commander clearly violated that prudent dictate. In an effort to ambush Cornwallis's force moving up from Charleston, Gates detached a company of Maryland Continentals, some artillery, and some North Carolina militia to join General Sumter on the Camden–Charleston road. Additionally, he sent Major Davie with a body of North and South Carolina mounted infantry to escort the Patriot wounded from Hanging Rock to a hospital in Charlotte. Fearful that any delay would allow Cornwallis to consolidate forces, Gates struck out for Camden on 27 July, arriving in the area north of the town on 11 August. Along the route of march, Caswell's North Carolina militia and Stevens's Virginians finally joined the column after it crossed the Pee Dee River in northern South Carolina. The best estimates of the numbers place Caswell's militia at about 2,000 effectives and Stevens's troops at 700–800 men once they rendezvoused. In the pre–Industrial Age, however, exact counts are difficult, particularly for militia. No commander on either side could count on militia reliability. Estimates for Caswell's North Carolinians range from 1,200 to over 2,100 men. At one point Colonel Marion and a small partisan band of perhaps 20 men joined the force; Gates immediately detached them on scouting and reconnaissance duty.

The general chose to march directly through the North Carolina Sand Hills rather than a longer route westerly through Salisbury and Charlotte, both Patriot strongholds likely to provide food and animal fodder. Subordinate officers, including de Kalb and Gates's adjutant, Col. Otho Holland Williams, recommended taking the longer but more sustainable route for its more-reliable food availability. The Sand Hills, essentially undeveloped pine barrens, offered little in the way of supply. Moreover, that region held danger in the form of Loyalists, many of whom had survived the Moore's Creek debacle four years earlier. These ethnic Scottish Highlanders, concentrated around the Cross Creek area, largely remained loyal despite oppression from Patriot authorities. Even if few took military action against the advancing Continentals, the fact that they could provide valuable intelligence to the British simply from troop-movement observation should have concerned Gates. On the march the men subsisted on green corn and unripe fruit, which caused considerable gastrointestinal distress, especially dysentery. Despite promises of food and spirits just ahead, none materialized as the weary and starving Continentals trudged through the oppressively hot and humid Carolina summer. The wear and tear on the troops, a condition noted by the militia commanders, eventually played out in their performance on the day of battle.

Meanwhile, Cornwallis had been active. Receiving Rawdon's report of Gates's approach to Camden, he departed Charleston on 10 August and arrived late in the evening three days later. Despite an apparent 1-to-2 disadvantage in numbers,

Cornwallis resolved to initiate battle, a decision certainly in keeping with his bold, aggressive nature. He reported to Lord Germain, "having left Charlestown sufficiently garrisoned and provided for a siege, and seeing little to lose by a defeat and much to gain by a victory, I resolved to take the first good opportunity to attack the rebel army."[22]

The numbers should have troubled Gates. While he claimed to have 7,000 effectives, the report of Adjutant Williams indicated only 3,200 men, among them just 900 Continentals. With this heterogeneous mix of troops, the general nevertheless ordered a night advance, a difficult maneuver even for well-trained troops, harder still for ill-disciplined and inexperienced militia. Accordingly, at 10:00 P.M. on the night of 15 August, the southern American army marched in column out of Rugeley's Mill toward Camden, ten miles distant, led by Armand's Legion, a polyglot and unusual unit composed of foreign mercenaries and British deserters. Close behind came the Maryland and Delaware Continentals, followed by Caswell's North Carolinians, with the Virginians acting as rear guard. Light infantry covered the line of march on the flanks, the standard pattern for moving troops in column. The march became a disaster. The terrain north of Camden was especially challenging, alternating between wooded areas and a single road bordered by swampy marshland. Exhausted, hungry, and undisciplined troops often fell out of formation. Stragglers wandered all about the countryside. Men fell ill to stomach disorders, having eaten only a quick molasses meal before the march. Discipline collapsed among the inexperienced militia.

Meanwhile, Cornwallis went about arranging his line of battle. He received reinforcements from Ninety Six—light infantry commanded by Lieutenant Colonel Nesbit Balfour—and others drawn from Hanging Rock and Rocky Mount, all in relatively fine physical condition compared to Gates's exhausted and ill-fed troops. Cornwallis must have felt that, although numbers likely fell in Gates's favor, the fact that the Patriots had been on a rough march for several days through inhospitable country while his own men remained rested and well nourished granted him the qualitative edge. The heat and humidity of a southern August and exhaustion—wonderful examples of the "friction" in warfare—played to Cornwallis's advantage.

While thoughts of a withdrawal in the face of a numerically superior opponent occurred to the earl, three factors mitigated against retreat. The earl realized that he "had the option to make, either to retire or attack the enemy, for the position at Camden was a bad one to be attacked in."[23] The town had been a gathering point for the many wounded from the previous engagements and those who succumbed to the general malaise and illnesses that typically overcame eighteenth-century armies in garrison towns in the hotter climates. By early August, over 800 sick and wounded men lay in Camden. To abandon so many to the enemy without a fight might well undercut the extraordinarily high troop morale generated by the string of real and apparent Crown victories since the previous autumn. Perhaps most importantly, the exceedingly high moral authority that Cornwallis had garnered from his troops, not only in the present conflict but also throughout his entire military career, would be diminished. That moral authority—based not only on his military leadership and command acumen, tactical and operational skills and accomplishments, concern for the health and welfare of the common soldier (all too often rare in the period), and his willingness to gladly suffer the privations of harsh campaigning alongside his men (starkly illustrated as the Southern Campaign unfolded)—was perhaps his greatest attribute as a commander. It could and should not be undone by a retreat; the earl would "stick and stay." In truth, to do otherwise would have been completely out of character for one of the boldest, most aggressive, offensive-minded, and risk-taking commanders of the age.

Marching out of the Camden encampment toward Rugeley's Mill, Lieutenant Colonel James Webster commanded the lead division, comprising the British Legion dragoons and several light infantrymen as an advance covering force, intended to be the first elements to make contact with the enemy, and the 23rd (Royal Welch Fusiliers) and 33rd (West Riding) Regiments of Foot. Next came Lord Rawdon's division of Provincial regiments—the Volunteers of Ireland, Tarleton's British Legion infantry, Lieutenant Colonel John Hamilton's Royal North Carolina Regiment, and the remaining men of Colonel Bryan's decimated North Carolina Loyalists. The 71st Regiment formed the rear guard. Unlike the desperate and struggling Patriot force, Crown troops demonstrated the value of discipline, training, morale, and experience as their night march proceeded up the post road with little trouble. In the humid heat of a Carolina summer night, the two armies marched in the dark toward each other. Rawdon's column boasted three of the most veteran, battle-hardened, disciplined, and capable of all the line regiments in America, all supported by the best and most experienced of the Provincials. Against this force, Gates could only rely upon the Delaware and Maryland infantry. The qualitative odds stood starkly against the Patriots.

Around 2:00 A.M. on the sixteenth, the lead elements of each army came into contact and exchanged volleys for several minutes until a charge by Tarleton drove the Patriot dragoons back toward their main body. A night engagement is always chaotic, and one can imagine the scene that then ensued. Despite all, officers on both sides handled their troops relatively well, and a sharp action resulted. Virginia militia firing from concealment in the woods eventually forced the British Legion to retire. As more British troops moved up, the Continentals retired under increasingly heavy fire until a counterattack led by Lt. Col. Charles Porterfield reestablished the tactical advantage and drove back the Loyalists.

Porterfield, mortally wounded in this action, had stabilized the front, allowing more of Gates's stragglers to catch up with their units. After sustaining a few casualties and taking some prisoners, both sides withdrew to reform. Gates, surprised to learn from these captives that he faced Cornwallis himself along with British regulars, not just Rawdon's Provincials, nevertheless chose to continue the engagement.

A hastily convened council of war confirmed this decision; only General Stevens voiced any opinion, that the Patriots had no choice but to continue the fight. One can only speculate, but the shock of having engaged British regulars surely must have stunned all present. But Stevens was correct. In the face of such an enemy and with Gates's force disorganized in the dark, to attempt a withdrawal courted disaster. Clearly, the fact that Cornwallis had marched out of Camden in the night with a significant and potent force indicated that he meant to fight; more importantly, he had the strength with which to crush the Patriots. There would be no standing behind a stockade and defensive works for this opponent. In period warfare, with forces standing so close to each other due to the weaponry and limited communications, it is axiomatic that when a unit loses its cohesion in the face of the enemy, heavy casualties result if the enemy's cavalry charges into the retiring—and often panicky or fleeing—infantry. Artillery in the form of the battalion guns, typically 3- or 6-pounders, tended to cause heinous casualties when firing canister or grapeshot into retiring infantry. As a veteran officer and for all his negative aspects, Gates understood this dynamic. He realized that he must chance a fight and hope that his militia would stand. He knew the Continentals would hold—beyond that only lay hope.

Cornwallis also realized that he faced the enemy's main body, but his situational dynamic proved far superior to the unfortunate Gates. Looking across the battlespace as daylight broke, the earl determined that he held an excellent position, with swampland on either side of his line inhibiting any enemy flanking motion. Although the Patriots occupied slightly higher ground, the elevation angle did not grant them any real advantage. With both sides taking a tactical pause to reform and reorganize, Cornwallis ordered his men to lie down and rest in preparation for the morning fight. The battlefield, five miles north of Camden, lay flanked on either side by marshy ground amid a pine forest astride the Camden–Charlotte post road and slightly east of the Wateree River. It gave Cornwallis a huge tactical advantage. A broad front battlespace often favors the numerically superior side, or at least provides some excellent tactical opportunities. With more troops and on a wide-open field, the numerically superior force can fight its inferior opponent to a draw in the center while using the extra troops for encirclement or outflanking maneuvers. If this dynamic occurs in period linear warfare, the outflanked force has but two realistic options—withdraw or

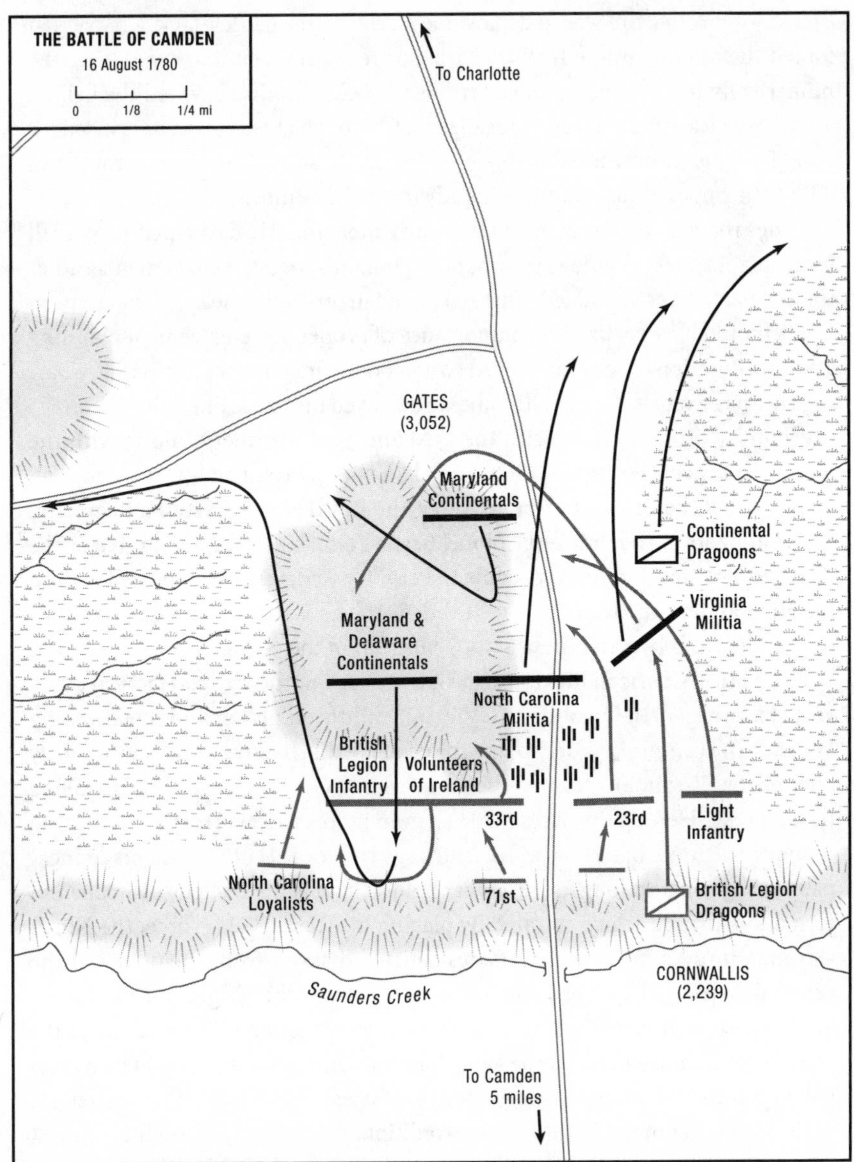


The Battle of Camden, 16 August 1780. Map by Erin Greb Cartography.

execute a "refuse the flank" maneuver. A second aspect of the terrain lay in the marshland on either side of the road. A common tactic once the infantry began exchanging volley fire was to deploy one's cavalry in a flank attack, a move that forced the opponent to either withdraw or reposition, either way placing the numerically inferior force in deep trouble. As Cornwallis surveyed the field, it must have pleased him no end to realize that, through chance, fate, or just deuced good fortune, he now faced an enemy who had to slug it out on a narrow front with little opportunity to utilize his advantage in numbers.

Gates made two critical errors that early morning. He developed no overall battle plan, thus individual commanders fought separate engagements rather than as part of a coordinated, unified effort. Surprisingly, the long-experienced Gates should have realized the importance of proper pre-engagement planning and coordination. The error proved costly. Following an opening artillery barrage from the rebels, Cornwallis quickly deployed his battle line, with Webster's division holding the right with the 23rd and 33rd Regiments along with the light infantry composite battalion.[24] Lord Rawdon's Provincials formed the left, composed of the British Legion infantry, the Royal North Carolina Regiment, the Volunteers of Ireland, and Colonel Bryan's North Carolina Volunteers. The depleted 71st stood in reserve, while the cavalry under Tarleton posted behind the Highlanders, ready to deploy as needed. The field artillery, composed of two 6-pounders and two 3-pounders, took position in the center.

When the American line formed, Gates made another crucial tactical error. He placed the North Carolina and Virginia militia on his left and center, facing Webster, the Carolinians occupying the center, while the somewhat more sturdy and reliable Virginians formed the far left flank; General Stevens commanded the left wing. Here again Gates made an even more critical error. It is one thing if one of the line's flanks caves in, its troops run, or it is otherwise made incapable of fighting; so long as the center holds, there is the nucleus of a coherent formation around which to rally. By placing his least reliable force, the North Carolina militia, in the center, Gates courted disaster from the outset. If the center collapsed, the Continentals on the right and the Virginians on the left would be isolated, separated, and in danger of annihilation in detail. Perhaps the reserve could move in to fill the gap left in the center, but that would be a great risk to run and too probabilistic to count on. Gates should have known better. He understood that in the British Army, traditionally, the best, most elite, or most senior units were always given the position on the right of the line, a practice called "fighting right-handed," which likely came from the typical medieval practice of the right being the sword hand. Why the Patriot commander chose to place his militia against Cornwallis's right is truly a mystery. Thus, against the disciplined and well-trained British regulars, the Virginia militia had little chance in a conventional, linear engagement. In truth, Gates lost the battle before the main fighting actually began.

The Continentals formed the Patriot right, facing the Provincials, with de Kalb commanding the right wing. Under the command of Brig. Gen. Mordecai Gist, the 2nd Maryland Brigade, consisting of three Maryland Continental Line regiments and a Delaware regiment, formed the heart and strength of the Patriot line. Gates positioned himself in the center and rear with Brig. Gen. William Smallwood's 1st Maryland Brigade, which acted as the reserve along with Armand's Legion, which also guarded the left flank. The artillery occupied the center, a position typically of great advantage. By just rotating guns left or right, an efficient artillery crew could cover much of the battlespace, especially in one as constricted and narrow as at Camden. But by being in the center with just the militia as their infantry protection, if those inexperienced troops did not hold but fled, the guns would be vulnerable to capture (or to being spiked by their crews) should the enemy overrun their position. While it takes a panicky soldier only a few seconds to race several yards toward safety, it takes several minutes to limber up a gun and pull it out of harm's way. Military history is rife with instances of field artillery overrun when their accompanying infantry breaks for the rear. The Marylanders in reserve, easily the finest, most capable unit in the Continental Army and a match for the best British regiment, were thus essentially out of the action when they should have been deployed on the front line against Webster's division. In placing one of his best units in the rear, Gates nullified what few qualitative advantages he actually held. A better deployment would have placed Smallwood to his left flank to shore up the wobbly militia and to provide the artillery with better protection.

Cornwallis struck first, ordering Webster to advance around dawn. In reaction, Stevens attempted to reposition his Virginians in support of Caswell's units. Right away, linear cohesion began to crumble. Typical of the probabilistic nature of war and the chaos of the battlefield, senior Patriot commanders began to make tactical errors based on incomplete situational awareness, a common effect, especially in period warfare. Colonel Williams believed that he saw confusion and disorder in the British right and convinced Gates to attack. The Patriot commander ordered Stevens to advance. It is dicey enough to expect militia to stand and fight against an oncoming regular force, but to order an offensive movement against such opponents stands little chance of success. Understandably, the Virginians did not race to the assault. In frustration, Stevens sent about fifty men ahead to open fire and take advantage of the perceived British disorder. Seeing this movement and interpreting it as Gates realigning his left, Cornwallis ordered Webster to assault the rebel line with haste before the enemy could reinforce it. Meanwhile, Rawdon's men opened fire on the Virginians as Stevens attempted his advance.

Many of the militia fired from behind trees and obstructions, but to little effect and with no coordination. Advancing with parade-ground precision, Webster's regulars commenced volley firing before coming to the "Charge Bayonet" position. In a single motion hundreds of British bayonets came to the ready as the line emerged from the dense smoke created by their volleys, made thicker by the damp summer air. The sight of the advancing redcoats and the sound of their "huzzahs" with each forward step and the rhythmic beating of the drums unnerved the inexperienced, undisciplined militia. Battle is an emotional and visceral experience; one can only imagine the fear and terror in those men as they looked across the field at the advancing line of British "cold steel." Many threw down their arms and fled to the rear, and with them all cohesion in the Patriot line dissipated. Seeing the Virginians' collapse, most of Caswell's North Carolinians did the same; only Col. Henry Dixon's unit of the North Carolina militia held firm. Smallwood attempted to move the Marylanders in reserve up to staunch the hemorrhaging line, though to little positive effect, and they too were driven back by the advancing red line. Gates's left crumbled in mere minutes. Cornwallis, in his after-action report to Lord Germain, stated: "Our line continued to advance in good order, and with the cool intrepidity of experienced British Soldiers, keeping up a constant fire or making use of bayonets as opportunities offered, and after an obstinate resistance during three quarters of an hour threw the enemy into total Confusion, & forced them to give way in all quarters."[25]

Events went better for the Patriots on their right. The Continentals stood their ground and even advanced against Rawdon's division through heavy volley fire. Despite the flight of the militia through the 1st Maryland Brigade, which temporarily disrupted their cohesion, the experienced and disciplined Marylanders quickly reformed and moved up to support de Kalb and the remaining Continental units. But with the rebel left flank gone, Webster executed a wheel maneuver, bringing the 23rd and 33rd into line on the remaining Continentals' left flank, into which they poured in volley after volley of enfilading fire. Despite their courage and steadfastness, the Continentals could not stay long in this cascade of bullets and withdrew in good order. De Kalb received multiple wounds while desperately attempting to rally his men, falling and left behind by his retreating men. Afterward, realizing the officer's identity, British troops propped the German against a wagon wheel for support. Cornwallis rode to the scene and ordered de Kalb removed by a litter for medical attention. He died of his wounds three days later and was buried with full military honors and a Masonic ceremony.[26]

Meanwhile, the rebel army fled the battlefield in small groups. Tarleton's dragoons chased the militia for over twenty miles. The Virginians, the initial cause of the left's disintegration, largely escaped. Cornwallis reported the rebel loss as between 800 and 900 casualties and 1,000 prisoners, including General Rutherford, that "vile and cruel incendiary."[27] Camden represented a stunning and complete victory of British arms, a tactical and operational achievement of huge importance. It demonstrated the superiority of well-trained, disciplined veteran soldiers over ill-trained, inexperienced forces in a conventional engagement. Camden also showcased the competency and superb field leadership of Cornwallis and several subordinate officers, most notably Lieutenant Colonel Webster and Lord Rawdon. In a single day the earl removed from the field a substantial enemy army and literally the only Continental forces of any consequence south of the middle colonies. Patriot losses amounted to 250 killed in action and a further 800 wounded. The losses to the militia units due to fearful, exhausted, and hungry men simply going home and retiring from the fight cannot really be calculated. On the Crown side, Cornwallis lost 68 men killed among 324 total casualties. In an act that will forever disgrace his reputation, upon seeing the flight of the militia, Gates mounted his horse, Fear Naught, and fled the battlefield, reportedly not stopping until he reached the safety of Charlotte, some sixty-five miles distant.[28] The general made Hillsborough by the nineteenth and desperately began to reconstitute his shattered army. Barely 700 men made it back to Hillsborough. As the refugees streamed into North Carolina, leaving the wreckage of a battle lost scattered over miles of country road—dead, dying, and wounded men; baggage; wagons; and supplies—to the British, North Carolina now seemed ripe for conquest.

While Camden represented a stunning tactical victory, it also sprang a strategic trap on Cornwallis. Flush with victory, he moved farther into the backcountry and away from his base of support and maritime sustenance at Charleston, which complicated his already tenuous supply and reinforcement situations. Doing this made the attacks by South Carolina partisans more deleterious while providing many more "targets of opportunity" for Marion and his peers. Partisan war typically results when one side in a conventional struggle is profoundly defeated, but the spirit that motivated people to take up arms still exists. That attitude and willingness to continue the struggle often takes the form of irregular warfare. In the South the surrender of Charleston in May 1780 and the outcome at Camden removed from the South its regular Continental forces, thus forcing partisan bands to emerge. The leaders of these irregulars owed little allegiance to either civil or military chains of command or authority, thus creating a nightmare scenario for the conventional-warfare-minded British. In a way, then, Cornwallis became a victim of his own success. Moreover, as he moved farther into the hinterland, his unreliable supply situation worsened. The earl can be blamed for launching off into the wilderness and abandoning his seaborne supply connection, but throughout the war the American Department remained oblivious to the supply situation, compounded by the inefficient and inadequate British supply system (highlighted in chapter 1). Then again, partisan attacks disrupted what logistical structure was in place.

Camden validated Cornwallis's theory of victory, that by smashing every regular Continental force, he would overawe and intimidate the rebels into submission and acceptance of royal rule, thus accomplishing the overall policy objective. Thus, he launched off on his North Carolina invasion with a faulty strategic assessment and a lack of understanding of the true nature of the war in the South. The earl never realized (or if he did, it was much too late) that the true center of gravity in the South lay in public opinion and the "hearts and minds," not victory in conventional combat.

As the campaign wore on, an increasingly debilitating factor set in—force attrition. Though Crown losses at Camden numbered barely over 300 men, it represented a 20-percent casualty rate among the regular line regiments, a factor that became increasingly critical in the coming months. Finally, Gates's defeat and humiliation brought into the fray perhaps the most strategically adept general officer in the Continental Army, Nathanael Greene of Rhode Island. But to Cornwallis, as he took in the events of the day and the utterly astounding results of the under-one-hour engagement, the Battle of Camden validated his operational and strategic concept of bold, aggressive offensive action; he now resolved to carry that concept forth into North Carolina.[29]

## A Season of Discord: Chesapeake Diversion, Autumn 1780

Cornwallis consistently advocated a diversionary action in the Chesapeake in support of his march into North Carolina. He understood that such an operation would necessarily force the Virginians to respond and would block any southerly movement by the Continental Army. Just after Camden, he again suggested the idea to Clinton. Further, he advised the CinC that the success of his proposed advance (as far as Hillsborough) and the plan to reestablish royal government and pacify the colony depended on the "operations which your Excellency may think proper to pursue in the Chesapeak [*sic*], which appears to me, next to the security of New York, to be one of the most important objects of the war."[30]

The Chesapeake concept had been in Clinton's mind from the start of the Charleston operation. Indeed, when he departed South Carolina, his orders anticipated a future campaign in that region. But he had cautioned Cornwallis that the highest priority was to defend the posts in South Carolina, especially Charleston. Further, operations into North Carolina should be along the Cape Fear River basin to maintain water communications with the coast; Chesapeake operations could commence in due course. One of the major waypoints along the road to Yorktown occurred when Clinton ordered 2,500 troops under Major General Alexander Leslie to the Chesapeake on 10 October with instructions to establish a defensive post in Hampton Roads and conduct raids as far north as Richmond. In December he detached Brigadier Benedict Arnold with a further 2,000 troops to Portsmouth, Virginia.

Yet every passing day placed Cornwallis in greater peril. By the time additional forces arrived in Virginia, the opportunity for effective and useful action had passed. The engagements at Cowpens, King's Mountain, and Guilford Court House had occurred by mid-spring, forcing Cornwallis's forlorn army to abandon North Carolina for want of supplies and men. It is possible that prompt British actions in the Chesapeake, regardless of the threat of summer disease, might have achieved some operational and strategic success. As it was, the dispatch of forces under Leslie in October, Arnold in December, and Major General William Phillips in the following spring proved too little, too late. While Arnold's force did some raiding around Richmond, French naval power held them hostage at their base at Portsmouth, a factor that negated any operational advantage.

Clearly, a differing strategic concept set in, one that increasingly debilitated southern-pacification efforts. It also created tension between the CinC and his principal field commander. In Clinton's original concept, Chesapeake operations required control of the South Carolina posts. By late summer, however, the earl took a different tack than his senior officer in New York. Cornwallis, though bold, was not completely foolhardy. He understood that his success required reinforcement and support from Clinton. In a letter of 29 August, in which he announced his intended course of action, Cornwallis reminded him of the absolute need to commence simultaneous actions in support of his own North Carolina operations or, in lieu of a diversionary expedition, at least a substantial reinforcement of his own dwindling command: "I most sincerely hope that Nothing can happen to prevent your Excellency's intended diversion in the Chesapeake. If unfortunately any unforeseen Cause should make it impossible, I should hope that you will see the absolute Necessity of adding some Force to the Carolinas."[31]

In the decisions made in the immediate post-Camden period, one sees several critical flaws in Cornwallis's strategic thinking. He failed to see that, while he might gain some operational success from the destruction of Continental forces, his campaign was doomed to failure in the absence of sufficient strength to consolidate victories. In terms of suppressing Patriot irregulars and partisans and in providing security for Loyalists such that they would play their expected role in the southern pacification, he simply lacked the numbers. One might even question his strategic judgment at this point in terms of South Carolina's security and thus the prudence of advancing north. As events played out, the partisans, while diminished by British and Loyalist actions, certainly remained undefeated, irritating, and destructive to the "clear and hold" strategy.

## Fishing Creek, 18 August 1780

Following Camden, the partisan war intensified. The stunning victory and resulting utter collapse of Continental military power in the Carolinas did not deter men like Marion, Sumter, and Pickens; rather, it had the opposite effect. Taking advantage of the victory, Cornwallis vowed to pursue and destroy the irritating partisans and deployed his best instrument—Banastre Tarleton and the British Legion. The ever-aggressive and offensive-minded Tarleton caught up with Sumter on 18 August at Fishing Creek, badly mauling his command in killing, wounding, or capturing over 500 men. In the precursor moves to the disaster, Sumter had decided to cooperate with the Patriot force approaching Camden. Accordingly, he sent Gates a proposal for taking control of the Santee ferries and river crossings. Given the difficulty of movement in the Carolinas, with numerous rivers running from the northwest out of the Appalachians and Piedmont foothills southeast toward the Atlantic, such control would have seriously impeded any rapid British movements. Gates agreed and ordered Sumter to move along the Santee and Wateree Rivers, taking control of all possible crossing points and watercraft. Sumter was reinforced on the fifteenth by Col. Thomas Woolford, with 100 Maryland Continentals and 300 North Carolina militia. Simultaneously, Gates ordered Marion to move up the Santee.

Flush with capable reinforcements, Sumter marched toward the Crown posts at Rocky Mount and Hanging Rock, sites of recent clashes. Finding them deserted since their garrisons had marched to reinforce Rawdon, he encamped and detached Col. Thomas Taylor with a small force to assault Carey's Fort on the Wateree. The hastily constructed redoubt, typical of the British effort to establish fortified posts, in reality represented more of a tempting target for the partisans than any real deterrent to their activity. Manned by a few Loyalists, the redoubt guarded the main Wateree ferry crossing about a mile south of Rocky Mount and roughly thirty miles from Camden (near present-day Ridgeway). Taylor's men achieved surprise and captured not only thirty prisoners but also significant supplies. Further adding to Crown logistical woes, Taylor intercepted a supply train en route to Camden from Ninety Six. This small but important action illustrates a fundamental command-and-control problem that complicated Cornwallis's efforts as he moved farther away from his seaborne sustainment. One of the most significant Patriot partisan contributions lay in the interdiction of supply and communications, which increasingly hampered and complicated British operations. Cornwallis paid a heavy price for his inability to destroy or at least minimize these partisan logistics-interdiction activities.

Alerted to a British crossing downriver from his position—likely Cornwallis coming up from Charleston—Sumter decamped and marched ten miles upriver. In failing to contest the earl's crossing, he essentially aided the British victory at Camden. While he might not have defeated the advancing forces from Charleston, he might have at least impeded their progress, thus allowing Gates to attack a greatly outnumbered (rather than reinforced) Lord Rawdon the next day. Such is the probabilistic nature of war. Once Gates's army dissolved under the weight of British volleys and bayonets, Sumter's command represented the only substantial Patriot force remaining in South Carolina. It instantly made him a target. Tarleton chased the fleeing Camden refugees several miles north, as far as Hanging Rock, before returning to Camden. Cornwallis then ordered him to pursue Sumter, who, slowed by the captured wagons and animals, appeared vulnerable. Setting out the next day with the British Legion, he advanced parallel to Sumter's line of march but on the opposite bank of the Wateree. Tarleton and his 350 men awaited their opportunity to strike the Gamecock. In truth, neither side knew of the other's actual presence across the river. Sumter encamped again at Rocky Mount on the seventeenth and the next morning marched out on the Catawba River road. Here he committed a mistake unforgiveable for an experienced commanding officer by failing to post scouts to reconnoiter his line of march or to ferret out the enemy's position. The error cost his command dearly. Reaching Fishing Creek at Cow Ford, he again encamped, settling into a garrison mentality whereby men traveled freely about the camp with weapons stacked or inside their Bell of Arms (a conical tent for stacking muskets in camp) and with cooking fires blazing. Tarleton lurked nearby. Alerted finally to Sumter's presence the previous night by the campfires, he silently crossed the river and stalked his prey. Leaving behind sixty slower-moving infantry, he mounted the remaining infantrymen on the dragoons' horses and, riding two by two, approached the Patriot camp. Captain Charles Campbell and an advance element rode ahead to scout the position and ran into Patriot patrols, which they dispatched quickly. A high ridge runs between the Catawba and Fishing Creek; Tarleton utilized this to his tactical advantage and drew his troopers into line of battle.

Sumter, who had been sleeping under a wagon, awoke to the shouts and cries of his surprised men and gunfire. He attempted to rally his troops, but the mounted infantry and dragoons had cut them off from their stacked arms. Carnage ensued. Sumter, helpless to rescue the situation, fled into the woods on horseback, apparently without his hat, boots, or saddle. Tarleton reported that his men captured a horde of enemy combatants, supplies, and weapons. In addition to the Patriot prisoners, the legionaries rescued 100 men who had been captured with the supply convoy and about 150 local residents taken earlier by Sumter.

Cornwallis now expected the colony to calm, stating in a report to Lord Germain on the twenty-first that "the rebel forces at present being dispersed, the internal commotions and insurrections in the province will now subside."[32] Here is seen a fundamental flaw in the entire British strategic concept for pacifying the colonies and returning them to allegiance. This rebellion was not like any other in these men's experiences and certainly not like previous Jacobite uprisings that had been crushed by brute military force. That Cornwallis and senior British officers still at this late date considered the American insurrection as one that could be crushed by military force illustrates the profound misunderstanding of its nature, especially in the South. This goes a long way toward explaining the equally profound strategic incoherence and inability to craft and execute an appropriate, effective strategy. It is beyond the scope of this analysis to explore the causes of the War of American Independence, but those dynamics help explain how the Southern Campaign unfolded from the Patriot side. These causes also explain the rapid Patriot resurgence in the Carolinas after Camden and Fishing Creek, a truly frustrating and bewildering scenario for Cornwallis as he pressed ever closer to his planned North Carolina invasion.[33]

## Musgrove's Mill, 18 August 1780

Despite the disasters at Camden and Fishing Creek, the speed with which the Patriots rebounded amazed the British. The affair at Musgrove's Mill on 19 August somewhat balanced the latter debacle. Known as the "Over-Mountain Men," Lt. Col. Isaac Shelby's militia from the Watauga settlements (now eastern Tennessee), joined with Georgians under Lt. Col. Elijah Clarke and South Carolinians under Lt. Col. James Williams, together about 200 mounted riflemen. Rifles and horses gave these men two distinct tactical advantages in the partisan struggles with the Carolina Loyalists—firepower with standoff distance and tactical mobility—keys that soon played large after the war widened into western North Carolina by October. At Musgrove's Mill on the Enoree River (near present-day Spartanburg), Colonel Alexander Innes's command of around 500 Loyalists doubled the Patriot numbers; the three officers nevertheless resolved to attack, using tactical deception to level the quantitative advantage. The Georgians crossed the river ford to seemingly stumble upon the enemy encampment, then quickly retreated in apparent flight as the Loyalists gave chase—into a trap. Luring the enemy to a prepared log-and-earth fortification, the Patriots opened fire against the charging

Provincial regulars, who came at them with fixed bayonets. Driving the Patriots back by sheer weight of numbers and aided by the charge's speed while the riflemen reloaded, Innes's men drove the Patriots into the surrounding woods. After a shot felled Innes, the attack disintegrated as the Patriots counterattacked, driving back the stunned and leaderless Provincials. In the melee that resulted, the Loyalists lost heavy casualties estimated at 150 killed or wounded and seventy captured. For the Patriots, casualties amounted to a dozen killed or wounded. Although the three officers contemplated a follow-up assault on Ninety Six, given the earlier Camden debacle and Sumter's loss the same day at Fishing Creek, they demurred, retiring away from major Crown forces.

For Cornwallis, the affair at the mill highlighted several negative trends in the evolving partisan insurgency. The injection of the Over-Mountain Men meant a new force of rugged, hardy opponents seasoned by the frontier struggle with the Cherokee and who had mastered the tactical arts of hit and run, ambush, sniping from a distance with rifles, and cover and concealment. Perhaps most importantly, these were men hardly likely to be intimated by threats and oaths. Additionally, a principal and highly successful Loyalist recruiter, Colonel Innes, had been lost. Finally, and perhaps most worrisome, a much smaller Patriot irregular force had crushed a Loyalist Provincial regiment of relatively well-trained and motivated troops by employing their inherent advantages in firepower and mobility. Since the British attempted to fight a conventional war against the irregulars with heavy infantry, smoothbore muskets, and bayonets—excellent in conventional linear battles in the open as at Camden—Musgrove's Mill should have been alarming. The affair further demonstrates the inappropriateness of the British tactical and operational concepts as to the employment of conventional forces in counterinsurgency operations, a conundrum that still flummoxes strategic planners hundreds of years later.

## The "Devil Himself": Nelson's Ferry, Blue Savannah, and Black Mingo Creek

What of Francis Marion? Thus far, he escaped undue attention from Crown forces. That dynamic changed dramatically in late August and September. Returning to the Low Country, he avoided contact and managed to place himself astride the vital logistics route between Charleston and Camden. Hearing of a supply column moving down from Camden with prisoners from Gates's army and halted at Nelson's Ferry across the Santee, he struck. Using surprise, speed, and a dawn attack, his men overwhelmed the small guard. In addition to the supplies, horses, and weapons, including arms and gear captured at Camden, he freed 150 Maryland Continentals. Interestingly, many Marylanders (probably more than half) chose to continue on to Charleston rather than back into the swamps with Marion. Most likely, as veterans of the Camden disaster, these dejected men believed that the Crown represented the winning side and decided to either stay out of the fray or even join the opposition. These actions represented a common dynamic in a civil war—individuals often change sides depending on the ebb and flow of events. Many troopers in Armand's Legion, the main Continental cavalry unit at Camden, started the war as British regulars, then deserted to the Patriot side.[34]

To avoid pursuit and capture, Marion's men took to the swamplands, where all efforts to root them out failed. Tarleton could not find the partisans and in frustration dubbed Marion the "Swamp Fox," a nickname immortalized ever since, remarking, "as for this damned old fox, the devil himself could not catch him!"[35] The Fox did not tarry long. Flush with the captured arms and the men freed at Nelson's Ferry, on 4 September he attacked the advance guard of a Loyalist force moving south, pushing them back. Once the main forces engaged, Marion felt the weight of numbers and withdrew to the safety of Blue Savannah, an island in the Little Pee Dee River. As the enemy approached, the fire from the undergrowth and thickets drove them back with heavy losses. With two significant wins, Marion's reputation grew as Loyalist support in the Pee Dee region waned.

Leveraging his run of successes, the Swamp Fox struck again on 28 September. A group of mounted Loyalists led by John Ball, a locally prominent rice planter, lay at Shephard's Ferry on Black Mingo Creek, which runs into the Black River. Being local men, Ball's troops knew the terrain and likely many in Marion's command. The Black Mingo Creek affair represented a growing dynamic in the Carolinas as the war deteriorated into civil strife. Ball positioned his men outside Willtown, a local village on the edge of a wood. Detecting Marion's approach at night, the Loyalists opened a deadly fire that initially drove back the Patriots. Marion then charged from three sides in a convergent attack. Suffering heavy casualties, Ball's men broke and fled. The Swamp Fox even captured the Loyalist commander's horse, which he promptly renamed Ball.

With these small but sharp actions in a span of a month, Marion demonstrated three essential dynamics. Despite the small size of his force—typically fifty men or less—the Swamp Fox showed the ability and willingness to take on much larger Loyalist formations in open combat. In the immediate post-Camden period, his actions reinvigorated Patriot spirits and enthusiasm while depressing Loyalist sentiment. No Crown supply or reinforcement convoy could travel safely through the countryside without fear of attack. Thus, Cornwallis and subordinate commanders detailed an increasing number of troops to escort duties, depleting their commands and diffusing Crown strength, a significant factor in subsequent North Carolina operations. Of perhaps even more critical importance, other than those serving directly with the British regular forces, no significant independent Loyalist force operated in South Carolina by summer's end. General Sumter, having escaped, began recruitment; Colonel Marion found safe haven in the Low Country swamps and forests, launching into what would become his forte—attacks on logistics and communication. Lieutenant Colonels Shelby, Clarke, Williams, Pickens, and Davie operated in western South Carolina. Given Cornwallis's aggressive nature, however, once he resolved to go on the offensive, he would do so even with the partisan diversions in his rear and the absence of support from the north, either a Chesapeake operation or a significant reinforcement. Complications loomed. As the Musgrove's Mill affair showed, the war had widened. Frontiersmen, previously minimally engaged, now joined the fight in force. Cornwallis's partisan, irregular problem expanded not only in quantitative terms but also spatially. With the frontiersmen's arrival, the entire South Carolina colony became the battleground in the autumn of 1780, with separate major partisan bands operating geographically: Marion in the Pee Dee and coastal region, Sumter in the Piedmont, and Pickens and the frontiersmen in the Appalachians and western foothills. These same frontiersmen would soon deliver a crushing blow to the earl's North Carolina invasion at an ancient volcanic plateau called King's Mountain.

There is a continuing question as to how Cornwallis's apparent lack of understanding or perhaps blatant disregard of the role of maritime power played into the coming catastrophe. To march into the Carolina backcountry while diluting forces to hold Charleston and other key posts in the absence of a reliable seaborne logistical chain could be interpreted as either folly or simple arrogance. The earl did express to Clinton the fear that disease, more prevalent along the coast than in the uplands, would decimate any reinforcements from New York until at least late autumn, and for this reason he seemingly eschewed any operation based on the Cape Fear River basin.[36] There existed a severe disconnect with Clinton's strategic concept in that he viewed North Carolina operations as merely an adjunct to the proposed Chesapeake operation. Cornwallis did not believe in that. Given his nature—making and executing decisions independent of higher command and with little to no regard for the value of naval cooperation—an element of uncertainty and disunity appeared that hampered the Southern Campaign for the remainder of the war. Despite the disadvantageous situation of a steadily eroding Loyalist force and the lack of a strong Chesapeake diversion, Cornwallis adhered to his plan to advance into North Carolina.

## "Fire and Sword": King's Mountain, 7 October 1780

With the resolve to press ahead despite the obstacles, Cornwallis implemented his campaign plan in September. The 7th Regiment of Foot (Royal Fusiliers) arrived from Charleston on the eighth, and with this reinforcement, the earl felt sufficiently strong to begin the march north by way of Hanging Rock and Waxhaws. He commenced the movement on 22 September with the ultimate objective of Hillsborough, where he hoped to reestablish royal authority and create a magnet for Loyalist support. Four days later the army reached Charlotte, which Cornwallis meant to use as the main Crown operating base for North Carolina. From an operational viewpoint, the decision made sense. Charlotte lay some sixty-five miles due north of Camden and astride the major north–south trade routes from central Virginia through the Piedmont and south to upper Georgia. Major Davie attempted a stalling attack, but his 150 horsemen could do little to halt the advance. While the move into North Carolina represented the next natural action based on the earl's strategic concept for ensuring the safety of South Carolina and Georgia, others viewed the move with trepidation. Charles Stedman, who served as commissary general to the army later commented that Cornwallis's decision seemed "to confound human wisdom . . . [and] derange the best concerted schemes [of men]."[37]

To cover his western flank, the earl detached Major Ferguson to operate west of Charlotte. The need to provide both flanking cover for the main force as well as to rouse the Loyalists into action prompted this action. In August the earl had indicated his intention to send the major into the mountains to cover the army's left flank with his newly constituted Loyalist corps; he had raised nearly a thousand recruits for his command in western South Carolina since his appointment as inspector of militia in June. Ferguson arrived in North Carolina on 7 September and promptly initiated action. At this point Cornwallis had some trepidation about the willingness of North Carolina Loyalists to rise again, perhaps due to the Ramsour's Mill affair. He wrote to Lieutenant Colonel Balfour: "Ferguson is going to advance with some militia and his own miserable naked corps to Gilbertown and Tryon County. I think it rather hazardous, but he says he cannot positively get them to stay longer where they are; and to be sure, this is a favorable time for advancing, and if ever those people will fight, it is when they attack and not when they are attacked."[38]

The major, inventor of the Ferguson breech-loading rifle, had won a few small skirmishes against local Patriot groups and felt confident in his mission.[39] Arriving at Gilbert Town, about fifty miles west of Charlotte, Ferguson released a prisoner to carry a word of warning to supporters of the rebel cause in the colony's western region. His threat of retribution rang loud: "if they did not desist from their opposition to the British arms, he would march his army over the mountains, hang their leaders, and lay their country waste with fire and sword."[40]

The infamous "fire and sword" message had profound results. Within days, local militia leaders throughout western North Carolina and Virginia collected their forces for a general rendezvous at Quaker Meadows on the Catawba River, about twenty-five miles northeast of Gilbert Town (near present-day Morganton). Those leaders included Lieutenant Colonel Shelby along with Lt. Cols. John Sevier, Charles McDowell, and William Campbell. Predominately mounted frontiersmen and armed with hunting rifles like Shelby's contingent, these frontier Patriots all came to be known as the Over-Mountain Men, as many hailed from the western side of the Blue Ridge Mountains. When threatened by a British officer with a large Loyalist force moving toward them, they reacted quickly and decisively. Joined at Quaker Meadows by a further body of North Carolinians under Col. Benjamin Cleveland, by 29 September, the assembled force of 1,300 mounted and superbly armed Patriots headed south toward the enemy. Although McDowell, as the senior militia officer, should have commanded, his fellow officers showed little confidence in his martial capability. In a move designed to prevent his embarrassment, he traveled north to Hillsborough to confer with Gates at Southern Department headquarters, ostensibly to request support and reinforcements. Campbell assumed command in McDowell's absence.

Ferguson initially retreated toward South Carolina once he realized the nature of the opposing force moving against him,. He sent messages to Cornwallis requesting reinforcement. After a feint of retreating to Ninety Six, the major moved north with renewed boldness and self-confidence, writing to the earl that "three or four hundred good soldiers, part dragoons, would finish this business."[41] But one wonders just how confident Ferguson really was, given that his letters to Cornwallis sought reinforcements. On 6 October he established a camp on the plateau of King's Mountain, just across the border into South Carolina. Unfortunately for Ferguson and his Loyalists, his two letters to the general failed in their intent. The first message of 30 September arrived at Cornwallis's headquarters on 7 October, while rebels intercepted the 6 October message sent from King's Mountain. From spies the Patriot leaders learned of Ferguson's intention to fortify King's Mountain and await reinforcement, setting the stage for a British disaster that rumbled through the remainder of the conflict like a Carolina summer storm.

Marching in a soaking rain, the rebel forces proceeded into South Carolina, covering the locks of their weapons with blankets and shirts to keep them dry. As they finally reached the base of King's Mountain by late afternoon of the seventh, the sun broke through. Forming into multiple columns that surrounded the Loyalist base, 900 Patriots selected from the force for their marksmanship skills prepared for a coordinated assault. Despite the thirty-mile march that had commenced the previous evening, anticipation and energy ran high as officers exhorted the men to take advantage of their shooting and concealment skills, a hallmark of the frontiersman.

A thousand North and South Carolina Loyalists waited on the summit. Additionally, Ferguson's force contained elements of several Provincial units, including the King's American Regiment (New York) and the New Jersey Volunteers, though these better trained, disciplined, and equipped troops amounted to only a hundred men.[42] Captain Abraham DePeyster from New York acted as the Loyalists' second in command. The ancient volcanic mountain rose from the flat plains below, visible from miles away, and is capped by a flat plateau that provided ideal ground for use of linear tactics. Unfortunately for the Loyalists encamped there, the heavily forested slopes gave the Patriots the tactical advantages of cover and concealment. Though Ferguson had posted pickets, apparently none saw the enemy horsemen assembling below. The Loyalists carried out their normal daily camp routine, unaware of the gathering storm.

The decision to attack straightaway allowed for tactical surprise, an advantage that outweighed the Patriots' fatigue. Dismounted, the Over-Mountain Men and militia separated and prepared for their convergent assault on the Loyalist camp. By 3:00 p.m., Shelby and Campbell's men approached the plateau from opposite directions using the dense foliage for cover. Not waiting for all the troops to take position, Shelby commenced firing from the north face of the mountain, followed quickly by Campbell's Virginians. Within a few minutes the entire rebel force advanced up the slopes. Ferguson rallied his men with the beating of quarters and by blowing his silver whistle, a common period communications medium. Attempting to form line at the crest of the plateau, which ran downward southwesterly at a slight angle for 600 yards, he quickly organized a bayonet charge. The Provincials advanced against Campbell's men, the first to reach the summit after scrambling over the rocky trails and through the thick, damp foliage. Though the charge succeeded in driving the Virginians back down the slope, the momentary success had perilous tactical consequences, removing one of the steadier units from the action at the summit just as the tardier rebel columns reached the plateau and opened fire.

Once the Provincials reached the base of the mountain, they came under intense and highly accurate fire from the retreating Virginians. Though an open field is excellent terrain for conventional linear tactics, to the frontier marksmen shielded at the edge of the plateau by rocks and trees, the open space provided an unimpeded field of fire. The rebel formation's irregularity and the terrain features provided one of the few instances in the war when the old myth of rebels "hiding behind rocks and trees" actually proved true. Unfortunately for Ferguson and his Loyalists, the Americans they faced that wet October afternoon possessed the frontier rifle and had been specifically selected for their shooting skill. The casualties among Ferguson's ranks grew horrendously as each minute passed.

The Provincials delivered three devastating bayonet charges against Campbell, each time his Virginians regained the plateau, driving his men down the mountain with casualties each time. Although each charge met with success, the Provincials' morale suffered each time the attackers returned to the plateau and delivered their murderous fire. While their own volleys might have done great damage at close range on a level battlefield, in having to shoot down the wooded mountainside, the Loyalists consistently fired too high and over the enemy's heads, causing few casualties. The battle against Campbell and the other Patriot columns reaching the plateau lasted about an hour, by which time the Loyalists, having suffered heavy casualties and pushed back up the mountain into their camp, fell into confusion and disorder. Several white flags came out as men attempted to surrender. Meanwhile, Ferguson sought to create a tipping point by a mounted charge with what few volunteers he could muster. As these men mounted up, riflemen just within the tree line shot them out of the saddle. Wounded in the hand himself, Ferguson frantically rode across and around the battlefield, rallying his men. Captain DePeyster urged an honorable surrender, but the Scotsman would have none of it. In company with a few other riders, the major charged the enemy and received at least seven rifle-ball wounds, killing him. Dragged along and into the woods by his dead foot still in the stirrup, the only native Briton at King's Mountain died near the northern end of the summit.

As casualties mounted, men panicked following the loss of their commander. DePeyster, now ranking officer, decided that surrender was the only way to stem the bloodletting. He requested a parley and quarter. Responding, Patriot officers shouted back that no quarter would be given until the Loyalists threw down their weapons. Corralled into a space barely sixty yards by forty yards, the Loyalists received fire at point-blank range for several minutes. The battle seemingly concluded, as often happens in the "fog and friction" of war, chance intervened. A Loyalist foraging party returned just as the apparent last shots rang out and, not understanding that surrender negotiations were ongoing, themselves opened fire, severely wounding Lieutenant Colonel Williams among others. In response, the Patriots, perhaps fearing the arrival of Tarleton's dragoons or similar reinforcements, again shot into the Loyalists packed together in the open, inflicting perhaps another hundred casualties before officers regained control of the situation. Many Patriots shouting "Tarleton's Quarter" assaulted and butchered unarmed and surrendering Loyalists in a mirror image of the Waxhaws Massacre until Lieutenant Colonel Campbell reasserted control.[43]

Killed-in-action reports vary for the Loyalists, ranging between 119 and 157 men, including Ferguson and several key officers. The victorious Patriots marched their nearly 700 prisoners toward Quaker Meadows and Gilbert Town, leaving behind a further 123 wounded Loyalists to die later on King's Mountain. Campbell's men stayed at the plateau to bury the dead hurriedly and unceremoniously. No one cared to tarry long on the battlefield; the fear of the omnipotent Tarleton guaranteed as hasty a Patriot departure as possible. With wounded men not easily transported except by wagons and left to suffer on the battlefield, the tragedy of American versus American in a nasty civil war compounded itself. This factor no doubt led to further recriminations and brutality in the post-Yorktown period, when the "Tory War" erupted in the Carolinas without the stabilizing influence of regular troops. The victors tried and convicted twelve Loyalists, hanging nine; three escaped. Most of the King's Mountain prisoners marched to Hillsborough eventually slipped away over the following months. Patriot losses amounted to less than a hundred casualties total.[44]

The action at King's Mountain further complicated the British strategic situation. Cornwallis had lost his left-flank covering force, while the Loyalist strategy suffered insurmountable damage. In a process begun earlier in the year at Ramsour's Mill, Ferguson's destruction accelerated the dynamic of a decline in both Loyalist recruitment in the Carolinas and Loyalist willingness to actively support Crown forces. King's Mountain demonstrated the fragility of a strategy based on a faulty net assessment—that hordes of Carolina Loyalists would flock to the king's colors. After Ferguson's defeat, Lord Rawdon expressed to Clinton the dismay of senior British officers at the lack of enthusiasm among Carolinians: "In short, Sir, we have a powerful body of friends in North Carolina—and indeed we have cause to be convinced, that many of the inhabitants wish well to His Majesty's arms; but they have not given evidence enough either of their number or their activity, to justify the stake of this province, for the uncertain advantages that might attend immediate junction with them."[45] Cornwallis blamed the lack of Loyalist enthusiasm on Patriot oppression and coercion. In this regard he was largely correct. Actions such as King's Mountain following closely after Ramsour's Mill did cow the western North Carolina Loyalists into inactivity. The earl discovered just how powerful this enthusiasm gap had become as he trudged through the North Carolina wilderness in the following winter and spring. Even before King's Mountain, Cornwallis had written in frustration to Clinton on 29 August: "We receive the strongest professions of friendship from North Carolina. Our friends, however, do not seem inclined to rise until they see our army in motion. The severity of the rebel government was so terrible and totally subdued the minds of the people, that it is very difficult to rouse them to any exertions."[46]

## Fish Dam Ford and Blackstock's Plantation, November 1780

Cornwallis fell back from Charlotte to Winnsborough, after which the majority of Crown action entailed efforts by various detachments to catch and destroy General Sumter's partisans. Tarleton, suffering from a fever and left behind when Cornwallis's army advanced to Charlotte, had placed Major George Hanger in temporary command of the British Legion. A contingent of the 71st under Major Archibald McArthur remained with the lieutenant colonel. Meanwhile Sumter regrouped. The general had been appointed commander of all South Carolina militia by Governor Rutledge, and Gates ordered him to advance toward the British position at Winnsborough, between the Wateree and Broad Rivers. This movement was intended to draw off forces from the main enemy body such that Brigadier General Smallwood might assault Winnsborough. The notion that Smallwood's decimated command could handle even a diminished British army is ludicrous, illustrative of Gates's complete lack of strategic and operational reality. The Marylander heard of Gates's impending relief from command and demurred attacking, leaving Sumter on his own. The Gamecock arrived at Moore's Mill on 7 November, thirty miles from Winnsborough. Pickets spotted and reported this movement. Cornwallis ordered a pursuit, and on the eighth Major Weymss departed Winnsborough with about 200 mounted infantry of the 63rd and forty dragoons from Tarleton's command. Local Loyalists reported that Sumter by then had moved to Fish Dam Ford, a few miles down the Broad River. The pursuing dragoons received details of the Patriot encampment, even to the exact location of the general's tent.

The aggressive Wemyss chose to assault even though severely outnumbered, Sumter having roughly 600 men after reinforcement by some Georgia militia a day earlier. At midnight Wemyss approached the camp with plans to attack before dawn, but alert pickets detected the enemy and opened fire, wounding the major in the arm and knee. A charge by dragoons went badly as well. Meanwhile, a party of dragoons approached Sumter's tent, who amazingly still slept despite the commotion. Awakened finally, he fought off his attackers, managed to slip under a tent flap, and disappeared into the dense woods—a second miraculous escape. A firefight then developed. With Lieutenant John Stark now in British command, he ordered his troops to charge with bayonets. The Patriots loosed a final volley before retiring toward the river. A group of South Carolina militia counterattacked, forcing Stark to withdraw, even abandoning his casualties. Both sides abandoned the area. In the morning the Patriots retook the campsite and treated wounded of both sides, capturing twenty-five prisoners, including Wemyss. Although he had garnered a horrific reputation for destruction and brutality, Sumter prevented his men from hanging the officer (who was later exchanged).

While ostensibly a small engagement with few casualties (less than fifty total), Fish Dam Ford represented a huge strategic communications win for the Patriots. Weymss, a notorious and hated figure, had been defeated. Perhaps more importantly, militia had beaten a regular force in open battle. Cornwallis immediately recalled Tarleton from chasing Marion and vowed to hunt down Sumter. The Gamecock, who showed an amazing ability to recover and recruit, if not much command talent in battle, now threatened important posts such as Ninety Six. Ranging about the countryside, his men attacked small Loyalist positions and eventually arrived at William Blackstock's plantation on the Tyger River. Reinforced by additional militia from Georgia under the command of Colonels Elijah Clarke, Benjamin Few, and John Twiggs, giving him over a thousand troops, and hearing that the pursuing Tarleton had divided his force, Sumter resolved to give battle. Tarleton detached a battalion to secure Brierly's Ford on the Broad River. Skirmishes ensued, but eventually the dragoons successfully crossed the river. Learning that Sumter intended to assault a Loyalist outpost on the Little River, only fifteen miles from Ninety Six, Tarleton resolved to attack even though numerically inferior.

Meanwhile, Sumter retreated to Blackstock's and established a strong defensive position. The high hills fronting the Tyger and the surrounding deep woods inhibited cavalry movement, while the split-rail fences and plantation outbuildings provided cover. Early in the morning of 20 November, Tarleton advanced on Blackstock's plantation with mounted infantry from the 63rd Regiment. Alerted to their approach, Sumter attacked once he realized that the British advance guard had taken position on a nearby hill to await the arrival of reinforcements. Tarleton dismounted his infantry, under Major John Money, and deployed them across a field, with the British Legion dragoons atop the hill preparing to charge. Sumter sent mounted militia to attack the dismounted infantry and 400 more troops in a direct assault against the hill. Sensing a slowness in the firing of the advancing Patriots, Money ordered a counterattack with bayonets. With no bayonets to repel the oncoming 63rd, the Patriots retreated to the plantation house, outbuildings, and the woods beyond; the British rushed headlong after them and into a trap. The Broad River Riflemen, posted in the structures, opened up a deadly fire that decimated the advancing troops. Back at the hill, the dragoons never realized the threat of the advancing enemy until caught in a hail of buckshot, which felled twenty of them in a single volley. Tarleton then organized a charge and rescued the surviving infantry, including Major Money, but at a high cost. Sumter, overly eager to get at the Green Dragoon, rode too close to the enemy and received wounds in the chest and shoulder. Once again, though, he eluded capture or death, albeit badly wounded and out of action for some time. The Gamecock would return.

Although Tarleton claimed a victory at Blackstock's Plantation, his losses belied such a boast. While details are sketchy, the probable numbers are close to two hundred British casualties compared to Patriot losses of less than ten men. Tarleton reported to Cornwallis: "Sumpter [*sic*] is defeated, his corps dispersed, and himself dangerously wounded. . . . But, my Lord I have lost men—50 killed and wounded and officers which are losses to the public service, . . . and every officer's horse, my own included, kill'd or wounded."[47]

The Patriot strategy of attrition by strategic defensive, which called for small incremental victories over detached forces and outposts, continued to both frustrate Cornwallis and wear down his manpower and material resources. Conversely, the successes further buoyed Patriot public support while depressing Loyalists. Wounded and out of action, Sumter on 11 December sent forces under Clarke and Few to attack a Loyalist column near Ninety Six at Long Canes, where the Patriots inflicted substantial casualties. Marion, having stayed inactive for some weeks, struck again at Halfway Swamp and Singleton's Mill the next day. The colonel's 700 men easily outnumbered the British 200. In a somewhat comical episode, the commander of the 64th Regiment of Foot, Major Robert McLeroth, realized the threat to his rear and challenged the Swamp Fox to a duel. When Marion's twenty picked duelists arrived at the designated spot, they saw the British column marching away to safety. Furious, they raced ahead and occupied Singleton's Mill and its outbuildings. As McLeroth approached, the defenders fled. The British officer soon found out why—the mill family all had smallpox. At Hammond's Store on 28 December, William Washington's dragoons, detached to raid and occupy British attention, attacked and crushed a large Loyalist force, inflicting 150 casualties and capturing a further forty. More striking and worrisome, Hammond's stood near the heavily Loyalist Ninety Six.[48]

Despite the need to suppress the growing and increasingly successful partisan problem, Cornwallis resolved to carry on and destroy the southern Continental army. True to his aggressive nature, he embarked upon this bold and risky move to regain the strategic initiative. Instead, it would lead only to disaster.

## "Rise, and Fight Again": Greene Takes Command, December 1780

Shortly after King's Mountain, Congress made a momentous decision, following General Washington's advice to replace Gates with Maj. Gen. Nathanael Greene as commander of the Southern Department. His appointment represented a sea change in Patriot leadership quality, strategic thinking, and operational ability in the South. Greene and Washington had developed a special bond of respect and confidence that had tremendous consequences for the cause of independence, all to Cornwallis's detriment. Known as "The Crab" by his troops due to a knee injury that gave his gait an unusual halting motion, he had no practical military experience when the rebellion broke out other than a few months serving as a private in the Kentish Guards, a Rhode Island militia unit. But Greene had powerful political allies. By the time the Rhode Islanders advanced north to help besiege Boston, he had been appointed a brigadier general and placed in command of the contingent. What he lacked in practical experience, he made up in technical and historical knowledge. When placed on the Continental Army establishment by Congress in July, Greene at thirty-three became the youngest general in the force. A voracious reader, he consumed numerous works on history, strategy, tactics, and military science. Greene soon proved his genius at organization and logistical management, also displaying an ability to play the consummate diplomat between divergent interests and personalities—all qualities that gave him a marked advantage over British forces once he moved south in 1780.

Through the campaigns of 1776–78, he commanded forces on Long Island, during the retreat across New Jersey, at the critical battles at Trenton and Princeton, and in the Philadelphia Campaign. At the Valley Forge winter encampment of 1777–78, the Rhode Islander showed his exceptional organizational and management ability as quartermaster general. The Quartermaster Department had never been quite up to snuff; Greene reorganized and made it a smooth-functioning staff unit. During the Rhode Island Campaign in the autumn of 1778, he served ably as an intermediary between the French and American officers, able to adapt to and work effectively with difficult alliance partners. This trait proved especially useful in the South, where he coordinated regular Continental operations with the typically independent-minded and often headstrong partisan leaders. The Rhode Island effort failed, but Greene set a standard for Allied working relations that transcended the typically difficult fragility of coalitions dynamics.

In the horrendous 1778–79 winter at Morristown, New Jersey, the most brutal of the entire century in the mid-Atlantic, the young general's quartermaster skills kept the army reasonably well fed, supplied, and frankly alive. As with most successful persons, he had enemies. Two such in Congress proposed to reorganize the Quartermaster Corps into a system of state consignments, an arrangement adopted by Congress but that proved hugely detrimental. Rather than a single entity led by a talented manager, Washington thus relied on the thirteen states to provide supplies for their own units within the army. This clumsy, inefficient arrangement nearly destroyed the Continental Army as a fighting force. Greene offered to resign. To shield him from such political attacks, Washington appointed him as commander at West Point in the wake of the Benedict Arnold treason scandal. Then as the southern situation collapsed, and with Gates, the darling of many in Congress, defeated and disgraced, Washington had the opportunity to recommend the right man as the new commander of the Southern Department to reorganize and revive the southern forces.

Greene headed south with orders to continue the ongoing irregular warfare against the British and Loyalists, aimed at the destruction of the Loyalist military ability and the complication of the British logistical situation. He arrived at Gates's headquarters at Charlotte on 2 December. There he found a gravely depressed, motley, and discouraged force of barely over 2,000 starving, ill-clad, and destitute troops; fewer than 1,500 were fit for duty. Greene reported to Washington that the troops appeared "literally naked, and a great part totally unfit for any kind of duty."[49] Despite the difficulties, the sad little army—facing winter's deprivations and the prospect of again fighting Cornwallis's seasoned regulars—represented the only force of any consequence south of Washington's main army near New York. If Greene failed, then Cornwallis might sweep up through North Carolina, Virginia, and Maryland to threaten Washington with a two-pronged attack. Additionally, Greene still had to contend with what remained of North Carolina loyalism. Though cowed by Ramsour's Mill and King's Mountain, a potent, existential force still lurked, especially in the Cross Creek and Tryon County areas, apparently awaiting only Cornwallis's arrival to emerge. If the earl pushed aside and destroyed the remaining Continentals, the chances for Loyalists executing the "hold" aspect of the Southern Strategy seemed very good indeed. Given this conundrum, Greene's strategic genius produced one of the most amazing and effective defensive campaigns in the history of warfare.

Upon relieving Gates at Charlotte, Greene displayed the energy, administrative acumen, and organizational skill that marked his career. He established a commissariat and appointed a capable quartermaster to address the chronic supply difficulties. Pressure placed on Virginia and North Carolina civil officials resulted in better, more reliable supply and logistics. Moreover, as an illustration of his ability to coordinate and cooperate with the irregulars that had so flummoxed the enemy, he immediately corresponded with Marion and Sumter in South Carolina and began unity-of-effort coordination and planning, a hallmark of Greene's southern tenure. In the northern campaigns he had developed a mistrust for militia based on their lack of reliability; nevertheless, the astute general realized that he had little choice but to incorporate them into his overall strategy of attrition. He explained his own southern strategy to Washington: "I see but little prospect of getting a force to contend with the enemy upon equal grounds . . . and therefore must make the most of a kind of partizan war."[50] It is important to note, however, that while he certainly believed in the value of irregulars and militia as force multipliers, Greene also understood that the final, culminating victory required regular troops in conventional battle. In this regard his views mirrored those of both Washington and Cornwallis. He stated to Sumter: "Partisan strokes in war are like garnishings on a table, they give splendor to the army and reputation to the officers; but they afford no substantial national security. They are matters that should not be neglected, and yet, they should not be pursued to the prejudice of more important concerns. You may strike a hundred strokes, and reap little benefit from them, unless you have a good army to take advantage of them."[51]

What of Greene's strategy for countering Cornwallis? There is an expression among modern military aviators: "high speed, low drag, speed is life." So it was with Greene. Acting the hare, he would wear down the British hound with speed and strategic mobility. He understood that Cornwallis's critical weakness lay in supply and logistics. Therefore, the farther away from the supply depots at Camden and elsewhere that he could lead Cornwallis, the better. Greene relied on the partisans to interdict and complicate Crown command, control, communications, and logistics. Unlike Cornwallis, he better understood the nature of the war in the Carolinas, particularly the use of terrain. He also recognized the critical potential of the southern water systems as barriers. On the journey to Charlotte, the general scouted river crossings, fords, and ferries in the various waterways crossing North Carolina from northwest to southeast. He also gathered boats and watercraft at key locations and staged them for rapid river crossings while denying these assets to the British. His locally raised troops also knew the terrain, intelligence that would help him stay ahead of the earl in the chase to come. Greene also enjoyed the services of expert cavalry under Colonels Lee and Washington.

Closely following the key tenet of the Fabian strategy, or attrition by the strategic defensive, to maintain one's force and only give battle when the potential rewards exceed the risk, Greene played a game of hide and seek until the decisive, culminating battle presented itself. In a classic Fabian strategy, one must accomplish four essential tasks: (1) exhaust the enemy first and prevent the destruction of one's own forces; (2) use sanctuary and tactical mobility to preserve one's own forces; (3) maintain close ties with civil authorities to ensure no premature commitment to battle; and (4) fight and win the culminating, decisive battle that convinces the enemy to quit the war. To accomplish these goals, Greene conceived of his forces as a "flying army" in that mobility, speed, sanctuary, and the employment of the partisans to frustrate and harass Crown forces represented the pathway to strategic success.

The story of the North Carolina Campaign of January to late April 1781 is that of Greene masterfully executing this strategy as Cornwallis thrashed about in frustration, chasing the elusive Rhode Islander. As Crown forces advanced into North Carolina in pursuit of the Continentals, Greene executed a brilliant operation: he "denied the enemy resources, limited their mobility while increasing his own and constantly wore down Cornwallis' forces to lead the British general into making mistakes."[52]

Unknown to the earl, another harbinger of ill fortune arrived in the South just after King's Mountain—Brig. Gen. Daniel Morgan, known as "The Old Wagoner." Morgan, who did great service with his riflemen during the Saratoga Campaign, had retired from the army over a lack of promotion and the appointment of Anthony Wayne to command the Corps of Light Infantry, a post he felt entitled to after Saratoga. Additionally, a medical issue—most likely sciatica and rheumatism—troubled the Virginian, so he retreated to his farm in Winchester. Greene convinced the "Old Wagoner" to return to active service, and Morgan obliged as commander of the Virginia Continentals sent to bolster the Southern Department. With this reinforcement, Greene then committed what most military theorists insist is a probable error—dividing one's forces in the face of an enemy, one numerically and qualitatively superior at that.[53] Napoleon Bonaparte successfully managed dividing forces, but his skill in maneuver lay in concentrating the separate columns at the key location at the ultimate moment. In Greene's plan, once each force reached the intended operating area, they stood over a hundred miles apart with no chance of quick mutual support. If boldness and risk taking is a mark of many successful commanders, then the Rhode Islander rates high on that scale. Yet it represented a huge gamble. In essence, by dividing his forces, Greene opened up the possibility of Cornwallis defeating him in detail. That destruction did not result had much to do with Morgan's tactical brilliance and military leadership. Greene had a practical reason for dividing the army—starvation. The Charlotte–Mecklenburg County area had been "picked clean" by various forces over the previous months, thus Greene had to find more reliable logistics, dividing his units to reduce the requirement for any one location.[54] Accordingly, he detached Morgan with a substantial force of Continentals and militia into western South Carolina, while he took the main body east and south to near Cheraw, South Carolina, at the headwaters of the Pee Dee River. In justifying his decision to split his army, Greene explained that the action

> makes the most of my inferior force, for it compels my adversary to divide his, and holds him in doubt as to his own line of conduct. He cannot leave Morgan behind him to come at me, or his posts of Ninety Six and Augusta would be exposed. And he cannot chase Morgan far, or prosecute his views upon Virginia, while I am here with the whole country open before me. I am as near to Charleston as he is, and as near Hillsborough as I was at Charlotte; so that I am in no danger of being cut off from my reinforcements.[55]

With these two superlative Patriot commanders now in the field, Cornwallis's task—and indeed the entire Southern Campaign—stood perilously close to the precipice of defeat.

The arrival of Major General Leslie in the Tidewater region of Virginia on 21 October boded well for Cornwallis's fortunes: the long-awaited Chesapeake diversion seemed at hand. Leslie's force quickly occupied the Hampton Roads area and awaited orders from the earl, under whose direct operational command Clinton had placed him. The ill effects of King's Mountain and the success of the partisan attrition strategy so distressed Cornwallis that he immediately ordered Leslie to proceed by sea to Wilmington, North Carolina, then to Charleston to reinforce his own depleted main body. This action nullified the possibility of a two-pronged assault as envisioned in the summer when British victory seemed imminent. An argument can be made that Clinton's six-week delay in dispatching Leslie had a significant effect on Ferguson's fortunes and ultimately on Cornwallis's as well. If Leslie's presence in the Hampton Roads area had come earlier, it may have resulted in the redeployment of Campbell's militia into southeastern Virginia (as actually occurred once Leslie did arrive in theater) rather than south into North Carolina to join with the Over-Mountain Men. These Virginians formed almost half of the Patriot force at King's Mountain, initiated the first assaults, and induced the Provincial infantry to charge three times down the mountain.

## "The Late Affair Has Almost Broke My Heart": Cowpens, 17 January 1781

Greene's bold move to divide his army created for Cornwallis a profound dilemma. Clearly, the earl now faced a general imbued with a keen strategic acumen and a firm grasp on the nature of the war in the South. While critics may argue that Cornwallis was the superior tactical battlefield general, Greene and the Patriot cause had the advantage of a clearer vision of the strategic imperative. Departing Charlotte on 20 December, Greene headed southeast toward the Pee Dee. Morgan, with the Maryland and Delaware Continentals under Lt. Col. John Eager Howard, supported by Virginia riflemen and Washington's Continental Light Dragoons, moved southwest. Charged with operating on the British left flank and threatening Ninety Six, Morgan covered nearly a hundred difficult miles to the Pacolet River, arriving on Christmas Day. In the realm of welcome Christmas gifts, he did well. Shortly afterward, Maj. Joseph McDowell brought in 190 North Carolina riflemen, veterans of King's Mountain. With a robust force of 800 skilled and experienced men, Morgan initiated his harassment operations, taking advantage of his dragoons and mounted riflemen's mobility and speed to dispatch several parties of isolated Loyalist bands while threatening Ninety Six, actions that forced Cornwallis to respond.

At Winnsborough, the earl knew he had to support Ninety Six, but Greene had moved to Hick's Creek on the Pee Dee. He resolved to mass as much strength as possible against Greene while detaching Tarleton to protect Ninety Six and hunt down Morgan. The imminent arrival of Leslie's force of over 1,500 men from Charleston bolstered the plan. With Morgan thrust out of the way, then superior numbers and experience could easily overwhelm Greene. While the earl was formulating his response to the Patriot moves, Morgan worried about his cavalry's safety near Ninety Six. He moved closer to cover the movements of Washington's dragoons, then began a withdrawal. Cornwallis ordered Tarleton to give chase. On New Year's Day 1781, the Green Dragoon moved north toward the Broad River with a potent thousand-man strike force of the dragoons and light infantry of his British Legion, elements of the 17th Light Dragoons, infantry of the 71st and 7th Regiments, and two Royal Artillery field guns. Charged to pursue Morgan with vigor, the stage was set for the coming showdown at Hiram Saunders's cow pens.[56]

By the fourth, Morgan's northeastward movement became apparent. Tarleton countered by advancing up the east side of the Broad River to the King's Mountain area to cut off his retreat. Four days later he arrived at the Enoree River, a tributary of the Broad. Meanwhile, Greene received the welcome reinforcement of the well-equipped and disciplined horsemen under Lieutenant Colonel Lee; these dragoons would play a significant role in the coming weeks. Straightaway, he detached Lee to operate with Colonel Marion in harassing the British right flank. From an operational and tactical viewpoint, Cornwallis had been outflanked, and the strategic imperative now lay in destroying the flankers before moving on Greene, thus alleviating the possibility of isolating him from Rawdon and Charleston in his rear. Although the earl held a momentary numbers advantage once he rendezvoused with Leslie, he found himself in a perilous situation as January advanced. Not waiting for the arrival of the reinforcements, he sent provisions to Leslie, whose men had been suffering from the rainy weather and poor roads as they slogged through the desolate backcountry. Cornwallis departed Winnsborough on the eighth to head into North Carolina, ordering Leslie to join him as quickly as possible.

On the frontier Tarleton crossed the Enoree at Musgrove's Mill and the Pacolet in pursuit of Morgan. On the sixteenth he arrived at the encampment at Thicketty Creek, but the Patriots had retired on the British approach, even leaving behind an unfinished breakfast. Forced back against the Broad River, Morgan decided to stand at Hannah's cow pens, a full seven miles from the only available ford across the rain-swollen river. For Tarleton, the ground there, bereft of undergrowth from cattle grazing and generally flat and open, represented excellent terrain for his horsemen. In the surrounding fields an occasional tree presented little impediment to linear troop movements. The rolling ground gave potential cover for either concealment or sanctuary from artillery fire.

Morgan understood his opponent's tactical concepts, which emphasized the shock of a fast-moving cavalry assault to break down a formation, then a follow up with infantry to destroy the shaken enemy. The general took a calculated risk in placing his men with their backs to the river but reasoned that this feature would stiffen the militia's resolve to stand and fight, given little hope of flight. With Cornwallis only thirty miles away at Turkey Creek and the usual unwillingness of militia to fight in another state, Morgan reasoned that they would have to stand or die fleeing. He admonished his enthusiastic but largely untrained militia to give a few sharp volleys and then retire, hoping that their fire would unhinge Tarleton's initial assault to the point that the better-disciplined Continental troops could withstand the attack.

As dawn broke on 17 January, Morgan arrayed his men in three lines. He placed several dozen Georgia and North Carolina riflemen in the first rank, roughly 150 yards ahead of the second line, with orders to fire two or three shots from fifty yards at officers and noncommissioned officers, then retire to their left behind the second rank of militia. The second line, consisting of South and North Carolina militia commanded by General Pickens, would then deliver the same and retire behind the third line by moving to the left to clear the field of fire. Just below the crest of a hill and thus not subject to British return fire, he posted his third line, the Continentals, Delaware and Maryland units commanded by Howard and supported on the flanks by more riflemen. In reserve, Washington's 120 dragoons and mounted militia stationed themselves behind a second ridge a half mile in rear of the Continentals, positioned for a flank assault once the battle became fully engaged.

Tarleton advanced with all haste in his usual manner—mobility and speed characterized his tactical concepts. By three in the morning of the seventeenth, he had his forces moving toward the river, with light and legion infantry in the vanguard. In the second column came the infantry of the two regular line regiments, with the cavalry and mounted infantry carrying the rear. Just before dawn Tarleton moved the cavalry into position ahead of the light infantry in tactical alignment for his preferred assault plan. By dawn, having driven in the Patriot pickets, the Green Dragoon pressed his men forward despite a hard four-hour march through heavy brush crossed by thick ravines and numerous creeks. The advance force soon encountered Morgan's first line, which inflicted several casualties on the Crown horsemen.

The impetuous Tarleton sensed an easy victory and pressed ahead. But he made several critical decisions that determined the battle's outcome. Tarleton decided

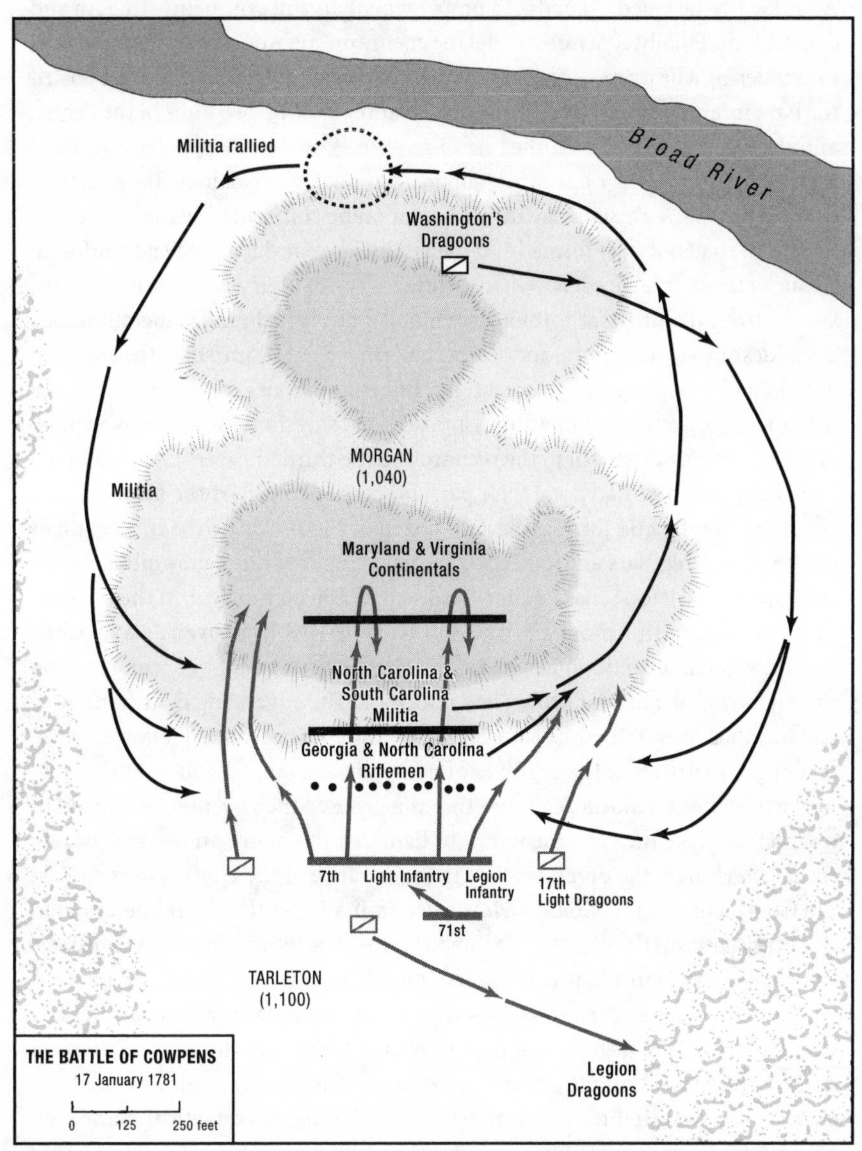


The Battle of Cowpens, 17 January 1781. Map by Erin Greb Cartography.

to engage a well-rested enemy in a firm defensive position with tired and hungry troops. He ordered a general advance well before all his forces were in place. Additionally, he failed to conduct a proper reconnaissance of enemy strength and dispositions. Finally, he assumed that the enemy militia would withdraw in panic, thus ordering a hasty cavalry charge. Spreading his line for battle, Tarleton posted the light infantry on his right, the legion infantry and the two guns in the center, and the 7th on his left, with the 71st in reserve. A squadron of horse advanced smartly but came under heavy fire, suffering significant casualties. Tarleton then decided to resolve the issue swiftly, whereupon he committed his second error, for the line had not fully formed and the assault became disjointed and confused. In one of those rare moments when militia carry out their assignment perfectly, volleys from the first two militia lines mauled the British, inflicting numerous casualties among the officers and senior ranks in only a few minutes. The charging men halted in stunned amazement, but hours and hours of drill and training prevailed; they reformed their lines and advanced again with fixed bayonets.

The militia's movement to the rear around the third line went well, but many men, believing they had done their part, proceeded to depart the field. Officers managed to rally and form up several dozen of them. Seeing the dispersion of the first-line irregulars and expecting the usual flight of the enemy militia in the second line, Tarleton sensed victory and sent his cavalry in against the disorganized militia. At this moment the Continental dragoons arrived and smashed into the right flank of the attacking infantry, who were also hit by accurate fire on their left from the militia, which had reformed. The advancing British infantry had lost the cover of their cavalry on their flanks. Disaster soon followed.

On the British left, the regulars of each side exchanged volleys for several minutes without making headway. Tarleton ordered the 71st, preciously held in reserve, to strike the Continental right flank. At this point an unusual occurrence determined the outcome. Seeing the advance of the Highlanders against the Continental right, Colonel Howard, commanding the third line, ordered the Virginians on the right of the line to "refuse the flank." But the Virginians, untrained in such intricate maneuvers, initially took the command as "retreat." Unlike in previous engagements, they remained in order, faced about, and smartly closed ranks. Seeing the retrograde movement, the Maryland and Delaware regiments started to do the same and retired. Realizing that his men had not been beaten and that they had merely misunderstood the tactical maneuver, Morgan took advantage of the error, to Tarleton's great detriment, by ordering Howard to continue to feign retreating until he reached a ridge crest about 100 yards in the rear of his original position.

The Highlanders, coming over the crest of the ridge saw the supposed retreat and charged with bayonets. While this action could unhinge a disorganized, wilting, or weak opponent, it also disrupts the tight linear cohesion of the attacking force. Individual officers and noncommissioned officers lose control as men surge ahead to reach the disjointed enemy, most of whom tend to turn and flee at this point. The very precise and deadly musket volleys from the highly trained, well-disciplined, and much-experienced British regulars were no longer possible as these men surged ahead. But when mounting a bayonet charge against an opponent who has not lost his cohesion, the attacker often encounters deep trouble. Such was the case at Cowpens. With the 71st shouting the "Huzzahs!" and coming on rapidly, Morgan halted the retiring line, ordered an about face, and gave the command to fire. The Highlanders received a withering volley at point-blank range. Simultaneously, Pickens's reformed militia came up on the Highlanders' left and rear and delivered devastating fire into the now-disorganized mass. If turnabout is fair play, the skill, training, and experience that the Continental troops had garnered since Valley Forge came to the fore. The Continentals surged forward in their own bayonet charge against the stunned Highlanders.

On the British right flank, Washington's cavalry, sensing the right moment, poured into Tarleton's disorganized dragoons, blowing past them and into the rear of the advancing center of enemy infantry. In an act that has haunted the 7th ever since, the panicked men of the regiment threw down their arms and shouted for quarter. The battle unraveled. The Highlanders, now engaged in the front, rear, and left, crumbled into a disorganized mob. Many soldiers continued firing, but with little effect. Seeing the rout, the legion dragoons, still unengaged in the rear, fled the battlefield when they might have counterattacked and salvaged the situation. Tarleton had lost control of his army. He sent in his remaining horsemen to support the 71st, but the horrendous Patriot fire drove them back. Reduced to hand-to-hand combat, the Highlanders laid down their arms; some panicked and fled. Tarleton attempted to rally his troops and save the guns to no avail. The Royal Artillery fought tenaciously, but they too were soon overwhelmed. A rout ensued. With his remaining few cavalry, Tarleton charged the oncoming horsemen, even managing to wound and dismount Washington. The feared Green Dragoon fled the field toward the Pacolet, pursued by Patriot cavalry.

Cowpens is one of the most complete battlefield victories in American history. With a loss of only 12 men killed and 61 wounded compared to British losses of 110 killed, over 200 wounded, and 830 captured, Morgan inflicted a devastating blow on the royal cause. Thirty-nine British officers perished out of sixty-six who started the battle. Cornwallis eventually made up the troop loses, but he could never make up the loss of prestige and reputation. The Patriots decisively defeated Tarleton, the most dreaded of Crown commanders. From a tactical viewpoint, the Green Dragoon committed the fundamental errors of overconfidence and arrogance. He allowed the assault to commence prematurely before his force had properly formed and ordered tired men into battle against a well-placed and rested foe. In his defense the unusually steady behavior of the Virginia militia could not be foreseen; their steadfastness in the face of a British assault had not hitherto been the case (as, for instance, in the Camden rout). Cornwallis confided to Rawdon on Cowpens a few days afterward, "The late affair has almost broke my heart."[57]

## "Strike Blows in the Air": North Carolina, January 1781

Following the King's Mountain and Cowpens debacles, Cornwallis faced an increasingly confident and growing rebel presence. King's Mountain compounded the negative public reaction to the Charleston proclamations and the Waxhaws strategic-communication disaster. Cowpens destroyed the British Legion as well as depleted two regular line battalions. Perhaps more importantly, the Continental Army and local militia together had finally defeated a skilled Crown force in an open, linear, conventional engagement, albeit not against the earl himself. Bereft of much of his light infantry, Cornwallis suffered a debilitating loss of reconnaissance, scouting, skirmishing, and fast-strike capability, assets he never rebuilt. The loss of this situational awareness and tactical mobility played an essential role in the Southern Campaign's breakdown.

Cornwallis, an intensely humane officer, typically chafed at the brutal treatment of rebel prisoners, particularly executions for treason. Nevertheless, he lost the public-relations battle. Technically, anyone committing treason by rebellion could be hanged. The earl tried to minimize such actions and keep to only the most important ringleaders, although he did order some executions for oath breakers, particularly those who had deserted the Loyalist militia and joined the Patriots. In his instructions to Lieutenant Colonel Turnbull at Camden once he departed for the first North Carolina invasion, the earl noted: "It is difficult to know what to do about prisoners. . . . If there are still several who were in our militia and afterwards joined the enemy, another example or two would be very proper. A certain number of the most violent and most capable of doing mischief . . . should be kept in prison to awe the enemy from putting any of our friends [Loyalists] to death."[58] To Lieutenant Colonel Cruger at Ninety Six, Cornwallis advocated that "in a civil war there is no admitting of neutral characters and that those who are not clearly with us must be so far considered against us as to be disarmed and every measure taken to prevent their being able to do mischief. At the same time, if they have been guilty of no new offenses, I would do it by the gentlest methods which the nature of that business will admit of, but I would do it effectually."[59]

Nevertheless, Cornwallis eventually realized that a firm hand had to be taken to pacify South Carolina. As John Ferling points out, "his actions were a hybrid of the velvet glove and iron fist."[60] The earl advised Lord Germain in his after-action report on Camden that he would "give directions to inflict exemplary punishment on some of the most guilty in hopes to deter others in future from sporting with allegiance, with oaths, and with the lenity and generosity of the British Government."[61] The examples of Major Weymss and others illustrate how certain officials took that order to heart. As a man wedded to the gentlemanly ways of eighteenth-century warfare, Cornwallis seemed out of his element in fighting a brutish, partisan civil war.

In dealing with such matters, there is always the question of how much retribution to inflict to tamp down rebel enthusiasm. It is an eternal struggle when crafting a counterinsurgency strategy. Often, too much harshness simply inspires more hardened determination and resistance. Too little violence, though, and neutrals feel free to join the rebels. That said, in this case the Loyalist reaction seemed to be the driving dynamic. Carolina Loyalists, who wished to see Cornwallis and Crown authorities destroy the rebellion with harsh punitive measures, chafed at their reluctance to employ such measures. The paroles offered in the May and June proclamations infuriated many of them. This dynamic goes a long way in explaining the lack of Loyalist enthusiasm and fear for Patriot retribution once the main army moved out, leaving them to provide their own security. Cornwallis's inability or unwillingness to crush the rebellion with the mailed fist simply undercut the "hold" aspect of the overall Crown strategy.

Making matters worse, Cornwallis had moved several hundred miles inland away from reliable seaborne supply. Although several bastions such as Camden and Ninety Six remained in Crown hands, the difficulty of moving supplies and reinforcements from Charleston in the face of the marauding partisan bands, especially Marion's, proved an increasingly dicey proposition. With winter approaching, foraging off the land would be equally problematic. Indeed, the problem of terrain, or rather the profound lack of appreciation for the nature of the terrain, further complicated the British situation. A valid criticism of Cornwallis throughout the campaign is his seeming disregard for the problem of logistical support once he moved inland. Yet the earl vowed to pursue the Continentals in winter despite the difficulty of the waterway crossings, lack of logistical support, and foul weather. While there are hints that he understood the dynamic relationship between the maritime dimension and logistics, as in his letter to Clinton regarding the proposed North Carolina invasion, he promptly violated his own caution in the 1781 campaign: "When the troops march into North Carolina it will be absolutely necessary to get supplies up some of the principal rivers of that province."[62] As will be seen, the failure to derive advantage from the British maritime superiority played large in the final year of the Southern Campaign. William Willcox, the eminent Clinton biographer, strikes true in his assessment of Cornwallis's failings:

> The Earl does not seem to have understood the two underlying necessities for British success in the South, sea power and loyalist support; and he certainly did not understand the connection between them. They were linked by logistics. An army that was out of touch with the sea was an army chronically short of supplies; it had to move in search of them or starve. Because it could not stay long in one area, it could not call out, protect, and organize the loyalists; therefore it could not hold territory. An army that held nothing, but merely marched through the countryside, would never force the Americans to battle; they might fight it on their own terms and in their own good time, or leave it to strike blows in the air.[63]

Therein lies the fundamental fatal flaw in the "clear and hold" strategy.

Despite the geographic factor, Cornwallis resolved to reenter North Carolina. Buoyed by the news of Brigadier Arnold's Virginia expedition and the imminent arrival of Leslie, Cornwallis pressed on with his plans. Leslie's forces arrived in Charleston on 14 December 1780. With the Brigade of Guards (composed of several companies each of the 1st, 2nd, and 3rd Foot Guards under Brigadier Charles O'Hara), the German (Hessian) Regiment von Bose, the King's American Regiment, a battalion of Loyalist light infantry, elements of the 17th Light Dragoons, artillery, German Jägers, and troops drawn from the 82nd and 84th Regiments of Foot, Leslie commanded some of the best soldiers in North America. While some of these units stayed in South Carolina, a great many of them rendezvoused with Cornwallis on 18 January 1781 as the earl launched his second North Carolina invasion. Arnold arrived in Virginia in December as well with a raiding force to continue Leslie's original mission and to create a diversion to draw Patriot attention away from Cornwallis. With Arnold's presence in Virginia, Greene's central source of supply and reinforcement was now threatened. Although British officers never fully trusted the recent convert now commanding a substantial force, no one doubted the general's tactical and operational genius. Not completely trusting the man, Clinton sent Lieutenant Colonels John Graves Simcoe, commanding the Queen's Rangers, and Thomas Dundas to keep watch over Arnold. He captured Richmond and marched to Portsmouth, at the mouth of Chesapeake Bay, where Major General Phillips took charge. Phillips arrived in Williamsburg in late April, and with the arrival of Arnold's command, his force there stood at about 3,500 effectives. Arnold returned to New York in June, after Cornwallis's arrival. Phillips's troops then joined with Cornwallis's army once the earl arrived in Virginia in late spring. Cornwallis had hoped that these forces represented, finally, the Chesapeake diversion he long requested. But the activities of these forces amounted to raids on a few supply posts and the burning some tobacco warehouses. Ultimately, these proved practically useless and disappointing to Cornwallis.

To compound the problems of unity of command and effort and the concomitant lack of strategic coherence, Clinton received no correspondence from his field commander between 18 January, when the earl informed the CinC of the intention to reenter North Carolina, and 10 April, after the arrival of his bedraggled army in Wilmington. Further complicating the British strategic situation, the April letters did not arrive at Clinton's headquarters until May, well after Cornwallis had already arrived in Virginia. Thus, for a critical four months, as Cornwallis thrashed about the North Carolina backcountry and eventually made his way to the coast, there was a complete loss of command, control, and communications between the primary decision maker (Clinton) and the operational field commander (Cornwallis). In most premodern warfare, once an army departed for a campaign or expedition, its commander, generally the monarch or a royal family member, made all the major strategic and operational decisions independent of the civil or military authorities at home. Communications limitations, time, and distance simply made any other regime impractical if not impossible. But in a glimpse of the future, the British dynamic reflected a very modern concept in civil-military relations. The civilian authority (Germain and the cabinet) made policy and provided the general strategic outline; strategy was determined by the military authority (Clinton) and then translated to executable actions, operations, and plans; and the field commander (Cornwallis) executed the operational plan. In this case that pattern actually existed for one of the first times in history, yet the mechanisms for effective command, control, and communications did not yet exist, especially in the rough country of the Carolinas.

From the strategic viewpoint, the Cowpens disaster forced Cornwallis into a potentially rash action in chasing Greene into North Carolina, despite leaving a substantial force in his rear. Given the earl's naturally aggressive and risk-taking nature, however, he could have hardly done anything else. Should the Cowpens catastrophe have convinced Cornwallis of the folly of mounting an invasion of North Carolina? A less aggressive, bold, and risk-taking officer might well have drawn back to await reinforcements, better weather, or orders from above. The rebuttal is simple—retreat was not in his nature. Indeed, Cornwallis had been focused on a North Carolina invasion since the beginning of the Southern Campaign. In his letter to Clinton on 6 August 1780, even before the Camden victory, the earl stated: "It may be doubted by some whether the invasion of North Carolina may be a prudent measure, but I am convinced it is a necessary one and that, if we do not attack that province, we must give up both South Carolina and Georgia and retire within the walls of Charlestown. Our assurances of attachment from our poor distress'd friends in North Carolina are as strong as ever, and the patience and fortitude with which these unhappy people bear the most oppressive and cruel tyranny that ever was exercised over our country deserves our greatest admiration."[64]

Additionally, Clinton's parting orders to the earl required him to hold Charleston, raise up the Georgia and South Carolina Loyalists, supply them arms, and to raid into North Carolina.[65] All these imperatives required open and reliable communications with the Charleston base. For Cornwallis, the partisans made his communications anything but reliable.

The ill effects of the partisan war on Loyalist commitment and support and the failure to secure pacification in South Carolina after Charleston's fall roiled the backcountry and undercut Crown efforts to restore royal government. As with the loyalty oaths that put neutrals and former rebels equally on "death ground," episodes such as the story of a Newberry District farmer named Waters illustrate the phenomenon:

> [Waters had a neighbor] who were [*sic*] in favor of the King [and] insisted on Waters subscribing an oath of allegiance to the King, which he refused to do, upon which they came to words. Waters was in the act of starting for home . . . when this neighbor seized a loaded rifle . . . and pursued, saying: "I will kill you unless you subscribe to the oath." Waters . . . snatched the gun from him and turned it upon him. When this fellow seized a stick and turned it upon Waters . . . [he] shot him. . . . Waters surrendered himself to the civil authorities, and was put in Ninety Six jail. Not long after . . . [his brother] and friends liberated him by cutting down the door in a dark night upon which Waters left immediately and took refuge in . . . North [Carolina] and there joined the army; and returning South with Green[e], fought.[66]

Clausewitz captures the difficulty of the hybrid war facing Cornwallis as he wintered over at Winnsborough contemplating another North Carolina foray: "The countryside . . . that greatly enhances the effectiveness of an insurrection is the scattered distribution of houses and farms. . . . [T]he most characteristic feature of an insurgency in general will be constantly repeated in miniature: the element of resistance will exist everywhere and nowhere."[67]

Leaving Rawdon in command of the various garrisons throughout South Carolina and Georgia, Cornwallis embarked on his winter campaign. To cover a possible line of retreat and to ensure a coastal port, he detached 300 troops to secure Wilmington, North Carolina. Perhaps he realized finally that seaborne supply represented his one great advantage, and the move inland diminished that factor. Despite the generally mild Carolina winter, a campaign during these months in the eighteenth century was fraught with hazards. In the absence of a reliable supply and depot system, both sides had to operate on minimal food and fodder and to rely on whatever supplies could be foraged. As 1780 rolled into 1781 and the Southern Campaign's final year, each side seemed like prizefighters, moving, jabbing, and waiting for the inevitable mistake to provide their chance to land a jarring blow. The earl, chastened by the King's Mountain and Cowpens defeats, resolved to press on with his plans. He advised Clinton that he intended to invade North Carolina, refusing to "give up the object of this winter's campaign." His strategic intent, as he advised Lord Germain, was to "penetrate to North Carolina, leaving South Carolina in security against any probable attack in my absence."[68]

As with the French revolutionaries chasing the elusive Scarlet Pimpernel in fiction, Cornwallis continued pursuing the Patriot partisans in the Carolinas in fact. He defeated one band after another only to find others popping up elsewhere, confounding his South Carolina pacification efforts in advance of implementing the next step in the Southern Strategy. He sought them here, he sought them there, he sought them everywhere. For Cornwallis, who by his nature and strategic concepts chased the illusive victory through conventional engagements, he saw the "clear" results of victories at Charleston and Camden crumble in the face of the partisan insurgency and its ill effect on the Loyalist "hold" element of the overall strategy.

*Siege of Charleston*, by Alonzo Chappel, 1862.
*Courtesy of the Anne S. K. Brown Military Collection, Brown University Library.*

*Opposite, top*
Adm. Charles Henri, comte d'Estaing. Portrait by Abbe de Haisne, 1782.
*Courtesy of the Anne S. K. Brown Military Collection, Brown University Library.*

*Opposite, bottom*
Gen. Sir Henry Clinton, K.B. Portrait by John Smart, 1780.
*Courtesy of the Anne S. K. Brown Military Collection, Brown University Library.*

*British Camp Scene*, by Henry William Bunbury, 1790.
*Courtesy of the Anne S. K. Brown Military Collection, Brown University Library.*

Vice Adm. Marriot Arbuthnot.
*Courtesy of the Anne S. K. Brown Military Collection, Brown University Library.*

Lieutenant General Charles, 2nd Earl Cornwallis.
*Courtesy of the Anne S. K. Brown Military Collection, Brown University Library.*

Lt. Col. Banastre Tarleton. Portrait by Joshua Reynolds, 1782.
*Courtesy of the Anne S. K. Brown Military Collection, Brown University Library.*

*Slaughter of Col. Buford's Regiment . . . Waxhaws.*
*Courtesy of the Anne S. K. Brown Military Collection, Brown University Library.*

Maj. Gen. Horatio Gates. 1777.
*Courtesy of the Anne S. K. Brown Military Collection, Brown University Library.*

*Battle of Camden—Death of de Kalb*, by Heppenheimer and Maurer, 1875.
*Courtesy of the Anne S. K. Brown Military Collection, Brown University Library.*

Maj. Gen. Johann de Kalb. Portrait by Henry Bryan Hall, 1870.
*Courtesy of the Anne S. K. Brown Military Collection, Brown University Library.*

*Death of Major Ferguson at King's Mountain*, by Alonzo Chappel, 1863.
*Courtesy of the Anne S. K. Brown Military Collection, Brown University Library.*

*Battle of Cowpens . . . Conflict between*
*Cols. Washington & Tarleton*, by Alonzo Chappel, 1858.
*Courtesy of the Anne S. K. Brown Military Collection, Brown University Library.*

*Col. Washington at the Battle of Cowpens*, 1820.
*Courtesy of the Anne S. K. Brown Military Collection, Brown University Library.*

*Opposite, top*
Lt. Col. Banastre Tarleton. 1782.
*Courtesy of the Anne S. K. Brown Military Collection, Brown University Library.*

*Opposite, bottom*
*Marion Crossing the Pedee*, by William Tyler Ranney, 1852.
*Courtesy of the Anne S. K. Brown Military Collection, Brown University Library.*

*Genl. Marion & the British Officer*, by Henry Warren, 1855.
*Courtesy of the Anne S. K. Brown Military Collection, Brown University Library.*

*The Rescue . . . Rescuing American Prisoners*, by Currier and Ives, 1876.
*Courtesy of the Anne S. K. Brown Military Collection, Brown University Library.*

*The Soldier's Pledge*, 1795.
*Courtesy of the Anne S. K. Brown Military Collection, Brown University Library.*

Maj. Gen. Nathanael Greene. Portrait by Charles Wilson Peale.
*Courtesy of the Anne S. K. Brown Military Collection, Brown University Library.*

Lieutenant Colonel Francis, Lord Rawdon. Portrait, as Earl of Moira in later years, by Joshua Reynolds, 1792.
*Courtesy of the Anne S. K. Brown Military Collection, Brown University Library.*

*Battle of Eutaw Springs*, by Alonzo Chappel, 1859.
*Courtesy of the Anne S. K. Brown Military Collection, Brown University Library.*

*Opposite, top*

Gen. George Washington. Portrait by Charles Wilson Peale, 1780.

*Courtesy of the Anne S. K. Brown Military Collection, Brown University Library.*

*Opposite, bottom*

Maj. Gen. Gilbert du Motier, marquis de Lafayette.

*Courtesy of the Anne S. K. Brown Military Collection, Brown University Library.*

*Below*

Rear Adm. François Joseph Paul, comte de Grasse.

*Courtesy of the Anne S. K. Brown Military Collection, Brown University Library.*

*Battle of the Virginia Capes*, by V. Zegg, 1962.
*Courtesy of the U.S. Navy Art Collection, Naval History and Heritage Command.*

*In the Trenches before Yorktown*, by Rufus Fairchild Zogbaum, 1881.
*Courtesy of the Anne S. K. Brown Military Collection, Brown University Library.*

*Siege of York-Town*, by Coudert, 1785.
*Courtesy of the Anne S. K. Brown Military Collection, Brown University Library.*

*The Surrender of Earl Cornwallis*, by William Hamilton, 1790.
*Courtesy of the Anne S. K. Brown Military Collection, Brown University Library.*

Lieutenant General Charles,
2nd Earl Cornwallis. 1781.
*Courtesy of the Anne S. K. Brown Military Collection, Brown University Library.*

CHAPTER 4

# "Fatal Infatuation"

## *Cornwallis Invades North Carolina*

When the reports of Major Ferguson's King's Mountain disaster arrived, Clinton became understandably concerned. Despite his hesitancy to further reduce his force in New York in the face of possible combined Continental and French actions, he detached units under Brigadier Arnold to Virginia with orders to strike at the Patriot supply depot at Petersburg and occupy a post at Portsmouth to take logistical advantage of supply and reinforcement by sea through Chesapeake Bay. As a further indication of Clinton's ultimate strategic intent, he foresaw Cornwallis in turn reinforcing the small expedition to the point that it could undertake offensive operations. It is clear that in late December 1780, the American CinC intended to undertake peripheral actions in Virginia and the Chesapeake region. What is also clear is that in so envisioning such operations, he expected Cornwallis to first subdue North Carolina and maintain control of South Carolina before any further movement northward. Herein lies the seed of the disastrous strategic incoherence that erupted in late spring of the following year.[1]

Much debate has occurred over the divergence of strategic concept between Clinton and Cornwallis over operations in North Carolina and Virginia. Yet as early as 6 November 1780, Clinton made clear his intentions that the earl should operate in North Carolina and establish a post at Hillsborough, supplied from the Loyalist enclave at Cross Creek. Further, the earl should establish a post and operating base at Portsmouth, Virginia, and "carry on desultory expeditions in Chesapeak [*sic*] till more solid operations can take place," using the troops sent from New York under Leslie. While he felt unable to detach a large number of the New York garrison to reinforce Cornwallis at this time, Clinton intended for his field commander to operate in Virginia and even suggested the possibility of taking up winter quarters at Portsmouth. In the absence of any communications between the CinC in New York and the field commander in North Carolina for almost four months from January to late April 1781, the earl's decision to abandon

North Carolina following Guilford Court House makes sense. At this point, then, strategic coherence does not seem to play a role. Both the overall commander and the subordinate field commander seem to be in synchronization on the intended objectives. Within weeks, however, profound strategic incoherence would set in, doing so in an ultimately decisive way.[2]

## "Infinite Danger in Proceeding": Cornwallis Prepares to Move North

For Cornwallis, the arrival of Leslie's reinforcements on 18 January 1781 and assurances of some possible, if limited, support from New York later made his resolve to march into North Carolina understandable and, certainly in his mind, justifiable. Clearly, his strategic assumptions revolved around a logistical concept—if he could control North Carolina, he could shut down the flow of supplies and reinforcements from the northern and middle colonies, thus starving the South Carolina partisans into irrelevancy. While the Marions, Sumters, Pickenses, and their ilk could readily obtain food, horses, and basic supplies from locals, they could not obtain gunpowder and replacement weapons. In the harsh, hot, and humid South Carolina and Georgia summers, eighteenth-century weapons exposed to the elements soon ceased to function. Supply from the North had to remain relatively free from Crown interference for the partisans to remain active.[3]

A winter campaign is problematic under any conditions at any place (except perhaps the arid and particularly hot regions). The Germans in the Soviet Union between 1941 and 1944 and Napoleon Bonaparte in Russia in 1812 absolutely learned that harsh lesson. In North America a winter campaign is fraught with similar danger. With the harvest done and little naturally growing fruit and vegetables for foraging, starvation in the field is the major problem apart from the cold temperatures. The normal pattern for the pre–Industrial Age military meant going into winter quarters typically by November or December at the latest. The campaign season began again in middle to late spring, though often not until summer. But the pattern proved different in the American War; Cornwallis had experienced it firsthand. Washington's strategic surprise at Trenton followed by the ambush of the earl's rear guard at Princeton in harsh winter weather convinced him that the normal patterns did not apply. Although winter campaigning in the somewhat warmer climate in the Carolinas and Georgia compared to the North appears less trying, temperatures as far south as northern Florida routinely dip below freezing in winter and snow (or ice) does occasionally fall. Compounding the difficulty of moving through the southern landscape in winter is the temperature variability. From day to day, one might experience below-freezing temperatures that soon moderate. Frozen dirt roads, ideal for cavalry and artillery movement, can become muddy quagmires within hours. Melting snows in the Appalachians, though not heavy, still cause flooding of the rivers flowing out of the mountains in late winter and early spring, creating difficult crossings. With limited infrastructure, such as bridges and ferry crossings, the swollen waterways created a nightmare for military operations, much to Cornwallis's chagrin as he discovered during his chase of Greene across the Carolina Piedmont, with its many wide and flooding rivers (including the Yadkin, Deep, Haw, and Catawba). Nonetheless, in the decision to engage in a winter campaign, the earl exhibited not only his characteristic aggressiveness but also his optimism and confidence in both his abilities and the stoutheartedness, vigor, discipline, loyalty, and military excellence of his troops. He placed overwhelming confidence in himself and his battle-tested and skilled veterans in overcoming the limitations and hazards of a winter wilderness campaign.

As Cornwallis's troops stepped off into the tan-brown bleakness of a Carolina winter, the South Carolina situation remained tenuous. He reported to Clinton that "the perpetual risings in different parts of this province, the invariable successes of all these parties against our militia, keep the whole country in continual alarm and render the assistance of regular troops every where necessary."[4]

The statement reveals a fundamental weakness in Cornwallis's highly aggressive "clear and hold" strategy. The need to maintain regular units at various outposts led to an inability to concentrate against Greene's forces in North Carolina and violated a fundamental principle of war—concentration—at least to the conventionally minded earl. With reduced numbers, once he finally engaged Greene at Guilford Court House in March, he had neither sufficient strength to overwhelm on the battlefield nor the capability to absorb horrendous casualties; disengagement from the Continentals and retreat to Wilmington inevitably resulted. Conversely, the need to man the outposts with regulars caused by the partisan activities and inability of the Loyalist militias to restore Crown authority throughout South Carolina undercut the entire strategy.[5] Cornwallis, like a boxer with one hand tied behind his back, charged forward into North Carolina seeking a decisive engagement with Greene.[6]

With the deteriorating security situation in South Carolina coupled with the loss of so many of his light forces, particularly the British Legion infantry along with several hundred men of the 71st and 7th Regiments at Cowpens, the earl could have taken a more prudent approach and retreated back into South Carolina to the safety of winter quarters to resupply, reinforce, and prepare for spring operations—a course most prudent commanders would have followed. Not so Cornwallis. To his mind, a bold thrust might well destroy Greene before the Rhode Islander could rendezvous with Morgan's detachment. Cornwallis might well then defeat each in detail, a classic tactic employed in later years with supreme precision by Napoleon. The destruction of the Continental Army's main southern force for the third time in less than a year might well cow the neutrals and buoy the Loyalists, reversing the tide in the Carolinas. If Cornwallis could do to Greene as he had to Gates at Camden, the "clear and hold" strategy might yet have a chance for success. Given his character and the potential gains, he launched the offensive, though he did have doubts. Admitting to Lord Rawdon the tenuousness of the Crown position, the earl acknowledged that the move against Greene brought "infinite danger in proceeding," yet he saw no alternative. To do otherwise invited "certain ruin in retreating." Despite the daunting situation created by Tarleton's debacle, Cornwallis appears to have been ever the optimist. It is a trait of highly successful commanders to express optimism in their ability to overcome disadvantage and adversity. Confidence in one's subordinates is another. Despite the hazards, Cornwallis expressed both of these critically important qualities—optimism and confidence in subordinates—stating to Rawdon that "O'Hara's brigade sets the example of rigid discipline and perfect good will on all occasions. Our men are healthy and full of zeal. If opportunity offers, I trust I shall send you good news."[7]

## "A Chain of Evils": The Loyalist Strategy Unravels

It is clear that following the King's Mountain debacle, Cornwallis had severe doubts about the efficacy of the Loyalist strategy and, indeed, the entire "clear and hold" concept. From his increasingly vitriolic observations in official correspondence regarding North Carolina Loyalists, a pattern of strategic thinking emerges that completely discounted the very foundation of the Southern Strategy, that southern Loyalists would turn out in significant numbers not only for active military duty but also in supplying the Crown forces and maintaining civil order by reinstituting functioning royal governance. In November 1780, for example, he expressed his frustration in harsh tones to Leslie: "We will then give our friends in North Carolina a fair trial. If they behave like men it may be of the greatest advantage to the affairs of Britain. If they are as dastardly and pusillanimous as our friends to the southward, we must leave them to their fate and secure what we have got."[8] Yet the importance of armed Loyalists rising in support of the Crown underlay the entire theory of victory behind the Southern Strategy. Cornwallis made this point clearly even as late as early January 1781, stating, "I would leave no means unattempted to arm America in our favour, which is the only chance of putting a favourable end to this war." Doubts must have been running through the earl's mind as he contemplated charging into the North Carolina hornets' nest unsure of Loyalist support. Yet as the optimist confident in his own and his troops' abilities and fortitude, he pressed ahead smartly.[9] Subordinate commanders also expressed misgivings regarding Loyalist enthusiasm. A frustrated Rawdon stated shortly after King's Mountain, referring to North Carolina Loyalists, "Not a single man attempted to improve the favourable moment or obeyed that summons for which they had been so impatient."[10]

British officers did not grasp the trends at play in terms of Loyalist turnout. The dynamics included the effectivities of the Patriot militia in suppressing the Loyalists, particularly in North Carolina before Cornwallis's arrival and after Ramsour's Mill and King's Mountain. While many Patriots turned out for temporary service with their local militias when called on by Greene and other Continental officers, many simply stayed close to home to protect property and family, a factor that inhibited local Loyalists from embodying; others simply joined bands of roving militia embarked on Tory intimidation. Formal bodies often received assignments to attack Loyalist units. Colonel Davie of North Carolina proved especially effective in this role. Leading a Patriot cavalry unit that initiated raiding into South Carolina soon after the loss of Charleston, Davie attacked, defeated, and dispersed two large Loyalist formations in a two-day period in September 1780.[11] As Cornwallis made his first foray into the Charlotte area, Davie crossed back into North Carolina and initiated highly effective interdiction and raiding operations. Additionally, other North Carolina Patriot officers, including William Davidson (now a brigadier general) and Jethro Sumner, conducted similar operations. The difficulties in controlling the Charlotte–Mecklenburg County region, known colloquially to British authorities as the "Hornets' Nest," moved Tarleton to comment that he found the area "more hostile to England than any others in America. The vigilance and animosity of these surrounding districts checked the exertions of the well affected, and totally destroyed all communication between the King's troops and the Loyalists in the other part of the province. . . . [T]he foraging parties were every day harassed by the inhabitants, who . . . fired from covert places, to annoy the British detachments."[12]

A second dynamic was how many enthusiastic Loyalists actually remained in North Carolina by late 1780. Put another way, would it not be rational to assume that the majority of those most willing to take up arms for the royal cause had already done so by 1780–81? Looking at the royal-force composition, one is impressed by the great number of Loyalists serving in the Provincial units in the South, including Colonel Bryan's North Carolina Loyalists and Colonel Innes's South Carolina Loyalists, both very large units. A great many Carolinians had already taken the king's shilling and, indeed, provided excellent military service throughout the campaign.

Above all, the psychology of the Carolina Loyalists must be considered. After years of abuse, harassment, and condemnation by their Patriot neighbors, could one have expected a large turnout unless the regular army showed that Crown forces could stay in place? Cornwallis made two forays into North Carolina, but there existed no credible military presence capable of supporting and sustaining the "clear and hold" strategy once he hastily departed back to South Carolina (the first time) and rapidly moved on to Tidewater Virginia (the second time). In the absence of such a supporting regular force, is it a surprise that local Loyalists proved unwilling to turn out? Here the human psychological factor has to be considered; to blame the Loyalists for the army's discomfiture seems hollow. A counter to Cornwallis's Loyalist perception came from the southeastern part of the colony, where, supported by the Wilmington garrison under Major James Henry Craig, local Loyalists maintained a robust resistance to Patriot activities throughout the summer and autumn of 1781. In South Carolina, despite the partisan activities, many Loyalists still operated.

Cornwallis, faced with the collapse of his irregular and unreliable allies, now reverted to his core strategic, operational, and tactical beliefs. If the Carolina Loyalists could not maintain or accomplish their role in the overall Southern Strategy, then the formally trained and conventional military man would carry out the mission with his own reliable and trusted troops—the regulars of the British Army and the increasingly skilled and experienced Provincial units. In abandoning the "clear and hold" strategy, the earl essentially rejected the foundational principal of the Southern Strategy and opted for a purely conventional military solution. As modern observers have learned, in an ideological or religious-based internecine struggle, such solutions are rarely successful. Military might utilized for an opponent's physical destruction must be combined with the elements of psychological warfare. In hybrid warfare, as had developed in the South following the fall of Charleston, a purely conventional military solution had little chance for success.

The fragility of British logistics; breakdown in command and control; increasing strategic incoherence between Cornwallis, Clinton, and Lord Germain; and, most importantly, the loss of active Loyalist support following King's Mountain, all combined to doom the earl's valiant little force as it struck out across the Carolina winter landscape. Clearly, the King's Mountain disaster had done more than simply strip Cornwallis of his Loyalist light infantry and Major Ferguson, a promising and talented if overly rash officer. It caused a strategic reassessment by the field commander that had ultimately disastrous consequences for the royal cause. As Clinton later remarked of King's Mountain, it "proved to be the first link in a chain of evils that followed each other in regular succession until they at last ended in the total loss of America."[13]

## "Absolute Necessity:" The Winter Campaign Begins, January 1781

Cornwallis commenced his march north on 8 January, and once Leslie joined up, he intended to catch Morgan's force and destroy it before the Old Wagoner could reunite with Greene's main body. Concurrent with his march into North Carolina, Cornwallis secured a potential seaborne logistics base by ordering Colonel Balfour in Charleston to detach a force to take Wilmington, some miles up the Cape Fear River from the sea and an excellent port facility. Accordingly, Balfour detached Major Craig of the 82nd Regiment to do the job. With six companies from his own regiment along with a body of invalids (soldiers medically unfit for regular combat duty) from other units left behind in Charleston to recover from illness, Craig set out on 21 January. The major's orders included not only taking Wilmington and Fort Johnson but also collecting boats to take supplies upriver to the Cross Creek settlement. Arriving on the twenty-eighth, Craig found the city and its supporting defenses practically unprotected; he occupied Wilmington after dispersing a New Hanover County militia force north of the city.[14]

While Wilmington offered an excellent base for seaborne supply, it also illustrated perhaps the most critical command-and-control vulnerability facing Cornwallis as he crossed the Carolinas' border—logistics. While operating near the coast, as happened during the New York and New Jersey Campaigns and the seizures of Savannah and Charleston, British forces could expect reasonable if not wholly satisfactory supplies, especially rations and animal fodder. Once a force moved inland, as Lieutenant General John Burgoyne had learned in 1777, British logistics failed with disastrous results—a lesson in military science that Cornwallis soon learned. With Wilmington, he had a secure operations base in North Carolina, except that it sat 300 miles away from his line of march; for that, it might as well have been on Mars. Given the difficulty of transportation over an undeveloped infrastructure, combined with Patriot interdiction operations, the city represented a useless asset so long as the army operated at a distance. Wilmington provided the advantage of a well-developed port to which the Royal Navy could bring in supplies and reinforcements or from which to evacuate troops, but unless the army remained within a day's march or thereabouts, it could provide little support to Cornwallis.

Similarly, the depot and magazine at Camden proved no more valuable. Although much closer than Wilmington at roughly sixty-five miles from Charlotte, with the South Carolina partisans in the field and highly effective against British supply convoys, even that shorter distance was far enough to prove burdensome and inadequate. Thus, thrashing about in the North Carolina backcountry, Cornwallis had little hope for obtaining British supplies, and as he learned bitterly, the intimidated local Loyalists had little to offer his hungry and footsore troops. The earl realized that factor too late, only acknowledging the reality once in Virginia by June that it had been "the want of navigation rendering it impossible to maintain a sufficient army in either of those provinces [North and South Carolina], at a considerable distance from the coast."[15]

Greene, in contrast, displayed a genius for logistics. Moreover, his strategic vision and operational artistry revolved around his understanding of this imperative. Perhaps his business background or his time as Washington's quartermaster general had taught him the criticality of reliable and constant logistical support. Regardless of the source of his understanding, whether innate or acquired, Greene comprehended the nature of the campaign in the Carolinas; more importantly, he visualized how to win the battle of supply. Cornwallis did not. The detrimental results of the earl's misunderstanding of the nature of the logistical dynamic soon played out in the red-clay mud and raging rivers of the southern winter landscape.

The army was encamped at Turkey Creek on the Broad River in North Carolina by mid-January when disaster struck the royal cause at Cowpens just across the border. With his left flank now exposed, Cornwallis faced the first of his great decision points as he advanced northward. In his subsequent decision, one sees the nature of this fundamentally offensive-minded (some might say "bloody-minded"), highly aggressive commander. In a letter to Clinton from the Broad River camp, Cornwallis assured his superior officer: "It is impossible to foresee all the consequences that this unexpected and extraordinary event may produce, but your Excellency may be assured that nothing but the most absolute necessity shall induce me to give up the important object of the winter's campaign."[16]

Already the difference in orientation between the two senior officers became apparent, with Cornwallis charging off into North Carolina despite the fundamental risks, while the more cautious, risk-averse, and pessimistic Clinton feared for the safety of New York in light of Washington's forces in New Jersey and the French contingent in Rhode Island under the comte de Rochambeau. Despite his caution and concern, Clinton did assure his subordinate of continued support, but the hint of doubt and pessimism prevailed as indicated by his less-than-optimistic caution that the "experiment [advance into North Carolina] will . . . be fairly tried. . . . [I]f it succeeds and we hold the entrance to the Cheasapeak [*sic*], I think the rebels will never attempt either of those provinces [North Carolina and Virginia]."[17] The potential for disaster created months earlier in the glow of profound battlefield victory as Clinton gave carte blanche to his subordinate field commander to implement essentially his own operations now came to be realized. The always confident and bold Cornwallis chased the elusive Greene through the southern wilderness while the uncertain and careful Clinton fretted over the consequences of too foolhardy a stroke, their varying and ultimately divergent strategies for the South driving a wedge between them. The strategic coherence that had characterized the Charleston operation and the Camden success now unraveled.

## "To the End of the World": The Hound Takes the Bait

After Cowpens, Morgan moved west to avoid being overtaken by the British main body. Two factors caused him to set his army in motion. First, he feared that Cornwallis would force his command into a disadvantageous engagement and resolved to retire farther northeast toward Salisbury, North Carolina. Second, due to his long-standing health problems, Morgan informed Greene that he would relinquish command to Brigadier Generals Pickens and Davidson. The confluence of these events caused Greene to reenter the fray, a decision that led to one of the most dramatic events that marked the Southern Campaign—the "Race to the Dan." For Cornwallis, though, Morgan still presented a problem. He took decisive action to cut off the Patriot force's retreat. Thus, an operational plan to destroy the various detachments of Greene's army emerged, with Morgan being its first target. If Cornwallis could get between the general and his line of retreat and destroy the Patriot force, he could make up for the losses at Cowpens and severely damage any chance of Greene reconsolidating his widely spread command. But a delay of two days at Turkey Creek until 19 January, while awaiting Leslie's arrival with reinforcements, gave Morgan the chance to escape. At this point the lack of good intelligence and situational awareness caused Cornwallis to make a significant tactical error. Believing that Morgan had headed for Ninety Six, the earl turned the army toward the Little Broad River. In actuality, Morgan headed in the opposite direction toward Ramsour's Mill and ultimately Sherrill's Ford on the Catawba River north of Charlotte. Upon discovering this, Cornwallis had his army race north into western North Carolina in pursuit. Burdened by the heavy equipment and wagons of a conventional army on the march and slowed by poor roads in a largely undeveloped wilderness, Crown forces advanced methodically, but slowly.

Having lost much of his light infantry at Cowpens, Cornwallis faced a dilemma. His army reached Ramsour's Mill on the twenty-fifth and halted. It had covered only seventy-two miles in seven days, hardly adequate to catch the more nimble Morgan, still a two-day march and two difficult river crossings ahead. In contrast, the Patriots had covered two river crossings and a hundred miles in just five days, an extraordinary feat given the weather and terrain conditions they faced. Despite leaving behind the heaviest baggage and the female camp followers, Cornwallis's pace hardly improved. The earl resolved to lighten the burden further, and at Ramsour's Mill had the baggage burned. To set the example, Cornwallis threw in his own possessions, followed by all the officers' baggage. Not even the officers' wine and the men's rum rations were spared, no doubt the cause for much angst among all ranks. Tentage went into the blaze as well, a bold step in the middle of winter. After this bonfire, only a few wagons to transport the ill and injured and necessary supplies remained. Apart from these, the army would advance with only what the men could carry in their haversacks and knapsacks. Cornwallis said of his decision to burn the baggage: "As the loss of my light troops could only be remedied by the activity of the whole corps, I employed a halt of two days in collecting some flour, and in destroying superfluous baggage and all my wagons, except those loaded with hospital stores, salt, and ammunition and four reserved . . . for sick and wounded. . . . I must in justice to this army, say that there was the most general and cheerful acquiescence."[18] Charles Stedman, a Loyalist serving as Cornwallis's commissary, confirmed the general's assessment of the men's reaction: "And such was the ardour both of officers and soldiers, and their willingness to submit to any hardship for the promotion of the service; that this arrangement, which deprived them of all future prospect of spirituous liquors, and even hazarded a regular supply of provisions, was acquiesced in without a murmur."[19]

Still, some men deserted, though surprisingly few, considering the general rate of eighteenth-century military desertion, particularly under such daunting conditions. Brigadier O'Hara, commanding the Brigade of Foot Guards, captured the attitude of the army on that cold winter's day as they set out again in pursuit of the enemy: "In this situation, without baggage, necessaries, or provisions of any sort for officer or soldier, in the most barren, inhospitable, unhealthy part of North America, opposed to the most savage, inveterate, perfidious, cruel enemy, with zeal and with bayonets only, it was resolved to follow Greene's army to the end of the world."[20]

Sergeant Roger Lamb of the 23rd Regiment of Foot (Royal Welch Fusiliers) commented in his memoirs on the egalitarianism displayed by Cornwallis in discarding his own camp gear, tentage, and personal belongings. Such an action in the eighteenth century, while perhaps not unheard of, certainly would have been unexpected and rare.[21] In terms of the moral authority it imparted to the earl, the effect was incalculable. Other commanders since Cornwallis have also shared in their troops' physical misery, such as German general Erwin Rommel in the Libyan desert campaign of 1941–42, who adopted the same privations as the men of his Afrika Korps and became legendary. The positive effect on the troops' morale, their eagerness to follow one's orders, their trust in the commander's judgment, and their willingness to suffer great privations in pursuit of the mission based on a commander's high degree of moral authority is of huge importance to an army's ultimate effectiveness and fighting ability. Lamb said of Cornwallis on the race across the Carolina Piedmont, with few rations or physical comforts, "in all this his lordship participated, nor did he indulge himself even in the distinction of a tent; but in all things partook our sufferings, and seemed much more to feel for us than for himself."[22]

That Cornwallis would attempt a winter campaign bereft of the ordinary necessities of an army on the march was not at all out of character. Earlier in the preceding summer, he had acknowledged the potential logistics problem of a campaign into North Carolina, warning Clinton that "the back part [western section] of that province is in a want of provisions nearly approaching to famine, so that it will be impossible to establish any post there until after the harvest."[23] Despite his own warning of the potential supply problem of an interior campaign, he embarked on the wild chase through the Carolina backcountry. Here one sees the risk-taking side of his generalship. That the necessary prudence to risk taking appears absent might also be argued. Perhaps he calculated that he could catch Greene and maybe Morgan, defeat them, and move into more hospitable winter quarters before supply problems overwhelmed his force. Then again, perhaps as he expressed to Rawdon, in his mind to retreat meant disaster. Whatever the thinking, the baggage burning represented a bold stroke that might have yielded excellent strategic effects. Cornwallis, ever the clever tactician, had responded energetically to the loss of his light forces at Cowpens. Tactically, he simply converted his entire army into a light, highly maneuverable, and agile striking force.[24] Reinforced by Leslie's command, he resolved to embark on his great quest—Greene's destruction. As the men stepped off from the encampments on the twenty-eighth, they had every reason to believe that the southern Continentals would be the next victims of British arms. Cornwallis cannot be faulted for assuming that the former Quaker he faced would be as easy prey as had Lincoln and Gates before him. The earl did not yet realize that Greene, the private with a limp in 1774 and the young brigadier in 1775, had become perhaps the most talented and astute strategic and operational field commander in the Continental Army by early 1781.

## The Race to the Dan River Begins

By most tactical considerations barring the logistics issue, Cornwallis held the advantage. He had created an essentially all-light and battle-hardened force capable of rapid movement even over the North Carolina Piedmont backcountry. Despite the lack of developed infrastructure, particularly roads, a winter campaign meant that on many days British troops could count on either frozen or at least hard-packed roadways. Spring rains later would turn travel into a difficult, muddy slog, but by then Cornwallis counted on having caught Greene. Except in exceptionally cold winters, the average daily temperature in western North Carolina could be frosty, though not as excessively frigid as in the northern colonies. But a critical vulnerability in Cornwallis's plan lay in another form of infrastructure, bridges—in that, there were hardly any. The North Carolina geography parallels that of South Carolina. Rivers flow out of the Appalachians in a south-by-southeast direction toward the coast. While they tend to be relatively narrow with few gorges or rapids, the problem for both sides was how to transport a force across. Some rivers, such as the Catawba above Charlotte, are relatively shallow. Others required ferries or boats and afforded few shallow fords. In this dynamic one sees the strategic brilliance of the former quartermaster Greene. In modern military parlance he "prepared the battlespace." Greene understood that the key to outrunning the aggressive earl lay in rapid river crossings and denying the opponent the same. Accordingly, he ordered the construction of a hundred large bateaux suitable for river crossings and staged them along his probable route of retreat. While perhaps anecdotal, stories abound regarding the Race to the Dan of British advance-scouting forces arriving at the southern bank of a river only to observe the rear guard of Greene's army disembark on the opposite bank. True or not, they capture the essence of the earl's dilemma. To Greene's advantage, every mile north moved the Continentals closer to their supply sources in Virginia, while Cornwallis moved ever farther away from his own at Camden, Winnsborough, and Wilmington, among others.

In preparation for a possible retreat, Greene also detached his quartermaster, Lt. Col. Edward Carrington, with orders to round up all the boats on the rivers between Charlotte and the North Carolina–Virginia border and station them on the Dan River. This prudent and forward-thinking move proved fortuitous in the coming weeks. As the combatants moved northeast toward Virginia, four large rivers—the Catawba, Yadkin, Deep, and Dan—made for a challenging journey. All had potentially fordable shallows; many fords and ferries existed along these water arteries. But the recent heavy winter rains meant that most areas approached flood stage; until each river crested, fording by men and horses proved difficult, deadly, and highly problematic. Boats and ferries thus took on an increased importance. From an operational viewpoint, with speed and mobility paramount to the two forces, Greene's orders to Carrington represented a singular advantage and, in truth, made possible the operational execution of a Fabian strategy. If one looks at the boats as the operational center of gravity, then Greene's foresighted action represents one of the most critical aspects of the entire campaign, illustrative of the man's strategic genius.[25] As the campaign in North Carolina unfolded, speed and rapidity of movement and maneuver became the guiding imperative for both armies; neither could be encumbered by a lengthy and burdensome supply train. In the Race to the Dan, Cornwallis required speed and mobility to catch his adversary, while Greene needed it to avoid being brought to bay. In the critical arena of logistical support, the Rhode Islander far outshone his British counterpart. Not only did Greene "prepare the battlespace" in terms of river crossings but also did so with food.

Prior to January 1781, Greene prepositioned over twenty supply depots throughout western North Carolina. He ordered local militia to gather milled grain and store it at various gristmills, most of which were owned by prominent Patriot militia officers. Typically, a three-day supply of stores would be deposited at each site. An eighteenth-century army could typically march between ten and fifteen miles per day for a stretch of roughly a week. Beyond that, the men required rest and recuperation, as did the animals pulling artillery and wagons. By prepositioning supplies along the likely route of march, Greene could be confident of a continuous supply. Cornwallis, conversely, could not. As the British forces reached the mills recently abandoned by the Patriots, they would likely find sufficient camping space and good water but not food. The farther north Cornwallis marched, the more critical became his food problem; forage could not help much. In the middle of winter, few locations still held more than a bare minimum of provision. Although there are no known statistics, one can be confident that if a prudent farmer knew that British forces were in the area, he likely would remove or hide all of his food and stores from the foraging parties. With the rapidity with which the Crown army advanced, these groups had little time to search for hidden stores—they simply had to move on and do so at a quick march. Even should they find a store of grain, the simple process of grinding wheat or corn to flour took time that Cornwallis could not afford. The campaign's nature for the earl made foraging operations difficult and ultimately ineffective. Greene retreated toward, not away from, reliable logistics support in Virginia, while for every mile traveled, Cornwallis and his men slogged deeper into the unfriendly North Carolina interior.

From a strategic viewpoint, Cornwallis's invasion might be valid had he possessed a robust logistics tail. That he did not bedeviled the earl to no end. Here again the misreading of the nature of the war compounded the British strategic difficulty. The entire Southern Campaign rested on the outpouring of Loyalist support, not only recruitment into Provincial and irregular units, but also incorporation into such auxiliary functions as sources of supplies, logistical means, and intelligence. Thus, entering the wilderness based on a false premise, he and his command paid a steep price for the misunderstanding. For Cornwallis, despite the increased mobility and rapidity of movement created by the baggage burning, a tenuous supply problem became ever more critical as he charged off across the Carolina winter wilderness in search of the culminating victory.

Greene had the advantage of situational awareness over the earl. He relied on locals for intelligence, which the Briton could not access. Once Cornwallis advanced away from the heavily Loyalist German and Swiss-German settlements on the Broad River near Ramsour's Mill and the Tryon County area, he entered Mecklenburg County, where the predominant Scotch-Irish and heavily Presbyterian Patriot supporters held sway.[26] This feature of immigrant settlement into western and central North Carolina meant that while some local Loyalists might surreptitiously support the rapidly advancing Crown force, in all likelihood the dominant Patriots across the entire Piedmont likely provided far-more-valuable intelligence to Greene. While this aspect of the Race to the Dan is hard to quantify in the absence of precise records, the nature of the population between the Catawba and the Dan Rivers suggests that Greene had an intelligence-collection and situational-awareness advantage. Further, he had the luxury of interior lines of communication. Simply put, in this context Greene retired into and through friendly territory that had already been well scouted. Patriots had seized control of local civil government early in the revolt, thus mechanisms for official support, bodies of organized local militia, and reliable supply depots already existed.

Once Cornwallis initiated the chase, Greene knew that he needed to concentrate all available forces as rapidly as possible. Should he be forced to turn and face the onrushing British, he needed maximum manpower. With only a sergeant's guard of Continental dragoons, an aide and a guide, the Patriot general set off to join Morgan as rapidly as possible, despite the danger of traveling through largely Loyalist-dominated country. If the earl demonstrated the characteristics of energy and boldness, the new Southern Department commander matched him in all respects. Crossing the 125 miles from Cheraw, South Carolina, to the Catawba, Greene reunited with Morgan in two days. Certainly, a less-daring officer might have opted to travel with the much slower main army. But Greene understood the necessity for speed and time as well as his opponent did. On reaching the Catawba and learning of Cornwallis's baggage burning, an exuberant Greene declared to Morgan, "Then, he is ours!" While other commanders might have preferred the safety of the Appalachians to the northwest, this profoundly gifted strategist understood that in drawing the British forces ever-deeper toward Virginia, he gained more advantage with every mile. Charged with such confidence despite his opponent's proven tactical skills, Greene could state with confidence that the earl was truly "ours."

Still, if Cornwallis managed to get between Morgan and the main body of Greene's army, he could defeat each in detail; rapid movements and forced marches might accomplish the task. Greene, to his dismay, had found Morgan in very poor health due to back problems, sciatica, and rheumatism, physical ailments that soon cost the general his most creative and inspirational subordinate. Nevertheless, he soon had Morgan's force moving north along the Catawba River with the mission of raising fresh recruits. Once Cornwallis breached the Catawba barrier, however, Greene realized that the earl threatened this force and hastily rode for Salisbury, ordering Morgan to rendezvous with the main army there. With Cornwallis moving closer, Greene could not tarry. Once his army was reunited, he would run, but to a purpose, executing a perfect example of the classic Fabian strategy. As Cornwallis's force attrited through sheer friction during these months, his chances for the hoped-for decisive victory evaporated. Greene's actions during the winter of 1780–81 illustrated his incredible foresight and extraordinary strategic vision.

## Cowan's Ford, 1 February 1781

Departing Ramsour's Mill on 28 January, Cornwallis's army moved to cross the rain-swollen Catawba River at one of the three passable fords, the two most likely being either the public Beattie's Ford, north of Charlotte, or the private Cowan's (or McCowan's) Ford farther south. Meanwhile, Greene determined to march north to remain beyond the earl's reach. Rapidly concentrating his dispersed command, the general realized that if Cornwallis could defeat in detail his various wings, North Carolina and subsequently Virginia and Maryland would lay open and vulnerable. As he departed South Carolina, Greene had ordered Major General Huger to march the army north from Cheraw to Salisbury. Weather and terrain coupled with the men's misery—cold, without tentage, many without shoes or boots, and all subsisting on little food—made for a laborious and difficult journey. Surprisingly, not a man deserted Huger, a testament to the army's character that moved to face the veteran and disciplined enemy. To impede the British advance at all potential fords of the north fork of the Catawba, Greene posted a strong guard of North Carolina militia and some units of Morgan's command. He detached Brigadier General Davidson with orders to impede the British crossing wherever it might occur, which led to one of the campaign's more dramatic episodes.

Arriving at the Catawba, Cornwallis realized that, although Morgan was encamped on the eastern side, the roaring waters could not be forded. He paused for a full two days. With this delay, the natural friction of war intervened. Had his forces been able to immediately cross the river and defeat any opposing militia as well as the scattered parts of Morgan's command, Cornwallis might well have caught Greene on the run. The two-day respite, though, allowed Huger's column, struggling up from Cheraw, additional time to march unimpeded toward

Salisbury. As the Catawba's waters receded by 31 January, Davidson posted troops at the fords the British would likely use. With 800 men he could not hope to prevent an enemy crossing, but he could impede it and further delay Cornwallis's advance. Beattie's Ford represented the more likely crossing point, so the general posted 300 men there, with a lesser number at Cowan's Ford to contest any movement there. Upon completion of a delaying action, Davidson would pull all his forces back to rendezvous with Greene near Salisbury. There is an old military maxim that he who attempts to defend everywhere, defends nowhere; such was the case with the crossing of the Catawba. Two tactical problems confronted Davidson. Guarding all of the potential crossing points diluted and spread thin his available forces. In addition, there was the question of the militia's reliability? The utter collapse of the North Carolina militia at Camden could not have inspired confidence in their steadfastness. True, they now defended their own state at this point, but when a force of steady, highly disciplined, veteran regulars pressed forward, typically even the most stouthearted militia flee. Additionally, they had performed exceptionally well at Cowpens, so perhaps Davidson hoped for the best. But there Morgan, in a brilliant tactical move, had put the Broad River to his rear, a factor that no doubt caused the militia to "stick and stay." Despite these potentially hazardous conditions, Greene had little choice but to trust that Davidson and the North Carolina militia would hold long enough to consolidate his forces at Salisbury. If Cornwallis crossed the river unimpeded and advanced swiftly before the Southern Department's army could coalesce, all might well be lost. At one in the morning on 1 February, Cornwallis's main force broke camp and marched for the Catawba—and into one of the most extraordinary and legendary events of the war.

To complicate the issue for the Patriots, the earl employed a deception. By making moves toward each of the possible fords, he forced Davidson to spread his forces to cover all contingencies. On 1 February Lieutenant Colonel Webster marched to Beattie's Ford with substantial forces and began an artillery barrage to play out the deception. With Webster on the march toward the more northerly ford, Cornwallis and O'Hara led the main body—the Brigade of Guards, the 23rd, Regiment von Bose, and some cavalry—toward Cowan's Ford. If the ruse worked, Cornwallis expected to outflank the militia. He had proven his skill at the tactical maneuver of "turning the flank" on several occasions, most notably at Camden. In eighteenth-century warfare the force that succeeded in outflanking the opponent, thus creating the opportunity to inflict enfilade fire, typically prevailed.

Geographically, Cowan's Ford split at midstream, but this feature would not have been readily apparent to one observing from the western bank, as the British did. A wagon crossing of about three to four feet in depth with a rocky bottom continued straight to the west bank, while a shallower ford, suitable for use by men and horses, angled right to the east bank a quarter mile from the wagon path. No one in the British command knew of this divergent variation except perhaps the Tory guide; it is not clear what if anything he said to Cornwallis or any other of the officers there. Arriving at the ford, the earl realized that, though the river was fordable by infantry and horse, it would be a dangerous undertaking. At 500 yards wide and moving rapidly, any man or animal that stumbled on the slippery stone bottom might be washed away. With the continuously pelting winter rain, he realized that the water level, even then up to the average soldier's waist and chest, would soon make the crossings impassible. Without accurate battlefield intelligence, the troops moved into the water at the deeper wagon crossing, not the better foot ford. True to his character and aggressiveness, Cornwallis ordered the advance. No one was to fire until they reached the opposite bank. Soldiers removed their cartridge boxes and held them and the muskets as high over their heads as possible or secured the leather boxes about their necks. Even in the best of conditions, the Brown Bess military musket typically misfired one out of every eight shots. Wet powder would guarantee a much higher misfire rate.

Covering Cowan's Ford with a few less-than-reliable militia and about 300 of Maj. Joseph Graham's cavalrymen, Davidson hoped to delay the British crossing. He had placed the bulk of his militia to defend the shallower portion, where infantry might cross, while only a smaller picket guard of twenty-five men covered the wagon ford. The general stationed his mounted troops several hundred yards to the rear.

Cornwallis, Leslie, and O'Hara led the crossing. Advancing four abreast, the soldiers struggled through the swift-moving, waist-deep, frigid water. In the early morning dimness, the British made the first hundred yards across before pickets discovered their movement. As the lead elements under Lieutenant Colonel Francis Hall of the 3rd Foot Guards reached midstream, random, uncoordinated fire came from the recently stirred rebel militia on the opposite bank. Some casualties fell from the shooting, including the horses of both Leslie and O'Hara; both officers almost drowned in the rushing water. Lieutenant Colonel Hall died of wounds while leading the crossing of the fast-moving river. Another shot wounded Cornwallis's horse, which struggled to the opposite bank before dying. Men slipped and fell as they hurriedly stumbled over mossy rocks. The swift current swept some downstream, particularly the wounded. Horses lost their footing, dumping riders into the murky, roaring water. Despite the current and enemy fire, the Guards pressed ahead and reached the bank in good order, then formed ranks and drove the militia off in disorder. Cornwallis later reported that the "Light Infantry [Guards Brigade], landing first, immediately formed, and in a few minutes killed or dispersed everything that appeared before them."[27]

Attempting to salvage the situation, Davidson rallied his cavalry and posted them on the river bank, but the morning cooking fires to their rear made them perfect silhouettes for British volleys; the cavalry soon dispersed, leaving Davidson dead from a shot to the heart. Once across, Cornwallis then turned his men upstream toward Beattie's Ford, where Webster crossed with no opposition. With their general killed, the militia hastily retreated up the Salisbury road, with Tarleton in hot pursuit. Although casualties on both sides remained light (only four Patriots died, including Davidson, with three captured), the Battle at Cowan's Ford gave a hint of the nature of the North Carolina operation. The steadfastness of the Guards in crossing a fast-moving river under heavy fire, maintaining disciplined unit cohesion with the general officers in the lead, illustrated to all that the coming campaign would be hard fought, rapidly moving, and aggressive.[28] It also indicated that geography would play a pivotal role throughout. Unfortunately for Cornwallis, the spatial advantage now favored the Patriots, not him. Morgan's men by now had escaped. Aware of the impending British crossing, the division broke camp and marched all night north toward Trading Ford on the Yadkin River, thirty miles away. With impassable roads and an exhausted force, Cornwallis knew that he had won only a local victory. Because of the crossing delay, the quarry now lay miles away and out of reach.

## "Judiciously Designed and Vigorously Executed": The Race Unfolds

Greene, meanwhile, had stayed in the Salisbury area, expecting to meet up with Davidson's men. Awaiting their arrival at Tarrant's Tavern, he heard distant gunfire as Tarleton's dragoons dispersed a gaggle of North Carolina militia.[29] Greene stayed in place at first, then departed only after he learned of the general's death and that Cornwallis had successfully crossed the Catawba. Stopping in Salisbury at Steele's Tavern, where the owners presented him not only a hearty breakfast but also a gift of coins for the cause, he quickly penned orders for Huger to rendezvous instead at Guilford Court House, some fifty miles northeast of the town. With Cornwallis across the Catawba and Tarleton already on the move, if Huger continued toward Salisbury, the earl could interdict him and destroy his column with overwhelming force.

Cornwallis must have determined that he would catch Greene and Morgan with their backs to the Yadkin River. With the winter floods and the river at a high stage, he calculated that he could trap the Continentals between it and the Catawba. Destroying more wagons to speed up the march by doubling up the teams and slogging through muddy lowlands and rushing creeks, Cornwallis drove his army forward through the Carolina wilderness. Entering Salisbury, the British learned that the quarry lay only a few miles ahead at Trading Ford on the Yadkin. Charged with this positive intelligence, Cornwallis believed that he would win the race, but weather and sheer exhaustion conspired to ruin his chances—that and Greene's careful advance preparations. Sending Tarleton ahead with some mounted troops, the earl hoped to trap the enemy. In the realm of counterfactuals, one can only wonder what might have happened if a reprise of Cowpens had occurred on the Yadkin—Tarleton versus Morgan and Greene, with the Patriots' backs to a river. But it was not to be. Due to rain, darkness, and bad roads, the dragoons did not arrive at the Yadkin until about midnight, capturing some abandoned wagons and driving off the militia posted on the southern bank to defend the ford. The bulk of Morgan's force had made the north bank in safety, leaving the British frustrated across the roaring Yadkin.

With boats previously gathered at the Yadkin, Greene's men crossed the river as the enemy approached. With no boats to be had and the Patriots encamped on the opposite shore, all the frustrated Crown forces could do was to fire a few artillery rounds across the river with no effect. At this point logistics again came into play. Cornwallis had to feed his hungry men and horses, which thus required a two-day stay in Salisbury. Adding to the delay, with no boats and the Yadkin now too deep for fording, Cornwallis had to divert fifty miles north to a passable ford upriver (Shallow Ford). After crossing the river, the earl learned from Loyalist observers that Morgan's force was heading for a rendezvous with the remainder of Greene's army, coming up from South Carolina, at the hamlet of Guilford on the Haw River. But yet another waterway intervened—the Deep River. Cornwallis again sensed an opportunity. He assumed that Greene had neither an opportunity to raise militia forces in the Piedmont nor a willingness to engage south of the Dan River.[30] He also believed that if he forced Greene upriver, the Rhode Islander could not cross due to a lack of boats. As is well known in strategic and operational thinking, the enemy always gets a vote, which is exactly what Greene intended. The Patriot commander believed that the further he could draw Cornwallis away from his logistical support bases at Wilmington and in South Carolina, the more in extremis the earl would find himself. The plan, though bold and daring, presented risks. Should Cornwallis actually succeed, engage Greene south of the Dan, and defeat him, then nothing stood in the earl's way to prevent his tapping the huge stores available in southern Virginia, previously untouched by the fighting. The two generals, like two aggressive prize fighters, stood toe to toe, each executing an extraordinarily risky gambit.

Once again, Greene trumped the earl. After the Rhode Islander had his forces across the Yadkin, which presented a huge tactical advantage for Greene and a detriment to Cornwallis, all the available boats lay on the northern bank, out of reach of the British. Four days later the earl's hopes of catching and defeating elements of a divided army ended as the forces under Greene, Morgan, and Huger rendezvoused at tiny Guilford Court House. With the addition of Lee's Legion, Greene now had a light-dragoon capability rivaling Tarleton's British Legion. Estimates put the Patriot army's strength at about 2,000 effectives. But such estimates deceive. With only roughly 1,400 Continental regulars, how certain could Greene be of the militia's reliability? True, they had done good service at Cowpens, but any prudent commander must always view local forces as a "random variable." Even with the expected arrival of well over a thousand Virginia militia, uncertainty prevailed. Would the Rhode Islander now turn and give battle? Estimates of Cornwallis's strength ran as high as 3,000 veteran, highly disciplined, and likely angry regulars. Many of those with him who had a mind to desert most likely had already done so, following the baggage burning at Ramsour's Mill, and simply faded into the wilderness.

Greene now faced one of those moments with which all field commanders must eventually grapple. The impetuous and bold Cornwallis would have no qualms—attack, attack, attack;. that was the Englishman's essential character. Greene, however, showed a more strategically calculating bent. If he committed to an engagement based on the hoped-for arrival of the Virginians and the excellent defensive characteristics of the Guilford Court House terrain and lost, the rebellion in the South might utterly collapse. Cornwallis, Clinton, and the British regulars would have thus defeated three Continental armies in less than a year. The gains of Ramsour's Mill, King's Mountain, and Cowpens, in terms of their positive psychological effect, would be dissipated. Loyalists would likely turn out in large numbers; southern Patriots—disheartened and depressed—might opt for the safety of declared neutrality or worse and sign the loyalty oath. With Greene out of the way, Cornwallis could advance into Virginia and join the Crown forces already there. The strategic effects of such a juncture would have been monumental. Many of the Saratoga and Cowpens prisoners of war kept in Virginia might be freed for further service. With newly arrived reinforcements from New York, Cornwallis would have a strike force capable of either consolidating control over the four southern colonies by sheer military might or of initiating a pincer movement against Washington's main body in conjunction with Clinton's forces moving out of New York. With Washington subdued, Rochambeau in Newport would certainly have to evacuate as soon as possible. With only the relatively tiny partisan bands in South Carolina and Georgia, resistance south of Pennsylvania would have been practically nil. The Swamp Fox and his partisans could not have survived very long in such an environment. Even if the New England and middle colonies remained in rebellion, the most economically valuable colonies of Virginia and the two Carolinas, with their commodities of tobacco, naval stores, and rice, would be under firm Crown control. Simply put, if Greene committed to battle too early and lost, Cornwallis and the British "clear and hold" strategy would prevail. Faced with the potential for disaster weighed against the possible gains, Greene opted to continue the chase. A council of war concurred. He would commit to battle, likely at Guilford, at some future point, but it would be under more favorable conditions. Clearly, the Patriot commander understood that the fate of the rebellion in the South lay in his hands alone.

To cover the retreat and harass the advancing British, Greene formed a light corps composed of Washington's cavalry, the infantry of Lee's Legion, 300 Continental infantry, and sixty Virginia riflemen. Although Greene desired that Morgan command the rear guard, the Old Wagoner's poor health finally brought the end of his active service; the gallant warrior returned to his Virginia farm and played no more role in the war. Col. Otho Williams assumed command of his division. A better substitute could hardly have been appointed, as would soon be demonstrated. Williams received simple orders—delay, harass, and misdirect. Maintaining contact with the British advance guard, usually forces under Tarleton, Williams would slow down the British river crossings by ensuring that there were no boats. In addition, by remaining in constant contact, he could convince Cornwallis that Greene's main force lay just beyond Williams, bound for the Dan River upper fords farther northwest from the army's true crossing points farther downriver at Boyd's and Irwin's Ferries. On the eighth Williams and his rear guard departed Guilford headed northwest. Two days later Greene marched toward the Dan in a different direction. Cornwallis took the bait. Believing Williams's command to be the Continental rear guard, with Greene's main body somewhere up ahead, the earl launched off in pursuit. His first move, a feint toward Hillsborough, was meant to draw Greene in that direction. Then, with a rapid turn toward Williams, Cornwallis planned to reach the Dan ahead of his opponent and wait in ambush. For Greene and the Patriots, operational deception in warfare could hardly have been accomplished more adroitly.

Seventy miles to the north of Guilford Court House lay the Dan River and safety. The same tactic that Greene had earlier used in dividing his force now gave Cornwallis another opportunity to defeat each in detail. Greene had to keep Cornwallis from coming between the main body headed toward the lower reaches and Williams's diversion force leading the earl toward the upper reaches. There were essentially two imperatives—speed and misdirection. Greene knew that boats awaited his army on the southern bank to take them to safety. For Williams, he had to maintain the deception that his small force represented the rear of the Continental army. Pickets patrolled the rear, creating the illusion of a large body of troops not far ahead. On any given night, fully half of his men stood picket duty or maintained a mounted patrol. With Tarleton's dragoons scouting ahead of the British main body, these men had to be seen and in numbers. To maintain the chase away from Greene and to prevent Cornwallis from catching and destroying his command, Williams allowed no more than a temporary pause each night, typically less than six hours. In a forty-eight-hour period, between the marching, scouting, picket duties, and brief rest stops, the men had only a few hours' sleep. One can imagine the weariness. On the other hand, every one of them knew what would happen if their pace slackened and the enemy caught up with them. Without tents, the men traveled light. Each day's march commenced by 3:00 A.M. The only meal pause came with breakfast once Colonel Williams deemed the force far enough ahead for safety.

At the same time as Greene departed Guilford, Cornwallis reached Salem (now Winston-Salem), a German Moravian backcountry village roughly twenty-five miles to the west. Simultaneously, Huger finally rendezvoused with Greene. With Morgan's troops already joined, Greene now had a fairly potent force of hardened Continentals, especially the 1st Maryland, one of the best-drilled and experienced regiments in the Continental Army. With the Patriot army now nearly whole (less only Williams's command), Cornwallis had lost the opportunity to confront and destroy the various detachments in detail. He now faced a greater challenge as both armies launched off in the final run toward the Dan. Snowstorms and rain alternated for the next several days. The Piedmont region of North Carolina does get occasional winter snow, but in general, even in February, the weather is tolerable. Each army slogged north knowing full well the importance of keeping their respective forces moving despite rough terrain, intolerable weather, and lack of food and supplies, and for Cornwallis, the galling lack of local Loyalist support. The earl, ever aggressive and energetic, urged his men forward much as Hannibal had driven his Carthaginian army over the Alps in 218 B.C.E., completely surprising the Romans as they emerged onto the north Italian plain. But unlike the stunned Roman consular generals, Greene knew full well the movements and location of his opponent, and although on the defensive, he lured Cornwallis farther and farther away from his logistical support while building his own numerical strength of both regulars and local militia. Here was Greene at his strategic best, and sadly for the royal cause, Cornwallis at his worst in terms of aggressive risk taking without the necessary prudence. This failing would soon cost him.

At night, as the temperature dropped, the ground became hard and frozen. That factor might have been a positive in that even severely rutted wagon roads were easier to traverse when frozen. But in daylight the top few inches typically melted, becoming muddy and sticky. Soldiers' shoes and boots got mired in gobs of sticky, irritating, red-clay mud. Despite this handicap, the armies accomplished incredible feats. Each side marched over thirty miles a day, an extraordinary achievement in winter in a wilderness with little food and rest. In one day, 13 February, they covered forty miles in a twenty-four-hour period. Even in the best of weather and terrain conditions, an eighteenth-century army did well to travel ten to fifteen miles in a day. Despite Williams's measures for speed against the swift-moving Cornwallis, occasional action occurred. For example, at one point a troop of Tarleton's scouts encountered elements of Lee's Legion forming the rear guard. Unfortunately for the British, eighteen men died and the remainder beat a hasty retreat. Nonetheless, the incident verified Williams's concern for his command's safety.

The colonel eventually turned east to rendezvous with Greene and Huger, assuming that they had reached the Dan River safely. For once, the earl's situational awareness proved correct. Detecting the direction change, he also turned east and continued the chase. A crisis moment had arrived for Williams. Had he swung east too early and committed a fatal error, now leading the enemy not away from, but directly toward Greene's army? O'Hara led the British advance element, a light infantry company (from the Brigade of Guards). Occasional clashes ensued as Williams's troops encountered O'Hara's lead scouts. But the ruse continued to work, with Williams leading O'Hara toward Dix's Ferry, some six miles downstream and to the east of Greene's destination at Irwin's Ferry. By the twelfth, the deception had been uncovered by Tarleton's dragoons, who discovered the route of the Continental main body toward the lower Dan. The chase tightened, with the British advance force coming literally within volley range of Williams's rear guard. But Greene reached Irwin's Ferry first and crossed successfully, while Williams's troops remained fourteen miles distant, O'Hara on their heels.

Despite the extraordinary exertions, the British chase came to naught. The advance scouts and dragoons under Tarleton reached Boyd's Ferry on the fourteenth. Once again they could only stare across an impassable river at the Patriots on the other side with all the available boats. Greene had reached Virginia. One can imagine Williams's anxiety, and relief, when on the fourteenth he received a message from Greene written at 5:30 p.m.: "All our troops are over and the stage is clear. . . . I am ready to receive you and give you a hearty welcome."[31] One can also imagine the emotions running through the hungry, footsore, exhausted soldiers as the word passed down the line. With huzzahs and cheers so loud that they could be heard by the British advance guard, the implication now became clear. By dusk of the fifteenth, Williams reached the ferry and quickly crossed. O'Hara arrived less than an hour later only to witness the last of the enemy making the opposite bank. Greene's army was safe and soon to be intact. The hare had outchased the hound. Tarleton later complimented his foe, stating, "Every measure of the Americans, during their march from the Catawba to Virginia, was judiciously designed and vigorously executed."[32]

From the first of February through mid-March, as the chase unfolded, Cornwallis had little communications with any subordinate commanders in South Carolina or with Clinton in New York. At Camden Lord Rawdon might have been in a position to assist the earl with a march north. From an operational aspect, such a move might have forced Greene into a more westerly direction as Cornwallis advanced from the Charlotte-Salisbury-Guilford axis while Rawdon moved through the Sand Hills, likely picking up Loyalist support from the Scottish Highlanders around Cross Creek. Thus pushing Greene farther away from his reinforcements and supplies north of the Dan, Cornwallis might have cornered the elusive Rhode Islander, outnumbered, with his back to the mountains. This operational alternative never developed and, in truth, probably could not have. Such a pincer movement required extensive coordination with frequent and continuous communications. Here again the failure of the Carolina Loyalists to provide material support played a role. Had they helped establish reliable communications between Cornwallis and the southern posts, such a coordinated operation might have developed. Instead, Rawdon sat idle in South Carolina with little knowledge of his commander's whereabouts. The youthful commander expressed his frustration to Balfour in Charleston and could only report that he suspected the army may have arrived in the Salisbury area.[33] Meanwhile, Cornwallis could only fire artillery rounds across a swollen river at an enemy that consistently and brilliantly eluded his pursuit.

In one of the most extraordinary occurrences in military history, the cold, exhausted, hungry men of the British and Continental armies, many without proper shoes or boots, had marched 230 miles in eight days, averaging 28 miles per day. Without boats to cross and faced with a march upstream for a ford, Cornwallis reluctantly admitted that he had been bested. On 21 February he wrote to Rawdon, expressing the frustration of having failed to overhaul and destroy Greene: "I tried by a most rapid march to strike a blow either at Greene or Morgan before they got over the Dan, but could not effect it." Cornwallis blamed his failure to catch the Patriots on the poor roads, the many waterways, and the destruction of bridges. The earl must have appreciated the brilliance of Greene, though he did not state as much. He turned his army toward Hillsborough, sixty miles to the south, arriving there by slow marches on 20 February.[34]

## "If He Persists in His Mad Scheme": Prelude to a Battle, February and March 1781

Had Cornwallis actually failed by not engaging Greene before he crossed into Virginia? It is often assumed to be the case. But to answer this question, a consideration of the actual strategic intentions and desired strategic effects is in order. In this context, the answer becomes simply yes and no. Flippancy aside, one must consider both aspects, intentions and effects. From a broader strategic sense, the objective of the entire Southern Campaign to date favors the positive response. The strategic imperative of destroying, chasing away, or otherwise nullifying the Continental Army in the Carolinas, Georgia, and the Floridas had been achieved. By late February 1781, no formal Continental command of any significance operated south of Virginia. Crown forces occupied key posts at Ninety Six, Georgetown (South Carolina), Augusta, and Camden. Significant coastal cities able to support naval operations, including Charleston, Savannah, Pensacola, Saint Augustine, and Wilmington, were safely in British hands. While the South Carolina partisan bands of Marion, Sumter, and others operated freely and irritatingly in the backcountry, they could not hold territory. A few defeats at the hands of Lord Rawdon and other regional commanders would certainly undo the irregulars. Although Continental forces and irregular troops had dealt significant body blows to the Crown cause at Ramsour's Mill, King's Mountain, Cowpens, and a host of smaller engagements in the backcountry, again, to what strategic purpose? Viewed in this light, Greene's escape had merely aided Cornwallis in accomplishing the strategic effect of his highly aggressive, bold, and risky thrust into North Carolina.

Viewed from the opposite tack, however, one can assess Cornwallis's strategic position as a failure. Indeed, he had driven out the Continentals and taken command of the lower South. But it was a matter of timing. As Cornwallis halted for a day before turning back toward Hillsborough, the Crown strategic situation appeared positive. Within weeks, however, the Southern Campaign had failed, utterly and completely. The tactical victory at Guilford Court House on 15 March (discussed below) coupled with the loss of Pensacola, West Florida, to Don Bernardo de Galvéz's Spanish army on 9 May dramatically altered the strategic situation. To effect this incredible change in the strategic situation, though, took some action on Greene's part. Had he remained north of the Dan, as many more timid officers might well have done, Cornwallis would have won. But the Rhode Island businessman of insignificant prewar military experience proved to be as bold and audacious a commander as his opponent. Greene understood that as gallant and brilliant as had been his wild chase to the river, in military terms—and more importantly, in terms of strategic communications and psychology—he had been defeated. Public opinion is ephemeral and fleeting. Certainly, the local Patriots regarded the general's accomplishment as a victory and would be temporarily buoyed. But, in reality, it could not last. With Greene in southern Virginia, how long would it have been before the Carolina Loyalists regained their confidence and rose up in defiance as the Southern Strategy envisioned? What of the British regular forces in Virginia? If Greene stood still awaiting reinforcements and supplies, with Cornwallis free to consolidate, regroup, recharge, and rally the Loyalists, how long might it be before he would be caught in a pincer between the Crown forces, with the Appalachians to his rear and nowhere to run? Greene then, in his winning the Race to the Dan, had established the conditions whereby he might be able to accomplish his objective of destroying British authority in the South, but he had not yet won the day. He desperately required the fundamental component of any Fabian strategy—the decisive, culminating, conventional victory. To obtain that objective, despite the fact that his expected reinforcements had not yet arrived, he understood that he must recross the Dan and in some fashion defeat Cornwallis in a stand-up, conventional, regular-forces battle. Weather made his decision somewhat easier. As the flooded river receded, Cornwallis might well have simply waited and then struck across the Dan himself. Ultimately, Greene knew that he had to defeat or somehow disable Cornwallis, which meant reengaging in North Carolina. On 18 February he sent Pickens, with a force of Maryland Continentals accompanied by Lee's Legion, back across the Dan with orders to harass Cornwallis and suppress Loyalist activity. This crossing represented the opening phase of the British month of discontent, March 1781.

In retrospect, while significant battles of the War of American Independence, such as Guilford Court House and Saratoga, are credited with the ultimate victory of the United States and its French allies and are traditionally viewed as the tipping or turning points, in reality, it was the simple decision of two field commanders that set in motion the chain of events leading ultimately to Surrender Field at Yorktown. With Cornwallis's departure from the Dan River region, Greene now had the strategic initiative. Reinforced by an ever-increasing number of North Carolina and Virginia militia, he marched back into North Carolina, intending to bring the exhausted British army to battle—but on his terms, not the earl's. Greene expressed his optimistic attitude to Gov. Abner Nash of North Carolina: "The moment the enemy moves towards Hillsborough I shall fall into their rear."[35] Cornwallis's retirement to that town and Greene's decision to recross the Dan ultimately determined the outcome of the war. Viewed in this light, the combination of both decisions in February 1781 represents the decisive moment of the struggle in the South that ultimately led to the outcome at Yorktown. Given this interpretation, then, on his arrival at the Dan on 15 February, Cornwallis had won the Southern Campaign. On his departure for Hillsborough, however, he lost the War of American Independence.

Despite the lack of a significant Continental force in the Carolinas and Georgia, the specters of the proclamations of the previous year and the disasters at Ramsour's Mill, King's Mountain, and Cowpens continued to exert their influence. At Hillsborough Cornwallis expected an outpouring of Loyalist support and recruits. This did not occur. In response to his proclamation inviting Loyalists to muster at Hillsborough under arms and with ten days' rations, few men came forward except in idle curiosity to see the army and then depart again. O'Hara commented: "I am certain that in our march of near a thousand miles, almost in as many directions, thro' every part of North Carolina, tho' every means possible was taken to persuade our friends as they are called and indeed as they call themselves to join us, we never had with us at any one time one hundred men in arms. Without the experiment had been made, it would have been impossible to conceive that government could in so important a matter have been so grossly deceived. Fatal infatuation!"[36]

On the twenty-third Cornwallis received word that Greene had recrossed the Dan River. Reinforced with Continentals sent from farther north and a significant body of Virginia and North Carolina militia, he now outnumbered Cornwallis, whose command had dwindled to roughly 1,600 troops. The earl understood the strategic imperative to defeat Greene so as to rally the North Carolina Loyalists and tamp down Patriot support. His opponent gave him the opening. Despite the woeful turnout of Loyalist support while the army rested at Hillsborough, Cornwallis had to act swiftly and decisively to defeat Greene before the balance of forces weighed too heavily in the Patriot's favor. He also needed a sound victory to convince the Loyalists of the invincibility of Crown arms, otherwise few would join "whilst doubt remained on their minds of the superiority of our arms."[37] However confident Cornwallis still might have felt in his chances for success, his cagy opponent suspected from the start of the merry chase that the earl had embarked on a lost cause. Here one sees the Rhode Islander's extraordinary strategic vision. Once Greene received sound intelligence that the Briton had burned his baggage at Ramsour's Mill, he commented to Huger, "I am not without hopes of ruining Lord Cornwallis if he persists in his mad scheme of pushing through the country."[38]

## Pyle's Massacre, 25 February 1781

In late February an event occurred that not only illustrates the frustration of reliance on the North Carolina Loyalists but also likely eliminated any hope of raising substantial forces from among the local population who, while they may well have been sympathetic to the royal cause, nevertheless had been cowed into inaction. Known variously as "Pyle's Massacre," "Action at the Haw River," and

"Pyle's Hacking Match," the incident highlights the increasingly barbaric nature of the Southern Campaign. In this action Lee's Legion struck a death blow to British hopes of a Loyalist uprising in the central Piedmont. The colonel had reported for duty with Greene's force on 13 January at the head of his legion. Composed of both cavalry and infantry, with the infantry typically riding double with the horsemen, the 280-man force (180 infantry organized into three companies, with the other 100 men divided among three troops of horse), Lee's Legion provided Greene a reliable, highly disciplined, and mobile scouting and skirmishing force. And its members wore short-tailed green uniforms, a factor that led to the Crown catastrophe on the twenty-fifth.

After turning from the Dan River, Cornwallis raised the Royal Standard and issued a proclamation calling on all Loyalists to "repair to Hillsborough with weapons and ten days rations."[39] Greene had earlier detached Lee back across the Dan to maintain a watch on the earl's movements. Two companies of Maryland Continentals accompanied the legion, and more reinforcements gradually joined up. Brigadier General Pickens later arrived with over 700 North and South Carolina militia and assumed overall command. The Patriot force had three essential missions: to harass and annoy Cornwallis, interdict and discourage potential Loyalist supporters, and, if possible, induce Tarleton to attack in hopes of finally eliminating his depleted force remaining from the Cowpens disaster. At this point entered Doctor John Pyle, a prominent Loyalist militia colonel who agreed to march his force of 300–400 men to Hillsborough to rendezvous with and join the main army. Having served at Moore's Creek in February 1776, been captured there, survived by providing medical services to his captors, and then witnessed five years of Patriot intimidation of his Loyalist neighbors, no doubt Pyle stood eager to wreak destruction on his oppressors. His men hailed from the region between the Haw and Broad Rivers, thus they had motivation to defend their own homes and families. Cornwallis detached Tarleton to bring this Loyalist force into camp safely. But the British Legion never reached the Loyalists; Lee's Legion did.

At midday on 25 February, Lee and Pickens attacked a Loyalist plantation near Hillsborough, an action that set in motion Pyle's destruction. The Patriot commanders hoped to find Tarleton's force at that site but discovered only a pair of British officers, Tarleton and his command having already moved on. Meanwhile, Pyle's Loyalists drifted about the countryside attempting to link up with the Green Dragoon. Late that afternoon, however, they met up with the Patriot force in search of Tarleton. Pyle had been instructed to rendezvous at the plantation. Although the doctor-colonel headed in the right direction, Tarleton could not be located. At this point the "fog and friction" of war came to bear. As dusk approached, two Loyalists emerged from the woods and, seeing green-coated legionnaires, assumed them to be from the British Legion. None of the men, including Pyle, knew what Tarleton looked like, and Lee employed a most successful deception by portraying himself as the notorious British officer.

The colonel sent one of the bamboozled Loyalists ahead to instruct Pyle to move off the road and allow "Tarleton's troopers" to pass and then fall in behind. Maintaining the deception, Lee forced the two captured British officers to accompany him. Meanwhile Pickens's infantry, easily identified as Patriots, moved stealthily through the woods on the flanks while the green-jacketed legionnaires paraded past Pyle's Loyalists. Once Lee reached Pyle, who had stationed himself at the far end of the line, both men shook hands and greeted one another. Various claims have been made about the subsequent turn of events. Lee later claimed that he intended to allow the Loyalists to lay down their arms and return home or to turn sides and join his command. His main concern was to continue chasing the real Tarleton; a few hundred ill-trained and poorly armed Loyalists really did not matter compared to the prize ahead. Some legends contend that some of Pyle's men detected Pickens's infantry in the woods and opened fire. Other stories assert that several of Lee's officers noted the red ribbons in the Loyalist's hats and feared that they had ridden into a trap, causing a general action to break out. Whatever the truth of the matter, the end result proved devastating for the Crown cause. As the action erupted, many Loyalists, believing that "friendly fire" had broken out, bellowed "Hurrah for King George" and similar shouts of recognition. Within ten minutes, ninety-three Loyalists lay dead, with many others wounded. The Patriots lost a horse.

Surprised and unprepared, Pyle's men had little chance. The Patriot legionnaires had already drawn sabers as if to render salutes and, being only a few feet apart, came onto the stunned Loyalists swiftly and without mercy. Colonel Pyle, although wounded, managed to crawl away from the scene, returned home, and survived the war. Lee did not order a pursuit, suspecting that Tarleton's force lay only a mile or two farther down the road toward Hillsborough. In fact, the Green Dragoon had set up camp for the evening at O'Neal's plantation and likely could not have arrived at the scene in time to intervene before nightfall. He learned of the massacre from wounded survivors who arrived at the camp about nightfall and complained that his men had attacked then. So successful had been Lee's ruse that at even this stage of the affair, many Loyalists still believed the action had been a "friendly fire" tragedy.

Tarleton, a man of incredible energy, aggressiveness, and active nature, immediately ordered his troopers to mount up. Simultaneously, however, he received orders from Cornwallis to return to Hillsborough straightaway. But just as the British Legion prepared to ride, Lee and Pickens arrived on the scene, intent on Tarleton's destruction. But for the gathering darkness, they might well have accomplished it, instead deciding to wait for daylight to attack. By morning, Tarleton, never one to tarry, had departed and slipped away.

What can be made of Pyle's Massacre? In terms of force strength, the surprised Loyalists would have added little to Cornwallis's military capability. The real damage to the royal cause was psychological. With the destruction of North Carolina Loyalist forces at Ramsour's Mill, King's Mountain, and now Pyle's Massacre, one can understand the reluctance of locals to support the army. In addition, the most valuable services that local sympathizers might have provided—food, supplies, and intelligence—were lost to the earl. Even hardcore supporters might contemplate the consequences of declaring openly for King George and Britain. Conversely, local Patriots had reason to become more active and support the rebellion. While the actual numbers are incalculable, neutrals also wished to protect themselves, their property, and their families. They could assess the situation themselves, and a great many likely declared for the Patriot cause, either openly or tacitly. Here is seen the value of Patriot "strategic communications." While the ruthlessness of Lee's legionnaires at Pyle's Massacre was and still is viewed as a clever use of operational deception leading to a valuable psychological victory, the actions of Tarleton's troops at the Waxhaws was and is still portrayed as wanton brutality and senseless slaughter. Such is the value of propaganda to the side that most successfully employs it.

The events of 25 February 1781 starkly illustrate another of the strategic problems plaguing the Crown's efforts in the South—a breakdown in command, control, and communications. Even in the most technologically robust conflict, communications fail. Certainly, in the pre–Industrial Age, with rudimentary communications by either personal presence or at best, written message, such failures occurred regularly. Thus, the fact that Colonel Pyle and his Loyalists and Tarleton and his legionnaires had no idea of each other's presence barely a mile or so apart is neither strange nor unusual. How fast can a mounted dragoon travel? Even in an unsophisticated infrastructure such as existed at the time in Piedmont North Carolina, the time to mount up and gallop that distance was measured in minutes. Had Tarleton been aware of the Loyalists' situation even a few minutes beforehand, the action might have turned out differently. The massacre may well have occurred, but, positing an alternative history, what might have been the result of the British Legion arriving at full gallop, weapons at the ready, with Lee's troopers in a disorganized state as always occurs during combat. If Tarleton had recovered the situation, as he was perfectly capable of doing, and inflicted a devastating defeat on the Continental dragoons and Carolina militia, might the reaction of the Carolina Loyalists to Cornwallis's presence and call to arms been different? Might Greene not have had the hundreds of North Carolina militia at the upcoming engagement at Guilford Court House? What if the two Loyalists had recognized any of the Patriots for who they were? What if Lee had not been such a good actor? What if Colonel Pyle had known Tarleton so as to recognize him, or even if he had stationed himself at the head of his troopers rather than at the rear along the Hillsborough road? While all such speculation (as are all historical counterfactuals) is interesting and does aid in strategic thinking and analysis, the fact remains that a lack of effective communications at the tactical level had a devastating consequence on Crown chances for success. It is foolish to state that this type of occurrence was unique or even extraordinary. Such tactical-communications breakdowns occur at every engagement in every conflict in history. What is significant here is that this particular instance had a far more consequential influence on the strategic situation than have most such occurrences. It is also symptomatic of the strategic problems facing Cornwallis throughout the post-Camden campaign, providing yet another causative explanation for the eventual march to Yorktown.

Pyle's Massacre illustrates the essential strategic dilemma facing Cornwallis and his subordinates. The bulwark of the Southern Strategy had always been Loyalist support. The British theory of victory underpinning the Southern Campaign and the "clear and hold" strategy assumed massive Loyalist physical and material assistance. This disaster further eroded what little Loyalist enthusiasm remained in North Carolina. The disappointing turnout at Hillsborough proved the ultimate failure of the Loyalist strategy. In the campaigns in the middle and New England colonies earlier in the rebellion, Lord Germain and his field commanders assumed that the rebellion's center of gravity lay in the cities—Philadelphia, Boston, New York, Charleston, and the rest. Only too late did they realize that the true center of gravity was two-fold—the Continental Army and its ability to remain viable as a symbol of hope and resistance, and, more importantly, public support. While Cornwallis recognized the criticality of destroying Greene and his Continentals, the lack of public support ultimately doomed his chances for achieving the policy objective of restoring the southern colonies to allegiance. In a civil war of neighbor on neighbor in which loyalties shift depending on the flow of events and personalities and in which hybrid warfare characterizes the conflict's nature, a conventional force-on-force strategy seldom succeeds. In this regard Cornwallis's ultimate lack of an appropriate strategic vision is glaringly apparent. Notwithstanding, the ever-aggressive, bold, and active nobleman resolved to chase down and destroy Greene's force, the object of his march into North Carolina and the immediate cause of the clash at Guilford Court House on 15 March.

## "Another Such Victory Will Ruin the British Army": Guilford Court House, 15 March 1781

Cornwallis bivouacked at Hillsborough for six days to allow his men to rest and recover from the exhausting chase. In Virginia Greene did the same. Horses proved especially problematic for the Patriots, even though Gov. Thomas Jefferson authorized the requisition of mounts from local farms. Despite the supply and reinforcement problems, Greene sought to keep in close contact with his adversary and on 23 February marched toward Hillsborough. His total strength increased to 2,600 men (1,000 Continentals and 1,600 militia) with the arrival of 600 Virginians under Brigadier General Stevens.[40] Pickens's South Carolinians and the light infantry and cavalry under Colonels Williams and Lee moved to within ten miles of the British camp, tempting the British lion to spring. But Cornwallis did not react in force, although several ambushes and small engagements occurred. In reaction to Pyle's Massacre and the continual harassment, coupled with the disappointing Loyalist turnout and the lack of local provisions, Cornwallis resolved to move against the forces operating on his flank. On the twenty-sixth he departed Hillsborough for the Haw River, encamping near Alamance (near present-day Burlington) the next day. This site, at the crossroads on the south side of Alamance Creek, gave him the option of a swift movement toward either Guilford Court House or Wilmington, still under the control of Major Craig's detachment and a secure base of seaborne supply. In a game of cat and mouse, both sides remained unengaged except for patrols and minor skirmishes between scouting and forage parties. Despite efforts by Cornwallis to provoke a general action, Greene refused to cooperate. On 6 March the earl recrossed the Haw in an attempt to bring on a general action. Again his adversary refused to comply; only a small skirmish cost each side minor casualties.

Greene encamped only fifteen miles north of the British position but moved his camp every other day to avoid a surprise attack as his numbers grew. By 10 March, he had received two brigades of North Carolina militia totaling just over a thousand men. Brig. Gen. Robert Lawson soon after arrived from Virginia with a thousand additional Virginia militia and 550 Virginia Continental regulars detached from Maj. Gen. Friedrich von Steuben's command in southeastern Virginia. By mid-March, the Patriot army mustered nearly 4,400 effectives (with as many as 1,600 being Continental regulars), a complete reversal of the balance of forces from a month earlier. Greene now came close to matching Cornwallis in regulars, and the nature of these troops would prove critical in the following days. Among the Continentals were several regiments of Maryland and Delaware infantry, regarded as some of the best in the army. Notably, the 1st Maryland Regiment had long been heralded as one of the best in the Continental Army and easily the equivalent of the most elite British regulars. This unit played a seminal role in the upcoming battle at Guilford Court House. Among the militia, subsequent events demonstrated that the Virginians stood fairly solid and a vast improvement over those who had cut and run at Camden the previous summer. The North Carolinians proved to be disappointing, however, an oddity since they were fighting on their home ground. Earlier, General Morgan had read the temperament of militia against Cornwallis's regulars, both British and Provincial, stating to Greene that if the Patriot militia stood firm, he would win; if not, he would lose. Nonetheless, the numbers stood in Greene's favor, and he determined to take advantage. Despite the apparent numerical superiority, the commanding general never fully trusted the militia. He expressed this sentiment to Governor Jefferson, stating of these men that they "soon get tired out with difficulties, and go and come in such irregular bodies that I can make no calculations on the strength of my army."[41]

Despite his militia concern, Greene resolved to face the earl in a conventional battle. Accordingly, on the fourteenth he positioned his army near Guilford Court House in the spot he had reconnoitered several weeks previously; he regarded the site as good defensible ground and awaited the arrival of his nemesis. The terrain south of the courthouse undulated, with a good stand of pine trees and the occasional hardwoods. In the field to the south, known as Hoskins's Fields, a split-rail fence provided some cover for defending troops. More importantly, the cornfields, open and cleared, provided an excellent field of fire for the ill-disciplined and hotfooted Carolina militia. If Greene could replicate the militia's success at Cowpens, he would gain a singular advantage.

Cornwallis now had been out-reinforced. He could muster only 2,200 men fit for duty, although British regulars composed the bulk of his force. Nonetheless, harsh conditions, continuous marches, poor food, and the rigors of the campaign all told on the command. Having burned the baggage in Tryon County weeks earlier, his troops slept in the open or constructed crude brush shelters called "wigwams" and subsisted on turnips and green corn. In the forty-eight hours preceding the battle at Guilford, the men had hardly any rations at all. Foul, cold, wet weather with soaking rains sapped the energy of the most confident and hardy troops. Cornwallis knew that he could not long sustain this position; so too did Greene. The Patriot commander understood that time was of the essence. If he tarried, either Cornwallis would slip away or his irregulars and militia would abandon him for home and the spring planting. He must strike soon. Almost simultaneously, both forces started marching toward each other. On the thirteenth Cornwallis advanced to Quaker Meeting House at New Garden, twelve miles south of the courthouse. Greene's force then lay at the Speedwell Iron Works, a few miles north.

The following day each army moved into position, with Greene forming his lines just south of the courthouse as the British marched up the New Garden Road, the major transportation route between Charlotte, Salisbury, and Hillsborough. The fifteenth broke with an early spring frost as Tarleton advanced up the road, leading the army in two columns. The main body with the artillery composed the first column, while to the right came Colonel Hamilton's Provincials and a dragoon force. Leading up to the courthouse, the ground rose gradually from Little Horsepen Creek along the road. Flanked on both sides by heavy woods, the gently rolling landscape, partially covered in cornfields, provided excellent terrain for the movement of cavalry and linear infantry formations. The long slopes allowed for militia in the front line to move off to the flanks and rear without interfering with the fire and movements of subsequent lines. Taking Morgan's example from the Cowpens victory, Greene placed the least experienced militia in the first line astride the New Garden Road some 400 yards north of the creek and roughly a half mile south of the courthouse. These two brigades of North Carolina militiamen, totaling just over 1,000 men and commanded by Brig. Gen. John Butler and Col. Pinketham Eaton, had just joined the army on 10 March. Although welcome, Greene intended to utilize them as had Morgan at Cowpens in the hopes that their fire, though likely disjointed and uncoordinated, might cause some casualties in the advancing British line. Butler's men positioned themselves on the west side of the road and Eaton's on the east behind a fence line. To protect their flanks, and no doubt to boost the men's confidence, Greene positioned Washington's cavalry and some Delaware Continentals on their right and Lee's dragoons, with 200 of Campbell's King's Mountain veterans, on the left. In truth, the Patriot commander badly botched his tactical arrangement. Unlike Morgan's deployment at the Cowpens, Greene placed his three lines several hundred yards apart, thus the lines could not support each other. Additionally, the wooded terrain further isolated them from one another. In essence, then, there would be three separate engagements, each with different dynamics, as the Crown forces advanced.

Some 300 yards to the rear of the first line, Greene positioned the Virginia militia of Stevens and Lawson. Many of these men had served in previous engagements and had the advantage of experience over the North Carolinians. Additionally, their position in the second line lay in dense woods. While the cornfields of the first line provided a field of fire and operating space for the Patriots, it also offered excellent ground for the British line and cavalry to maneuver. But once the advancing redcoats reached the adjacent woods, this advantage for the defenders disappeared. Clearly, Greene expected much more from the Virginians in the second line. Northeast of the second line and a farther 500 yards back stood the Continentals under General Huger, just in front of the

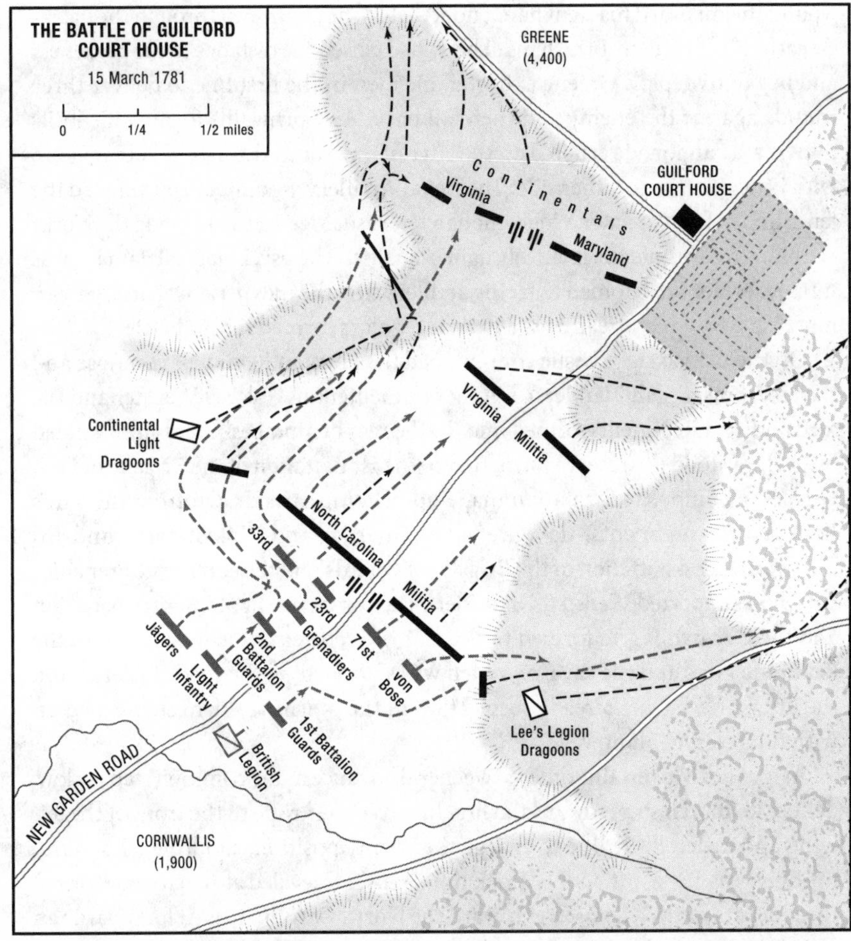


The Battle of Guilford Court House, 15 March 1781.
*Map by Erin Greb Cartography.*

courthouse where the land slopes down into a cleared area. These experienced troops of the Maryland, Delaware, and Virginia Continental Line formed the backbone of Greene's command and had seen the most action of any troops in the South. They would be a match for the best of the British line. Greene also posted two 6-pounder guns with the Marylanders. The open meadow below provided an excellent field of fire.

The first skirmish, involving Tarleton's advance guard and a patrol of Lee's dragoons, occurred roughly four miles south of the courthouse. Although the hasty midmorning encounter resulted in few casualties, Tarleton received a wound that maimed his right hand; nonetheless, he continued through the battle. By early afternoon, the British main body had closed the distance to the battlefield and began to deploy. Greene exhorted his men in the first line to deliver three rounds against the enemy and then fall back. As Cornwallis formed his units into line, a cannonade erupted on the edge of the woods that lasted half an hour, with little damage to either side. The Royal Artillery 3-pounders pummeled the fence line in front of Eaton's men, though few casualties accrued among the North Carolinians. Despite the relatively light casualties, the psychological damage was immense. Not accustomed to facing artillery fire, the inexperienced militiamen must have felt great dread as the British regulars formed line of battle.

On the British right Leslie commanded the Hessian Regiment von Bose and the 71st (Fraser's Highlanders). On the left Lieutenant Colonel Webster and the 23rd and 33rd Regiments formed line. To the rear behind Leslie and commanded by O'Hara stood the reserve formation of the 1st Battalion of the Brigade of Foot Guards, a composite formation made up of companies drawn from the three Foot Guards regiments—1st (Grenadier Guards), 2nd (Coldstream), and 3rd (Scots). The 2nd Battalion of the Brigade of Guards and the composite grenadier battalion supported Webster. On the left. The composite light infantry battalion and the German Jägers formed to the rear of Webster in the woods and to the left of the guns and the cavalry, which was stationed on the road. Tarleton and the dragoons, having already seen action in the morning skirmish, formed up with the reserve infantry.

At 1:30 P.M. Cornwallis ordered a general advance at the common step (a slow, deliberate march step) toward the first line. Webster rode to the front of the left wing and ordered the line to charge the enemy position, shouting, "Forward, my brave fusiliers!" At double quick time, muskets leveled at "Charge Bayonet," the redcoats hurled themselves toward the North Carolinians. At forty yards an unusual dynamic occurred. Generally, once a bayonet attack commences, forward momentum takes hold and the charge rolls forward in a hurly burly fashion. But, strangely, the advancing British line stopped, arms raised to the recover position (firelock with fixed bayonet raised vertically at the left shoulder). Lamb noted the unusual pause in the forward momentum. Much like the dreadful quiet before a tornado strikes, the advancing British line halted momentarily just yards from the North Carolina militia: "It was perceived the whole of their force had their arms presented, and resting on a rail fence. . . . [T]hey were taking aim with the nicest precision. At this awful period a general pause took place; both parties surveyed each other for the moment with the most anxious suspense."[42]

Leslie shouted orders to the troops, and the advance recommenced. At nearly point-blank range, the Carolinians fired off their first volley, doing great devastation to the British ranks. A return volley then plowed through the Patriot line. The second and third rebel volleys caused even greater devastation, but the regulars pressed forward. Against the British bayonets, the militia had no chance. Panic ensued as the infantry reached the fence line. Men raced for the woods. All efforts by their officers to form them into a cohesive unit and to fall back on the second line to support the Virginia militia failed as terrified men fled through the second line, unencumbering themselves of knapsacks, canteens, and weapons. Only a few men of Eaton's brigade recovered their nerve and formed up with Campbell's riflemen and Lee's Legion infantry on the flank to retire in good order. Cornwallis had won the engagement of the first line, but with significant casualties. The second line awaited.

Despite the flight of the first line's center, the flanks held steady. As the victorious British passed through, they received fire from Lee's Legion, Campbell's riflemen, and the Delaware Continentals. To counter the emergent threat, the British line wheeled to the left and right. Into the center came the 2nd Battalion Guards and the Guards Grenadiers, creating a horseshoe formation. Pushing ahead through the woods, O'Hara's 2nd Battalion, the 33rd, and the grenadiers drove Stevens's Virginia militia brigade out of their positions and back to the right, thus clearing the woods of rebels on the British left. The second line had been breached, though with similarly heavy British casualties. Meanwhile, the 23rd and 71st thrust up against the stouter Virginian left on the east side of the road. In a bold move Webster ordered his now-unengaged left wing to continue the advance on against the third line of Continentals. Accordingly, the 33rd, Guards Light Infantry, and Jägers drove forward. As individuals and small parties of Virginians emerged from the woods, it became apparent to the men drawn up on the road in front of the courthouse grounds that the second line had failed and that the following redcoats, though reduced by serious casualties, were taking dead aim at their position.

Greene had the fortunate advantage of having the 1st Maryland and the 5th Virginia Regiments in the third line facing Webster. These men would not flee from the redcoats then reforming their line on the wood's edge. Webster, however, had taken a bold gamble. Unsupported and with the British right wing still clearing the woods east of the road of the remaining Virginia militia, he had advanced to within forty yards of a stout enemy, unsupported on his flank and perilously overextended. The Continentals loosed a frightful volley that staggered the British advance. Sensing the danger, Webster executed a retrograde movement to the relative shelter of a ravine to await the British right wing and center. Had Greene ordered an immediate counterattack against the unsupported Webster, he might well have carried the day. He did not. Greene feared that the probable losses to his forces from such a strike would undercut his strategy of attrition. As each minute passed, chances for a stunning Patriot battlefield victory ebbed away. Meanwhile, in the woods a third bayonet charge finally cleared out the last of the Virginians, freeing the British right and center for action against the Continentals. Greene had lost his moment. The entire British line swung about to confront his third line.

In the attack on the third line, an extraordinary event occurred. The Guards 2nd Battalion, commanded by Lieutenant Colonel Duncan Stuart, faced the relatively inexperienced and newly recruited 2nd Maryland Regiment. Unlike their more veteran 1st Maryland counterparts, these men had not faced troops such as the Foot Guards. The raw Marylanders literally fled without firing a round, to the profound amazement of the advancing British. Seeing a momentary advantage created by the gap in the Continental line, the Guards surged forward. But, to their detriment, the Patriots reacted swiftly and decisively. In a simultaneous reaction to the Guards running into their line, the 1st Maryland wheeled about to face the threat while Washington rushed his dragoons into their exposed right flank. It is a maxim in linear warfare that to be outflanked generally meant destruction. In their zeal to have at the fleeing Marylanders, the Guards committed a horrendous tactical blunder. Stuart fell in the melee as did many of his men. O'Hara received a second wound that day but, though briefly surrounded by Continentals, escaped when several soldiers rushed to his defense. From a position several yards back, the Royal Artillery detachment under Lieutenant John McLeod had been firing grapeshot into the rebel ranks. As the Guards retreated under the dual envelopment of the 1st Maryland and the Continental dragoons, no doubt many suffered from this "friendly fire." Nonetheless, McLeod's cannonade broke up the Continental counterattack and allowed the 2nd Guards Battalion to escape the trap. Though wounded, O'Hara organized a retreat, and the bulk of the battalion escaped the rebel pincers. Seeing McLeod's now-exposed guns and Cornwallis nearby, Washington reformed his dragoons for a second charge. The earl immediately saw the danger and ordered McLeod to fire grapeshot at the advancing horsemen, a swift reaction that broke up the charge.[43]

At this point the battle disintegrated for Greene and the Continentals. His two best chances to destroy a sizeable portion of the opponent's forces—Webster's wing earlier and then the 2nd Guards—had been lost. Compounding the problem, Lee pulled his legionnaires from the battlefield as the Regiment von Bose oblique marched to the right (at an angle to the original direction of the forward advance so as to move laterally while maintaining the line facing the opponent). With no cover on his left flank, a furious Colonel Campbell reluctantly retired with his riflemen. The other unit facing these rebel forces, the 1st Guards Battalion, wheeled around to come in on the Continental left. With the survivors of the 2nd Guards Battalion on their right flank, the 23rd Foot advanced. The 2nd Battalion of the 71st coming up the road fell in on the Guards' right flank, and several hundred British troops surged forward toward the Continental position. Faced with the loss of all of his first- and second-line forces and pressed at all points by the weight of the entire British army, Greene ordered a retreat at roughly 3:30 P.M. Cornwallis attempted a pursuit, but his men, marching and fighting since before dawn with no food or rest, could not answer the order. Greene thus collected his forces and stragglers and made his way back to the camp at Troublesome Creek, out of danger and out of British reach. Cornwallis's casualties were horrendous. With ninety-three dead on the field, including Stuart, and 439 wounded, including O'Hara, Webster, and Tarleton, his army suffered 25-percent casualties, a devastating loss in any age of warfare. With military medicine still in a primitive state and made worse by the absence of adequate field care or hospitals, many of the wounded soon joined death's ranks. With seventy-eight killed in action, 183 wounded, and two guns captured by the Royal Welch Fusiliers, Greene's losses appeared much lighter. But when considering the hundreds of militia who fled—and thus could be counted as missing—overall Patriot casualties look astounding.

By the tenets of eighteenth-century warfare, Cornwallis had won the laurels of combat. The enemy retreated; he held the field. Total Patriot casualties of killed, wounded, and missing (again, however, mostly from local militia simply heading home rather than reporting for further duty), from a purely statistical viewpoint, seemed devastating. While perhaps a tactical triumph, from the strategic viewpoint, Guilford Court House represented yet another costly Crown victory. With nearly a quarter of his force killed or wounded, the earl had spent his power. He had failed to destroy Greene, as he had done to Gates at Camden. Many of his best troops lay dead or dying that early spring Carolina evening. Heavy rains soon soaked the red clay into thick mud. With no tents or food, the living suffered through a bitter night. Fifty more men died in the darkness, likely from exposure. No food was to be had by the survivors for a full forty-eight hours. Cornwallis sent his after-action report to both Lord Rawdon and Lord Germain on the seventeenth. What sounded on paper like a significant victory failed to capture the huge strategic problem now confronting the earl and his depleted and exhausted force.[44] On the day following the battle, the lieutenant general wrote an order to be read to his troops: "Lord Cornwallis desires the officers and Soldiers to accept of his warmest acknowledgments for their very extraordinary valour displayed by them in the action of yesterday; he will endeavor to do justice to their merit in his presentation to their Sovereign and the Commander-in-chief and shall consider it the greatest honour of his life to have been placed at the head of so gallant an army."[45]

Such complimentary words from a commander to his troops forms a critical aspect of that officer's moral authority. In this case, for a member of the peerage, the pinnacle of aristocracy, to address an eighteenth-century army, while not necessarily unusual, was certainly powerful. In this age the common public perception of the British soldier, however unfair and misguided, portrayed the typical recruit as a ne'er-do-well, vagrant, criminal, or worse who had no options other than to join the army. In fact, depending on the recruitment region for a particular regiment, the typical soldier might be a younger son of a yeoman farmer who, due to his junior position in the family, would not inherit property and thus a means of living. He might be a younger son of a tradesman or craftsman with older brothers more likely to take over the family business. For elite families, younger sons typically obtained a king's commission in either the army or the Royal Navy or opted for the clergy since, by primogeniture, the eldest son inherited the estate. In the Scottish Highlands, so valued was military service that the officer raising a unit personally selected the men—to not be chosen represented an immense embarrassment.[46]

Brigadier O'Hara captured the essence of the battered army after Guilford Court House. In a letter to his friend, the former prime minister the Duke of Grafton, he wrote:

> No zeal or courage is equal to the constant exertions we are making; Tho' you will not find it in the Gazette, every part of our army was beat repeatedly, on the 15th March, and were obliged to fall back twice. The Rebels were so exceedingly numerous, as to be constantly to oppose fresh troops to us, and to be in force to our Front, Flanks, and Rear: It is impossible to say too much in praise of our Officers and Men in a conflict that lasted near two hours, tho' so powerfully out-number'd, their Spirit and constancy never forsook them, and at length Crowned their manly exertions with Victory.[47]

Could Greene have destroyed Cornwallis had he ordered a final counterattack rather than retiring to safety? Perhaps. But there is the omnipresent "fog and friction" of warfare. Had the Patriot commander realized the extent of the British casualties, he might have ordered a shattering counterattack. Given his aggressive bent, Cornwallis, if placed in the same situation, might well have done so. Greene, on the other hand, was more of a strategic thinker than an operational artist. Tactically astute and effective in combat, Cornwallis always displayed a debilitating strategic obtuseness. While clearly not of the caliber of a Benedict Arnold or several other Continental Army senior officers tactically, Greene clearly demonstrated the most pronounced and critical strategic acumen of the entire conflict. Other historians might well argue this point, and fair enough—that is perhaps a debate for another venue. Nonetheless, Greene displayed profound strategic vision. Yes, he might well have destroyed the crippled British force had he known of its condition and had he ordered a counterattack. This proposition will remain in the great realm of the unknown. Despite what he may or may not have known at the moment, Greene understood that he had stood toe to toe with the most talented British field commander and against the most veteran, hardened, and skilled British army of the war; he had held his ground while inflicting serious damage. He also understood an overarching imperative of a successful Fabian strategy—do not allow the enemy the culminating battle until he has been sufficiently weakened. Greene's actions and orders to withdraw clearly indicate that he understood that imperative to preserve his force. In this regard, while Cornwallis may have tactically won the field that day, Greene clearly won the strategic victory. Guilford Court House came as a direct consequence of decisions made in late February—by Cornwallis to retire to Hillsborough and by Greene to recross the Dan and reengage. The battle was one in a chain of events set in motion by those decisions that led inexorably down the road to Yorktown. In London, when reports of the engagement finally reached the government in early June, the opposition leader Charles James Fox is reputed to have stated, "Another such victory will ruin the British Army."[48]

## "Sad and Fatal Effects": The Retreat to Wilmington

Faced with the consequences of the Race to the Dan and his inability to destroy Greene, Cornwallis now confronted a horrific choice that surely violated every notion of the offensive-minded Englishman: he must retreat. With the dead and dying all about him, with no rations and little chance for foraging parties to gather anything of value in the late winter in the face of roving Patriot bands, and with no prospect of reengaging the enemy, Cornwallis made his fateful decision to withdraw to Wilmington. His foresightedness in sending Craig to capture the port on the Cape Fear River now proved propitious. Nevertheless, two hundred miles across potentially hostile territory now faced the survivors. O'Hara captured the essence of the meaningless tactical victory at Guilford Court House and the inordinate British casualties. To Grafton he bemoaned the "sad and fatal effects" of the loss of British casualties that day.[49]

One hope shone brightly for some relief—the Scots Highlander settlements around Cross Creek. The Highlanders, who had raised hundreds of warriors five years earlier, might provide succor and hope despite their great losses at Moore's Creek Bridge. Essentially passive since that disaster, the Highlanders, still overwhelmingly Loyalist, might prove a salvation in the wilderness. The example of Captain Peter Carpenter, the only surviving company commander of the dramatic Loyalist defeat at Ramsour's Mill in June 1780, is instructive. Having recovered from his wound, Carpenter readily agreed to allow elements of Cornwallis's force to encamp on his plantation a few miles from the mill. But it being January and firewood a necessity, the soldiers chopped up a section of the Loyalist's split-rail fences. Carpenter was so incensed by that action that as soon as the British forces departed on their chase of Greene, he signed the "Oath of Allegiance to the State of North Carolina" and paid a hefty fine in cash and, interestingly, 520 pounds of fresh beef. He rebuilt his fences in stone—no mean feat in western North Carolina—determined to build a fence that the British could not burn down.[50] How many other Captain Carpenters existed among the formerly ardent southern Loyalists is unknown. But the probability that many Loyalists had simply given up the fight gets to the critical miscalculation inherent in British strategic thinking.

Accordingly, on 18 March, leaving behind the most seriously wounded to the care of British medical staff and Greene's surgeons, the army marched for the safety of the settlements at Cross Creek, the Cape Fear River, and ultimately Wilmington in search of rations, relief, and reinforcement. Greene immediately followed, sending Lee's Legion ahead to maintain contact with the retreating British. But the Patriot commander faced looming trouble himself. With the militia enlistments expiring, most of those men opted to return to their homes, a quite understandable mindset given that spring-planting time had arrived. Greene now faced a dilemma: should he continue the harassment of Cornwallis or break off the action? He opted for the latter and on 29 March informed Washington in New Windsor, New York, of his decision to advance into South Carolina to confront Lord Rawdon and threaten Charleston. Greene proposed to force Cornwallis to abandon North Carolina to defend his posts in the lower Carolina. Such a move would free North Carolina officials to raise men for military service without fear of British actions. The Rhode Islander pointed out that such a move "is warranted by the soundest reasons both political and military."[51] To mask his intentions and keep his movements invisible to Cornwallis, though, he kept Lee engaged in harassment operations, giving the impression of continued pursuit. The ruse worked—the earl retreated toward safety.

Cornwallis drove his exhausted army across the Carolina Piedmont. With the decision to retreat made, a numerically superior enemy in the field close at hand, and a starving army in unfriendly territory, Cornwallis dared not tarry. Arriving at Cross Creek on 1 April, the army found little relief. No supplies had been moved up from the coast, while few of the local Highlanders joined the force. The bedraggled army pressed on toward Wilmington along the King's Highway, parallel to and along the west bank of the Cape Fear River, arriving a week later, exhausted and hungry. The trip had been appalling. Faced with little food or time to forage, soldiers broke into homes along the way and plundered whatever could be hauled away, sparing neither Loyalist nor Patriot. Cornwallis summed up the difficulties upon reaching Wilmington, informing the American secretary that "provisions were scarce, not four days' forage within twenty miles—and to us the navigation of the Cape Fear River to Wilmington impracticable, for the distance by water is upwards of a hundred miles, the breadth seldom above one hundred yards, the banks high [among other things, affording concealment to harassing Patriots], and the inhabitants on each side generally hostile."[52]

More wounded died along the line of march, including Lieutenant Colonel Webster, who had received wounds to his arms and a leg at Guilford. Cornwallis grieved for the loss of one of his closest friends and most talented subordinate commanders. Lamb reported that Webster's death so grieved Cornwallis that on receiving the report, the earl turned and looked at his sword, exclaiming, "I have lost my scabbard."[53]

The army arrived in Wilmington on 7 April. For several days, Cornwallis attended to administrative matters, such as arranging for prisoner exchanges with Greene and promotions and transfers for officers, while the army recovered its fighting strength and soldiers healed wounds. O'Hara, wounded twice in the chest and thigh, recovered sufficiently to return to duty. Cornwallis considered his various strategic options. By mid-April, the growing dispute between Clinton and the earl over where the main combat operations should occur became apparent. In a report to Lord Germain, Clinton hinted, however subtly, at the festering discord. The CinC cautioned the secretary, "I cannot agree to the Opinion given me by Lord Cornwallis . . . that the Chesapeak [*sic*] should become the Seat of War even if necessary at the expense of abandoning New York: as I must ever regard this post to be of the utmost Consequence."[54] The fact that Cornwallis reported directly to Germain from Wilmington as well as to Clinton as indicated by his letter of 18 April illustrates the growing strategic incoherence characterized by the breakdown in unity of command. From a purely military standpoint, for a field commander to report directly to the political authority while on campaign injects an element of uncertainty and, more critically, undercuts unity of command and effort. The earl's next move—the march into Virginia—broke open the simmering disagreement between the CinC in New York and his field commander regarding the follow-on course of action and the proper utilization of Cornwallis's diminished, but still viable, field force. By the early summer, the rift threatened not only the Southern Campaign's objectives but also British dominion over its North American colonies.

The campaign in North Carolina had come to naught. Hundreds of slain Loyalists, Provincials, and British regulars attested to the strategic defeat. While resting his army at Wilmington, Cornwallis captured two of the fundamental problems facing British efforts in the south in a 10 April letter to Major General Phillips, who would soon depart for operations in Virginia in the final phase of the Southern Campaign: "I have had a most difficult and dangerous campaign and was obliged to fight a battle two hundred miles from any communication. . . . The idea of our friends rising in any number and to any purpose totally failed, as I expected; and here I am, getting rid of my wounded and refitting my troops at Wilmington."[55]

Further illustrating the unraveling of the Loyalist strategy, Clinton remarked to Lord Germain that the North Carolina invasion was made "in the hope that Lord Cornwallis's Success amongst out Friends in North Carolina, which was the principal Object of his March into that Province, would have been such as to have restored it, and South Carolina to Tranquility."[56]

The faulty net assessment by British authorities at all levels as to the viability of a military strategy based on Loyalist support had become strikingly apparent by the time Cornwallis's exhausted, hungry, and ragged troops limped into Wilmington. The earl must surely have regretted burning his baggage at Ramsour's Mill in January and the attempt to chase Greene without adequate supply or access to seaborne logistical support. At least he now acknowledged that dynamic, which explains his willingness to stay close to the coast and to follow readily Clinton's orders to establish a naval operating base on the Chesapeake.

In terms of the Loyalist strategy's failure in the Carolinas, with the costly victory at Guilford Court House and the inability to destroy Greene's force, Cornwallis acknowledged the obvious in a letter to Lord Germain two days after the battle justifying his actions in light of the overall strategic objective. He had gone into the fight convinced that a resounding battlefield victory would finally rouse the Loyalists to action and that "it would be impossible to succeed in that great object of our campaign, the calling forth [of] the numerous loyalists of North Carolina, whilst a doubt remained on their minds of the superiority of our arms."[57] In seeking a purely tactical military decision, Cornwallis again displayed his striking lack of an overarching strategic vision. He had operationalized the British strategy, assuming that tactical skill and operational artistry would win the day and reverse Crown fortunes. Clearly a man of tremendous energy, courage, and dogged determination, much beloved by his troops and inherently bold and daring, Cornwallis lacked that one essential element—the ability to visualize the larger strategic picture. Greene, on the other hand, while not as tactically talented as the earl, nonetheless, possessed that vision. With the Race to the Dan and the Guilford Court House fight, Cornwallis had risked all and lost. He had drawn to an inside straight, but the better cards lay in the opponent's hand.

## "In Quest of Adventures," April 1781

Cornwallis now faced a monumental strategic decision. He had essentially three options. One would be to wait at Wilmington and restore his spent force to good health and then evacuate by sea. The North Atlantic hurricane season technically begins about early June, but the most dangerous periods are August and September. Therefore, he had several weeks to restore his fighting strength and allow the walking wounded to fully recover. From Wilmington by sea, he could make sail for Charleston so as to move inland in support of Lord Rawdon, holding the critical post at Camden. This action might nullify Greene, but it would be an expression of defeat, something the earl's character and personality could not abide. The sacrifices had been too great to admit that the struggles through the Carolinas had been all for naught and to essentially start the process over again. On the other hand, this course likely would ensure that South Carolina could be preserved and defended. Greene would not have the forces available to confront the combined strength of Rawdon and Cornwallis and most likely would have had to retreat back into North Carolina or even Virginia, thus ensuring a stalemate. Some subordinate officers viewed this option differently. O'Hara stated that once Greene entered South Carolina, "a general Revolt will take place and we shall certainly lose the Carolinas for ever. . . . I believe we shall endeavor to join Major General Phillips who is said to be at Petersbourg at the Head of the Jame's [*sic*] River in Virginia."[58]

Another alternative for an evacuation by sea would be to make sail for the Chesapeake for operations in that region. Clinton had already made it clear that he intended some form of actions there, and his dispatch of Leslie, Arnold, and Phillips into Virginia so indicated. With Cornwallis safely in the Tidewater at Portsmouth, Norfolk, or up the James River closer to Richmond and Petersburg, the British could launch the longed-for culmination of the Southern Campaign—the conquest of Virginia. With the French still enjoying the Newport summer and Washington near New York, if the garrison could checkmate any Franco-American interference, Cornwallis, reinforced and refreshed, might run wild in Virginia without serious Continental opposition. Once secured, Rawdon from South Carolina and Cornwallis coming down from Virginia might well regain the strategic initiative against Greene. With his main sources of supply and reinforcements from the middle colonies and Virginia cut off, the Rhode Islander would wither on the vine. Evacuation by sea and a subsequent amphibious landing in the Chesapeake Bay presented a viable and strategically sound option. It combined the traditional advantages of joint army-navy expeditionary warfare, which had proven so effective against New York, Charleston, and Savannah.

A different option for the earl lay overland. Wilmington is only a few day's march from Camden or Charleston. Once recovered by May or June, the army could march south and rendezvous with Rawdon for operations against Greene and the South Carolina partisans. Some strategic analysts have interpreted this move as dangerous and overly risky, claiming that there were too many rivers to cross between Wilmington and Camden. The opportunity for Greene to ambush Cornwallis at a crossing seemed high. This interpretation, frankly, does not stand up to scrutiny. The advantages that Greene enjoyed were interior lines of communication. Anything north of South Carolina represented interior lines for him. The Patriot commander had the ability to scout out the terrain and more importantly stage boats and ferry craft, leaving the British to mutter obscenities from the opposite bank. No such advantage accrued to Greene should he try to interdict and ambush Cornwallis's advance. To do so meant crossing in between the two main British forces. Cornwallis also enjoyed a direct line of march to either Charleston or Camden, while Greene, starting from a more westerly position, likely could not conceal his movements, thus negating any sort of ambush. Alternately, Cornwallis could travel by sea, negating any confrontation with Greene; in fact, on 24 April he ordered Balfour in Charleston to send transport boats to Wilmington. Perhaps this action represented an operational deception since, without a doubt, Greene would soon hear of the departure of the craft from Charleston. Whether this thought occurred to Cornwallis or not, the effect would be to freeze Greene in place, preventing him from moving north with a superior force to intercept Cornwallis or place Wilmington under siege. And the transports could ferry the sick, wounded, and invalids back to more secure Charleston, thus freeing Cornwallis from the burden of medical care and thus increasing his mobility.

As to Greene and his move into South Carolina, he did have a head start, having departed the Guilford area in early April. But should he attempt to besiege Camden, he risked an Alesia sort of double siege, with Rawdon at Camden playing the role of Vercingetorix to Greene's Julius Caesar. He would surely have to withdraw before Cornwallis arrived. Then, combined with Rawdon's force, the numerical odds would again favor the earl, with Greene well outside his interior lines of communication. Should Cornwallis have taken this option? Perhaps. But again, to do so meant admitting that Greene had won the day and that the sacrifices in North Carolina were for naught. Cornwallis was unlikely to pursue this course.

The final option lay in a march north toward Virginia and, in combination with the forces already present there, wreak destruction on that vital colony. If Virginia fell, the Crown would be in a position to negotiate a settlement with the remaining rebellious colonies. From a strategic-coherence viewpoint, this option aligned with Clinton's concepts of the appropriate operations. Cornwallis thought the same. While he might have chaffed at abandoning North Carolina, he proposed that "a serious attempt upon Virginia would be the most solid plan, because successfull [*sic*] operations might not only be attended with important consequences there but would tend to the security of South Carolina and ultimately the submission of North Carolina."[59]

The earl reasoned that the key to controlling the Carolinas lay in cutting off supplies and reinforcements coming through Virginia. He would later justify this thread in his strategic thinking in a report from Williamsburg in late June 1781, after he had left North Carolina and marched into Virginia, by informing Clinton that "the men and riches of Virginia [are] furnishing ample supplies to the rebel southern army."[60] But before then, by 23 April he had received firm intelligence that Greene had indeed marched into South Carolina, clearing the way for his army to move north without interference. Cornwallis decided to make for the Old Dominion. With a badly mauled force, he dared not engage Greene again in an open battle, but had expressed the opinion to Clinton that the key to victory in the Carolinas lay in Virginia.[61] In essence, the earl simply moved his spatial orientation northward. If in his strategic concept the conquest of North Carolina would have meant starving the South Carolina Patriots of reinforcements and logistics, why would not the same dynamic apply to Virginia? He could not wait for new orders from Clinton and made preparations for the march north. Departing Wilmington on the twenty-fifth, he was determined to make Virginia the seat of war. In so doing, the earl set in motion the last great act of the War of American Independence and unleashed the gremlin of strategic incoherence on his road north. Virginia, then, became his next target. In a moment of candor as he departed Wilmington, Cornwallis wrote, "our experience has shown that their [Loyalists] numbers are not so great as had been represented and that their friendship was only passive: For we have received little assistance from them since our arrival . . . and altho' I gave the strongest and most publick assurances that . . . I should return to the upper Country [Piedmont and Hillsborough areas], not above two hundred have been prevailed upon to follow us either as Provincials or Militia."[62]

Cornwallis expressed his frustration and obvious impatience in a letter to Major General Phillips. The exasperated earl showed again his natural inclination for aggressive, decisive action: "Now, my dear friend, what is our plan? Without one we cannot succeed. . . . If we mean an offensive war in America, we must abandon New York and bring our whole force into Virginia; we then have a state to fight for, and a successful battle may give us America. If our plan is defensive, mixed with desultory expeditions, let us quit the Carolinas . . . and stick to our salt pork at New York, sending now and then a detachment to steal tobacco."[63]

References to New York, desultory operations, and sticking to one's rations clearly slapped at Clinton's strategic concept and Cornwallis's view of his more defensive-minded superior. The letter illustrates the growing rift between the two officers that by June became full-blown antagonism. In a more diplomatic tone, as would be expected from a junior to a senior officer, Cornwallis said essentially the same thing to Clinton, but the prodding for a more offensive orientation is quite clear. Clinton no doubt chaffed at the veiled assault on his leadership and lack of offensive spirit. In a letter penned the same day as the note to Phillips, Cornwallis chided the CinC: "I am very anxious to receive your Excellency's commands, being as yet totally in the dark as to the intended operations of the summer. I cannot help expressing my wishes that the Chesapeak [*sic*] may become the Seat of War. . . . Until Virginia is in a manner subdued, our hold of the Carolinas must be difficult, if not precarious."[64] In truth, on his own accord, two weeks later Cornwallis led his troops north toward the Old Dominion and, like it or not for Clinton, made Virginia the "Seat of War," an action that soon brought ruin to British North America.

While Cornwallis made for Wilmington, Greene marched to South Carolina with 2,600 men, almost two-thirds of them Continentals. The last of his forces departed the Guilford area on 2 April. His plan called for cooperation with local partisans. Correspondence went out to the major leaders, including Pickens, Sumter, and Marion. Close, coordinated operations would characterize the war in South Carolina and along the Georgia border in 1781 and 1782. The cumulative effect of these activities by the time of the Yorktown Campaign in Virginia would be the almost complete loss of British control over the South, with the exception of Savannah and Charleston, and the utter unhinging of the Southern Strategy.

The British strategic disadvantage as of April 1781 now burgeoned as the controversy over the earl's advance into Virginia and the Chesapeake further poisoned relations between Cornwallis and Clinton. With it came the utter breakdown of British unity of command, unity of effort, strategic cohesion, and strategic leadership, with decisive results for America's future. Before departing Wilmington, an exasperated earl declared, "I am tired of marching about the country in quest of adventures."[65] More specifically, Greene's successful implementation of a Fabian strategy undid Cornwallis's invasion and set him on the road to Virginia and disaster. The frustration in the British inability to counter the Patriot's Fabian strategy shows in the observations of an anonymous British officer: "As we go forward into the country the rebels fly before us, and when we come back they always follow us. Tis almost impossible to catch them. They will never fight nor totally run away, but keep at such a distance that we are always a day's march from them. We seem to be playing at Bo Peep."[66]

On 25 April 1781 Cornwallis and his army marched north toward Tidewater Virginia, crossing the Roanoke River on 13 May. British major military operations finally moved to the Chesapeake, the final seat of war. With the decision to abandon North Carolina, Cornwallis, like another highly aggressive, bold, and risk-taking commander two thousand years earlier, had crossed his Rubicon.

CHAPTER 5

# "WHAT IS DONE, CANNOT NOW BE ALTERED"

## *THE SOUTHERN CAMPAIGN DRAWS TO A CLOSE*

Many controversies and questions surround the actual operational execution of the Southern Campaign, among them the question of what might have occurred had Rear Admiral Thomas Graves won the Virginia Capes engagement of 5–9 September 1781. What if Cornwallis had managed to evacuate his force to Gloucester Point and thus negate the Franco-American siege at Yorktown? What if Clinton had not issued the damning proclamations of May and June 1780? But perhaps the most heated controversy surrounds Cornwallis's decision soon after Guilford Court House to strike out for Virginia rather than return to South Carolina. This move initiated the campaign's final phase, which ended in October with the Yorktown surrender, and revealed a severe lack of strategic coherence between the triad of Lord Germain, Clinton, and Cornwallis. This dynamic has come to be known as the "Clinton-Cornwallis Controversy," which broke out in the press and public arena following the generals' return to Britain. The argument inspired a lively public debate between the two men as to the greater responsibility for the debacle in Virginia. In a series of articles in the press and pamphlets, the two officers argued for months. Ultimately, public and official opinion sided with Cornwallis. The debate again emerged in the late nineteenth century when the American historian Benjamin Franklin Stevens transcribed the body of this printed material in a two-volume edition appropriately titled *Clinton-Cornwallis Controversy Growing Out of the Campaign in Virginia, 1781*. In the twentieth century various historians tended to side with whichever commander they favored; even now, the argument still rages. Despite all the agonizing over where ultimate blame lay, the central issue for analysis is not determining who was mainly responsible, rather it lies in determining what effect the decisions of each player in the drama—Clinton, Cornwallis, and

Germain—played on the breakdown of strategic coherence and the attendant loss of unity of command and control.

## A New Seat of War: Virginia, 1781

By mid-April, Cornwallis determined to advance into Virginia and saw offensive operations there as the key to victory in the South. Major General Phillips arrived in the Chesapeake in late March, which gave Cornwallis hope for a successful campaign. Of his decision to march north, he informed Lord Germain that, given the minimal North Carolina Loyalist turnout and the difficult terrain, "cut with numberless Creeks & rivers and the total want of navigation, which renders it impossible for our army to remain long in the heart of the Country, [it] will make it very difficult to reduce this province [North Carolina] to obedience by a direct Attack upon it."[1]

It is interesting to note that Cornwallis finally acknowledged the logistical problems he had created for his force by the movement into the Carolina frontier as opposed to operations along the coast. Perhaps he counted too heavily on supplies provided by the Loyalists, which by April he realized would not be forthcoming. In this light he does show some measure of the ability to make strategic reassessments, a necessity for a strategic decision maker given the nature of war, with interactivity and adaptation as fundamental dynamics. He further stated to the secretary: "I take the liberty of giving it as my opinion that a serious attempt upon Virginia would be the most solid plan, because successful operations might not only be attended with important consequences there, but would tend to the security of South Carolina, & ultimately to the submission of North Carolina."[2]

Yet in this endeavor lay the seeds of strategic catastrophe, as the offensive-minded Cornwallis clashed with the more cautious Clinton over the focus and direction of Virginia operations. In truth, Clinton had his own command-and-control problems as Germain put pressure on him to mount offensive operations southward: "I doubt not that you will avail yourself of his [Washington's] weakness, and your own great superiority, to send a considerable force to the head of the Chesapeak [*sic*], as soon as the season will permit operations to be carried out in that quarter. I flatter myself the southern provinces will be recovered to his Majesty's obedience before the long-promised succours . . . can arrive from France."[3] Germain made the point even more forcefully in May, stating to Clinton that "it was a great mortification to me to find . . . your ideas of the importance of recovering that province [Virginia] to be so different from mine."[4] With the situation in constant flux, a more or less uncontrollable field commander, and the threat of Washington and the French, Clinton, ever cautious, decided not to commit further forces to the southern effort despite pressure from Whitehall. Indeed, in his letter of 13 April, the senior commander hinted that he did not intend to move the seat of war to the Chesapeake.[5]

On 25 April Cornwallis, with his force of just over 1,400 men, marched out of Wilmington and headed north to Virginia. The march represented a major diversion and further strained his already rocky command relations with Clinton. In heading for Virginia rather than returning to Charleston by either land or sea, Cornwallis stretched his original orders far beyond Clinton's original intent. The earl justified his actions by expressing fear that Major General Greene, now operating in South Carolina, would march north to cut his lines of communication with Phillips in the Virginia Tidewater. To add to the growing discord, he departed Wilmington without direct orders to do so, which would be required of any substantial movement when the initial operational imperative, that of defending Charleston and the South Carolina and Georgia posts, had changed. But had it changed? In his departing orders from Charleston, Clinton had given the "outlines of [his] intentions where your Lordship is likely to bear a part." The CinC informed the general: "When your Lordship has finished your campaign [to pacify South Carolina], you will be better able to judge what is necessary to be done to secure the south and recover North Carolina. . . . [A]fter leaving a sufficient force in garrison in Charlestown . . . , I should wish you to assist in operations which will certainly be carried on in Chesapeak [*sic*] as soon as we are relieved from our apprehensions of a superior fleet and the season will admit of them in that climate."[6] Granted, a commander's intent is typically long on broad-brush strategic objectives and short on operational details. One can see from these orders how Cornwallis might broadly interpret his scope of action. To Clinton, the Chesapeake meant establishing a presence that could control the narrow strip of land between the bay and mountains (the Delaware Neck) to interdict supplies and reinforcements flowing from the North into the Carolinas. It also would establish a safe haven for Loyalists from which to conduct operations against Virginia, Delaware, and Maryland Patriot interests. Clearly, Clinton did not mean to move the seat of war from New York to Virginia, yet Cornwallis's taking the commander's intent to the ultimate interpretation of his operational prerogatives did exactly that. Thus, the breakdown in British strategic coherence and unity of command and effort worsened as the earl's devastated army marched north out of Wilmington.

From Clinton's perspective, operational execution of his plans called for a slow, methodical, and deliberate advance northward along the coast, with naval support assured. Moves up the Cape Fear River maintained the sea link and allowed for a rendezvous with potentially powerful Loyalist forces at Cross

Creek. As the coastal plain and Tidewater regions became pacified, inland operations would tamp down Patriot activities and restore royal control. From there, detachments from Cornwallis's command could cooperate with forces sent from New York in a pincer movement on the Chesapeake Bay. Assuming that Germain sent reinforcements to America, a dubious hope based on actions to date, Clinton would then move against Pennsylvania and trap Washington between two large forces. Failing reinforcements, the CinC intended to establish a forward operating base on the Chesapeake from which the Royal Navy could operate. New York and Charleston anchored these operations. In gradually pacifying areas from an expanding arc emanating out from Charleston, Wilmington, and the Chesapeake station, Loyalist sanctuaries would be established, Loyalists encouraged to turn out in numbers, and territory regained for the Crown. In theory, Clinton's operational concept captured the essentials of the "clear and hold" strategy, had much merit, and could be accomplished given the resources. But it required patience and, above all, superb operational command and control. Cornwallis, though, was anything but a patient man, and so the specter of strategic incoherence reared up almost immediately. The Camden victory injected a caustic element of "victory fever" into the earl's plans. Rather than sticking to the coastal route, he chose to march toward the North Carolina Piedmont and Charlotte, a move that ultimately resulted in King's Mountain, followed by Cowpens. Cornwallis argued that bringing forces near the coastal lowlands and tidewater marshes prior to winter risked debilitation by rampant disease. Yet even subordinate officers questioned the earl's decision. Tarleton, for example, argued for the Cape Fear move to establish water communications prior to an inland advance, but his headstrong commander chose otherwise.[7]

Strategic incoherence emanated from the top. Germain, loathe to issue definitive orders, shied away from such commands to his CinC in New York. Rather, he issued vague suggestions about the preferred strategy and resultant operations. Instead of either sending definitive orders or establishing broad strategic objectives—the role of the civil authority in a properly functioning civil-military relationship—he split the middle, never directly ordering Clinton to conduct specific operations or providing his commander with realistic, achievable strategic guidance. Germain operated in a different world reality, claiming that Crown forces would soon retake Virginia and that Washington's army lay on the verge of disintegration. As another example, he counted troops as present and fit for duty simply based on muster reports, blissfully ignoring the reality that, at any given moment, up to a third of the army lay ill with all manner of sicknesses and maladies. Decisions more properly determined at the field level were made in Whitehall and transmitted through vague messages. Indecisiveness reigned. Cabinet-level decision making in Lord North's government typically drifted month to month, and no definitive guidance crossed the Atlantic. For example, a replacement for the irascible Vice Admiral Arbuthnot and the sending of reinforcements to Clinton are decisions that should have been made swiftly by the cabinet. They were not. As this strategic drift worsened in early 1781, from Clinton to Cornwallis and Germain to Clinton, events in Virginia started the march toward disaster for the royal cause. The strategic triad irrevocably shattered.

A critical step in Clinton's Chesapeake plan included sending Brigadier Arnold into Virginia to conduct raids and establish an initial operating post on the bay, most likely at Portsmouth, Virginia, and conduct raids into the hinterland. Arnold would take up the task initially assigned to Major General Leslie. In response to the British presence at Portsmouth and concerns for Virginia's safety, Washington detached Maj. Gen. Gilbert du Motier, the marquis de Lafayette in late February with 1,200 Continentals to confront Arnold. These troops provided the dynamic for the growing conflict as the summer progressed and forces on both sides collected and increased. In early February a small flotilla of French warships commanded by Captain le Gardeaur de Tilly departed Newport for operations in Hampton Roads against the small Royal Navy force covering and supporting Arnold. Although the force encountered no opposition—the British ships had moved up the Elizabeth River into shallow water—the trend of an increasing French naval focus on the Chesapeake Bay already existed. Additionally, Washington and General Jean Baptiste de Donatien de Vimeur, the comte de Rochambeau started consultations that led to the Franco-American operation against Cornwallis in the autumn. At this time, the two commanders agreed to send 1,200 French troops to Virginia in support of Lafayette. But Arbuthnot, still on the American station and sortieing out of Lynnhaven Bay near Norfolk on 16 March, engaged the French force ferrying these men off the Chesapeake Capes. While the Royal Navy suffered more damage than their French opponents, the brief action caused the French squadron to return to Rhode Island with the troops. In this first significant combat of the Virginia Campaign, the advantage lay with the Crown's forces. But perhaps more importantly, the French finally recognized the criticality of active engagement with the British and cooperation in combined operations with the Patriot forces. As Cornwallis and his meager army trod across North Carolina toward Virginia, they had no idea of the coalescence of forces now coming together and aimed at their destruction.

In response to the French attempt to reinforce Virginia, Clinton dispatched 2,000 British troops under Phillips to reinforce Arnold. A force of twenty warships ferried the men to Hampton Roads. Phillips's orders carried the germ of the coming disaster. In addition to supporting Arnold and placing himself under Cornwallis's command, he was to harass rebel positions, interdict supplies, and establish a defensible post on the Chesapeake from which ships of the line could anchor and operate. A week before the earl departed Wilmington, Phillips commenced his raiding activities, directed initially at Richmond. Attempting to impede Phillips's advance, a large force of Virginia militia engaged the marauding British near Petersburg. After a sharp fight, the redcoats drove off the Virginians and commenced a destructive raid, concentrating on foodstuffs and tobacco. Ordered by Cornwallis to rendezvous at Petersburg, Phillips occupied the town, where he died of typhus on 15 May, five days before the earl arrived. The British had lost yet another superior senior commander, and for Cornwallis, a close friend. Adding to the usual campaign difficulties, Phillips had found Arbuthnot as obstreperous and difficult to work with as had Clinton. Until the navy could guarantee security from French activities in the Chesapeake, British actions in Virginia had to be cautious. Arbuthnot seemed unwilling or unable to pursue French naval forces, either at Newport or in the bay. To the army commanders, the vice admiral represented a hindrance, not a help.

Cornwallis had executed a fait accompli. The earl sent word of his plan to Clinton only after arriving at Petersburg, almost a hundred miles into Virginia from North Carolina. In his mind a retreat now back toward Charleston or even Wilmington would be a major psychological blow to British pride and morale. Given his personality, Cornwallis was not likely to take such a step unless ordered or forced to do so. In May 1781 neither possibility seemed likely. Clinton reluctantly acquiesced: "what is done, cannot now be altered: and as your Lordship has thought proper to make this decision, I shall most gladly avail myself of your very able assistance in carrying on such operations as you shall judge best in Virginia."[8] Nevertheless, the CinC reiterated that he had varied his instructions to other forces at various times in reaction to Cornwallis's situation. While strategic reassessment is a necessity, the problem for the British in 1781 lay in the fact that the commander and his subordinate worked at cross-purposes and had a differing concept of the desired strategic effects—in fact, of the exact object of the campaign. This deteriorating relationship starkly illustrates the problem of unity of command and effort and the disastrous unraveling of British strategic coherence. Cornwallis strongly asserted that Virginia had become the essential battleground, repeating in his 26 May letter from Petersburg, "if offensive war is intended, Virginia appears to me, to be the only Province, in which it can be carried on, and in which there is a stake, but to reduce the province and keep possession of the country a considerable army would be necessary."[9]

While the earl believed Virginia to be the focal point of the war, Clinton still advocated a thrust against Philadelphia. It is odd as to why he would consider the recapture of that city as a war winner, given that he not only took part in the previous Pennsylvania Campaign of 1777 but also commanded the evacuation of the city in 1778, when Washington's meager and starving army represented the only opposition. Now, however, General Rochambeau sat at Newport with thousands of excellent, well-trained, and well-equipped French troops. In essence, by diluting forces for a move on Philadelphia, Clinton might as well trade New York for Philadelphia. Unless he intended or hoped to draw out the enemy into a decisive engagement, the CinC's fixation on Philadelphia is mystifying in retrospect unless his long-range plan encompassed establishing coastal enclaves built around the control of key ports such as Philadelphia, Annapolis, New York, Savannah, Charleston, Wilmington, Norfolk, and perhaps even Boston. Lord Barrington, then secretary at war, had proposed such a strategy, with naval command of the seas enforcing an economic blockade and commerce control in the rebellion's early years. An enclave strategy had the salutary effect of providing a protected area for Loyalists as well as the ability of Crown authorities to support their business and industry while hampering rebels outside the protected areas. But both the king and Germain preferred the iron-fisted, crush-the-rebellion-by-brute-force approach; thus, the coastal-enclave idea died swiftly. While this plan might have provided a viable strategic alternative by the summer of 1781 and might have given Britain a much stronger bargaining position in any treaty negotiations, there is no evidence to suggest that Clinton had this strategic approach in mind with the assault on Philadelphia and control of the Chesapeake.

For him, with Cornwallis now in Virginia, there still existed strategic possibilities. If the earl could disrupt communications and logistics flowing south to Greene, he might still save Charleston and South Carolina. If Cornwallis moved farther north into Maryland, Clinton might finally close off the Delaware Neck. Alternately, he could leave a small army in Virginia and pull troops back to New York for operations against Washington and the French in Rhode Island. While some strategic options remained, at the heart of it, Clinton still opposed major operations in Virginia and had no real hope for substantial Loyalist support there. As late as mid-June, he argued against such a course: "experience ought to convince us, that there is no possibility of restoring Order in any rebellious Province . . . without the hearty Assistance of numerous friends. These my Lord: I think are not to be found in Virginia. . . . [T]hey are not to be found in great numbers anywhere else, Or that their exertions, when found, will answer our expectations. . . . [T]hey are gone from us, and I fear, are not to be recovered."[10] Here is the ultimate expression of the "clear and hold" strategy's complete failure, and indeed, that of the entire Southern Strategy's foundations of reliance on Loyalist turnout. With the lack of faith in future positive results from offensive operations in Virginia, the CinC continued: "I beg leave to recommend it to you, as soon as you have finished your active operations you may now be engaged in, to take a defensive station in any healthy situation you chuse [*sic*] (be it at

Williamsburg or York Town). And I would wish in that case that, after reserving to yourself such troops as you may judge necessary for an ample defensive and desultory movements . . . for the purpose of annoying the enemy's communications, destroying magazines, etc, . . . [troops] may be sent to me in succession as you can spare them."[11]

Clearly, by early June, Clinton intended to withdraw into a defensive mode and to simply react to enemy movements while defending New York and Charleston and conducting minor harassment operations in the Chesapeake using a defended naval station as the operating base—Portsmouth or Yorktown as suggested by his correspondence to Cornwallis. Like it or not, his subordinate's aggressive actions had forced the CinC's hand. It should be noted that Clinton never directly ordered Cornwallis to fortify Yorktown specifically, despite the earl's later claims. He did, however, direct him to establish a suitable defensive post capable of supporting a naval station on the bay. Assumptions can be deadly. The concept of a naval operating base assumed that Britain would maintain command of the sea in the theater, which ultimately proved a false hope.

Cornwallis, to his credit, finally realized the vacancy of a strategy calling for holding and defending multiple inland posts. Not only did he accept that such isolated posts could not be held and that North Carolina remained unconquerable, but he also proposed a concentration of forces in Virginia to destroy the enemy in detail as the best option. The logic of this position called for annihilating Lafayette, thus cutting off Greene from sustainment from the north and allowing Crown forces in South Carolina to give the Rhode Islander a merry chase. From there, British forces could mount a coordinated pincer movement against Washington, finishing with a joint army-navy operation against the French in Newport. When the center of gravity is considered, the rebellion could continue indefinitely so long as a viable force of the Continental Army remained in the field; it could not long survive the army's elimination, a fact that Washington and the more sensible politicians in Philadelphia understood all too well. To further explore this counterfactual argument, even though Cornwallis had suffered grievous casualties in the Carolinas, had he and Clinton agreed on the Virginia concept and implemented this strategic option, Crown arms would have, in a mere year and a half, destroyed three Southern Department major field forces (Lincoln at Charleston, Gates at Camden, and Lafayette in Virginia) and neutralized the remaining one (Greene in South Carolina). From this point, Washington would be vulnerable to attack from two directions by an army filled with hardened combat veterans charged with victory. While it is interesting to explore such strategic alternatives, the simple matter is that, again, Clinton and Cornwallis worked at cross-purposes; thus, the loss of the ever-critical unity of command and effort ensured the coming disaster at Yorktown.

While Cornwallis lacked the necessary strategic vision needed to carry him through to victory, this statement captures the essence of one of the great blunders of overall British strategic thought and decision making. In assuming that a city, in this case Philadelphia, represented the center of gravity for the rebels, the loss of which would induce them to negotiate terms (likely based on those offered by the Crown in 1778, which essentially were the demands of 1775 but without independence), the man most responsible for actual operations totally misjudged the true nature of the war. In this, what Clausewitz succinctly asserts as the "first, the supreme, the most far-reaching act of judgment that the . . . commander [has] to make," understanding the true nature of the conflict, Clinton missed the mark with his focus on Philadelphia.[12] Cornwallis, to his credit, understood that a concentration of forces against a divided enemy represented the best hope for victory over the Continental Army. He had learned the price of dividing his forces, first at King's Mountain and then at Cowpens. As of the late spring of 1781, he now eschewed holding multiple posts and instead advocated concentrating his forces. Yet neither officer ever truly comprehended the most critical strategic imperative. The true path to ultimate victory in the South lay in winning the "hearts and minds" of the populace, the single-most-important rebel center of gravity. In this regard, neither commander's plan was adequate.

## The Lion Humbled: South Carolina, 1781

As Cornwallis retreated toward Wilmington and salvation, Greene moved south after Guilford Court House to fill the vacuum. With the earl thrashing about in coastal North Carolina and then moving on to Tidewater Virginia, the Rhode Islander saw the opportunity to attack the more strongly defended posts in South Carolina, including Camden and Ninety Six. While the partisans there could harass and complicate Crown logistics and communications, they could not amass sufficient military power to take the larger posts. With Greene's Continentals freed from the threat of Cornwallis and Tarleton, Patriot strategy took a significant turn, with the objective now of destroying any British control of the countryside by reducing and capturing their major forward operating posts. The first target represented the most important—the post and magazine at Camden.

Greene had earlier sent Colonel Lee's dragoons to cooperate with Colonel Marion. The Swamp Fox attempted to take Georgetown, the primary coastal post north of Charleston, in late January, but his lack of artillery prevented success. In response, a two-pronged British attack resulted in the Wiboo Swamp engagement on 6 March. In this marshy terrain, movement was restricted to raised causeways; Marion took advantage of the geography to ambush and harass the advancing enemy columns. Ultimately, the expedition failed. In late April Marion struck again, this time at Fort Watson on the Santee River, where the Camden–Charleston road crossed. Control of the post cut Camden's connection to the coast. Brigadier General Sumter had previously failed to take this fort, but the opportunity to isolate Camden could not pass. With the bulk of the garrison out on a "search and destroy" mission, Marion and Lee constructed a siege tower (a "cavalier") that allowed them to shoot over the tops of the walls and take the post. With Fort Watson neutralized, the road to Camden lay open.

Lord Rawdon, now a twenty-seven-year-old brevet major general commanding all Crown forces south of Virginia, resolved to take the fight to Greene. His determination resulted in the Battle of Hobkirk's Hill, north of Camden, on 25 April. With 900 men, anchored by the 63rd Regiment, he marched out to assault Greene's 1,200-man force on a ridge known as Hobkirk's Hill. Rawdon used his riflemen to snipe at officers and noncommissioned officers as the Patriots had done so successfully at Cowpens. The battle gradually evolved into a linear contest won tactically by Rawdon but, as with Guilford Court House a month earlier, strategically by Greene. While the Patriots lost 132 killed and wounded, Rawdon lost over a third of his force. From the strategic-effects viewpoint, Hobkirk's Hill represented an immense Patriot victory. Unable to ensure Camden's safety afterward, Rawdon evacuated his troops, destroyed the fortifications and excess stores, and burnt much of the town itself. The major upcountry post and the linchpin of efforts to control the hinterland and subdue the partisans was lost. Rawdon realized that with the limited manpower available, he could not defend all the posts and decided to consolidate as much as possible by abandoning them. He informed Cornwallis that "the situation of affairs in this province has made me judge it necessary for a time to withdraw my force from the Back Country and to assemble what troops I can collect at this point."[13]

Taking advantage of Rawdon's withdrawal to Charleston, Sumter took Orangeburg on 11 May, capturing its British and Loyalist defenders as well as a large supply stores. On the road junction between Augusta, Charleston, and Ninety Six, Orangeburg's loss further complicated Crown reinforcement and supply movements. Lee, operating separately from Marion, assaulted a strongly held post at Fort Granby and forced its surrender on 15 May. The colonel's dragoons also captured Fort Galphin, on the Savannah River twelve miles south of Augusta, in a two-day action, 19–21 May. Georgia now came under threat of Patriot attack as post after post fell to the combined Continental dragoons and Patriot partisans. By the end of May, five critical points had been lost to the Crown, with only Georgetown on the coast and Ninety Six in the uplands remaining along with Augusta to the south. Greene turned his attention to the critical Georgia city, which had been quiet for months. The plan of attack developed during a meeting of the major Patriot partisan commanders and Greene. The major general would besiege Ninety Six while Pickens's South Carolinians, Georgia militia under Lieutenant Colonel Clarke, and Lee's Legion would strike Augusta.

At Augusta, a substantial force under Colonel Brown guarded two forts—Grierson and Cornwallis—which became the initial objectives. Grierson fell relatively quickly. The better-defended Fort Cornwallis presented a tactical problem. Since the besiegers had no artillery to pound its stockade walls, they erected a tower that allowed riflemen to pick off defenders from above. Brown and 300 Loyalists finally surrendered on 5 June. With Augusta again in Patriot hands, royal control over Georgia crumbled; only Savannah remained as a lone outpost of any consequence. Ninety Six, however, presented a different problem. In a heavily Loyalist and populous area of South Carolina, Lieutenant Colonel Cruger, a New York Loyalist, held the post with 550 men of De Lancey's Brigade as well as New Jersey and South Carolina Loyalists.[14]

Its defenses based on an earthwork dubbed Star Redoubt, Ninety Six represented the most extensive British inland fortification south of New York. The Royal Engineers, using the *trace italienne* design common in Europe since the sixteenth century, had extensively improved the fort, replete with star-design bastions providing crossfire, fraise, sloped walls with a firing step, and two blockhouses, all surrounded by a dry ditch. The critical vulnerability lay in the water source west of the village and fort. In accordance with his new operational plan, Lord Rawdon sent orders to Cruger to abandon Ninety Six, but the Patriots intercepted the letter, leaving Cruger determined still to defend his post. Now leading a thousand troops, Greene besieged the post. Thaddeus Kosciusko, a Polish volunteer in the Continental Army and an expert military engineer, recommended focusing all efforts on the Star Redoubt, using standard siege tactics of constructing approaching parallels connected by zig-zagging communications trenches. A cavalier tower allowed riflemen to snipe at the defenders, thus minimizing hazards to the diggers.[15] The Patriot works crept ever closer, but delays allowed the British to react. On 31 May Cruger reported that Greene was "now within one hundred and fifty yards of our Star Redoubt, the principal work, and approaching with great rapidity."[16]

Rawdon countered. Having received reinforcements from Ireland, he raced with these fresh troops to relieve the siege.[17] Despite Patriot reinforcements—Lee and Pickens arrived in time to participate, fresh from their Augusta success—the defenders scotched all of Greene's siege efforts. Patriot attempts to control the water supply similarly failed as the stout Loyalist defense held. In an attempt to slow up Rawdon, Greene detached Pickens and Washington's cavalry to harass the relieving force. Meanwhile, he attempted a last assault, which made it into the fortifications, only to be pushed back. With Rawdon's substantial relief force approaching, Greene lifted the siege on 19 June, having lasted twenty-eight days, and retreated into North Carolina. Rawdon arrived two days later.

Due to the summer heat and casualties from heat exhaustion and other summer maladies, Crown forces could not pursue Greene. Many of the newly arrived troops, still dealing from the usual infirmities of sea travel, suffered terribly in the Carolina warmth and humidity. Malaria and dysentery wore down both armies; neither had the ability to fight. Rawdon ordered Ninety Six abandoned and returned to Charleston, his own health in collapse. Greene moved his suffering troops to the Santee High Hills to recover. Meanwhile, Marion finally captured Georgetown on 6 June. With the abandonment of Ninety Six and the loss of Georgetown, British efforts to control the hinterland totally collapsed. Only Charleston, Savannah, and their immediate environs remained in Crown hands, a sad remnant of the victorious position only nine months earlier. With Rawdon returning to England due to debilitating illness, command in Charleston devolved to Lieutenant Colonel Alexander Stewart (or Stuart). In late summer Greene received Continental reinforcements and substantial local militia. He decided to march on Charleston. Stewart resolved to block him and established a strong position based on a plantation house at Eutaw Springs. The final great conventional battle of the Carolinas campaigns resulted.

## "Bloody and Obstinate": Eutaw Springs, 8 September 1781

The plantation at Eutaw Springs sat astride the Charleston road fifty miles northwest of the city at Nelson's Ferry on the Santee River. As Greene approached on 8 September, his force included 900 Continentals from Virginia, North Carolina, Maryland, and Delaware, many of whom had significant combat experience at Cowpens and other engagements. His cavalry included Washington's dragoons and Lee's Legion as well as Lt. Col. Wade Hampton's South Carolina horsemen. South Carolina militia and state troops (somewhat better trained, equipped, and drilled than normal militia) formed a large portion of Greene's troops. In total, the Rhode Islander could muster about 2,000 effectives against Stewart's approximately 2,200 men of the 3rd, 63rd, and 64th Regiments as well as New York Loyalists under Cruger; South Carolina Loyalists served as cavalry. Stewart collected the grenadier and light infantry companies from the 3rd, 19th and 30th Regiments, forming a battalion under Major John Marjoribanks of the 19th Regiment of Foot; this unit played the most critical role in the coming fray.[18]

Greene formed two lines, with the militia in front backed up by the Continentals. They struck the British camp by surprise and initially pushed back the enemy. Stewart and other officers rallied their troops and formed them in line, firing volleys at the advancing Patriots. When the militia line wavered under the fusillade, the Continentals moved ahead against the volley-firing British, now recovered from the initial shock. At this point the chaos of war set in, and Greene's assault faltered. Having overrun the British camp, the militia started plundering tents and stores, especially the rum. All discipline and cohesion broke down. The men having suffered numerous privations over the past few months, perhaps the militia's loss of discipline is understandable, if not forgivable. A second, more tactical event occurred that doomed Greene's chances for victory. On the British right, Marjoribanks's flank battalion had already done considerable damage to the Patriot cavalry, wounding and capturing Colonel Washington. Marjoribanks then retired several yards into a strong position protected by the plantation garden wall and part of the palisade recently thrown up. From here his men fired into the left flank of the Patriot's main line, inflicting numerous casualties. When the Continentals and militia buckled, Stewart attacked the Patriot right flank, forcing Greene to withdraw back to the High Hills area.

Once again, Greene had lost or at least drawn in open, conventional combat. Nonetheless, once again, in the great scheme of things, it did not matter. Although he lost fewer troops than Greene, Stewart had to fall back to Charleston, leaving Greene and the Patriot partisans in control of the backcountry. Stewart described the action at Eutaw Springs, which lasted a full three hours, as "bloody and obstinate."[19] Nevertheless, Greene accomplished his strategic imperatives. He had maintained his forces in the field and not allowed the enemy to destroy him. He had found sanctuary, by capturing in detail through subordinate commands, all the critical enemy posts in the backcountry from which the opponent might mount operations against him. Again, Greene had successfully conducted a Fabian strategy. Although he did not win the decisive, culminating, conventional battle necessary for the strategy's completion, he had set the table for General Washington to do so in Virginia a month later. Greene accomplished what the Continental Army commander in chief had sent him south to do. In short, while in Virginia Cornwallis struggled to find a winning strategy, in the Carolinas and Georgia, the Southern Strategy of "clear and hold" had utterly and fatally collapsed.

## Pensacola and the Loss of West Florida, 1779–81

A perhaps less understood aspect of the Southern Campaign, though certainly one that complicated Crown efforts to pacify the South, lay even farther south in West Florida. Spain entered the fray in 1779 as a traditional Bourbon ally. The Spanish had no real interest in American independence; they simply wanted back

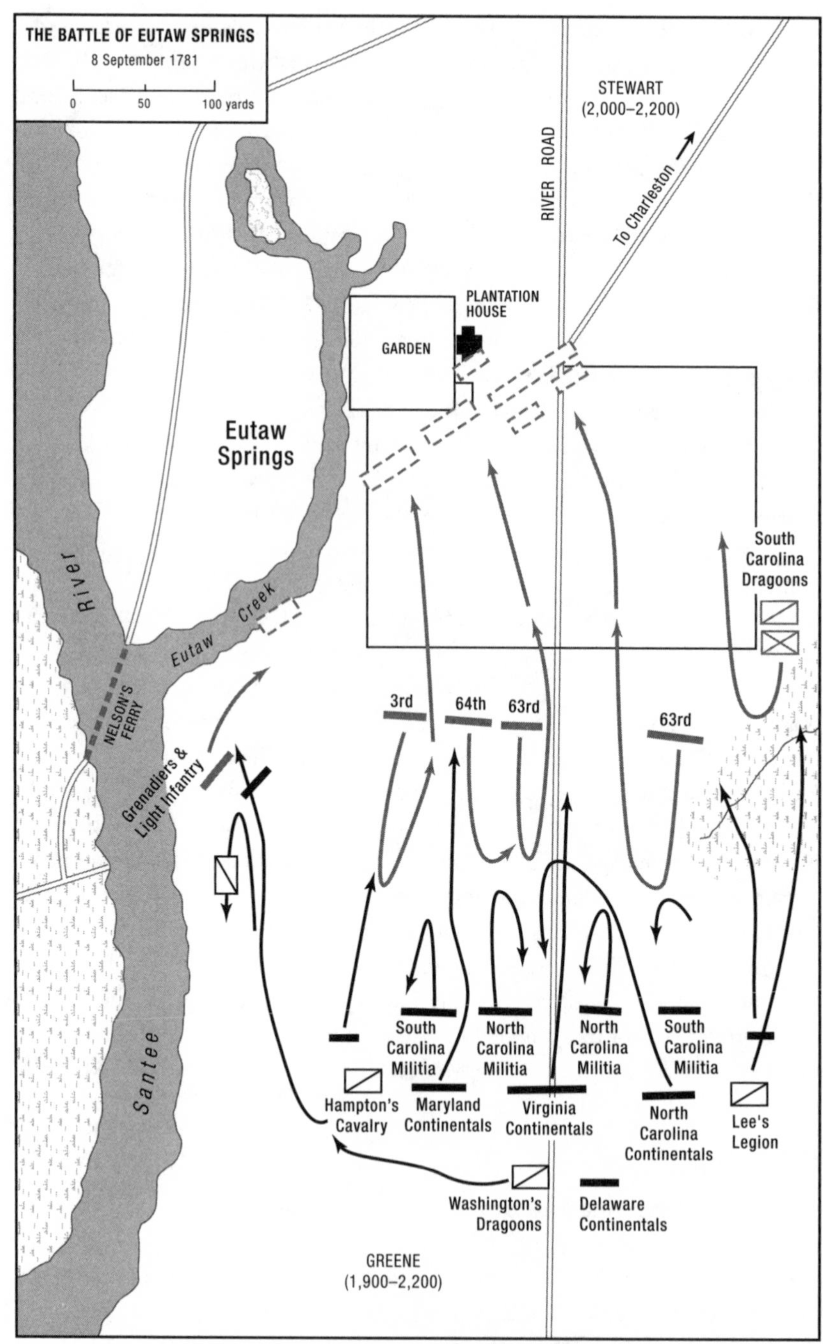


The Battle of Eutaw Springs, 8 September 1781.
*Map by Erin Greb Cartography.*

possessions lost in the several Anglo-French/Spanish conflicts of the previous nearly two centuries, including Jamaica, Minorca, Gibraltar, and the Floridas. In 1780–81 the Spanish, operating out of New Orleans and Havana under Governor General Don Bernardo de Galvéz, executed one of the most successful operations in their military history. Galvéz captured British posts throughout the Mississippi River region and, most importantly, in March 1781 besieged and captured Pensacola, the capital of West Florida. Spanish actions, therefore, created not only a two-front war for Cornwallis in the Carolinas but also drew off thousands of troops who might have made a substantial difference in the operations in North and South Carolina. With Spain now actively involved, the British strategic situation altered dramatically.[20]

With East and West Florida solidly Loyalist, troops based in Saint Augustine represented an existential threat to Georgia and South Carolina. Following rebel victories in 1775–76, whereby Patriot governments took control of local governments in both Carolinas and in Georgia, thousands of Loyalists fled south into the Floridas for refuge. Royal Governor Tonyn created a potent raiding force from among these refugees, including Thomas Brown, who played a large role in the Southern Campaign. Tonyn appointed "Burntfoot" Brown as colonel and commander of a Loyalist partisan force known as the King's Rangers, or more colloquially as Brown's Florida Rangers. Eventually, the unit became more formalized as the East Florida Rangers and conducted operations throughout Florida, Georgia, and occasionally South Carolina.[21] Throughout the years prior to the Crown invasion and capture of Savannah and Augusta, Brown and the Rangers conducted raids against southern Georgia. Cattle thievery represented their primary activity, for East Florida could not feed itself without imports; the Georgia Patriot government had prohibited food exports to Saint Augustine. But the unit tended to aggravate Augustine Prevost, military commander in East Florida, due to their unwillingness to cooperate with regular-army authorities. The major general threatened to cut off all military aid to the Florida Loyalists unless the rangers operated under his command; the governor pointed out that as colonial militia, Brown's unit remained strictly under his control. By 1779, the dispute ended when the East Florida Rangers came into the American Establishment and thus under the command and control of regular military authorities. In West Florida, under Royal Governor Peter Chester, the West Florida Royal Foresters operated. Despite the troubles with militia experienced by British authorities, Patriot military officers had even greater difficulties. Patriot militia attempts to invade Florida to eliminate the irritating Loyalist partisans failed several times throughout 1776–78.

By 1779, the strategic situation altered in the Patriot's favor as Galvéz began systematically capturing West Florida outposts along the Mississippi River and farther inland. An abortive Crown attempt from West Florida to take New Orleans placed Pensacola and Mobile in jeopardy when Galvéz responded. Despite Major General John Campbell's best efforts, the failure of Commodore Sir Peter Parker, commanding the West Indies squadron out of Jamaica, to provide naval support to the expedition for fear of French and Spanish attacks in the Caribbean doomed the attempt. Campbell pleaded with British authorities for assistance, but little came from his efforts.[22] With the failure to take New Orleans, Baton Rouge in 1779 and Mobile in 1780 soon fell to Galvéz. Pensacola followed in May 1781.

The royal governor of Jamaica, who shouldered the military responsibility for Pensacola, vainly attempted to save the city following the loss of Mobile, less than fifty miles away from the capital. A hurricane in 1780 delayed Galvéz, who was determined to strike as soon as possible. Commanding an amphibious force from New Orleans and Havana, he landed at Santa Rosa Island just off Escambia Bay in March 1781. Attempting to save Pensacola from bombardment, Campbell withdrew his forces to Fort George. Galvéz commenced a siege in late April. In one of those probabilistic events so typical in the chaos of war, on 8 May a Spanish artillery round landed in an ammunition-storage site near the fort. The resulting explosion killed a hundred soldiers and wounded considerably more. Faced with this sudden catastrophe, the following day Campbell surrendered the fort and over a thousand troops. Unable to care for such a huge number of prisoners, the Spaniard paroled his captives, who eventually returned to Britain. Although Galvéz did not invade the more populous and better-defended East Florida, the loss of so many troops in a fruitless defense severely hampered Rawdon's efforts to hold South Carolina. Had those men been available, it is possible that he might have defeated or destroyed Greene's army or at least have retained the key posts at Camden, Georgetown, and Ninety Six. Spanish actions in West Florida represent an excellent example of sequential operations working in tandem to produce a cumulative effect, in this case the almost complete loss of Crown control over the southern hinterland and the collapse in Georgia and the Carolinas of the "clear and hold" strategy.[23]

Through both of these dynamics—Spanish actions in Florida and Greene's in South Carolina—the Southern Strategy crumbled. Unable to counter the partisans and hold the interior posts, British commanders retreated to Charleston and safety. By the time of Yorktown, only Charleston, Wilmington, and Savannah remained firmly in Crown hands. South Carolina pacification efforts had ended; the only option was to hold the coastal posts and await events. In Florida the empire crumbled further with the loss of West Florida. Both campaigns had cost thousands of British and Loyalist casualties. Had Cornwallis, operating in the Carolinas and Virginia, been able to use those troops, the Yorktown surrender might never have happened.

## The Virginia Campaign, Spring and Summer of 1781

All told, by early summer, Cornwallis now had his largest force of the campaign, at 7,200 effectives, against Lafayette commanding half as many troops. But on reading Phillips's orders from Clinton, the earl had to have been dismayed by the intended nature of operations. Was this plan not simply one to send out detachments to steal tobacco that he had so recently derided? Nonetheless, he resolved to carry out the commander's intent; he would continue the economic strategy of attacking Patriot resources and establish an operating post on the Chesapeake. Further, upon arrival in southern Virginia, he finally and completely disregarded Loyalist support, constituting the final collapse of that aspect of strategy around which so many hopes and plans revolved. Illustrative of this changed attitude, Cornwallis later issued a decree on 9 August as he entrenched at Yorktown, demanding that all inhabitants in and around the county must

> repair to Head Quarters at York Town on or before the 20th day of Aug to deliver up their Arms, and to give their Paroles, that they will not in future take any part against His Majesty's Interest. And they are likewise directed to bring to Market the Provisions that they can spare, for which they will be paid reasonable prices in ready money. And notice is hereby given, that those who fail in complying with this Order will be imprisoned when taken, & their Corn and Cattle will be seized for the use of the Troops.[24]

The implementation of this aggressive economic policy went forward with great vigor. Cornwallis and his subordinates, frustrated by the inability to stamp out rebel activity despite battlefield victories, took the new plan to heart. In a swift-moving raid Tarleton even seized some Virginia legislators, acquired tons of stores, and missed capturing Governor Jefferson at Monticello by a bare ten minutes. Other actions, mainly of an economic-warfare nature, continued throughout the summer; the defense of posts no longer constituted a key objective as it had in South Carolina. Additionally, Cornwallis's forces struck at the state's military capability by destroying arms, military stores, and foodstuffs. Private property had no sanctity as swift-moving cavalry raided and burned plantations and farms, confiscated stores, freed slaves, and destroyed anything of military or economic value that could not be carted away. Although much of the light-force capability had been lost in the previous battles, Cornwallis still had suitable units with which to carry out the sequestration campaign, including over 500 mounted hussars and light dragoons of Lieutenant Colonel John Graves Simcoe's Queen's Rangers and remnants of the British Legion. This cavalry gave the earl a substantive body capable of rapidly striking any enemy force and conducting economic raids. Using confiscated horses, an additional

800 infantry mounted up for raids that often covered between thirty and seventy miles per day. No plantation, farm, or town from the Tidewater to the Blue Ridge Mountains remained safe from Cornwallis's mounted warriors. Adding to Patriot concerns, Lafayette's Continentals could not hope to match this mobility, which created fear and doubt among troops concerned about ambush and sudden attack. To address the fears, Lafayette always kept a distance of at least twenty to thirty miles from Cornwallis, which had the effect of giving British cavalry free rein to operate without opposition or interference. Local authorities found few militiamen willing to turn out for fear of identification and having their property attacked, destroyed, or confiscated without payment.

Despite the intensity of this economic strategy, random acts of plunder and terror did not fit the new strategic-effects concept. Cornwallis prohibited individual foraging and marauding as detrimental to the campaign, the objective of which lay in demonstrating that rebellion and support of independence incurred a dreadful economic price. Perhaps this is a case not of winning friends, but of influencing people. Cornwallis issued explicit Rules of Engagement concerning the campaign as illustrated by the General Orders issued to "prevent the scandalous practice of taking Horses from the Country people." Under his procedural guidelines, receipts would be issued and payment made based on the individual's "past and future Conduct."[25] Additionally, thousands of slaves fled their masters and flocked to the security of British forces in hopes of emancipation, which further undercut the Virginia plantation-and-commodities-based agrarian economy. Escaped slaves served British forces in auxiliary roles as spies, guides, laborers, and servants, a dynamic that created a force-multiplier effect and addressed one of the chief deficiencies of the previous Carolina campaigns—that of a lack of accurate, timely local intelligence. Thus, economic warfare to ensure appropriate behavior became the new key to strategic victory in the South.

If the strategic situation looked positive for Cornwallis in early June 1781, the perception was transitory as additional forces against him started in motion. In March French rear admiral François Joseph Paul, comte de Grasse departed Brest with twenty ships of the line bound for the West Indies but available for combined and joint operations in the colonies. Added to the Newport squadron now commanded by Commodore Jacque Melchior Saint-Laurent, comte de Barras, France would have a numerical superiority over Royal Navy forces in North American waters. Whitehall responded meekly. Rear Admiral Robert Digby, Arbuthnot's designated relief, departed Britain with only three ships of the line. On 10 June roughly 800 troops of the Pennsylvania Continental Line under Brig. Gen. Anthony Wayne rendezvoused with Lafayette, allowing him to commence more-active operations. The Frenchman followed Cornwallis as the British main body moved back down the James River toward Williamsburg. But his orders required him to avoid direct conflict with the larger British force while doing his utmost to interfere with the enemy's raiding activities. More importantly, Greene still ran wild in South Carolina. If a key objective of the economic campaign had been to deny resources to the Continental forces in the Carolinas, the plan failed. Even though troops such as Wayne's Pennsylvanians went to Lafayette instead of Greene, the Southern Department commander continued to overrun post after post in the South Carolina backcountry in cooperation with the local partisans. Many supplies and weapons captured in these actions made their way into Greene's camp along with locally procured food and fodder.

Other circumstances drove a knife into the heart of Cornwallis's hope for a successful Virginia Campaign. In May Washington and Rochambeau met for a conference in Wethersfield, Connecticut, to coordinate operations. Washington advocated a combined attack on New York, while the French wished to send support to Lafayette in Virginia. Through the interception of a courier to Lafayette, Clinton learned of Washington's proposal and concluded that the real Continental threat lay to New York. Only too late did he realize that while the two allies had initially agreed on the American's proposal, the plan quickly changed to the French concept for operations against Cornwallis. Clinton's reluctance to denude his New York garrison is understandable, but for the royal cause, his faulty intelligence of the opponent's intentions meant that once the enemy plan and movement became obvious in late September, there was little time to react and reinforce Virginia.

Germain advised Clinton that de Grasse had sailed but could not say whether the squadron was heading to the Indies or Virginia. This uncertainty caused Clinton to recall troops from Cornwallis and to prepare for a defensive struggle wherever the Allies should strike.[26] The earl, though disappointed and in disagreement, nevertheless prepared to strip his forces of the units demanded by the CinC's orders, which arrived at his headquarters on 25 June. But he would not retire from Virginia without a fight. Using a slave posing as a deserter to misinform the enemy of his intentions, Cornwallis lured the impetuous Wayne into a trap near Green Spring Farm on 6 July. Convinced that the British had crossed the James River and that only elements of the British Legion still lay on the north bank, the Pennsylvanian surged forward. To further the ruse, Cornwallis stationed his main force in dense woods, leaving only pickets in sight. Wayne took the bait and sent his Continentals forward, confident of an easy victory. Only the courage of their commander, their own bravery under trying circumstances, and the onset of darkness saved the Pennsylvania Line from destruction. Green Springs had been a close-run affair. Upon hearing of the engagement, Greene complimented the youthful Frenchman and Wayne but cautioned the Pennsylvanian to be leery of Cornwallis. Greene advised him by letter to "be a little careful and tread softly, for, depend upon it, you have a modern Hannibal to deal with in the person of Lord Cornwallis."[27]

The Allies could not have realized the great fortune that Clinton was about to deliver. Having captured French messages and secret instructions from King Louis XVI in early June indicating that the de Grasse expedition represented the last effort from France in support of the Patriots, Clinton determined to ride out the storm (to use a metaphor) and assume a defensive posture, or "the policy of avoiding all risks as much as possible, because it was now manifest that, if we could only persevere in escaping affront, time alone would soon bring about every success we could wish."[28] There is controversy as to when the actual messages were finally deciphered, but the cogent point remains—the CinC went into a defensive mode.[29] With Clinton in this mindset and Cornwallis, reinforced by Phillips's troops and determined to subdue Virginia by aggressive operations as the new seat of war, strategic incoherence and a complete loss of effective command and control could be the only result. To complicate the situation further, Admiral Sir George Rodney, in ill health, departed the West Indies for England on 1 August with three ships. Commodore Parker at Jamaica, despite requests for support, failed to send ships north. The admiral also had indications that de Grasse intended to make for the Chesapeake but failed to pass that intelligence on to Graves in New York before he left. Rodney, who later defeated de Grasse at the Battle of the Saintes, might have been the man to salvage the naval situation. Rear Admiral Sir Samuel Hood, the number two in seniority, might have done so as well. Graves, however, was definitively not that man. Hood departed the West Indies, bound for the Chesapeake, on 10 August with only fourteen ships of the line, compared to de Grasse's twenty-eight, for what came to be a decisive engagement, the Battle of the Virginia Capes. Despite indications of the French admiral's movement north and the march of the now-combined Allied army into New Jersey on 19 August, Graves and Clinton seemed blissfully unaware of the coming catastrophe.

Arriving in Tidewater Virginia, Cornwallis received three letters in quick succession from his commander. The first, dated 29 May, informed the earl of Clinton's displeasure with the move into Virginia. The second and third letters, dated 8 and 12 June, instructed Cornwallis to send forces to reinforce New York and for an assault on Philadelphia. Clearly, Clinton, imbued with a defensive mindset, failed to see an opportunity for choking off Greene in South Carolina while drawing out the Franco-American forces to their destruction. Nonetheless, Cornwallis complied with the orders and readied a force to move toward Pennsylvania. Then on 20 July he received a countermanding order. Clinton had once again altered his plan, now instructing Cornwallis to recall any troops still under his control and to fortify Old Point Comfort. Hastily debarking his forces, the earl sent engineers to assess the designated region, which proved incapable of supporting large warships since proper defensive works could not be constructed due to the unsuitable soil and terrain. A further order dated 11 July arrived amid these movements, Clinton instructing Cornwallis to occupy and fortify a post on the York River to further support Old Point Comfort.[30] These had been the original orders to Phillips: "If the Admiral, disapproving of Portsmouth and requiring a fortified station for large ships in the Chesapeak [*sic*], should propose York Town or Old Point Comfort, if possession of either can be acquired and maintained without great risk or loss, you are at liberty to take possession thereof."[31] Cornwallis inherited the concept and proceeded to implement the plan. To compound his senior's worries, the earl insisted on retaining his entire force for the new post's defense, thus shutting off that manpower source for either a New York or Philadelphia operation. Once again the two generals worked at cross-purposes.

Clearly, the naval imperative became imminently more critical. For the Virginia campaign to succeed, naval support, particularly in the face of growing French maritime power, had to play a leading role and that required a defendable, reliable, and adequate operating base with proper anchorages. After consulting the temporary North American station commander, Rear Admiral Graves, Clinton proposed Old Point Comfort as the preferred site. Phillips had previously rejected Portsmouth, and Cornwallis expressed this view as well for reasons of defense consideration and health concerns for the men. Furthermore, based on his engineers' assessment of Old Point Comfort, the earl also rejected this location because it could not control movement into the James and York Rivers and lay too far north to protect a fleet anchored in lower Hampton Roads. He opted instead for the village of Yorktown, situated on the south side of the York River and only a few miles from Williamsburg. Located on the narrow York Peninsula, with the York River to the north and the James to the south, the only escape route, should the position become untenable, was northwest up the peninsula, which an enemy blocking force could easily prevent. The only other option—evacuation by water—required good weather and maritime control, neither of which could be guaranteed. In retrospect, the choice of Yorktown seems odd. With a much smaller force of less capable troops, Lafayette had managed to maintain contact with Cornwallis's army and conduct continuous observation while simultaneously blocking a retreat toward Williamsburg and Richmond. Additionally, land-based supplies could no longer reach British forces, thus making control of the Chesapeake a fundamental requirement and a critical vulnerability. Instead of waging his preferred offensive in the South and destroying the Continental forces under Greene in South Carolina and Lafayette in Virginia, Cornwallis now became simply a garrison commander.

The grand plan to overawe the South by British military might and secure its peace and allegiance through the rising of the Loyalist population had withered away in the heat of a southern summer. Confused, defensive, desultory, and lacking in any sort of war-winning strategic vision, British decision makers compounded the problem repeatedly. In London Germain expected and demanded the massive rising of Loyalists and stuck to his concept from the initial phases of the campaign. In New York Clinton waffled as to which strategy to pursue—a highly offensive, maximum-effort conventional campaign to destroy the enemy's war-making capability, or a purely defensive enclave strategy that relied upon the occupation of key cities. Finally, he chose the defensive, informing Cornwallis that "until the season for recommencing operations in the Chesapeak [*sic*] shall return, your Lordship . . . must, I fear, be content with a strict defensive."[32]

Slogging through the Tidewater countryside toward the hamlet on the York River in the heat and humidity of a late Virginia summer, Cornwallis must have felt neutered, abandoned, and betrayed by his senior officer. He commented in a letter to Lord Rawdon that he suspected that the CinC was "determined to throw all the blame on me, and disapprove of all I have done, and that nothing but the consciousness that my going home in apparent disgust would essentially hurt our affairs in this country could possibly induce me to remain."[33] This profound lack of strategic cohesion would, within weeks, result in the resolution of affairs—and not to Britain's advantage. In effect, Clinton's orders to occupy and fortify a post on the Chesapeake and to send forces to New York to either defend the city or take part in a campaign against Philadelphia meant the doom of what in retrospect might have been a winning strategy. Economic intimidation enforced by overwhelming military presence to ensure good behavior, while harsh and destructive, might have resulted in pacification. In the end, addressing the concerns and demands of 1775–76 by the civil and political authorities had to be accomplished lest the spirit of independence break out again. But from the military aspect, Cornwallis had hit on a potentially effective plan for securing the South. Once again, a lack of unity and strategic coherence intervened; on 2 August 1781 Cornwallis tied himself irrevocably to the defense of the Yorktown post.

## "A Measure of the Utmost Importance": Battle of the Virginia Capes, 5–9 September 1781

Great, cataclysmic events often turn on single episodes of random chance. Such was the case in the early autumn of 1781 as Cornwallis established a defended naval station in Tidewater Virginia. That random chance occurred at the Battle of the Virginia Capes, 5–9 September, as several tactical decisions resulted in a rare Royal Navy loss to the French navy in combat. The defeat of Rear Admiral Graves's squadron by French forces under Rear Admiral comte de Grasse not only doomed Cornwallis but also made possible the conditions whereby the Franco-American force under the command of Washington and comte de Rochambeau forced his surrender in October, thus effectively ending the War of American Independence.

In truth, Graves need not have lost the engagement; he might well have accomplished his assigned mission of securing the mouth of Chesapeake Bay and establishing local sea control in support of Cornwallis at Yorktown. But there were five critical tactical errors committed by the British in the course of the engagement on 5 September and in the days following. Had any of those decisions been different, the war might have taken a vastly more dramatic turn, perhaps in Britain's favor. Traditional historiography blames Graves for poor tactical decision making. Many recent naval historians are kinder on Graves and harsher on Rear Admiral Hood's tactical decisions. Additionally, the misunderstanding of tactical intentions due to poor visual signaling certainly contributed to British difficulties.

The communications failure between London and New York continued to prove problematic. Although Lord Germain sent a vaguely worded warning to Clinton in early April 1781 regarding de Grasse's probable movements, he assumed that Royal Navy forces on North American and West Indies stations would outmatch any French forces and aggressively pursue them. Further, Germain failed to add that the enemy fleet could be expected to arrive in theater by August.[34] Unable to maintain an effective distant blockade against the main French operating base at Brest, the Royal Navy allowed de Grasse to sortie for North American waters on 22 March. Operating in the West Indies, the admiral took the island of Tobago and threatened more damage to British interests. He received constant and urgent requests from Rochambeau for naval support, funds to pay his troops, and at least 5,000 reinforcements to bolster Washington's Continental forces posted in a covering position outside New York.

In late July de Grasse made a fateful determination: He would sail to the Chesapeake to support his countryman commanding Continental troops in southeastern Virginia, General Lafayette. The admiral embarked three French regiments then serving with the Spanish and concluded a deal with the Spanish whereby they would guard the Caribbean and thus protect his rear. Finally, on 5 August, led by the flagship, the 110-gun first-rate *Ville de Paris*, the fleet departed Martinique. Twenty-eight ships of the line, seven frigates, two cutters, and fifteen auxiliary merchantmen sailed north. Transiting through the Bahamas Channel without difficulty, along the way they captured several British ships, including one transporting Lord Rawdon, who was making his way back to England in ill health. The fleet dropped anchor in Lynnhaven Bay (off present-day Virginia Beach) on 29 August. Opposing them at Yorktown lay only the 44-gun HMS *Charon*, two lesser frigates, and six sloops. On 9 June Rochambeau and his army marched out of Newport, Rhode Island, toward New York. De Grasse's naval presence became an essential element in the Yorktown affair. Bolstered by French sea power, the Allied move now placed Crown forces in great peril.

From the British perspective, the situation could hardly have been worse. With most of the available naval strength still in the Caribbean under Admiral Rodney and his subordinate Hood, Graves had only six ships of the line in New York with which to confront de Grasse's twenty-eight. Moreover, Graves did not receive word of the French movement until late August. Two frigates sent north by Hood to alert Graves and to carry Rodney's order that he should rendezvous with Hood off the Chesapeake, HM Sloop *Swallow* and HMS *Active*, failed to warn him of Hood's and de Grasse's movements. *Swallow* arrived in New York to find Graves on patrol near Boston, having received erroneous intelligence from London that a French supply convoy was bound for that city or Newport, and was captured by privateers while searching for the squadron. American privateers also captured *Active*. Rodney soon turned over command to Hood and returned to England with three ships of the line. Hood, with fourteen sail, set course for Virginia on 10 August, only a few days behind the French. The British ships, with copper-sheathed hulls and taking a more direct route, reached the Chesapeake ahead of de Grasse but departed for New York when no evidence of French warships could be found.[35] The traditional interpretation has Hood stopping in Chesapeake Bay at Cape Henry and the Capes of the Delaware; recent examinations of several ship's logbooks, however, indicate that Hood sailed directly for New York and simply assumed that de Grasse had not arrived at either location.[36]

The French dropped anchor in Lynnhaven Bay four days later. To complicate the British situation, Barras departed Narragansett Bay on 25 August with his Rhode Island Squadron, carrying the heavy siege guns. Had Graves gotten underway for the Chesapeake just a week earlier, he would have rendezvoused with Hood sailing north and could have been in possession of the bay well ahead of the French. The West Indies Squadron's arrival on 28 August and the strident urging of Hood prompted Graves to set a southerly course on 31 August, though far too late to reverse the growing crisis. Reportedly, Hood burst in on a meeting between senior commanders with the exclamation: "Whether you attend the army in Rhode Island [Rochambeau] or seek the enemy at sea, you have no time to lose. Every moment is precious."[37]

Outside New York, Washington's planned assault fell apart. Although reinforced by the French army, probes of the city's defenses revealed no weaknesses.

Additionally, a convoy arrived early in August with 3,000 German troops to bolster Clinton's position. The odds had shifted, and not in the Allies' favor. Finally, word arrived that de Grasse had sailed for the Chesapeake. The northern plan was undone. Without overwhelming naval support and the reinforcements aboard de Grasse's transports, no assault on New York could be mounted. Washington then made one of the most critical decisions of his career: "Matters having now come to a crisis and a decisive plan to be determined on, I was obliged, from the shortness of Count de Grasse's promised stay on this coast, the apparent disinclination of their Naval Officers to force the harbor of New York and the feeble compliance of the states to my requisition for men . . . , to give up all idea of attacking New York; and instead to remove the French Troops and a detachment from the American Army . . . to Virginia."[38]

Eventually, Clinton recognized the enemy movement and reacted. Writing to Cornwallis on 2 September, he warned: "Mr Washington is moving an army to the southward with an appearance of haste; and gives out that he expects the cooperation of a considerable French armament. Your Lordship, however, may be assured that if this should be the case, I shall either endeavor to reinforce your command by all means within the compass of my power; or, make every possible diversion in your favor."[39] In a case of too little, much too late, his subordinate in Virginia was doomed the moment the Allied force departed their camps near New York and made doubly so as French warships dropped anchor in Lynnhaven Bay. Further undercutting any hope of reinforcement or rescue, as Royal Navy forces approached the mouth of the Chesapeake in the early morning of 5 September, the dynamics of naval dominance that have characterized most of Britain's conflicts did not play to British advantage.

Admiral de Grasse's warships rode at anchor in three lines in Lynnhaven Bay. As the anchorage came into clearer view, Graves realized that his nineteen warships faced twenty-four of the enemy's. With a great disparity in total guns but with the advantage in speed due to the copper-sheathed hulls and by holding the weather gage, Graves began his approach just past ten in the morning. Sighting the British squadron, the French slipped their anchors and mooring cables and attempted to sortie. The incoming tide prevented immediate movement, as did the need to tack to windward to clear Cape Henry, but by 2:00 p.m. the *Ville de Paris*, holding the middle station, cleared the cape. At this point the first critical tactical decision appeared. While a more aggressive commander might have ordered a general chase to catch the slower-moving or immobile French struggling with the incoming tide and attack their van before the full squadron could form a tight line of battle, Graves formed a line-ahead column formation as delineated in the standing Royal Navy *Fighting Instructions*.[40] He afterward stated to Lord Sandwich, first lord of the Admiralty, "My aim was to get close, to form parallel,

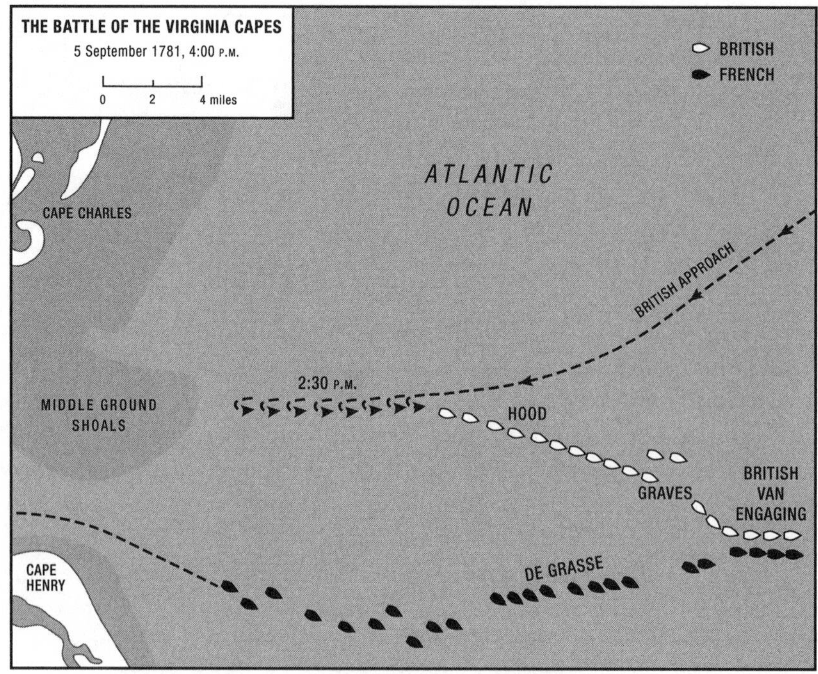


The Battle of the Virginia Capes, 5 September 1781.
*Map by Erin Greb Cartography.*

extend with them, and attack all together." Hood severely criticized Graves for not attacking the vulnerable van quickly, commenting, "Had such an attack been made, several of the enemy's ships must have been inevitably demolished in half an hour's action, and there was a full hour and half to have engaged it before any of the rear could have come up."[41] Had a general chase been ordered rather than forming the line of battle, Graves's warships might have destroyed or disabled a significant portion of the French squadron before de Grasse could bring his center and rear divisions into action.

Advancing from seaward and the east but still well north of the French line and seeing that his lead ship sailed dangerously close to the Middle Ground shoals, approximately five miles northwest of Cape Henry on the westward leg of his approach, Graves wore (haul about to an opposite tack by jibing) and reversed course at about 2:30 P.M., a move that placed him on the same heading as the French, his second critical tactical decision. The maneuver cost him his speed-and-mobility advantage as the British ships struggled with the same tide and wind as the French. Graves then executed a turn, called in modern naval parlance a "turn together true," whereby all ships change course to the new heading simultaneously.

While this maneuver maintains the same true bearing of each ship to the others, the relative bearing alters. Ships that had been in the rear division now composed the British van. Commanded by Rear Admiral Francis Drake, these vessels were in poor condition after months on station in the warm Caribbean waters. The turn placed them directly against the strength of the French column, while the more capable British vessels under Hood occupied the rear of the line. The more correct maneuver would have been a "Corpen turn," whereby the lead ship, upon execution, comes to the new course, while all others maintain their course and adjust speed to keep their relative position in line. When each ship reaches the turning point of the lead vessel, it comes about to the new heading. In this way true bearing changes while relative bearing is maintained. The practical result is that, had this been done, the first units to engage the French would have been Hood's far-more-capable and combat-ready ships.

When Graves gave the turn order, his squadron lay too far north of the struggling French line, thus in order to engage, Drake's ships, now in the lead, steered south by southeast toward the French at a steep angle rather than in a tight line closely parallel to the enemy. Seeing that the approach angle was too wide, at 2:30 Graves issued the order to the lead ship, HMS *Shrewsbury*, to "lead more to starboard, or towards the enemy." This third tactical decision created a dogleg approach, whereby individual ships followed the leader and approached the French line one at a time. The angle of approach was at least three points of sail, or approximately thirty-four degrees. Here the "turn together true" would have been the better maneuver, though still placing Hood's division in the rear. In turning to a new southeasterly course together and thus forming a line of bearing, the entire British line would have approached the French simultaneously. Then a follow-on turn back to the original heading would place Graves's line alongside de Grasse's and on a parallel course. At 3:46 P.M. Graves signaled to "bear down and engage the enemy." Thus, when the order to engage came, all of the rear division and many of the center division ships were still angling down toward the French line.

With the windward gage and speed advantage, the Royal Navy could have inflicted horrendous casualties on the struggling French, especially their outgunned van. But with this approach, the French center came into action before the bulk of the British warships assumed their position in the battle line. An approach more to the south and closer to the enemy formation prior to the turn maneuver would have placed Graves's line more closely parallel to the enemy's while still maintaining the his advantages on the approach run. The practical result of the steep approach angle and turn in succession meant that each ship came into battle line successively, engaging the French but with a significant lag time between each ship hauling into station, thus losing the advantage of concentrated firepower delivered over a short period against a disjointed enemy.

As the British line approached, by some mistake the flagship, HMS *London*, still flew the line ahead (a single-file column formation, usually with the guide ship at the head and all ships following in the guide's wake) signal for several minutes before being hauled down. According to Hood and many other sources, this signal remained hoisted for a full ninety minutes (until about 5:30 P.M.) while the engage the enemy signal also flew. With contradictory signals in the air, ship captains took individual initiative, some closing with the enemy on their own and some maintaining line ahead. Hood did not order his division to engage the enemy until the line ahead signal was hauled down. (Graves claimed that this occurred at 4:11 P.M., but with ship's logs reporting different execution times, the issue is still hotly debated.) In the chaotic melee that followed, all tactical cohesion disappeared. The flagship charged ahead to engage the enemy, only to foul the line of fire of ships that had maintained line ahead. The van division suffered half the total damage and casualties for the entire British squadron as it engaged the French lead ships. Within an hour, the center divisions of each line came into action; due to the tactical and maneuvering problems, however, only a dozen of the nineteen British ships saw actual action, and of them only eight were heavily engaged versus fifteen Frenchmen. Here occurred the fourth critical tactical decision. Hood claimed that he strictly adhered to the line ahead signal rather than order his division, now in the rear, to charge ahead and engage the enemy. Thus, very few of his ships actually engaged the French. Had Hood been more aggressive, ignored the signals problem, and ordered his division into immediate action, the entire tenor of the battle might have changed in favor of the British. With approaching sunset, Graves ordered a pause in the action at 6:30 P.M., which meant that Hood never did catch up to the French line.

The flag signals problem exacerbated the lack of a standard signals instruction and commander's intent as expressed in the *Additional Instructions.* Admiral Rodney demanded strict adherence to the commander's intent, with no individual initiative. In Hood's defense, he simply followed the familiar West Indies pattern, which used the standing *Admiralty Instructions* and Rodney's *Additional Instructions.* Vice Admiral Arbuthnot, Graves's immediate predecessor, had issued his own additional fighting instructions in 1779–80 and, in 1781, issued supplemental instructions accompanied by a listing of more than forty signals. The West Indies Squadron did not have these signals and fighting instructions until they arrived off Sandy Hook, New Jersey. With little opportunity to coordinate on the *Additional Instructions* in use on the American Station, tactical incoherence thus injected itself.[42] Despite this dynamic, Hood could have been more aggressive. Article XXI of Rodney's *Fighting Instruction* specified, "Whereupon, every ship in the squadron is to steer for the ship of the Enemy which, from the dispositions of the two squadrons, it must be her lot to engage, not withstanding the signal for the Line ahead will be kept flying."[43]

A more Nelsonian initiative, despite the signal and commander's intent instructions, might have yielded a different result. Hood fumed at the lack of tactical acumen throughout the engagement, even though in retrospect his decisions formed part of the problem. He remarked in a private letter to Assistant Secretary of the Admiralty George Jackson that finding the French fleet at anchor and straggling in their attempt to get underway to form line of battle "afforded the British fleet a most glorious opening for making a close attack to manifest advantage, but it was not embraced."[44] While an immediate attack on the French van as it pulled away from the slower-moving center might have achieved the "most glorious opening," there were potentially two critical downsides to an immediate attack with all ships that could bring guns to bear. First, Graves did not know the total number of French ships of the line as he approached. There could have been potentially thirty-six (twenty-nine from de Grasse and seven from Barras). Second, Graves, having not worked with the West Indies Squadron, had not had the opportunity to assess the capabilities and professional acumen of Hood's commanding officers. Thus, it is likely that he thought it safer to use the standard line ahead parallel approach attack formation, whereby he could exercise tighter command control.[45] Additionally, there is the danger of a general chase order, whereby the first ships to engage suffer great damage due to the enemy's ability to concentrate fire. Yet that is precisely the situation created by the steep angle approach. As a result, HMS *Shrewsbury* and HMS *Terrible*, the two van lead ships, endured significant damage, so much so that *Terrible* had to be scuttled. In retrospect, why not a general chase?

For four days, the two squadrons shadowed each other and held contact down the North Carolina Outer Banks. Once again Graves missed an opportunity to undercut the French advantage, his fifth decisive tactical decision. Given the British speed advantage, he might have slipped away in the dark, regained the Chesapeake, and established local sea control, which would have made the Allied position weaker. Hood, in a flag conference aboard *London*, stridently advocated this course of action, but Graves worried about the damage to his ships and the French numerical advantage; he chose not to attempt a run for the Chesapeake ahead of de Grasse, who indeed worried that the British would take such action. Accordingly, the French admiral ordered a return to Chesapeake Bay on the evening of the ninth. The force under Barras, composed of eight escorts and ten transports, having avoided enemy contact by skirting wide around the two squadrons, sailed into the bay that same day, carrying the French siege artillery, the deciding factor in Cornwallis's destruction. Graves thus lost the opportunity to "steal a march." Faced with crippled ships, outnumbered, and frankly outfought, he ordered a return New York.[46] Hood commented dryly, "I was distressed that Mr Graves did not carry all the sail he could also, and endeavour to get off the Chesapeake before him [de Grasse]; it appeared to me to be a measure of the utmost importance to keep the French out, and if they did get in they should first beat us."[47]

While counterfactual arguments are an interesting analytical tool and "what ifs" are for contemplation only, it is interesting to speculate the consequences of the British tactical decision making. Would the Allied army have marched on in light of Crown control of the lower Chesapeake? What might have happened had they embarked on the transports, not knowing of Graves's presence, only to arrive at the James River loaded with troops facing enemy ships of the line? Would de Grasse have been willing or able to reengage Graves in a role reversal of the fifth?[48] What if Graves had sailed earlier from New York and blocked French entry into the bay? What if de Grasse had divided his force, leaving part of it in the West Indies (as Rodney expected), or what if Rodney had not depleted his force in his return to England? What if the British ships had been better handled tactically? Despite these open questions, the loss of the command of the sea at the mouth of the Chesapeake played a significant role in the unfolding British disaster. In bitter commentary to his brother and others, Hood excoriated his senior officer for his tactical and operational decisions, particularly in not being aggressive in reaction to French movements.[49]

Whatever might have happened to save Yorktown and the army, it did not. On the thirteenth a council of war held between the flag officers onboard HMS *London* determined that, since the French had already returned to the Chesapeake and the squadron had suffered badly in the engagement of the fifth, a return to New York represented the only reasonable option.[50] As the dejected force sailed into New York Harbor to an anxiously waiting crowd on 19 September, one can only imagine the onlookers' thoughts and apprehensions. The Battle of the Virginia Capes cost the Royal Navy ninety killed and 246 wounded. More importantly, it cost them the war in America. Had Graves succeeded and driven off de Grasse, he would have reestablished British command of the sea in Chesapeake Bay. With Clinton moving several thousand troops to relieve Cornwallis unimpeded by the French navy, the final major land battle of the war in North America might have been at Yorktown, but instead of a beleaguered garrison pummeled into submission by French siege guns, it might well have been the decisive battle that Cornwallis had sought since Camden the year before. The Allied army could have been caught in a pincer movement between the two forces of Clinton and Cornwallis. But that is speculation.

Given its worldwide maritime struggle against the Bourbon powers—France and Spain—and the Dutch, Britain probably would have concluded some negotiated settlement with the American Patriots. Perhaps that would result in some form of American independence, perhaps not. What can be safely asserted is that had Graves defeated the French at the Battle of the Virginia Capes, the outcome of the War of American Independence would likely have been dramatically different. In war, small episodes of random chance often yield great results.

## "Mortification": Yorktown, September–October 1781

Cornwallis arrived at Yorktown on 2 August and immediately established his headquarters at Thomas Nelson's house on the southeastern end of town. A prosperous community dealing in the tobacco trade, Yorktown had once been the principal port on the Chesapeake, but by 1781, it had been eclipsed by other locations. To fortify the site, Cornwallis erected a series of inner and outer works that formed a crescent from riverbank to riverbank around the town and its port area. The outer defensive works stood a half mile out from the town center. Several creeks and ravines cut through the area between the two sets of works, providing an additional measure of defensive protection against a landward assault. As strong points to anchor the line, the earl constructed ten redoubts around the inner works. Redoubts 9 and 10, which would play a critical role in the upcoming struggle, dominated the left of the British position to the southeast in an area of level ground most likely to be the focus of any attack. For artillery, all the light fieldpieces moved into fourteen batteries. Eighteen-pounders drawn from the frigates anchored in the river supplemented these guns, with the warships providing additional artillery coverage. Across the river at Gloucester Point, the defenders constructed a triangular palisade-style fort and a series of earthworks along the bluff overlooking the river. Suffering from the heat, meager rations of poor quality, brackish water, and periodic desertions, especially among the German units, the army pressed ahead with construction through the dog days of August.

The first week of September brought unkind news. Cornwallis received a warning from Clinton that Washington had departed from New York and would likely move toward Virginia. The letter also expressed the CinC's assurance of reinforcements and aid. Having heard of the arrival of de Grasse on 30 August, such promises of support raised hopes in the British camp.[51] Cornwallis, in a curt and alarming letter, informed Clinton of the French admiral's arrival in strength: "Comte de Grasse's fleet is within the Capes of the Chesapeak [*sic*].

Forty boats with troops went up the James River yesterday and four ships lie at the entrance of this river [York]."[52] The hunter now became the hunted. The distant, sustained cannonade heard on the fifth gave evidence that the Royal Navy had arrived in force, but the return of the French to the Chesapeake several days later squashed any hopes of immediate relief. Realizing his danger, the earl devised a breakout plan to confront Lafayette at Williamsburg. Executing a nighttime forced march, his army would surprise the Continentals at daybreak. Yet in a decision completely out of character, though probably based on Clinton's assurances that 4,000 reinforcements had embarked their vessels and only awaited the right sailing conditions, Cornwallis called off the breakout attack on Lafayette.[53]

The same day that Clinton's letter of 6 September arrived, Washington and Rochambeau rode into Williamsburg. All the players were now in place. While Cornwallis awaited the promised relief, Washington acted. Although his main body had not yet arrived, the Allied commander posted available forces to impede any British escape attempt either up the York River or across to Gloucester Point. By the twenty-first, the entire Allied army arrived safely with no enemy interference. De Grasse agreed to keep his French squadron on station in the Chesapeake until at least 1 November. On 27 September Washington initiated the final great event of the War of American Independence—the Siege of Yorktown. The following day before dawn, in the dry and still-warm early Virginia autumn, the Allied army marched out of the Virginia capital toward the hamlet on the York, with Continentals in the lead. By late afternoon, British pickets reported the presence of French troops on the Williamsburg Road and exchanged shots before retiring inside the breastworks. By evening, Allied forces took up positions around the British works. The French occupied the left and northwest sector, with their left flank resting on the river and their right at the Continentals' left position, near a marsh. Washington stationed his Patriot forces to the south and southeast of the town to the river below it. The Allied line ran roughly a mile out from the British fortifications. The following day Washington moved his position closer to the enemy redoubts,. drawing fire from British gunners against the troops in the open. Fortunately for the Patriots, the barrage did little damage, and the python-like squeeze commenced a process that lasted for three weeks as the Allies conducted a classic, European-style siege. In New York the CinC recognized the peril, advising Lord Germain: "We are therefore no longer to compare Forces with the Enemy, but to endeavor to act in the best Manner we can against them. . . . With what I have, inadequate as it is, I will exert myself to the utmost to save Lord Cornwallis . . . [and would assure] his Lordship that I would either reinforce him by every possible means in my Power, or make the best diversion I could in his favor."[54]

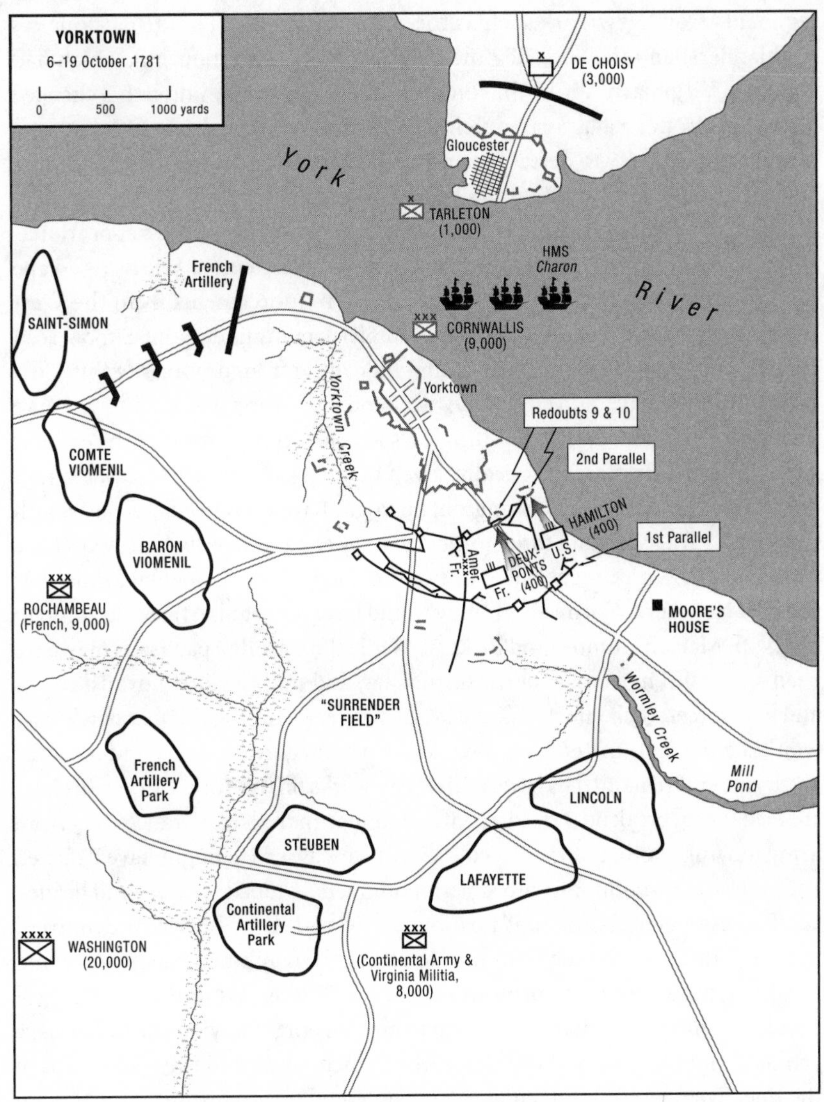


The Siege of Yorktown, 6–19 October 1781.
*Map by Erin Greb Cartography.*

As the Allied army fanned out into the encircling positions, Cornwallis again faced his usual operational situation—numerical inferiority. Although he had his greatest force of the entire Southern Campaign—over 7,000 men, including regiments from New York such as the 76th Regiment of Foot (MacDonald's Highlanders) and the 80th Regiment of Foot (City of Edinburgh), which had arrived in Virginia in April—the contradictory orders from Clinton that changed his actions from an aggressive offensive to a passive enclave defensive had cost him the opportunity to defeat the enemy in detail. Had he destroyed Lafayette before the arrival of Washington's force, his position would have been immeasurably improved. On the other hand, once he knew of de Grasse's appearance, why not attack Lafayette and avoid the potential encirclement before his escape route closed? Even with the arrival of French reinforcements from the West Indies under Maj. Gen. Claude-Anne-Montbleru, marquis de Saint-Simon, seen coming up the James River by boat after offloading from de Grasse's ships, the earl could then have moved north with a force of over 7,000 men to conduct a pincer operation against Washington's army in conjunction with the New York garrison. Or more practically, given Clinton's reluctance to come out of his garrison to confront Washington, he might have marched back into South Carolina with a more than three-to-one manpower advantage to destroy Greene's Continentals. With Greene out of the way and no viable Continental formations south of New York, Cornwallis finally would have the regular-troop strength to deal with Marion, Sumter, and Pickens. While the Carolina partisans may have been successful in small actions, skirmishes, and raids against Loyalist bands and light forces, their effectiveness against an overwhelming number of regulars would be suspect. Instead, counter to his usual aggressiveness and hunt for battle, the earl remained passive in his breastworks on the York. Cornwallis later claimed that to break out risked a confrontation with the larger Franco-American army moving south, but that force was still days away. He might have defeated Lafayette and Saint-Simon with superior numbers, escaped the trap, and headed south after Greene. Numerous possibilities existed that Cornwallis demurred to take.[55] Tarleton pleaded with him to attack the combined enemy force and break out, but apparently Cornwallis relied on Clinton's assurances of relief. He should not have. With Barras's arrival from Newport, carrying the heavy siege artillery, and the return of de Grasse, the French numbered thirty-six ships of the line. Even with reinforcements, Graves would be heavily outnumbered on the water. Knowing these odds, it is even stranger that Cornwallis did not take his young subordinate's recommendation and attempt an escape.[56]

The Allied army under Washington and Rochambeau consisted of French and Continental regulars and Patriot militia. With seven infantry line regiments totaling about 7,000 troops, an artillery component of 600 men, and cavalry totaling above 600 troopers, the French alone matched Cornwallis in numbers. More importantly, they brought siege guns and mortars. From the Continental Line, Washington fielded three divisions under Major Generals Lafayette, Benjamin Lincoln, and Baron Friedrich von Steuben, the Prussian officer who brought German drill, discipline, and tactical proficiency to the army in the winter at Valley Forge.[57] All told, the Continentals numbered just over 5,000 troops. The Virginia militia, under Gen. Thomas Nelson, took up a position on the far right of the Allied position, forming three brigades of 3,200 men.

Facing this combined force of over 15,000 troops, Cornwallis had approximately 7,500 effectives; due to the poor food and water combined with various illnesses, notably the "bloody flux" (dysentery), on any given day his real strength fell considerably lower. Many of these troops had been part of his command from the campaign's beginning, or before the North Carolina invasion, and included the Brigade of Guards; the 23rd, 33rd, and 71st Regiments of Foot; the 82nd Regiment's light infantry company; Tarleton's British Legion; Hamilton's North Carolina Volunteers; and the Regiment von Bose. Troops that had arrived with Arnold and Phillips were the two light infantry battalions drawn from different regiments; the 17th, 43rd, 76th, and 80th Regiments of Foot; the Provincials of Simcoe's Queen's Rangers; and three German regiments. In addition, 900 marines detached from the fleet filled out the command and manned the naval guns brought ashore. A scattering of dragoons, Royal Artillery, and German Jägers rounded out the besieged force. Cornwallis's hopes for relief rose when he received a letter from Clinton, dated 24 September, informing him that over 5,000 troops comprised the relief expedition. The correspondence further advised him that additional warships had arrived that day, with three first rates to escort the convoy.[58] Cornwallis penned a brave response that evening, but surely the lack of haste must have distressed him; Clinton had indicated an almost two-week delay in sailing. In as diplomatic and positive language as he could muster, the earl acknowledged the relief force but pointed out that he "had ventured these last two days to look General Washington's whole force in the face in the position on the outside of my works and I have the pleasure to assure Your Excellency that there was but one wish throughout the whole army, which was that the enemy would advance."[59] Perhaps a more direct response might have made the point more cogent. For example, when faced with blocking the Scottish Covenanter Army's invasion into northwest England during the Second British Civil War, Major General John Lambert had sent letter after letter to Parliament requesting reinforcements and supplies—to make the point, his letter of 20 July 1648 simply stated, "Haste, Haste, Post Haste!"[60] For Clinton, he could do little in a timely fashion until Graves returned since an overland march would take weeks. Sea transport was faster, thus the squadron's return represented the critical issue.

Complicating the rapidly unfolding crisis, London's attitude illustrated a profound lack of understanding as to the situation on the ground. Germain, in his 2 May 1781 letter, expressed "mortification" that Clinton proposed to remove forces from the Virginia theater for operations farther north. Further, Germain, having placed the issue before George III, advised Clinton, "I am commanded by His Majesty to acquaint you, that the recovery of the Southern Provinces, and the Prosecution of the War by pushing Our Conquests from South to North, is to be considered as the Chief and principal Object for the Employment of all the Forces under your Command, which can be spared from the defence of the Places in His Majesty's Possession, until it is accomplished."[61] In a single stroke the American secretary, normally given to broad platitudes and sweeping strategic conceptual thoughts, roiled the already shaky strategic coherence and command relationships in theater. In invoking the king's opinion, he implied that for Clinton, he had no choice but to prosecute the war in Virginia. The question remained—conduct an offensive seek-and-destroy operation of the sort Cornwallis preferred or a defensive and cautionary action. Germain in the same letter did provide the caveat that, given weather and seasonal conditions, the king granted his commander full authority to conduct more northerly operations. Similarly, the monarch did not wish for Clinton to "restrain . . . from availing yourself of any favorable Event, or change of Circumstances," but rather, the war should be conducted in accordance with the established plan, that the taking and abandonment of posts would accomplish nothing in terms of the overarching national policy of restoring allegiance in the rebellious colonies.[62]

To further reinforce London's attitude, Germain's letter of 7 July 1781 all but destroyed any plan to withdraw forces from Virginia to relocate the main thrust to the middle colonies. Though not a specific order, it stated that "it gave His Majesty much satisfaction to find, by these Dispatches [previous Clinton correspondence describing Cornwallis's advance into Virginia], that you had so fully adopted the Plan suggested to you, of pushing the war to the Southward with all the force you could spare from the Defence of New York."[63] The letter, received on 10 October as plans moved ahead for a relief force from New York, underscored for Clinton the lack of support for his strategic concept from London and no doubt reminded him that ultimate strategic decision-making authority had been taken out of his hands and assumed three thousand miles away. Such micromanagement of the theater commander's discretion to determine force disposition and the thrust of the campaign in a dynamic and changeable environment further compounded an already strained and brittle strategic cohesiveness. Combined with the distance from North America to Britain and the concomitant communications delay, the ability to assess the situation on the ground and to react swiftly had been devastated.

In Yorktown, in a sign of the growing desperation of the besieged forces, the lack of fodder caused the British to kill over 600 horses and dump their carcasses into the river. The horrible stench must have added to the dismal atmosphere inside the beleaguered garrison. In the first week of October, little fighting occurred, though much activity went on behind Allied lines. There, soldiers dug entrenchments, filled sandbags, and built gabions, fascines, abatis, and stakes—materials of a standard siege. Meanwhile, the Royal Artillery and marines fired their guns on any target of opportunity that presented itself. On the evening of 2 October the ships at anchor in the York opened fire on the Allied positions to cover the crossing of cavalry over to Gloucester Point to provide support for a foraging party. Washington, however, had stationed 1,500 Virginia militia to impede any such breakout attempt. Additionally, the Patriot commander sent over 1,400 French troops and 800 marines drawn from the French fleet to support the militia. As Tarleton's legionnaires and Simcoe's rangers returned from their foraging foray with loaded wagons, the French and militia struck, inflicting many casualties. Although the Crown forces returned to Yorktown without further incident, this proved to be the last major forage of its kind on the Gloucester side, further contributing to the growing starvation inside the garrison.

On the night of 6–7 October, the Allies completed and opened their first parallel. With pickaxes, gabions, and shovels in hand, 1,500 men moved out into the open to construct the parallel trench in a single night. At only 800 yards from the defenses, this parallel trench ran for 2,000 yards, from Yorktown Creek in the center of the Allied line to the river, and at spots ranged from 600 to 800 yards from the enemy lines. Supported by a French diversionary attack against Cornwallis's left and the lighting of large campfires in the center of the line, both of which drew British fire, the men toiled away and soon filled the gabions with dirt and sand from the four-foot-deep trench. Having neither spotted nor heard the work, at dawn the astonished defenders realized that the enemy had entrenched only a few hundred yards distant. On the ninth, with batteries finally in place, French artillery opened fire late in the afternoon; the first rounds killed several officers of the 76th Regiment. One by one the Allied barrage beat down the defensive works and, more critically, silenced all the artillery on the British left. On the tenth the French Grand Battery opened fire with 18- and 24-pounders and heavy siege mortars. No longer did the British have the advantage of shot weight. That night hot shot set HMS *Charon* and two transports ablaze in the anchorage, costing Cornwallis potential firepower and mobility and prompting him to order the scuttling or burning of several other ships.

Word of further delay in New York reached Cornwallis during the night of the tenth. Clinton now advised that the relief force could not sail for at least two more days. The CinC's words could not have encouraged the earl: "I have reason to hope from the assurances given me this day by Admiral Graves that we may pass the bar [a sandbar outside New York Harbor] by the 12th October if the winds permit and no unforeseen accident happens. This however, is subject to disappointment."[64] Reason to hope? If the winds permit? No unforeseen accident? Subject to disappointment? One can only imagine Cornwallis's thoughts as he read that letter while artillery and mortar rounds screamed over the breastworks, exploding within his lines. By the evening of the eleventh, the earl realized the virtual hopelessness of the situation. Over fifty enemy guns lobbed rounds and hot shot into the town and defenses. Cornwallis informed his commander that day, "we cannot hope to make a very long resistance." In a poignant postscript appended later that afternoon, he added, "Since my last letter was written, we have lost 30 men." Two hours later he noted: "Last night the enemy made their second parallel at the distance of 300 yards. We continue to lose men very fast."[65]

Meanwhile, senior officers in New York had debated plans for the rescue for days. Major General James Robertson, military governor of New York, proposed embarking up to 5,000 troops on any available ships in hopes that they could run through the French blockade. But without other general officer's support, his proposal died. Indications from Yorktown that the post could hold out for several more weeks induced a fatal lack of immediacy. Indeed, Cornwallis himself indicated in mid-September that he could hold the post until the end of October based on his provisions. Another possibility considered would allow Graves's entire squadron to run the blockade and evacuate the troops; but what then of the escape once the French had been alerted? Naval commanders opposed this option as untenable and foolhardy. As the days passed, the relief force's sailing date moved from 5 October to the eighth and on to the twelfth. Not until the seventeenth did the ships depart New York Harbor, and only by the nineteenth could the transports make way toward the Virginia Capes due to contrary winds. By then, the garrison had capitulated.

Begun on the night of the eleventh, the Allied diggers and sappers constructed the second parallel trench, 500 yards closer to the British lines. With the completion of the second line, Redoubts 9 and 10 came into prominence. To advance farther toward the town, the Allies had to neutralize these two fortified positions anchoring the British left on the river. Accordingly, on the night of the fourteenth, two storming parties of 400 men each, drawn from the French grenadiers and chasseurs and the Continental Light Infantry, made their way toward the enemy positions under cover of darkness. At Redoubt 9, defended by Hessians, the French attack momentarily stalled when discovered by a sentry as the advance men hacked away at the abatis and lay fascines to fill the protective trench. Within minutes, however, the chasseurs overcame the defenders, and the survivors surrendered. At Redoubt 10 the light infantry, under Lt. Col. Alexander Hamilton, advanced quickly and quietly with bayonets and unloaded muskets. With only seventy men, the defenders had little chance as the attackers rushed the redoubt entrance and front, not even bothering to hack away the abatis. The capture of Redoubt 10 took only ten minutes. The British left now lay wide open. Within hours the Allies moved batteries into the captured works; the second parallel now extended the entire length of the front.

On the sixteenth Cornwallis made one last desperate attempt to break out. A force of 400 men attacked the point where the French and Continental forces joined. The assault force managed to break into the second parallel and move down each side, killing defenders and spiking guns by breaking off the tips of their bayonets in the touchholes; within hours, however, the spiked guns returned to action. The raid, while courageous and bold, ultimately accomplished nothing. Meanwhile, in a last gamble, Cornwallis sent word across the river to Tarleton to prepare to attack the enemy force covering Gloucester so the earl's forces could evacuate Yorktown and escape across the river. At eleven that night a thousand men of the Guards, 23rd Foot, and light infantry crossed over in flatboats, taking an hour to reach Gloucester, after which the boats returned to the Yorktown side. Continuing in the run of ill fortune that characterized Cornwallis's time in Virginia, a squall blew up, making any further crossings impossible. Realizing that to divide his forces any further in the face of the enemy invited an attack on both fronts, and given that he could not get his entire army across in a single night, even though the storm moderated, he ordered the men to return.

On the morning of the seventeenth, Cornwallis and O'Hara assessed the grim situation. With only a single gun left firing, and that with just a few rounds left, the earl called a council of war. With ammunition nearly exhausted and the dead and wounded increasing by the hour, the senior officers realized that all hope had drained away. They had fought a courageous fight, and by the laws of war in such a hopeless situation, an honorable surrender was acceptable. All agreed. Cornwallis dictated a letter to Washington: "Sir, I propose a cessation of hostilities for twenty-four hours, and that two officers may be appointed by each side to meet at Mr Moore's house to settle terms for the surrender of the posts at York and Gloucester."[66] At ten in the morning, a lone drummer appeared on the parapet and beat the "parley." A British officer waving a white handkerchief descended the works. Firing ceased as an American officer blindfolded the Briton and escorted him to General Washington. To his request, the Virginian replied that a negotiation would be acceptable. That night the British destroyed as much hardware, arms, and ammunition as possible; either scuttled or burned the last remaining ships in the harbor; and blew up the town's powder magazine. Early on the eighteenth, Washington delivered his terms, which included that all soldiers and sailors would be regarded as prisoners of war. The commissioners for each side met in the afternoon at the Moore House behind Allied lines. By midnight, they had worked out all details for a formal surrender to occur on the afternoon of the nineteenth.

## Surrender Field, 19 October 1781

In accordance with the surrender terms, the Allies marched out at noon on the nineteenth and formed lines in a field down the Williamsburg Road from Yorktown. At two o'clock the roll of drums and shrill pitch of fifes and bagpipes was heard from the town as the British forces marched out of their breastworks. O'Hara led the column, carrying the earl's sword. Cornwallis, as had many in the army, had endured three separate bouts of malaria during the campaign and that afternoon remained at his quarters with a case of dysentery. Believing that the French general commanded the Allied forces, O'Hara attempted to surrender his sword to Rochambeau, who directed him to Washington, indicating that the Virginian commanded the Franco-American army. Swinging his mount over to Washington, O'Hara again offered the sword, which the general refused. O'Hara apologized for Cornwallis's absence, after which Washington indicated that his second in command, Benjamin Lincoln, would conduct the surrender. Of the British garrison, only 3,500 soldiers, marines, and sailors emerged from the town to "ground arms" that October afternoon, so devastating had been the illness and casualties. In last acts of defiance, angry veterans of the brutal struggle they had endured since the landing at Simmon's Island near Charleston, which held such high expectations months earlier, expressed their passionate feelings. At the concurrent surrender ceremony on the Gloucester side, Tarleton's British Legion defiantly rode out with drawn sabers. Two officers of the 23rd, both designated to board a transport ship to Charleston by the terms of the surrender, each wrapped the regiment's king's and regimental colors around their bodies under their uniforms. So it went on the saddest of days for British arms. Surgeon James Thacher of the Continental Army captured the surrender event's somber mood, commenting in his *Journal:* "At about twelve o'clock, the combined army was arranged and drawn up in two lines extending more than a mile in length. The French troops, in complete uniform, displayed a martial and noble appearance. . . . The Americans though not all in uniform nor their dress so neat, yet exhibited an erect and soldierly air, every countenance beamed with satisfaction and joy. The concourse of spectators from the country was prodigious, in point of numbers was probably equal to the military, but universal silence and order prevailed."[67]

From the British side, troops—sullen, exhausted, and angry—marched to what became known as Surrender Field. Many had helped consume the rum stores rather than surrender such prizes. Surliness characterized many as emotions overtook many others. One can only imagine the thoughts and feelings of the troops who had fought, starved, lost friends and comrades, and chased the elusive rebels for mile after mile over the southern countryside since early the previous year. These men, especially those who had served in the South from the campaign's beginning, had seen victory after victory at Camden, at the Catawba, at Guilford Court House, and at Green Springs. Now they surrendered.

Dr. Thacher, several days later, witnessed a moment epitomizing the incredible and thorough defeat of Cornwallis and his skilled, disciplined, experienced army: "While in the presence of General Washington, Lord Cornwallis was standing with his head uncovered, his Excellency said to him politely, My Lord, you had better be covered from the cold; his Lordship applying his hand to his head replied, 'it matters not, Sir, what comes of this head now.'"[68]

---

In the Scottish Highlands there existed in the eighteenth century an age-old tradition. When war came, the men of a clan lined up at attention. The chief, or in the eighteenth century the officer warranted to raise troops, walked down the line, examining every clansman, and choosing the men to serve in his unit. To every selectee the officer offered a pinch from his snuff mull, a sign of acceptance into the unit. To be selected represented a great honor; to be rejected meant embarrassment and dishonor. For those men of Scotland, of whom many served in the 71st, 76th, 80th, and North Carolina Loyalist Highlanders, derived from a martial culture in which military service to the clan and chieftain was the highest honor, the surrender at Yorktown must have been especially galling.[69] Captain Samuel Graham of the 76th Regiment of Foot (MacDonald's Highlanders) recorded that day in his memoirs: "[T]he garrison marched out betwixt the two lines of American and French troops reluctantly enough, and laid down their arms. A corporal next to me shed tears, and, embracing his firelock, threw it down, saying, 'May you never get so good a master.'"[70]

CONCLUSION

# "Peril and Delusion"

## *The Judgment of History*

The fault, dear Brutus, is not in our stars, But in ourselves.

—William Shakespeare, *Julius Caesar (act 1, scene 2, lines 140–41)*

Niccolo Machiavelli, the sixteenth-century Italian diplomat, philosopher, historian, military designer, and political commentator, observed that "everyone may begin a war at will but not finish it thus."[1] A thorough examination of the strategic decision making and the resultant operational execution of the Southern Campaign of 1778–81 indicates that at all levels of command and decision making, from the civil authority in London to the theater command in New York to the field command, British understanding of the nature of the War of American Independence was severely flawed. Based on false or misguided assumptions, especially as to the willingness of Loyalists to turn out in great numbers and to support the field forces, the strategy for pacifying the southern colonies one at a time from Georgia northward had no real chance for success. Added to this witch's brew of profoundly poor net assessment was the breakdown of strategic cohesion between the triad of decision makers—Lord George Germain, the American secretary in London; General Sir Henry Clinton, the commander in chief in New York; and Lieutenant General Lord Charles Cornwallis in the field. Finally, the command and control, especially exemplified by the horrific logistics and internal communications problems created by the army moving inland away from seaborne support and compounded by the partisans within the irregular warfare that erupted, added to the difficulty of conducting a military campaign at a distance in the eighteenth century. All these dynamics combined to undercut any chance for Crown strategic success in the South.

A critical concept is that of a "war within a war within a war." In broader terms, one can think of the American War experience as a revolutionary or "peoples" struggle, aimed at a profound change in the political and constitutional order, within a regional war (Canada, East and West Florida, and the thirteen colonies in rebellion), all within a global war after France, Spain, and the Dutch joined in against Britain (thus moving the battle front to the West Indies, Gibraltar, the Indian Ocean, and other regions). In terms of the British strategic conundrum after 1778, the kingdom had to fight essentially three different wars with limited resources and manpower, a situation exacerbated by the immense downsizing, especially in the Royal Navy, that had occurred after the Seven Years' War. Each conflict had profoundly different requirements. While the various officials in London struggled with the problems inherent in prosecuting multiple forms of war on a global scale, a similar context confronted Clinton, Cornwallis, and Crown forces in the South. Indeed, within this geographic context of wars within wars, Britain also fought a hybrid war composed of three different types: conventional, irregular, and revolutionary. Cornwallis, though a brilliant tactical and operational commander, nonetheless represented the conventional European officer schooled in the linear tactics and military theories of the seventeenth and eighteenth centuries. Perhaps no British commander stood prepared by experience, training, or disposition to conduct successfully the types of typical military operations required to attain strategic victory in the South.

Other difficulties brought on by a lack of strategic cohesion between civil and military authorities, the loss of command of the sea in September 1781, profound logistical problems, and the lack of Loyalist support made the ultimate task of restoring royal allegiance and authority in the southern colonies practically impossible. Indeed, the Southern Campaign required not only the "One Great Director" in London but also an astute military commander in North America. Either Clinton or Cornwallis could have played that role. Neither did, nor could they be expected to do so. The task simply lay beyond the scope of British resource capability and institutional organization of the day. With multiple offices responsible for supply and the lack of cooperation between ministries and departments compounded by the communications difficulties, the British administrative system was simply not up to the requirements of conducting a large-scale and distant colonial war. It would have required a depth of strategic leadership that few, if any, eighteenth-century officers possessed. Perhaps George Washington or Nathanael Greene came closest to this ideal, both Patriot generals possessing the strategic acumen and leadership traits required to prosecute and coordinate the three types of war—conventional, irregular, and revolutionary—all at the same time.

Ira Gruber, the historian of the Howe brothers (who preceded Clinton and Arbuthnot in command), points out that one of the difficulties in planning and subsequently executing British strategy for the war lay in the fact that none of the chief players had any relevant strategic and operational planning experience or expertise; only Cornwallis had attended a military academy. The central military and naval commanders, including Clinton, his predecessors Sir Thomas Gage and Sir William Howe, and the major naval officers in theater, all had led significant commands at the tactical level (individual ships, regiments, or battalions), but they lacked overall commander-in-chief experience. Unit-level commands allowed each officer to build reputations on "courage, tactical skill and administrative talent rather than on strategic insight." Yet no military authority in a major command position in the colonies had the requisite strategic- or campaign-level planning expertise to overcome the considerable challenges facing British efforts to crush the rebellion and restore allegiance to the Crown.[2]

Similarly, the principle decision makers in London, including King George III, the earl of Sandwich at the Admiralty, and Lord Germain, lacked the requisite strategic and operational planning experience and ability. Only General Amherst, who had held major command in North America during the Seven Years' War, possessed significant strategic planning experience. But even as CinC of the Army from 1778 on, he had little influence over the war's strategic and operational direction based on the constitutional peculiarities of the British military and naval system. Amherst, though, refused the command in North America, perhaps realizing the futility of that effort. The judgment of the American secretary's biographer is telling. He says of Germain: "Under his direction of the American war, the British cause in the colonies moved from the decent and possible to the indefensible and hopeless."[3]

To the question originally posed of good strategy badly executed or simply a bad strategy, an argument can be made either way. The strategy of a methodical advance through the South northward establishing Loyalist dominance, restoring royal authority and security, and relying on an outpouring of local Loyalist support and participation (the "clear and hold" strategy) had merit. It might have achieved its intentions had the initial strategic assumption played out as anticipated. In reality, the operational execution was, to borrow a phrase, "a bridge too far." No British military commander at the time exhibited the strategic ability to conduct a successful campaign given the dynamics in the South. Therefore, "badly executed" might be better thought of as perhaps "incapable of being well executed."

Questions arise in terms of "simply a bad strategy." Was the confidence in the Loyalist outpouring and the ability to cow the rebels by regular military operations and pure force an example of not understanding the true nature of the war? Was the strategy unattainable from the start, considering the available resources in manpower, ships, and logistics? Was the strategy simply too fragile or brittle to withstand the normal "fog and friction" of war when combined with the inevitable interaction and adaptation on the enemy's part? These are basic questions that all played into the ultimate British failure in the Southern Campaign and get to the heart of the question.

Once the two generals returned to Britain, a pamphlet war broke out regarding the blame for the American debacle. Cornwallis accused Clinton of failing to support his Virginia operations with sufficient troops and in ordering him to an indefensible post at Yorktown. Clinton countered, arguing that the earl should not have advanced into Virginia so hurriedly and so far from his primary operational base at Charleston. He also contended that Cornwallis should have heeded his warnings on the inadvisability of moving into Virginia and that his suggestions to fortify Yorktown were not firm orders. Ultimately, public opinion sided with Cornwallis. Regardless, the endgame remained. In 1783 the independent United States of America emerged on the world scene with the signing of the Treaty of Paris and the end of hostilities. Alan Valentine ultimately credits Germain for the loss of the colonies: "With the American war virtually ended, every leading general who had tried to implement the strategy formed in Whitehall had ended that service in anger if not in disgrace. . . . [They] all made their mistakes, but each was the victim of ineptitudes greater than his own. The chief formulator of that strategy had not yet met his own day of reckoning."[4]

So what is the assessment of the British strategic failure in terms of those dynamics proposed at the outset of this study—strategic coherence, strategic leadership, and theory of victory? To summarize the most essential points:

1. The British war effort suffered from a profound lack of strategic and operational coherence and a devastating breakdown in unity of command and effort as each node of the strategic and operational decision-making triad worked at cross-purposes, with differing concepts of the appropriate overall strategy and resultant operations.
2. Strategic leadership failed in terms of the inability to recognize and implement an appropriate strategy and its resultant operational execution, particularly the seapower aspect, while the key field commander, though of a bold and aggressive nature, substituted operational brilliance for strategic acumen when faced with a master strategist as his key opponent.
3. The British theory of victory proved woefully flawed and failed to comprehend the true nature of the rebellion in the South, exemplified by the faulty Loyalist strategy and by placing the population on "death ground" with the various counterproductive proclamations and mandatory oaths.[5] Sir John Fortescue captures the vacancy of the Loyalist strategy in his history of the British Army: "The mere fact that the British Ministry rested its

> hopes on the co-operation of American loyalists was sufficient to distract its councils and to vitiate its plans. . . . [O]f all foundations on which to build a campaign this is the loosest, the most treacherous, the fullest of peril and delusion. . . Their purpose being vague and unconfirmed, the Ministers proceeded without any idea of what an army could or could not do, or of the force that was required for any given object."[6]

Clausewitz reminds the student of war that "the political object is the goal, war is the means of reaching it, and means can never be considered in isolation from their purpose."[7] In other words, in all manner of discussions, deliberations, and decisions surrounding warfare, civilian and military leaders must hold in their minds exactly why they are pursuing a course of violence. Overly bold, aggressive conventional operations against the Continental Army forgot that the primary policy objective of the Southern Campaign was to pacify the public and return them to allegiance. The resultant chase of Greene, an ineffectual response to the partisan threat, and proclamations that inflamed and demoralized Loyalists and forced former rebels and neutrals to swear allegiance or be considered enemies all combined to undercut the ultimate political objective of pacification and returning the southern colonies to the Crown. Operationally, the chase through the vast, undeveloped southern terrain in hopes of inspiring the populace to turn out in great numbers to restore royal government while crushing any conventional opposition proved a hopeless endeavor. As Cornwallis charged off with his army in search of regular formations to destroy, Patriots simply filled the vacuum left by his departure. As Lord Rawdon withdrew from the South Carolina posts of Ninety Six and others, Patriots simply moved in. Since British forces could never consolidate control and ensure the security of territory other than a few protected enclaves (Charleston, Ninety Six, and Wilmington, for example), once Crown troops moved on, local Loyalists never had the opportunity to execute the fundamentally critical "hold" aspect of the Southern Strategy. Valentine aptly describes the failure of "clear and hold": "Cornwallis might lead his sweltering troops across the marshy plains and sandy foot-hills of the South, but the paths their troops had cut would close in behind them like the vanishing wake of a passing ship."[8]

On 20 October 1781 the captured commander of Crown forces in the South wrote to inform his commander in chief in New York that the Southern Campaign had ended: "Sir, I have the mortification to inform your Excellency that I have been forced to give up the posts of York and Gloucester and to surrender the troops under my command by capitulation on the 19th instant as prisoners of war to the combined forces of America and France."[9] With these few words, Lieutenant General Charles, 2nd Earl Cornwallis announced not only the failure of the Southern Strategy but also the failure to subdue the rebellion in the North American colonies and restore their allegiance to the British Crown. As Cassius cautioned Brutus in Shakespeare's play on the rise of Julius Caesar to tyrannical power, so too must the judgment of history conclude that the blame for Great Britain's loss of the American colonies lay not with the Fates, but within itself.

# Appendix

## *Short Biographies*

### *Sir Henry Clinton, KB (1730–1795)*

Clinton first served as an officer of an independent company of New York militia and fought at the 1745 siege of Louisburg. Commissioned as a captain in the 2nd Foot Guards (Coldstream Guards) in 1751, by 1758 he assumed a lieutenant colonelcy in the 1st Guards (Grenadier Guards) before becoming colonel in 1762. He participated in the Seven Years' War on the European continent from 1760 to 1762 and served as an aide de camp to Prince Ferdinand of Brunswick. Promoted to major general in 1772, he also took up a seat in Parliament for Boroughbridge and later Newark-on-Trent. Clinton arrived in Boston in May 1775 and commanded Royal forces at the Battle of Bunker (Breed's) Hill in June. He commanded the failed Charleston expedition in 1776 and returned in time to participate in the 1776 New York offensive. Receiving a knighthood in the Order of the Bath (KB) and promotion to lieutenant general in April 1777, he returned to the colonies after a brief stay in England. In May 1778 he relieved Sir William Howe as CinC in North America with a temporary promotion to full general "in America." In 1780 he personally commanded the British siege of Charleston, South Carolina, before returning to New York. Following the Yorktown surrender, Sir Guy Carleton relieved him as CinC in North America. Promoted to general in 1793 and appointed as governor of Gibraltar, Clinton died before assuming the office.

### *Charles Cornwallis, KCG, 2nd Earl and 1st Marquess Cornwallis (1738–1805)*

From a prominent Suffolk family and educated at Eton and at Clare College, Cambridge, Cornwallis, during his early military career, served as ensign, 1st Foot Guards; captain, 85th Regiment of Foot; brevet lieutenant colonel, 12th Regiment of Foot; and colonel, 33rd Regiment of Foot. He was promoted to major general in 1775, lieutenant general in 1777, and general in 1793. In Parliament

Cornwallis voted against the Stamp Act and advocated addressing colonial grievances. Arriving in the American colonies in 1776, he participated in the failed Charleston offensive and the New York Campaign; then the Battles of Princeton, Brandywine, Germantown, and Fort Mercer in 1777; and Monmouth Court House in 1778. He commanded all Crown forces in the southern colonies from June 1780 until the surrender at Yorktown, Virginia, in October, 1781. Elevated to Knight Companion of the Garter (KCG) in 1786, Cornwallis became governor general and CinC in India (1786–93), where he instituted civil and military administrative reforms and defeated Tipu Sultan of Mysore, thus assuring British domination. Elevated to marquess and appointed lord lieutenant and CinC in Ireland (1798–1801), Cornwallis defeated the Wolfe Tone rebellion and French invaders at Ballinamuck in 1798. Cornwallis was instrumental in the Acts of Union of 1800, leading to the creation of the United Kingdom. He led the British delegation at the Peace of Amiens negotiations with Napoleonic France in 1802. In his final service, Cornwallis again took up the governor generalship of India in 1805 but died of a fever soon after his arrival.

### *Patrick Ferguson (1744–1780)*

During the Seven Years' War, Ferguson served in the Scots Greys and later commanded a company of the 70th Regiment of Foot in the West Indies. Inventor of the breech-loading Ferguson rifle, he arrived in the colonies in 1777 in command of his rifle corps. Wounded at Brandywine, he returned to duty as a major in the 71st Regiment of Foot (Fraser's Highlanders). At Charleston in 1780, Sir Henry Clinton appointed him inspector of militia charged with recruiting Loyalist volunteers in South Carolina and Georgia. Sent into North Carolina to raise troops and protect Cornwallis's left flank, Ferguson issued the "fire and sword" proclamation, which enraged the Over-Mountain Men of the frontier. When Ferguson occupied a position at King's Mountain on the Carolina border in October 1780, the Over-Mountain Men and Virginia militia attacked, killing Ferguson and killing or capturing his entire Loyalist force.

### *Horatio Lloyd Gates (1727–1806)*

Gates obtained a commission in the 20th Regiment of Foot and participated in the War of the Austrian Succession (1740-48). Promoted to major during the French and Indian War (1754–63), he excelled at military administration but retired following the war's end. Selling his major's commission, he immigrated to Virginia in 1772. In 1775 Congress commissioned him as a brigadier general and adjutant general of the Continental Army. Promoted to major general in 1776, he assumed command of the Northern Department in August 1777 and commanded the forces that defeated Lieutenant General John Burgoyne in the Saratoga Campaign. In

May 1780 Gates assumed command of the Southern Department. Soundly beaten at the Battle of Camden in August 1780, he was relieved by Nathanael Greene in December. The Camden affair effectively ended Gates's military career.

### *George Germain (born George Sackville), 1st Viscount Sackville (1716–1785)*

Germain began his military career in the 7th Horse but took up a lieutenant colonelcy in the Gloustershire Regiment of Foot. Breveted to colonel, he participated in the Battle of Fontenoy in 1745 during the War of the Austrian Succession and became colonel of the 20th Foot and 7th Irish Horse. He served as a member of Parliament for Portarlington until 1761. With the Seven Years' War and promotion to lieutenant general, he assumed command of the British forces under Duke Ferdinand of Brunswick. At the Battle of Minden (1759), he refused to launch an attack despite several orders, resulting in his being court-martialed for cowardice and cashiered. In November 1775 he replaced Lord Dartmouth as secretary of state for the colonies and assumed responsibility for ending the American rebellion. The fall of the North ministry in 1782 due to Yorktown ended his political career, however, he was elevated to the peerage as Viscount Sackville.

### *Nathanael Greene (1742–1786)*

Born into a Rhode Island Quaker family, Greene studied military affairs rather than becoming a pacifist. He helped form the Kentish Guards, a militia unit, in 1774, serving in the ranks. In May 1775 he was promoted to command the Rhode Island Army of Observation at the siege of Boston. He later was commissioned as a brigadier and then major general in the Continental Army, commanding divisions during the northern campaigns, notably at the Trenton attack of Christmas Day, 1776. At the winter encampment at Valley Forge in March 1778, he became quartermaster general, making brilliant use of his business and logistical skills. He returned to field command at the Battle of Monmouth Court House (1778). Washington appointed Greene to command West Point after Benedict Arnold's treason, then in 1780 sent him to command the Southern Department. From December 1780 until the end of the war, Greene operated in the Carolinas, tactically losing battles at Guilford Court House in March 1781 and Hobkirk's Hill in April but demonstrating his strategic brilliance in flummoxing British efforts to pacify the South. Following the war, he established an estate in Georgia but died shortly thereafter.

### *Benjamin Lincoln (1733–1810)*

Lincoln's first military experience came in 1755, when he joined the 3rd Regiment of the Suffolk County (Massachusetts) militia; though seeing no action, he was promoted to major (1763) and lieutenant colonel (1772). Promoted to major general of the Massachusetts militia (1776), he participated in the defense of New York. Resultantly, Congress commissioned him as a major general in February 1777. Lincoln commanded the Continental right at the Battle of Bemis Heights during the Saratoga Campaign (1777), where he sustained a wound in the ankle. After convalescence, he rejoined the army in August 1778 and traveled south to command the Southern Department. Taking personal command of the defenses of Charleston, Lincoln surrendered the city (and himself) in May 1780. Later exchanged for a British general, he rejoined Washington's main force and served as second in command at Yorktown, where he accepted the British surrender. Following the war, Lincoln served two years as secretary at war under the Articles of Confederation and later led the Massachusetts militia in suppressing Shays's Rebellion (1786–87).

### *Daniel Morgan (1736–1802)*

A prosperous Virginia farmer, Morgan served during the French and Indian War with British forces as a teamster but was punished for striking a superior officer. In 1775 he formed a rifle company that served in the siege of Boston and then participated in the failed invasion of Canada, where he was captured. Released in 1777, Morgan raised a Continental Line regiment and assumed command of the Provisional Rifle Corps. He joined the army opposing Burgoyne in New York and was instrumental in the Saratoga victory (1777). Throughout the war in the North, he became increasingly irritated at a lack of promotion. Plagued by health issues, in 1779 Morgan resigned and returned to Virginia, but he came back on active service after the Battle of Camden. Sent by Greene to operate on Cornwallis's left flank, he defeated Tarleton at the Battle of Cowpens in January 1781. Morgan resigned again due to health, but later commanded troops as a major general during the suppression of the Whiskey Rebellion (1794) and then served in the U.S. House of Representatives.

### *Charles O'Hara (1740–1802)*

At the age of twelve O'Hara became a cornet in the 3rd Dragoons and at sixteen a lieutenant in the 2nd Foot (Coldstream) Guards . During the Seven Years' War, he served as an aide-de-camp to the Marquis of Granby. Promoted to lieutenant colonel, he commanded the newly acquired Senegal colony. Arriving in America in July 1778, O'Hara assumed command of the Brigade of Guards as a brigadier general in October 1780, joining Cornwallis in South Carolina as second in command. Badly wounded, he nonetheless survived the Battle of Guilford Court House in March 1781 and had the unfortunate duty of surrendering the army at Yorktown due to Cornwallis's illness. Promoted to major general, O'Hara took up the governorship of Gibraltar in 1792. Promoted to lieutenant general, he led an assault during the siege of Toulon in 1793, was captured, and spent two years as a prisoner. Exchanged for the comte de Rochambeau in 1795 and promoted to general, O'Hara again became governor of Gibraltar in 1795.

### *Francis Edward Rawdon-Hastings, 1st Marquess of Hastings, KG, PC (1754–1826)*

Commissioned as an ensign in the 15th Regiment of Foot in 1771, Rawdon was promoted to lieutenant in the 5th Regiment of Foot and arrived in Boston in 1774. Earning distinction at the Battle of Bunker (Breed's Hill) and promoted to captain in the 63rd Regiment, he participated in the events of the northern- and middle-colony campaigns and as an aide-de-camp to Sir Henry Clinton. He raised the Volunteers of Ireland, made up of immigrant Irish Loyalists, which fought throughout the Southern Campaign. Despite his youth, he commanded the British left wing at the Battle of Camden in August 1780. With Cornwallis's invasion of North Carolina in 1781, Rawdon remained behind to command all Crown troops in South Carolina and Georgia. Ill, he departed for Britain in July 1781 but was captured by the French navy en route. In 1793, promoted to major general, Rawdon commanded on the Continent while becoming the 2nd Earl of Moira. In 1803, promoted to general, he assumed the post of CinC, Scotland. Three years later he entered British politics. Appointed governor general of India in 1812, he defeated numerous native attempts to expel the British and was elevated to Marquess of Hastings in 1816. In 1824 Rawdon-Hastings was appointed governor of Malta. He also was appointed as a Knight of the Garter (KG) and a member of the royal Privy Council (PC).

### *Sir Banastre Tarleton, 1st Baronet, GCB (1754–1833)*

Son of a prominent Liverpool merchant and politician, Tarleton studied law at Middle Temple and University College, Oxford. He purchased a cornetcy in the 1st Dragoon Guards in 1775 and arrived in America in 1776. With rapid promotions, he became commander of the British Legion, a New York Loyalist dragoon unit that went to the Carolinas for participation in the Southern Campaign. Known for his bold and aggressive offensive actions, Tarleton earned a reputation for not only effectiveness but also brutality. At the Battle of Cowpens in January 1781, Morgan finally defeated him. Later in Virginia Tarleton commanded Gloucester Point, across the York River from Yorktown. Following the war, he entered Parliament representing Liverpool and served until 1812. Although promoted to major general in 1794, lieutenant general in 1801, and general in 1812, Tarleton never again commanded in combat. Created baronet in 1815, he was made a Knight Grand Cross of the Order of the Bath (GCB) in 1820.

# Notes

## Abbreviations

| | |
|---|---|
| C-CC | Benjamin Franklin Stevens, *The Campaign in Virginia, 1781: An exact Reprint of Six rare Pamphlets on the Clinton-Cornwallis Controversy*, 2 vols. (1888; reprint, Charleston, S.C.: Nabu, 2010) |
| HMC | Historical Manuscripts Commission |
| TNA CC PRO 30/11 | Cornwallis Correspondence, The National Archives, Kew, U.K. |
| TNA CO 5 | Letter Books of the Colonial Office, America and West Indies, The National Archives, Kew, U.K. |
| TNA HQ PRO 30/55 | Headquarters Papers of the British Army in North America, 1775–1784 (Dorchester Papers), The National Archives, Kew, U.K. |

## Introduction. British Strategic Leadership and the Southern Campaign

Epigraph: Carl von Clausewitz, *On War*, ed. and trans. Michael Howard and Peter Paret (Princeton, N.J.: Princeton University Press, 1976), 88–89.

1. For an analysis of British strategic thinking, see Ira D. Gruber, "British Strategy: The Theory and Practice of Eighteenth-Century Warfare," in *Reconsiderations on the Revolutionary War: Selected Essays*, ed. Donald Higginbotham (Westport, Conn.: Greenwood, 1978), 14–31.
2. Jeremy Black, "British Military Strategy," in *Strategy in the American War of Independence: A Global Approach*, ed. Donald J. Stoker et al. (London: Routledge, 2010), 58.
3. All war is complex, and the same conflict often experiences multiple forms of fighting, from large conventional warfare of nation-state versus nation-state or alliance down to small-unit or individual irregular, insurgency, or (what has been a traditional concept) guerilla warfare. Within a conflict, particularly between a great power and a less militarily capable opponent, the lesser combatant often uses a hybrid strategy to weaken the stronger entity through attrition, or a war of exhaustion. These multiple modes of warfare may occur simultaneously or sequentially within the same conflict. They may be coordinated to some degree between the conventional military authority

and irregular fighters, as in the Southern Campaign, or they might be completely random, as also seen frequently in the South. Hybrid warfare certainly describes the struggle during the Southern Campaign as conventional forces engaged in the linear warfare of the period while partisans of both sides engaged in irregular warfare, often based on local political, social, or economic rivalries with little relation to the broader picture of independence or allegiance. This hybrid warfare made British efforts to subdue the South dramatically more difficult. For an excellent case-study analysis of hybrid warfare throughout history, see Williamson Murray and Peter R. Mansoor, *Hybrid Warfare: Fighting Complex Opponents from the Ancient World to the Present* (New York: Cambridge University Press, 2012), 72–103.

4. The operationalization of strategy essentially means that one assumes that operational success equates to strategic success. Forces often conduct operations simply because that is what they are good at rather than because it accomplishes a specific strategic objective. Napoleon's invasion of Russia in 1812 and Hitler's Operation Barbarossa in 1941 are two commonly cited examples of the operationalization of strategy. So too was Gen. Erich Ludendorff's 1918 Michael Offensive on the western front, whereby frustrated subordinate commanders begged him for an explanation for what their specific operations intended to achieve strategically. The general simply ignored them, maintaining an attitude of attack it because it is there.
5. Ira D. Gruber, "Britain's Southern Strategy," in *The Revolutionary War in the South: Power, Conflict, and Leadership, Essays in Honor of John Richard Alden*, ed. W. Robert Higgins (Durham, N.C.: Duke University Press, 1979), 205.
6. Clausewitz, *On War*, 190–92.
7. Jones to Vice Admiral Kersaint, 1791, in *Warrior's Words: A Quotation Book: From Sesostris III to Schwarzkopf, 187 B.C. to A.D. 1991*, ed. Peter G. Tsouras (London: Cassell, 1992), 378.
8. Sun Tzu, *The Art of War*, ed. and trans. Samuel B. Griffith (New York: Oxford University Press, 1963), 66.
9. Bevin Alexander, *How Great Generals Win* (New York: W. W. Norton, 1993), 35–36.
10. Clausewitz, *On War*, 102. Clausewitz characterizes coup d'oeil as "the quick recognition of a truth that the mind would ordinarily miss or would perceive only after long study and reflection."
11. Basil H. Liddell Hart, *The British Way in Warfare* (New York: Macmillan, 1933), 94.
12. Martin Van Creveld, *Command in War* (Cambridge, Mass.: Harvard University Press, 1985), 18, 26–27.
13. Mitchell M. Zais, "Strategic Vision and Strength of Will: Imperatives for Theatre Command," in *The Challenge of Military Leadership*, ed. Lloyd J. Matthews and Dale E. Brown (Washington, D.C.: Pergamon-Brassey's, 1989), 85.
14. A "theater," or "theater of operations," is a modern term to describe a geographical region wherein war is fought. As such, eighteenth-century commanders would not have used the term per se but certainly understood the concept. In the War of American Independence, one might think of the various theaters as the New England and Canadian, middle colonies, southern, and West Indies. As the war turned global with French, Spanish, and Dutch intervention, it is useful to think in terms of the North American, Mediterranean, home islands, and Indian Ocean theaters.
15. There is a tendency to refer to the adversaries as Americans (or colonials) and British. But the war was both a rebellion against Britain and a civil war between Americans.

With an estimated 430 different Loyalist units embodied at some point, and with over 10,000 Loyalists in arms in 1780 alone in Provincial line regiments, it is erroneous to refer to the colonials in rebellion as the "Americans." Therefore, this study uses the terms "rebel" or "Patriot" to describe those opposing Crown authority and "Loyalists" for those who maintained their allegiance to Britain.

16. Andrew Jackson O'Shaughnessy, *The Men Who Lost America: British Leadership, the American Revolution, and the Fate of the Empire* (New Haven, Conn.: Yale University Press, 2013).

17. George Washington, Nathanael Greene, and Daniel Morgan clearly fit in this category of exemplary adversaries. It should be noted that the extraordinarily positive command relationship between Washington and the comte de Rochambeau played a critical role in the almost frictionless Yorktown Campaign, a dynamic that seems somewhat amazing considering the negative attitude toward provincials and colonists that generally characterized the European empires of the day.

18. "Report of conversation with L[ord] [James] D[rummond] and [William] Tryon," 7 Feb. [1776], ser. 1, vol. 13, item 36, Henry Clinton Papers, William L. Clements Library, University of Michigan, Ann Arbor.

## Chapter 1. Command and Control and the Southern Strategy

1. See Lois G. Schwoerer, *"No Standing Armies!": The Anti-Army Ideology in Seventeenth-Century England* (Baltimore: Johns Hopkins University Press, 1974).

2. It should be noted that in the eighteenth century, popular opinion cannot be viewed as it is in the twenty-first century. While the mass of the populace certainly held specific views on issues, in terms of influencing political decision making and national policy, such popular opinion carried little weight. What mattered and influenced decision making and policy were the opinions of the nobility, gentry, and major commercial and mercantile interests.

3. Quoted in Stephen Conway, "The Politics of British Military and Naval Mobilization, 1775–83," *English Historical Review* 112, no. 449 (Nov. 1997): 1193.

4. Paul H. Smith, "The American Loyalists: Notes on Their Organization and Numerical Strength," *William and Mary Quarterly*, 3rd ser., 25, no. 2 (Apr. 1968): 259–77. Some examples are the British Legion, made up of primarily New Jersey, New York, and Pennsylvania Loyalists; North Carolina Volunteers; Royal North Carolina Highlanders; South Carolina Loyalists; Volunteers of Ireland; and Queen's Rangers. Much will be heard from all these units in the subsequent operational narrative.

5. The Royal Navy had shrunk from 90,000 personnel in 1763 to 16,000 by 1775 and from 100 ships of the line in 1763 to 66 in 1775, many of which were old, decrepit, and in bad repair. For example, after the French entered the war in March 1778, the Royal Navy had 41 percent of its assets on American station, with 47 percent in European waters. By 1779 only 9 percent remained on American station, with 33 percent in the West Indies. Thus, a difficult situation in terms of providing escorts for convoys from Britain became far more complicated.

6. Clinton to Eden, New York, 1 Sept. 1780, Sir Henry Clinton, *The American Rebellion: Sir Henry Clinton's Narrative of His Campaigns, 1775–1782, with an Appendix of Original Documents*, ed. William B. Willcox (1954; repr., Hamden, Conn.: Archon Books, 1971), 456.

7. R. Arthur Bowler, "Logistics and Operations in the American Revolution," in Higginbotham, *Reconsiderations on the Revolutionary War*, 71. For expert analysis of the British supply and logistical problems, see R. A. Bowler, *Logistics and the Failure of the British Army in America, 1775–1783* (Princeton, N.J.: Princeton University Press, 1975). Other excellent studies on the logistical dynamics include David Syrett, *Shipping and the American War, 1775–83: A Study of British Transport Organization* (London: Athlone, 1970); Norman Baker, *Government and Contractors: The British Treasury and War Supplies, 1775–83* (London: Athlone, 1971); and John Brewer, *The Sinews of Power: War, Money, and the English State, 1688–1783* (New York: Alfred A. Knopf, 1989).
8. John R. Tokar, "Redcoat Resupply: Strategic Logistics and Operational Indecision in the American Revolutionary War, 1775–1783" (School of Advanced Military Studies, U.S. Army Command and General Staff College, Fort Leavenworth, Kans., 1999), 16.
9. Rotton to Amherst, 12 Feb. 1780, TNA CO 5/123, as quoted in Alan Valentine, *Lord George Germain* (Oxford: Clarendon, 1962), 433.
10. Piers Mackesy, *The War for America, 1775–1783* (Lincoln: University of Nebraska Press, 1992), 17.
11. Germain to Clinton, Whitehall, London, 8 Mar. 1778, HMC, *Stopford-Sackville Papers*, 2:99.
12. Mackesy, *War for America*, 54.
13. There were several Jacobite rebellions, centered primarily in the Highlands of Scotland, in support of the House of Stuart, deposed in the Glorious Revolution (known by some as a revolt) of 1689. Harsh military measures suppressed these risings.
14. For analyses of Germain, see Arthur Herbert Bayse, "The Secretary of State for the Colonies, 1768–1782," *American Historical Review* 28, no. 1 (1922): 13–23; and Valentine, *Germain*.
15. The best biography of the earl of Sandwich, which also captures the essence of strategic leadership and coordination with the cabinet, Germain, and the army, is N. A. M. Rodger, *The Insatiable Earl: A Life of John Montagu, Fourth Earl of Sandwich, 1718–1792* (New York: W. W. Norton, 1993).
16. Knox to Germain, Whitehall, London, 31 Oct. 1780, HMC, *Stopford-Sackville Papers*, 2:215.
17. William B. Willcox, "The British Road to Yorktown: A Study in Divided Command," *American Historical Review* 52, no. 1 (Oct. 1946): 3.
18. Alfred Thayer Mahan, *The Influence of Seapower upon History, 1660–1783* (New York: Hill and Wang, 1957); Julian S. Corbett, *Some Principles of Maritime Strategy* (1911; repr., Annapolis: Naval Institute Press, 1988).
19. Clinton to Arbuthnot, New York, 9 Dec. 1780, HMC, *Stopford-Sackville Papers*, 2:199.
20. Quoted in O'Shaughnessy, *Men Who Lost America*, 232.
21. Jeremy Black, *Parliament and Foreign Policy in the Eighteenth Century* (Cambridge, U.K.: Cambridge University Press, 2004), 105–6.
22. B. D. Bargar, *Lord Dartmouth and the American Revolution* (Columbia: University of South Carolina Press, 1965), 164.
23. O'Shaughnessy, *Men Who Lost America*, 67.
24. Valentine, *Germain*, 375.
25. Quoted in Willcox. "Yorktown," 3. The secretary was an administrative assistant and not a cabinet officer. He did, however, deal with a comprehensive accounting

of the war's financial aspects. For a thorough picture of the command-and-control problems created by Germain and his direct communications with Cornwallis, see C-CC.

26. Dartmouth to Gage, Whitehall, London, 2 Aug. 1775, HMC, *The Manuscripts of the Earl of Dartmouth*, vol. 2, *American Papers* (London: His Majesty's Stationary Office, 1895), 1412; J. D. Barnhart, *Henry Hamilton and George Rogers Clark in the American Revolution: With the Unpublished Journal of Lieut. Gov. Henry Hamilton* (Crawfordsville, Ind., 1951), as quoted in Bargar, *Lord Dartmouth*, 170–71.
27. Carleton to Johnson, Montreal, Can., 17 July 1775, TNA CO 5/253/7.
28. See chapter 2 for details of the Cherokee War.
29. For more on the Indian dynamic in the South, see John R. Alden, *John Stuart and the Southern Colonial Frontier: A Study of Indian Relations, War, Trade, and Land Problems in the Southern Wilderness, 1754–1775* (Ann Arbor: University of Michigan Press, 1944); Andrew M. Davis, "The Employment of Indian Auxiliaries in the American War," *English Historical Review* 2, no. 8 (Oct. 1887): 709–28; Philip M. Hamer, "John Stuart's Indian Policy during the Early Months of the American Revolution," *Mississippi Valley Historical Review* 17, no. 3 (Dec. 1930): 351–66; James H. O'Donnell, *Southern Indians in the American Revolution* (Knoxville: University of Tennessee Press, 1973); and Helen L. Shaw, *British Administration of the Southern Indians, 1756–1783* (1931; repr., Norwalk, Conn.: AMS, 1981).
30. Captain George Smith, *A Universal Military Dictionary* (London: Printed for J. Millan, 1779), 28. For analysis of the roles that blacks played in support of the Crown, see Alan Gilbert, *Black Patriots and Loyalists: Fighting for Emancipation in the War for Independence* (Chicago: University of Chicago Press, 2012); Michael Lanning, *African Americans in the Revolutionary War* (New York: Kensington, 2000); and Jim Piecuch, *Three Peoples, One King: Loyalists, Indians, and Slaves in the Revolutionary South, 1775–1782* (Columbia: University of South Carolina Press, 2008).
31. Martin to Dartmouth, HMS *Syreen* off North Carolina, 10 Mar., 20 Apr., 30 June, 16 July 1775, TNA CO 5/318; K. G. Davies, ed., *Documents of the American Revolution, 1770–1783*, 20 vols. (Shannon: Irish University Press, 1976), 9:213.
32. Dartmouth to Howe, Whitehall, London, 22 Oct. 1775, TNA CO 5/92.
33. Details of the Moore's Creek Bridge episode are found in Robert O. DeMond, *The Loyalists in North Carolina during the Revolution* (1930; repr., Baltimore: Clearfield, 2009); Duane Meyer, *The Highland Scots of North Carolina, 1732–1776* (Chapel Hill: University of North Carolina Press, 1987); and Hugh F. Rankin, "The Moore's Creek Bridge Campaign, 1776," *North Carolina Historical Review* 30 (1953): 23–60.
34. Cornwallis to Germain, 16 May 1776, TNA CO 5/396; Martin to Germain, 21 Mar., 5 July, 7 Aug. 1776, TNA CO 5/93; Campbell to Germain, 8 July, 29 Nov. 1776, TNA CO 5/318. All of these express the same sentiment that ill fortune caused the failure of southern Loyalists. That belief persisted in British official circles as the war progressed.
35. Wright and Campbell to Germain, 30 July 1779, TNA CO 5/98/210; 7 Aug. 1779, TNA CO 5/98/212; 11 Sept. 1779, TNA CO 5/98/381.
36. Simpson to Germain, 28 Aug. 1779, TNA CO 5/97/265. For Simpson's reports, notably in May 1780 after the fall of Charleston, see Simpson to Germain, 15 May 1780, "James Simpson's Reports on the Carolina Loyalists, 1779–1780," ed. Alan S. Brown, *Journal of Southern History* 21, no. 4 (Nov. 1955): 518–19.

37. Bourcher to Germain, Nov. 1775, HMC, *Stopford-Sackville Papers*, 2:19.
38. Eden to Dartmouth, Annapolis, Md., 29 Jan. 1773, TNA CO 5/87/1285.
39. See David Hackett Fischer, *Washington's Crossing* (New York: Oxford University Press, 2004), 162–77. Fischer examines the variety of ways in which local populations accommodated themselves to whatever power dominated an area at a given time, repeatedly switching allegiances.
40. Balfour to Germain, Charlestown, S.C., 16 Jan. 1781, HMC, *Stopford-Sackville Papers*, 2:197.
41. Sir John Fortescue, *A History of the British Army*, 20 vols. (London: Macmillan, 1902; repr., East Essex, U.K.: Naval and Military Press, 2004), 3(2):206.
42. Sir John Fortescue, *The War of Independence: The British Army in North America, 1775–1783* (1911; repr., London: Greenhill Books, 2001), 21.
43. Paul H. Smith, *Loyalists and Redcoats: A Study in British Revolutionary Policy* (Chapel Hill: University of North Carolina Press, 1964), ix.
44. Germain to Clinton, Whitehall, London, 8 Mar. 1778, TNA CO 5/95/94.
45. George III to Lord North, London, 18 Nov. 1774, *The Correspondence of King George the Third from 1760 to December 1783, printed from the Original Papers in the Royal Archives at Windsor Castle, arranged and edited by the Hon. Sir John Fortescue*, 6 vols. (London: Macmillan, 1927–28), 3:153.
46. Germain to Clinton, London, labeled "Most Secret," 5–8 Mar. 1778, TNA HQ PRO 30/55/9/996; HMC, *Stopford-Sackville Papers*, 2:94.
47. Germain to Clinton, Whitehall, London, 21 Mar. 1778, TNA HQ PRO 30/55/9/1031.
48. Valentine, *Germain*, 341.
49. Clinton to Germain, New York, 4 Apr. 1779, TNA HQ PRO 30/55/16/1885.
50. Clinton to Germain, New York, 27 July 1778, TNA CO 5/96/62.
51. For a discussion of the orders from Germain to Clinton regarding launching a southern campaign, see Mackesy, *War for America*, 232–34. Germain's letter of 5 August to which Clinton refers is in TNA CO 5/96.

## Chapter 2. The Southern Campaign Begins

1. The regiment still exists in the British Army as the 4th Battalion of the Rifles. In previous years the unit, redesignated as the 95th Rifle Regiment and no longer associated with North America, fought extensively in the Napoleonic Wars and especially during the Waterloo Campaign. The 95th also served as the unit for the historical Sharpe series by Bernard Cornwell and the novel *Rifleman Dodd* by C. S. Forester.
2. Tonyn to Amherst, St. Augustine, East Fla., 19 Jan. 1778, War Office 34/144/42, The National Archives, Kew, U.K. (hereafter TNA WO); Tonyn to Amherst, St. Augustine, East Fla., 14 Nov. 1778, TNA WO 34/111/184.
3. For details of the various agreements and treaties that established the boundary lines, see Louis De Vorsey Jr., *The Indian Boundary in the Southern Colonies, 1763–1775* (Chapel Hill: University of North Carolina Press, 1961).
4. Griffith Rutherford to the North Carolina Committee of Safety, 12 July 1776, *Colonial and State Records of North Carolina*, vol. 10 (Chapel Hill: University of North Carolina Library, 2004), 662.

5. Clarence W. Griffin, *The History of Old Tryon and Rutherford Counties, North Carolina, 1730–1936* (Spartanburg, S.C.: Reprint Company, 1982), 35; William L. Sherrill, *Annals of Lincoln County, North Carolina, Containing Interesting and Authentic Facts of Lincoln County History through the Years 1749 to 1937* (1937; repr., Baltimore: Regional Publishing, 1972), 25.
6. Following his defeat at Savannah, Howe was court-martialed and acquitted but still relieved of command in the South. He joined Washington in May 1779 and failed in the attempt to capture Verplank's Point on the Hudson River. Howe later sat on the court-martial of Major John Andre. He saw no further significant action and, following the war, returned to his New Hanover County plantation near Wilmington.
7. Bevin Alexander, in *How Great Generals Win*, defines convergent assault as an attack from multiple fronts or angles more or less simultaneously that forces the opponent to defend at all points, thus weakening and causing disruption to defensive arrangements. Alexander advocates that all successful generals use convergent assault.
8. For details of the fight at Savannah and Campbell's report, see Archibald Campbell, *Journal of an Expedition against the Rebels of Georgia in North America*, ed. Colin Campbell (Darien, Ga.: Ashantilly, 1981); Robert S. Davis Jr., "The British Invasion of Georgia in 1778," *Atlanta Historical Journal* 24 (1980): 5–25; and Alexander A. Lawrence, "General Robert Howe and the British Capture of Savannah in 1778," *Georgia Historical Quarterly* 36 (1952): 303–27.
9. Clinton to Campbell, New York, 8 Nov. 1778, TNA HQ PRO 30/55/13/1585; Clinton to Prevost, New York, 8 Nov. 1778, TNA HQ PRO 30/55/13/1539.
10. For comprehensive studies of Benjamin Lincoln, see David B. Mattern, *Benjamin Lincoln and the American Revolution* (Columbia: University of South Carolina Press, 1995); John C. Cavanaugh, "The Military Career of Major General Benjamin Lincoln in the War of the American Revolution" (Ph.D. diss., Duke University, 1969); and Carl P. Borick, *A Gallant Defense: The Siege of Charleston, 1780* (Columbia: University of South Carolina Press, 2003).
11. Adm. J. C. Wylie, USN, proposed an analytical model for strategic planning called "sequential and cumulative operations"—a sequence of planned operations in support of the overall strategy wherein every event depends on the previous event's success, running concurrently or consecutively. Cumulatively, they lead to the achievement of the desired effect. The Southern Strategy is an excellent example of the sequential leading to the desired cumulative effect, or the pacification of the South one colony at a time, starting in Georgia and moving up through Virginia. See J. C. Wylie, "Excerpt from 'Reflections on the War in the Pacific,'" in *Military Strategy: A General Theory of Power Control* (Annapolis: Naval Institute Press, 1989), App. A, 118.
12. Thomas Brown was captured in the loss of Augusta in June 1781, but a prisoner exchange freed him. He operated out of Savannah and Saint Augustine until the war's end. On the ceding of East Florida back to Spain, Brown moved to the Bahamas, where he again established a substantial estate. Wounded sixteen times in action and having established three great estates while losing two in Georgia and later in north Florida, the resilient Brown finally died on Saint Vincent in the West Indies in 1825.
13. In a "refuse the flank" movement, the threatened flank executes a "right about turn" (about face) followed by a left or right wheel, depending on which side of the line they are on. Once this gate swing is complete, the troops form essentially an L-shaped line, and they execute another "right about turn." In this way they face the attacking

force on both fronts. The negative aspect is that this maneuver cuts the firepower of each front.

14. Details of the Battle of Kettle Creek can be found in Robert S. Davis Jr., *Georgians in the Revolution: At Kettle Creek (Wilkes Co.) and Burke County* (Easley, S.C.: Southern Historical, 1986), and State of Georgia, *Kettle Creek: The Battle of the Cane Brakes, Wilkes County* (Atlanta: Historic Preservation Section, Office of Planning and Research, Dept. of Natural Resources, 1975).
15. There is some debate over how long the battle actually lasted. Some sources claim five minutes, others twenty. Whatever the time frame, it did not last long.
16. The "Tory War" that erupted in the Carolinas following the Yorktown surrender is emblematic of this civil war. While the depredations of the French troops at Savannah did not start the violent cycle, their action nonetheless helped stoke the internecine conflict, which grew ever more intense as the Southern Campaign progressed.
17. Polish count Kazimierz Pulaski arrived in America in 1777, and though not immediately commissioned in the Continental Army, he volunteered as a staff officer to Washington. He distinguished himself at Brandywine in September, and Congress consequently commissioned him brigadier general and commander of the horse. On 28 March 1778 Congress created the Pulaski Legion, consisting of sixty-eight dragoons and 200 infantry. Though a small command, Pulaski retained his general officer rank. He took part in the Charleston defense against Prevost's attack in May 1779. Although the legion emerged badly mauled at Charleston, reconstitution efforts paid off. The legion marched south with Lincoln to the siege of Savannah in September. Pulaski acted as the primary intermediary between the French and Americans during that operation.
18. Evacuated to the Continental Navy warship *Wasp*, Pulaski died en route to Charleston for medical attention and was buried at sea on 11 October.
19. Clinton to Germain, New York, 23 Dec. 1779, TNA CO 5/99(1)/29.
20. Clinton to Eden, New York, 19 Nov. 1779, *Facsimiles of Manuscripts in European Archives Relating to America, 1773–1783*, ed. Benjamin F. Stevens, 25 vols. (London, 1889–95), 10:1032.
21. Clinton to Eden, New York, 11 Dec. 1779, ibid., 10:1034.
22. Clinton to Germain, New York, 20, 21 Aug. 1779, TNA CO 5/98.
23. For an excellent analysis of the friction between Clinton and Arbuthnot and the resultant lack of joint operational cooperation, see William B. Willcox, *Portrait of a General: Sir Henry Clinton in the War of Independence* (New York: Alfred A. Knopf, 1962), 322–46.
24. Cornwallis to Clinton, 4 Apr. 1779, Clinton, *American Rebellion*, 138, 401; William Knox to Duncan Drummond, Whitehall, London, 10 Apr. 1779, TNA CO 5/97/369. Knox was Lord Germain's secretary while Drummond served as Clinton's aide-de-camp.
25. Cornwallis to William Cornwallis, Culford, 5 May 1779, HMC, *Report on Manuscripts in Various Collections*, vol. 6, *The Manuscripts of Miss M. Eyre Matcham, Captain H. V. Knox, Cornwallis-Wykeham-Martin* (London: His Majesty's Stationary Office, 1909), 319.
26. Germain to Clinton, Whitehall, London, 4 Nov. 1779, TNA HQ PRO 30/55/20/2408.

27. Clinton to Cornwallis, Headquarters near Charleston, 23 Apr. 1780, TNA CC PRO 30/11/2/5.
28. Ira D. Gruber, ed., *John Peebles' American War: The Diary of a Scottish Grenadier, 1776–1782* (Mechanicsburg, Pa.: Stackpole Books, 1998), 287.
29. Mackesy, *War for America*, 268.
30. For a reprint of the several pamphlets published by both generals to prove the other was at fault, see C-CC.
31. Clinton to Germain, New York, 22 May 1779, TNA CO 5/97/679.
32. The 33rd Regiment was Cornwallis's own regiment; accordingly, the earl and Webster were close friends. Tarleton, an officer of the 1st Dragoon Guards, took command of the British Legion, a Provincial Loyalist unit composed of both dragoons and infantry. Ferguson, a major in the 71st Regiment of Foot, was appointed inspector of militia by Clinton on 22 May 1780, charged with raising Loyalists troops, particularly in the Tryon County, North Carolina, region.
33. The British Legion was raised in New York in July 1778 and placed first on the American Establishment as the 5th American Regiment, March 1781, then on the British Establishment, December 1782. For a history of this and other units that participated in the War of American Independence, see Philip R. N. Katcher, *Encyclopedia of British, Provincial, and German Army Units, 1775–1783* (Harrisburg, Pa.: Stackpole Books, 1973).
34. Clausewitz, *On War*, 88–89.
35. These units were the 23rd, 33rd, and 64th Regiments of Foot; Ferguson's American Volunteers; Tarleton's British Legion; New York Volunteers; Queen's Rangers; North Carolina Volunteers; South Carolina Royalists; and Lieutenant Colonel Francis, Lord Rawdon's Volunteers of Ireland. Many of these troops formed the core of Cornwallis's army that charged through the Carolinas and Virginia.
36. Clinton to Cornwallis, Headquarters near Charleston, 23 Apr. 1780, TNA CC PRO 30/11/2/9.
37. Sun Tzu, *Art of War*, 77–78.
38. Clinton to Phillips, New York, 26 Apr. 1781; C-CC, 1:435–40.
39. Johann von Ewald, *Diary of the American War: A Hessian Journal*, trans. and ed. Joseph P. Tustin (New Haven, Conn.: Yale University Press, 1979), 235–36.
40. Clinton to Cornwallis, Charlestown, S.C., 6 May 1780, TNA CC PRO 30/11/2/28.
41. Ewald, *Diary*, 237.
42. It is not clear as to whether or not Clinton actually had hot-shot ovens within the siege works; nevertheless, simply the threat would have caused great angst in Charleston.
43. Clinton to Germain, Charlestown, S.C., 13 May 1780, TNA CO 5/99(2)/181.
44. Clausewitz defines the culminating point as "strategic attacks that lead up to the point where their remaining strength is just enough to maintain a defense. . . . Beyond that point the scale turns and the reaction follows that is much stronger than the original attack." *On War*, 528.
45. Proclamations of 22 May, 3 June 1780, TNA CO 5/99(2)/300, 302.
46. For an analysis of Clinton's perception of the public reaction to the proclamations, especially his of 3 June, see Willcox, *Portrait of a General*, 321.
47. Clinton to Cornwallis, *Romulus*, 8 June 1780, TNA CC PRO 30/11/2/106, with enclosure "Subscribers to the address, 2/110/D."

48. Raised in Canada from disbanded Highland regiments and taken on to the regular establishment in January 1779, the 2nd Battalion arrived in Charleston in April 1781 and fought at the Battle of Eutaw Springs.
49. Rawdon to Cornwallis, Camden, 7 July 1780, TNA CC PRO 30/11/2/252.
50. Cornwallis to Arbuthnot, Charlestown, S.C., 29 June 1780, TNA CC PRO 30/11/77/18.
51. Clinton to Germain, Charlestown, S.C., 4 June 1780, TNA CO 5/99(2)/299; Clinton to Germain, Charlestown, S.C., 13 May 1780, TNA CO 5/99(2)/248.
52. Tarleton to Cornwallis, Waxhaws, S.C., 30 May 1780, TNA HQ PRO 30/55/23/2784.
53. Tarleton to Cornwallis, Waxhaws, S.C., 30 May 1780, TNA CO 5/99(2)/308.
54. Clausewitz, *On War*, 85.
55. Jim Piecuch, *The Blood Be upon Your Head: Tarleton and the Myth of Buford's Massacre, The Battle of the Waxhaws: May 29, 1780* (Lugoff, S.C.: Woodward Corp., 2010), 40.
56. Germain to Clinton, Whitehall, London, 5 July 1780, C-CC, 1:229.
57. Amherst to Germain, London, 1 July 1780, TNA WO 34/191/101; Clinton to Germain, Charlestown, S.C., 13 May 1780, TNA CO 5/99(2)/248.
58. The battle site is on a hill overlooking the river in the present-day city of Lincolnton, North Carolina, which is named, ironically, after Maj. Gen. Benjamin Lincoln. There are various spellings, including "Ramsour," "Ramsaur," and "Ramseur"; however, "Ramsour" is the most accepted for the mill and battle.
59. The Royal North Carolina Regiment, under Lieutenant Colonel John Hamilton, was actually raised in Charleston in the spring of 1780, served at the siege of Charleston and the Battles of Camden and Hanging Rock, and sent to Saint Augustine in November 1782.
60. Despite his Loyalist sentiments, Captain Peter Carpenter, in the summer of 1776, led his militia company in the Rutherford expedition against the Cherokees during the Second Cherokee War. He would later make a claim for expenses incurred of £487–13–6, a considerable sum in the eighteenth century. See Treasurer's & Comptroller's Papers, North Carolina Military Papers, North Carolina State Archives, Raleigh. As the battle concluded, though wounded in the abdomen by a musket ball, the captain swam to safety across the South Fork River, where his family later found him and carried him to his plantation four miles away. To cleanse the wound, they passed a silk handkerchief through his abdomen. Captain Carpenter lived to 1817, but Ramsour's Mill ended his military adventures. He provides a significant case study in that his actions following Lord Cornwallis's North Carolina invasion in January 1781 illustrate the increasingly grim situation for Crown forces in terms of inspiring Loyalist turnout and support. More will be said of Captain Carpenter in chapter 4.
61. Sources for the Battle of Ramsour's Mill include DeMond, *Loyalists in North Carolina;* William A. Graham, "The Battle of Ramsaur's Mill, June 20, 1780," *North Carolina Booklet* 4, no. 2 (June 1904); Hugh F. Rankin, *North Carolina in the American Revolution* (Raleigh: Historical Publications Section, Division of Historical Resources, Office of Archives and History, North Carolina Department of Cultural Resources, 1959); William L. Carpenter, *The Battle of Ramsour's Mill* (Lincolnton, N.C.: Lincoln County Historical Association and Lincoln County Museum of History, 1992); Sherrill,

*Annals of Lincoln County, North Carolina*, 36–40; and Robert C. Carpenter, *Carpenters a Plenty* (Baltimore: Gateway, 1982), 497–8.

62. Cornwallis to Clinton, Charleston, S.C., 30 June 1780, TNA CC PRO 30/11/72/18.
63. Wemyss to Cornwallis, Cheraw Court House, S.C., 20 Sept. 1780, TNA CC PRO 30/11/3/80.

## Chapter 3. Partisan Warfare in the Carolinas

Epigraph: Baroness Emma Orczy, *The Scarlet Pimpernel* (1905).

1. Sun Tzu, *Art of War*, 77–78.
2. John Buchanan, *The Road to Guilford Courthouse: The American Revolution in the Carolinas* (New York: John Wiley and Sons, 1997), 89.
3. "Address of the People of Fincastle County, Virginia, to the Delegates from that Colony, who attended the Continental Congress," 20 Jan. 1775, Documents of the American Revolution, American Archives, University of Chicago Libraries.
4. Proclamation issued by Lieutenant Colonel Innes, Broad River, S.C., 14 June 1780, TNA CC PRO 30/11/2/157; Cornwallis to Wemyss, Charlestown, S.C., TNA CC PRO 30/11/78/52.
5. Cornwallis to Clinton, Charlestown, S.C., 15 July 1780, TNA CC PRO 30/11/72/30.
6. Cornwallis to Clinton, Charlestown, S.C., 6 Aug. 1780, TNA CC PRO 30/11/72/36.
7. Cornwallis to Clinton, Charlestown, S.C., 15 July 1780, TNA CC PRO 30/11/72/30.
8. Cornwallis to Clinton, Charlestown, S.C., 6 Aug. 1780, TNA CC PRO 30/11/72/36.
9. Cruger to the officer commanding at Camden, Ninety Six, S.C., 4 Aug. 1780, TNA CC PRO 30/11/63/13.
10. Cornwallis to Clinton, Charlestown, S.C., 10 Aug. 1780, TNA CC PRO 30/11/72/40.
11. Clinton to Cornwallis, Headquarters, Philipsburg, N.Y., 14 July 1780, TNA CC PRO 30/11/2/296.
12. Cornwallis to Clinton, Charlestown, S.C., 30 June 1780, C-CC, 1:224.
13. Cornwallis to Clinton, Charlestown, S.C., 6 Aug. 1780, TNA CC PRO 30/11/72/36.
14. Ibid.
15. Ibid.
16. Rawdon to Cornwallis, Camden, S.C., 3 Aug. 1780, TNA CC PRO 30/11/63/9.
17. Rawdon to Cornwallis, Camden, S.C., 11 Aug. 1780, TNA CC PRO 30/11/63/34.
18. See Elizabeth A. Fenn, *Pox Americana: The Great Smallpox Epidemic of 1775–82* (Boston: Hill and Wang, 2002).
19. "Return of the troops etc at Camden," 13 Aug. 1780, Camden, S.C., TNA CC PRO 30/11/103/3.
20. Cornwallis to Clinton, Charlestown, S.C., 14 July 1780, C-CC, 1:233.
21. Clausewitz, *On War*, 204.
22. Cornwallis to Germain, Camden, S.C., 21 Aug. 1780, TNA CC PRO 30/11/76/9.
23. Ibid.
24. It was common in the eighteenth century to form all of the light and grenadier companies from the line regiments into separate battalions. For example, the British forces that engaged the Massachusetts militia at Lexington Common in April 1775

were the light infantry under Major John Pitcairn of the marines, composed of the light companies drawn from the line regiments based in Boston.

25. Cornwallis to Germain, Camden, S.C., 21 Aug. 1780, TNA CC PRO 30/11/76/9.
26. Both Cornwallis and de Kalb were said the have been Freemasons, which was quite common in Britain and America among the aristocracy of the day, therefore, the story has much credibility.
27. Cornwallis to Clinton, Camden, S.C., 29 Aug. 1780, TNA CC PRO 30/11/72/47.
28. This according to General Otho Holland Williams's report of the battle.
29. An excellent primary source for all the major engagements from the British perspective in the Southern Campaign is Roger Lamb, *An Original and Authentic Journal of Occurrences during the Late American War from Its Commencement to the Year 1783* (Dublin: Wilkinson and Courtney, 1809). A sergeant in the 23rd Royal Welch Fusiliers, Lamb wrote an articulate and detailed account of the campaign from the soldier's perspective based on his diary.
30. Cornwallis to Clinton, Camden, S.C., 23 Aug. 1780, C-CC, 1:259.
31. Cornwallis to Clinton, Camden, S.C., 29 Aug. 1780, C-CC, 1:261–64.
32. Cornwallis to Germain, Camden, S.C., 21 Aug. 1780, TNA CC PRO 30/11/76/9.
33. For a better understanding of the ideological and philosophical causes of the War of American Independence, see Bernard Bailyn, *The Ideological Origins of the American Revolution* (Cambridge, Mass.: Harvard University Press, 1967); Gordon Wood, *The Radicalization of the American Revolution* (New York: Alfred A. Knopf, 1992); and Pauline Maier, *From Resistance to Revolution: Colonial Radicals and the Development of American Opposition to Britain, 1765–1776* (London: Routledge and Keegan Paul, 1973).
34. Cornwallis to Cruger, Camden, S.C., 27 Aug. 1780, TNA CC PRO 30/11/79/39.
35. Quoted in Walter Edgar, *South Carolina: A History* (Columbia: University of South Carolina Press, 1998), 235.
36. Cornwallis to Clinton, Charlestown, S.C., 14 July 1780, TNA CC PRO 30/11/72/26.
37. Charles Stedman, *The History of the Origin, Progress, and Termination of the American War*, 2 vols. (1794; repr., Charleston, S.C.: Nabu, 2010), 2:15.
38. Cornwallis to Clinton, Charlestown, S.C., 6 Aug. 1780, TNA HQ PRO 30/55/25/2949; Cornwallis to Balfour, Camden, S.C., 29 Aug. 1780, TNA CC PRO 30/11/79/45.
39. Even though Ferguson demonstrated the power and accuracy of his breech-loading rifle in 1776, the concern was that the troops would use up too much ammunition too fast, leaving them vulnerable. This attitude affected all armies until at least the mid-nineteenth century. Consequently, only a hundred rifles were manufactured. Ferguson commanded a rifle company that fought at Brandywine in September 1777 but was disbanded shortly thereafter. In a 1776 demonstration in London, while lying on his back using a lady's hand mirror to aim, he hit a target at 100 yards six times in less than a minute in the rain.
40. Quoted in Lyman C. Draper, *King's Mountain and Its Heroes: History of the Battle of King's Mountain, October 7th, 1780, and the Events Which Led to It* (1881; repr., Charleston, S.C.: Nabu, 2010), 169.
41. Ferguson to Cornwallis, Bufflow Creek, N.C., 5 Oct. 1780, TNA CC PRO 30/11/3/189.

42. The King's American Regiment and New Jersey Volunteers had been raised in 1776 following the British victories at Long Island and New York.
43. Captain DePeyster's report is given in DePeyster to Cornwallis, Camp near Gilbert Town, N.C., 11 Oct. 1780, TNA CC PRO 30/11/3/210.
44. See Anthony Allaire, *Diary of Lieut. Anthony Allaire of Ferguson's Corps* (New York: New York Times, 1968), 31–36. Allaire's diary was first published in Draper, *King's Mountain.*
45. Rawdon to Clinton, Camp between Broad River and Catawba, S.C., 29 Oct. 1780, TNA CO 5/101/43.
46. Cornwallis to Clinton, Camden, S.C., 29 Aug. 1780, TNA CC PRO 30/11/72/47.
47. Tarleton to Cornwallis, Camp at Blackstock's Plantation, Tyger River, 22 Nov. 1780, TNA CC PRO 30/11/4/173.
48. Rawdon to Cornwallis, Camden, S.C., 13 Dec. 1780, TNA CC PRO 30/11/4/321; Rawdon to Cornwallis, Camden, S.C., 13 Dec. 1780, TNA CC PRO 30/11/4/323; Coffin to Rawdon, English Plantation, S.C., 13 Dec. 1780, TNA CC PRO 30/11/4/319.
49. Greene to Washington, Camp Charlotte, N.C., 7 Dec. 1780, Nathanael Greene, *The Papers of General Nathanael Greene*, ed. Richard K. Showman et al., 9 vols. (Chapel Hill: University of North Carolina Press, 1991), 6:543.
50. Quoted in Terry Golway, *Washington's General: Nathanael Greene and the Triumph of the American Revolution* (New York: Henry Holt, 2005), 232.
51. Greene to Sumter, Camp on the Pedee, South Carolina, 8 Jan. 1781, Greene, *Papers*, 7:74–75.
52. For a thorough discussion of Washington's Fabian strategy, see Donald Stoker and Michael W. Jones, "Colonial Military Strategy," in Stoker et al., *Strategy in the American War of Independence.*
53. Clausewitz, *On War*, 204; Sun Tzu, *Art of War*, 139.
54. Greene to Baron Steuben, Cheraws on the East side of the Pedee, South Carolina, 28 Dec. 1780, Greene, *Papers*, 7:11.
55. Greene to unknown, Camp on the Pee Dee River, S.C., n.d., ibid., 175.
56. Cornwallis to Clinton, Camp on Turkey Creek, Broad River, S.C., 18 Jan. 1781, TNA CO 5/101/214. Saunders was a Loyalist. The more common name is Hannah's Cowpens. The best secondary source on the Battle of Cowpens is Lawrence E. Babits, *A Devil of a Whipping: The Battle of Cowpens* (Chapel Hill: University of North Carolina Press, 1998).
57. Cornwallis to Rawdon, Buffalo Creek, N.C., 21 Jan. 1781, TNA CC PRO 30/11/84/78.
58. Cornwallis to Turnbull, Camp on Waxhaw Creek, S.C., 13 Sept. 1780, TNA CC PRO 30/11/80/22.
59. Cornwallis to Cruger, Camden, S.C., 4 Sept. 1780, TNA CC PRO 30/11/80/5.
60. John Ferling, *Almost a Miracle: The American Victory in the War of Independence* (Oxford: Oxford University Press, 2007), 458.
61. Cornwallis to Germain, Camden, S.C., 20 Aug. 1780, TNA CC PRO 30/11/76/1.
62. Cornwallis to Clinton, Charlestown, S.C., 14 July 1780, TNA CC PRO 30/11/72/26.
63. Willcox, *Portrait of a General*, 353.
64. Cornwallis to Clinton, Charlestown, S.C., 6 Aug. 1780, TNA CC PRO 30/11/72/36.
65. Clinton to Cornwallis, Headquarters, Charlestown, S.C., 1 June 1780, TNA CC PRO 30/11/61/3.

66. P. M. Waters statement, quoted in John W. Gordon, *South Carolina and the American Revolution: A Battlefield History* (Columbia: University of South Carolina Press, 2002), 96.
67. Clausewitz, *On War*, 480.
68. Cornwallis to Clinton, Camp at Turkey Creek, Broad River, N.C., 18 Jan. 1781, TNA CC PRO 30/11/5/47; Cornwallis to Germain, Guildford, N.C., 17 Mar. 1781, TNA CC PRO 30/11/5/281.

## Chapter 4. Cornwallis Invades North Carolina

1. Clinton to Cornwallis, New York, 13 Dec. 1780, TNA CC PRO 30/11/4/316.
2. Clinton to Cornwallis, New York, 6 Nov. 1780, TNA CC PRO 30/11/4/35.
3. For a fuller examination of Cornwallis's concept that to control South Carolina, he must control North Carolina, see P. Smith, *Loyalists and Redcoats*, 155–56.
4. Cornwallis to Clinton, Wynnesborough, S.C., 6 Jan. 1781, TNA CC PRO 30/11/72/75.
5. Lord Rawdon commanded all posts, stations, and forces in South Carolina. These included a mixed force of British and Provincial regulars, Loyalist militia, Lieutenant Colonel Brown's corps, and the Florida Rangers at Augusta; the 7th Regiment of Foot with Cruger's and Allen's battalions at Ninety Six; Innes's South Carolina Loyalists, the New York Volunteers, Rawdon's Volunteers of Ireland, and the 63rd and 64th Regiments of Foot at Camden; Colonel Fanning's Loyalists at Georgetown; and various German forces and the 82nd and 84th (Royal Highland Emigrants) Regiments at Charleston, along with a few smaller outposts.
6. Cornwallis to Clinton, Wynnesborough, S.C., 6 Jan. 1781, TNA CC PRO 30/11/72/75. Cornwallis took with him into North Carolina the Brigade of Guards, the Regiment von Bose, the Jägers, Tarleton's British Legion, the 23rd and 33rd Regiments of Foot, and the 2nd Battalion, 71st Regiment.
7. Cornwallis to Lord Rawdon, Ramsour's Mill, N.C., 25 Jan. 1781, TNA CC PRO 30/11/84/83.
8. Cornwallis to Leslie, Wynnsborough, S.C., 12 Nov. 1780, TNA CC PRO 30/11/82/32.
9. Cornwallis to Rawdon, McAlister's, S.C., 12 Jan. 1781, TNA CC PRO 30/11/84/57.
10. Rawdon to Clinton, Camp between the Broad River and the Catawba, S.C., 29 Oct. (also dated 28 Oct.) 1780, TNA CC PRO 30/11/3/297.
11. An excellent reference for the activities of Davie and other North Carolina Patriot units is Hugh F. Rankin, *The North Carolina Continentals* (Chapel Hill: University of North Carolina Press, 1971).
12. Banastre Tarleton, *A History of the Campaigns of 1780 and 1781 in the Southern Provinces of North America* (1787; repr., New York: Arno, 1968), 160–61.
13. Clinton, *American Rebellion*, 261.
14. Craig to Balfour, Wilmington, N.C., 4 Feb. 1781, TNA CC PRO 30/11/5/67; Cornwallis to Clinton, Wynnesborough, S.C., 6 Jan. 1781, TNA CC PRO 30/11/72/75.
15. Cornwallis to Clinton, Williamsburgh, Va., 30 June 1781, TNA CC PRO 30/11/74/18.
16. Cornwallis to Clinton, Camp at Turkey Creek, Broad River, N.C., 18 Jan. 1781, TNA CC PRO 30/11/5/47.
17. Clinton to Cornwallis, New York, 13 Dec. 1780, TNA CC PRO 30/11/4/316.

18. Cornwallis to Germain, Guildford, N.C., 17 Mar. 1781, TNA CC PRO 30/11/5/281.
19. Stedman, *Origin, Progress, and Termination of the American War*, 2:326.
20. O'Hara to the Duke of Grafton, Wilmington, N.C., 20 Apr. 1781, Acc. 423/191, Grafton Papers, Suffolk Record Office, Bury St Edmunds, U.K.
21. Witness the actions of Sir Thomas Fairfax, the parliamentary cavalry commander in northern Britain in 1643, who rode in the saddle for three days while seriously wounded in the wrist such that it "made the bridle fall out of my hand: which, being among the nerves and veins, suddenly let out such a quantity of blood [that] I was ready to fall from my horse." Fairfax successfully led the retreat of his defeated force to the safety of Hull following its thrashing at the Battle of Adwalton Moor in July 1643. See Stanley D. M. Carpenter, *Military Leadership in the British Civil Wars, 1642–1651: 'The Genius of This Age'* (London: Cass, 2005), 23.
22. Lamb, *Journal*, 381.
23. Cornwallis to Clinton, Camden, S.C., 2 June 1780, TNA CC PRO 30/11/72/16.
24. All British line units had trained in light infantry operations while in Nova Scotia in early 1776 awaiting embarkation for the New York operation, therefore the transition to a light force was relatively easy. For an analysis of this dynamic, see Spring, *With Zeal and Bayonets Only*.
25. See Lawrence E. Babits, "Greene's Strategy in the Southern Campaign, 1780–1781," *Air Force Journal of Logistics* 8, no. 1 (Winter 1984): 10–14.
26. There are a number of excellent studies of the Scotch-Irish in the Carolina Piedmont at the time of the American War. For a more in-depth look at the settlers and culture that dominated the region, see Charles Woodmason, *The Carolina Backcountry on the Eve of the Revolution*, ed. Richard J. Hooker (Chapel Hill: University of North Carolina Press, 1953).
27. Cornwallis to Rawdon, Salisbury, N.C., 4 Feb. 1781, TNA CC PRO 30/11/85/1; O'Hara to the Duke of Grafton, Wilmington, N.C., 20 Apr. 1781, Acc. 423/191, Grafton Papers.
28. The crossing of the Catawba on 1 February 1781, while considered a civil action for which no battle honors could be awarded, is a famous and venerated event in the lore of the modern British Guards regiments. The site of the crossing is now under Lake Norman, following the construction of a dam in the twentieth century. Prior to the lake's filling, an oak tree that had been a sapling on the day of battle was cut, dressed, and preserved. In June 1992, at the 350th anniversary celebration of the founding of the Scots Guards (3rd Foot Guards in 1781), the 3rd Foot Guards in America, a War of American Independence reenactment unit, presented to the officers' mess of the 2nd Battalion, Scots Guards at Edinburgh Castle a plaque on which was mounted a reproduction small sword. The plaque was made from a piece of the harvested oak tree.
29. Tarrant's Tavern is sometimes seen as Torrence's or Tarrences's Tavern.
30. Cornwallis to Germain, Guildford, N.C., 17 Mar. 1781, TNA CC PRO 30/11/5/281.
31. Greene to Williams, Irwin's Ferry, Va., 14 Feb. 1781, Greene, *Papers*, 7:287.
32. Tarleton, *Campaigns of 1780 and 1781*, 229.
33. Rawdon to Balfour, Camden, S.C., 6 Feb. 1781, TNA HQ PRO 30/55/28/3324.
34. Cornwallis to Rawdon, Hillsborough, N.C., 21 Feb. 1781, TNA CC PRO 30/11/85/9.
35. Greene to Nash, Halifax County, Va., 17 Feb. 1781, Greene, *Papers*, 7:302.
36. O'Hara to the Duke of Grafton, Wilmington, N.C., 20 Apr. 1781, Acc. 423/191, Grafton Papers.

37. Cornwallis to Germain, Guildford, N.C., 17 Mar. 1781, TNA CC PRO 30/11/5/281.
38. Greene to Huger, Sherrads Ford, N.C., 30 Jan. 1781, Greene, *Papers*, 7:220.
39. "A Proclamation By the Right Honourable Charles Earl Cornwallis, Lt. General of His Majesty's Forces," Hillsborough, N.C., 20 Feb. 1781, TNA CC PRO 30/11/5/83.
40. In truth, Greene was as frustrated with the Virginia militia's reliability as was Cornwallis with the North Carolina Loyalists'.
41. Greene to Jefferson, Near the High Rock Ford, N.C., 10 Mar. 1781, Greene, *Papers*, 7:419.
42. Lamb, *Journal*, 361.
43. A long-persistent myth based on Henry Lee's recollection of events claims that Cornwallis ordered McLeod's guns to fire on the melee to extricate the 2nd Guards Battalion, knowing full well that many of his own troops would be hit. Larry Babits has addressed this issue, finding that none of the British or Patriot participants commented on the alleged orders. Having said that, perhaps the legend's persistence says much about Cornwallis's reputation for bold, decisive command leadership and his willingness to make difficult and agonizing decisions in the chaos of combat. See Larry Babits and Joshua B. Howard, *Long, Obstinate, and Bloody: The Battle of Guilford Courthouse* (Chapel Hill: University of North Carolina Press, 2009), 161.
44. Cornwallis to Germain, Guildford, N.C., 17 Mar. 1781, TNA CC PRO 30/11/76/38; Cornwallis to Rawdon, Guildford, N.C., 17 Mar. 1781, TNA CC PRO 30/11/75/14.
45. Quoted in Mark Urban, *Fusiliers: The Saga of a British Redcoat Regiment in the American Revolution* (New York: Walker, 2007), 247.
46. Stanley D. M. Carpenter, "Army," in *Britain in the Hanoverian Age, 1714–1837*, ed. Gerald Newman (New York and London: Garland, 1997), 28; Carpenter, "The British Army," in *A Companion to Eighteenth-Century Britain*, ed. H. T. Dickinson (Oxford: Blackwell, 2002), 475–76; Carpenter, "Patterns of Recruitment of the Highland Regiments of the British Army, 1756 to 1815" (Master's thesis, University of St Andrews, Scotland, 1978).
47. O'Hara to the Duke of Grafton, Wilmington, N.C., 20 Apr. 1781, Acc. 423/191, Grafton Papers.
48. Quoted in Franklin Wickwire and Mary Wickwire, *Cornwallis: The American Adventure* (Boston: Houghton Mifflin, 1970), 311.
49. O'Hara to the Duke of Grafton, Wilmington, N.C., 20 Apr. 1781, Acc. 423/191, Grafton Papers.
50. Part of the walls remain today as a line of stones on the ground. The Tory Confiscation Laws of 1777 and 1779 gave each North Carolina county officials the authority to seize the land and property of Loyalists. The Lincoln County (previously Tryon County) commissioners recorded on 19 September 1782: "Petter [*sic*] Carpenter [headed the list of 34] Names of those that is supposed to come under the Confiscation Act." In the Court of Sessions in October 1783, the commissioners reported that they had confiscated 520 pounds of fresh beef from Carpenter worth "$28 3/4 or Specie £11 and 10 shillings." See Confiscation Papers and Lincoln County Court Minutes for 1782 and 1783, North Carolina State Archives, Raleigh.
51. Greene to Washington, "Head Quarters at Col Ramsay's on Deep River, North Carolina," 29 Mar. 1781, Greene, *Papers*, 7:481.
52. Cornwallis to Germain, Wilmington, N.C., 18 Apr. 1781, TNA CC PRO 30/11/5/254.

53. Lamb, *Journal*, 360.
54. Clinton to Germain, New York, 23 Apr. 1781, TNA CO 5/102/42.
55. Cornwallis to Phillips, Wilmington, N.C., 10 Apr. 1781, TNA CC PRO 30/11/85/31.
56. Clinton to Germain, New York, 23 Apr. 1781, TNA CO 5/102/42.
57. Cornwallis to Germain, Guildford, N.C., 17 Mar. 1781, TNA CC PRO 30/11/5/281.
58. O'Hara to the Duke of Grafton, Wilmington, N.C., 20 Apr. 1781, Acc. 423/191, Grafton Papers.
59. Cornwallis to Germain, Wilmington, N.C., 18 Apr. 1781, TNA CC PRO 30/11/5/270.
60. Cornwallis to Clinton, Williamsburgh, Va., 30 June 1781, TNA CC PRO 30/11/74/18.
61. Cornwallis to Clinton, Wilmington, N.C., 10 Apr. 1781, TNA CC PRO 30/11/5/209.
62. Cornwallis to Germain, Wilmington, N.C., 18 Apr. 1781, TNA CC PRO 30/11/5/270.
63. Cornwallis to Phillips, Wilmington, N.C., 10 Apr. 1781, TNA CC PRO 30/11/85/31.
64. Cornwallis to Clinton, Wilmington, N.C., 10 Apr. 1781, TNA CC PRO 30/11/5/209.
65. Cornwallis to Phillips, Wilmington, N.C., 10 Apr. 1781, TNA CC PRO 30/11/85/31.
66. *Observations of an Anonymous British Officer* (1777), quoted in Dave Richard Palmer, *George Washington's Military Genius* (Westport, Conn.: Greenwood, 1975), 137.

### Chapter 5. The Southern Campaign Draws to a Close

1. Cornwallis to Germain, Wilmington, N.C., 18 Apr. 1781, C-CC, 1:416–18.
2. Ibid.
3. Germain to Clinton, Whitehall, London, 7 Mar. 1781, TNA CO 5/101/156.
4. Germain to Clinton, Whitehall, London, 2 May 1781, TNA CO 5/101/311.
5. Clinton to Cornwallis, New York, 13 Apr. 1781, TNA HQ PRO 30/55/29/3446.
6. Clinton to Cornwallis, Head Quarters, Charlestown, South Carolina, 1 June 1780, TNA CC PRO 30/11/2/68.
7. Tarleton, *Campaigns of 1780 and 1781*, 171.
8. Clinton to Cornwallis, New York, 29 May 1781, C-CC, 1:493–98.
9. Cornwallis to Clinton, Bird's Plantation north of James River, Va., 26 May 1781, C-CC, 1:487–91.
10. Clinton to Cornwallis, New York, 11 June 1781, TNA CC PRO 30/11/68/14.
11. Ibid.
12. Clausewitz, *On War*, 88–89.
13. Rawdon to Cornwallis, Camp at Monk's Corner, S.C., 24 May 1781, TNA CC PRO 30/11/6/106.
14. Raised in New York by Brigadier Oliver de Lancey in 1776, two of the three battalions fought throughout the South Carolina and Georgia Campaigns, disbanding in New Brunswick in 1783. Cruger commanded the 1st Battalion.
15. Rawdon to Balfour, Blake's Plantation, S.C., 9 June 1781, TNA CC PRO 30/11/6/210.
16. Cruger to Rawdon, Ninety Six, S.C., 31 May 1781, TNA CC PRO 30/11/6/212.
17. The troops from Ireland were the 3rd, 19th, 30th Regiments of Foot and a detachment of the Guards. Some joined Cornwallis in Virginia, with the remainder going to

South Carolina. Rawdon to Cornwallis, Charlestown, S.C., 5 June 1781, TNA CC PRO 30/11/6/174.

18. The battalion's parent regiments had arrived in South Carolina in June 1781.

19. Stewart to Cornwallis, St. Clair's Plantation, S.C., 26 Sept. 1781, TNA CC PRO 30/11/6/399; Stewart to Cornwallis, Flood's Plantation, S.C., 19 Sept. 1781, TNA CC PRO 30/11/71/30.

20. For detailed analyses of Florida's role in the War of American Independence, see Martha C. Searcy, *The Georgia-Florida Contest in the American Revolution, 1776–1778* (Tuscaloosa: University of Alabama Press, 1985); J. Barton Starr, *Tories, Dons, and Rebels: The American Revolution in British West Florida* (Gainesville: University Press of Florida, 1976); J. Leitch Wright Jr., *Florida in the American Revolution* (Gainesville: University of Press Florida, 1975); Gary D. Olson, "Thomas Brown, Loyalist Partisan and the Revolutionary War in Georgia, 1777–1782," *Georgia Historical Quarterly* 54 (1970): 1–19; and James W. Raab, *Spain, Britain, and the American Revolution in Florida, 1763–1783* (Jefferson, N.C.: McFarland, 2007).

21. The East Florida Rangers, raised along the East Florida–Georgia border, fought throughout the Southern Campaign, merging in 1782 with the Georgia Loyalists. Tonyn to Clinton, St. Augustine, East Fla., 29 May 1779, TNA HQ PRO 30/55/16/2016.

22. Extracts of Campbell's letter, Pensacola, West Fla., 11 Sept. 1779, TNA CO 5/99(1)/89; Tonyn to Clinton, St. Augustine, East Fla., 23 Dec. 1779, TNA HQ PRO 30/55/20/2494.

23. For details of the siege of Pensacola, see William S. Coker and Robert R. Rea, *Anglo-Spanish Confrontation on the Gulf Coast during the American Revolution* (Gulf Coast History and Humanities Conference, 1982); Virginia Parks, ed., *Siege, Spain and Britain: Battle of Pensacola, March 9–May 8, 1781* (Pensacola: Pensacola Historical Society, 1981); and N. Orwin Rush, *Spain's Final Triumph over Great Britain in the Gulf of Mexico: The Battle of Pensacola* (Tallahassee: Florida State University, 1966).

24. Cornwallis Proclamation, Yorktown, Va., 9 Aug. 1781, TNA CC PRO 30/11/101/34.

25. General Orders, 28 May 1781, "Orderly Book, H.B.M. 43d Regiment of Foot General Orders, From 23 May to 25 August 1781," Add. Mss. 42,449, British Library, London.

26. Clinton to Germain, New York, 18 May 1781, TNA CO 5/102/109.

27. Quoted in Henry P. Johnston, *The Yorktown Campaign and the Surrender of Cornwallis, 1781* (New York: Harper and Brothers, 1881), 68.

28. C-CC, 1:43n6.

29. For a discussion of the intercepted letters controversy, see Willcox, *Portrait of a General*, 394–97.

30. Clinton to Cornwallis, New York, 11 July 1781, TNA CC PRO 30/1/68/43.

31. Instructions to Major General Phillips, 10 Mar. 1781, TNA CC PRO 30/11/74/57.

32. Clinton to Cornwallis, New York, 11 July 1781, TNA CC PRO 30/11/68/43.

33. Cornwallis to Rawdon, Portsmouth, Va., 23 July 1781, TNA CC PRO 30/11/88/46.

34. Germain to Clinton, Whitehall, London, 4 Apr. 1781, TNA CO 5/101/84/169.

35. Sheathing hulls in copper plates reduced underwater marine growth, a major speed-limiting factor for wooden-hulled vessels.

36. See Michael J. Crawford, "New Light on the Battle off the Virginia Capes: Graves vs. Hood," *Mariner's Mirror* 103, no. 3 (2017): 337–40.

37. French Ensor Chadwick, ed., *The Graves Papers and Other Documents Relating to the Naval Operations of the Yorktown Campaign, July to October, 1781* (New York: Naval History Society, De Vinne, 1916), lxviii; C-CC, 1:21.
38. George Washington, diary, 14 July 1781, Washington, *The Writings of George Washington: Being His Correspondence, Addresses, Messages and Other Papers, Private and Public*, vol. 8, ed. Jared Sparks (Boston: Russell, Odiorne, and Metcalf, 1835), 134.
39. Clinton to Cornwallis, New York, 2 Sept. 1781, TNA CC PRO 30/11/68/77.
40. See Julian S. Corbett, ed., *Fighting Instructions, 1530–1816*, Publications of the Navy Records Society 29 (London: Spottswoodie, 1905).
41. Graves to Sandwich, HMS *London*, 14 Sept. 1781, John Montagu, Earl of Sandwich, *The Private Papers of John, Earl of Sandwich, First Lord of the Admiralty, 1771–1781*, ed. G. R. Barnes and J. H. Owens, 4 vols. (London: Navy Records Society, 1932–38), 4:181–82; Hood to Sandwich, HMS *Barfleur*, 6 Sept. 1781, Hood, *Letters of Sir Samuel Hood*, ed. David Hannay (London: Navy Records Society, 1895), 31.
42. For a more thorough analysis of the signals and instructions dynamic, see Peter Padfield, *Maritime Supremacy and the Opening of the Western Mind: Naval Campaigns that Shaped the Modern World, 1588–1782* (London: John Murray, 1999), 263.
43. Adm. Sir George Rodney, "Sailing and Fighting Instructions," Article XXI, TNA PRO 30/20/19.
44. Hood to Jackson, HMS *Barfleur* off the Delaware, 16 Sept. 1781, Chadwick, *Graves Papers*, 86–91.
45. As proposed in Kenneth Breen, "Graves and Hood at the Chesapeake," *Mariners' Mirror* 66 (1980): 63–64.
46. Graves to Admiralty, Battle Report, HMS *London*, 11 Sept. 1781, Admiralty Papers 1/489/419, The National Archives, Kew, U.K. (hereafter TNA ADM).
47. Hood to Jackson, HMS *Barfleur*, 16 Sept. 1781, Chadwick, *Graves Papers*, 86–91.
48. The eminent naval historian and Naval War College professor Rear Adm. Alfred Thayer Mahan has argued that had Graves taken station in the Chesapeake, de Grasse, on joining with de Barras, would most likely have declined to confront the British, allowing for the reinforcement or evacuation of Cornwallis's forces. See Alfred Thayer Mahan, *The Major Operations of the Navies in the War of American Independence* (London: Sampson Low, Marsten, 1913), 184.
49. Hood to his brother, HMS *Barfleur*, 24 Aug. 1782, Hood Letters, National Maritime Museum, Greenwich, London, MKH/501/MS52/060.
50. Graves Memorandum, HMS *London*, 13 Sept. 1781, TNA ADM 1/489/435/155.
51. Clinton to Cornwallis, New York, 2 Sept. 1781, TNA CC PRO 30/11/68/77.
52. Cornwallis to Clinton, Yorktown, Va., 2 Sept. 1781, TNA CC PRO 30/11/74/82.
53. Clinton to Cornwallis, New York, 6 Sept. 1781, TNA CC PRO 30/11/68/81.
54. Clinton to Germain, New York, 7 Sept. 1781, TNA CO 5/103/124.
55. For Cornwallis's explanation, see C-CC, 1:76–77.
56. Tarleton, *Campaigns of 1780 and 1781*, 374–75.
57. Lincoln had been exchanged for Major General Phillips and another general officer captured at Saratoga. At Yorktown he was second in command to Washington.
58. Clinton to Cornwallis, New York, 24 Sept. 1781, TNA CC PRO 30/11/68/83.
59. Cornwallis to Clinton, Yorktown, Va., 29 Sept. 1781, TNA CC PRO 30/11/74/93.

60. Lambert to Speaker of the Commons William Lenthall, Barnard Castle, 20 July 1648, *Journal of the House of Commons*, 5:646, 650.
61. Germain to Clinton, Whitehall, London, 2 May 1781, TNA CO 5/101/307.
62. Ibid.
63. Germain to Clinton, Whitehall, London, 7 July 1781, TNA CO 5/101/146.
64. Clinton to Cornwallis, New York, 30 Sept. 1780, TNA CC PRO 30/11/68/91.
65. Cornwallis to Clinton, Yorktown, Va., 11 Oct. 1781, TNA CC PRO 30/11/74/103.
66. Cornwallis to Washington, "York in Virginia," 17 Oct. 1781, TNA CO 5/103/275.
67. James Thacher, *A Military Journal During the American Revolutionary War, from 1775 to 1783, Describing Interesting Events and Transactions of this Period with Numerous Historical Facts and Anecdotes* (1823; repr., Cranbury, N.J.: Scholar's Bookshelf, 2005), 346.
68. Thacher, *Military Journal*, 362.
69. Although the 80th Regiment was raised in Edinburgh, by the 1770s many Highlanders had moved to Edinburgh and Glasgow and then later volunteered for army service from those cities.
70. Samuel Graham, *Memoir of General [Samuel] Graham: With Notices of the Campaigns in which He Was Engaged from 1779 to 1801, Edited by His Son, Colonel J. J. Graham* (Edinburgh: R. and R. Clark, 1862), 64 (19 Oct. 1781).

## Conclusion. "Peril and Delusion"

1. Niccolo Machiavelli, *Discourses on Livy*, trans. Harvey Mansfield and Nathan Tarcov (Chicago: University of Chicago, 1996), 147 (bk. 2, chap. 10).
2. Ira D. Gruber, "The Origins of British Strategy in the War for American Independence," in *Military History of the American Revolution: Proceedings of the Sixth Military History Symposium, United States Air Force Academy, 10–11 October 1974*, ed. Stanley J. Underdal (Washington, D.C.: Office of Air Force History, Headquarters USAF and Air Force Academy, 1974), 38–51.
3. Valentine, *Germain*, 398.
4. Ibid., 424–25.
5. Sun Tzu, *Art of War*, 134.
6. Fortescue, *History of the British Army*, 3(2):168–69.
7. Clausewitz, *On War*, 87.
8. Valentine, *Germain*, 426.
9. Cornwallis to Clinton, Yorktown, Va., 20 Oct. 1781, TNA CC PRO 30/11/74/105.

# Bibliography

## Primary Sources

"Address of the People of Fincastle County, Virginia, to the Delegates from that Colony, who attended the Continental Congress," 20 January 1775. Documents of the American Revolution, American Archives, University of Chicago Libraries.

Admiralty Papers. The National Archives, Kew, U.K.

Allaire, Anthony. *Diary of Lieut. Anthony Allaire of Ferguson's Corps.* New York: New York Times Press, 1968.

Army War College Historical Section. *Historical Statements Concerning the Battle of Kings Mountain and the Battle of the Cowpens, South Carolina.* Washington, D.C.: Government Printing Office, 1928.

Baurmeister, Carl Leopold. *Revolution in America: Confidential Letters and Journals 1776–1784 of Adj. Gen. Major Baurmeister of the Hessian Forces.* Translated by Bernhard A. Uhlendorf. New Brunswick, N.J.: Rutgers University Press, 1957.

Brown, Alan S., ed. "James Simpson's Reports on the Carolina Loyalists, 1779–1780." *Journal of Southern History* 21, no. 4 (November 1955): 518–19.

Campbell, Archibald. *Journal of an Expedition against the Rebels of Georgia in North America.* Edited by Colin Campbell. Darien, Ga.: Ashantilly, 1981.

Chadwick, French Ensor, ed. *The Graves Papers and Other Documents Relating to the Naval Operations of the Yorktown Campaign, July to October, 1781.* New York: Naval History Society, De Vinne, 1916.

Clinton, Sir Henry. *The American Rebellion: Sir Henry Clinton's Narrative of His Campaigns, 1775–1782, with an Appendix of Original Documents.* Edited by William B. Willcox. 1954. Reprint, Hamden, Conn.: Archon, 1971.

———. *The Narrative of Lieutenant-General Sir Henry Clinton, K.B., Relative to His Conduct during Part of His Command of the King's Troops in North America: Particularly to That Which Respects the Campaign Issue of 1781.* Farmington Hills, Mich.: Gale ECCO, 2010.

———. *Observations on Mr. Stedman's History of the American War.* Farmington Hills, Mich.: Gale ECCO, 2010.

———. *Observations on Some Parts of the Answer of Earl Cornwallis to Sir Henry Clinton's Narrative.* Farmington Hills, Mich.: Gale ECCO, 2010.

———. Henry Clinton Papers, 1738–1850. William L. Clements Library, University of Michigan, Ann Arbor.

*Colonial and State Records of North Carolina*. Vol. 10. Chapel Hill: University of North Carolina Library, 2004.

Confiscation Papers and Lincoln County Court Minutes for 1782 and 1783. North Carolina State Archives, Raleigh.

Corbett, Julian S., ed. *Fighting Instructions, 1530–1816*. Publications of the Navy Records Society 29. London: Spottswoodie, 1905.

Cornwallis, Charles. *An Answer to that Part of the Narrative of Lieutenant-General Sir Henry Clinton, K.B., Which Relates to the Conduct of Lieutenant-General Earl Cornwallis, during the Campaign in North America, in the Year 1781*. Farmington Hills, Mich.: Gale ECCO, 2010.

Cornwallis Correspondence. The National Archives, Kew, U.K.

*The Cornwallis Papers, Abstracts of Americana*. Edited by George H. Reese. 1859. Reprint, Charlottesville: University Press of Virginia, 1970.

*The Cornwallis Papers: The Campaigns of 1780 and 1781 in the Southern Theatre of the American Revolutionary War*. 6 vols. Edited by Ian Saberton. Uckfield, U.K.: Naval and Military Press, 2010.

*Correspondence of Charles, First Marquis Cornwallis*. Edited by Charles Derek Ross. Cambridge, U.K.: Cambridge University Press, 2011.

*The Correspondence of King George the Third from 1760 to December 1783, printed from the Original Papers in the Royal Archives at Windsor Castle, arranged and edited by the Hon. Sir John Fortescue*. 6 vols. London: Macmillan, 1927–28.

Dann, John C., ed. *The Revolution Remembered: Eyewitness Accounts of the War for Independence*. Chicago: University of Chicago Press, 1980.

Davies, K. G., ed. *Documents of the American Revolution, 1770–1783*. 20 vols. Shannon, Ire.: Irish Universities Press, 1976.

Döhla, Johann Conrad. *A Hessian Diary of the American Revolution*. Translated and Edited by Bruce E. Burgoyne. Norman: University of Oklahoma Press, 1990.

Ewald, Johann von. *Diary of the American War: A Hessian Journal*. Translated and Edited by Joseph P. Tustin. New Haven, Conn.: Yale University Press, 1979.

———. *Treatise on Partisan Warfare*. Translated and Annotated by Robert A. Selig and David Curtis Skaggs. Westport, Conn.: Greenwood, 1991.

Graham, Samuel. *Memoir of General [Samuel] Graham: With Notices of the Campaigns in which He Was Engaged from 1779 to 1801, Edited by His Son, Colonel J. J. Graham*. Edinburgh: R. and R. Clark, 1862.

Grafton Papers. Suffolk Record Office, Bury St. Edmunds, U.K.

Greene, Nathanael. *The Papers of Nathanael Greene*. 9 vols. Edited by Richard K. Showman, Dennis M. Conrad, Roger N. Parks, and Elizabeth C. Stevens. Chapel Hill: University of North Carolina Press, 1991.

Gruber, Ira D., ed. *John Peebles' American War: The Diary of a Scottish Grenadier, 1776–1782*. Mechanicsburg, Pa.: Stackpole Books, 1998.

Hanger, George. *The Life, Adventures, and Opinions of Colonel George Hanger*. 2 vols. Charleston, S.C.: Nabu, 2010.

Harcourt, William. *The Harcourt Papers*. Vol. 11. Edited by Edward Harcourt. Oxford: Oxford University Press, 1880.

Headquarters Papers of the British Army in North America, 1775–84 (Dorchester Papers). The National Archives, Kew, U.K.

"Headquarters Papers of the British Army in North America." In *Report on American Manuscripts in the Royal Institution of Great Britain (Dorchester Papers)*. Vol. 1. Edited by Benjamin Franklin Stevens and Henry J. Brown. London: His Majesty's Stationery Office, 1904.

*Historical Manuscripts Commission. Report on the Manuscripts of the Late Reginald Rawdon Hastings, HMC 78*. Vol. 3. London: His Majesty's Stationary Office, 1928–47.

———.*The Manuscripts of the Earl of Dartmouth*. Vol. 2, *American Papers*. Fourteenth Report, Appendix, Part 10, London: His Majesty's Stationary Office, 1895.

———. *Report on Manuscripts in Various Collections*. Vol. 6, *The Manuscripts of Miss M. Eyre Matcham, Captain H. V. Knox, Cornwallis-Wykeham-Martin*. London: His Majesty's Stationary Office, 1909.

———.*Report on the Manuscripts of Mrs. Stopford-Sackville, of Drayton House, Northamptonshire*. 2 Vols. London: His Majesty's Stationary Office, 1904–10.

Hood, Sir Samuel. Hood Letters. National Maritime Museum, Greenwich, London.

———. *Letters of Sir Samuel Hood*. Edited by David Hannay. London: Navy Records Society, 1895.

———. Papers of Admiral Samuel Hood. National Maritime Museum, Greenwich, London.

Hough, Franklin Benjamin. *The Siege of Savannah by the Combined American and French Forces under the Command of Gen. Lincoln and the Count D'Estaing in the Autumn of 1779*. 1866. Reprint, New York: Da Capo, 1974.

*The Journal of Alexander Chesney, a South Carolina Loyalist in the Revolution and After*. Edited by E. Alfred Jones. Columbus: Ohio State University, 1921.

Lamb, Roger. *An Original and Authentic Journal of Occurrences during the Late American War from Its Commencement to the Year 1783*. Dublin: Wilkinson and Courtney, 1809.

Letter Books of the Colonial Office, America and West Indies. The National Archives, Kew, U.K.

Mackenzie, Roderick. *Strictures on Lt. Col. Tarleton's "History of the Campaigns of 1780 and 1781, in the Southern Provinces of North America."* Farmington Hills, Mich.: Gale ECCO, 2010.

Montegue, John, Earl of Sandwich. *The Private Papers of John, Earl of Sandwich, First Lord of the Admiralty, 1771–1781*. 4 vols. Edited by G. R. Barnes and J. H. Owens. London: Navy Records Society, 1932–38.

Motier, Gilbert. *Lafayette in the Age of the American Revolution: Selected Letters and Papers, 1776–1790*. 5 vols. Edited by Stanley J. Idzerda. Ithaca, N.Y.: Cornell University Press, 1977–83.

"Orderly Book, H.B.M. 43d Regiment of Foot General Orders, From 23 May to 25 Aug 1781." Additional Manuscripts 42,449. British Library, London.

Original Correspondence of the Secretary of State. Letter Books of the Colonial Office, America and West Indies. The National Archives, Kew, U.K.

Rodney, Sir George. "Sailing and Fighting Instructions." The National Archives, Kew, U.K.

*The Siege of Savannah in 1779, as Described in Two Contemporaneous Journals of French Officers in the Fleet of Count D'Estaing*. Edited by Charles C. Jones Jr. 1874. Reprint, New York: New York Times and Arno Press, 1968.

Stedman, Charles. *The History of the Origin, Progress, and Termination of the American War.* 2 vols. 1794. Reprint, Charleston, S.C.: Nabu, 2010.

Stevens, Benjamin Franklin, ed. *The Campaign in Virginia, 1781: An exact Reprint of Six rare Pamphlets on the Clinton-Cornwallis Controversy.* 2 vols. 1888. Reprint, Charleston, S.C.: Nabu, 2010.

———, ed. *Facsimiles of Manuscripts in European Archives Relating to America, 1773–1783.* 25 vols. London, 1889–95.

Tarleton, Banastre. *A History of the Campaigns of 1780 and 1781 in the Southern Provinces of North America.* 1787. Reprint, New York: Arno, 1968.

Thacher, James. *A Military Journal During the American Revolutionary War, from 1775 to 1783, Describing Interesting Events and Transactions of this Period with Numerous Historical Facts and Anecdotes.* 1823. Reprint, Cranbury, N.J.: Scholar's Bookshelf, 2005.

Themistocles. *A Reply to Sir Henry Clinton's Narrative. His Numerous Errors Are Pointed Out, Conduct of Lord Cornwallis Vindicated from Aspersion. Includes the Public and Secret Correspondence.* Farmington Hills, Mich.: Gale ECCO, 2010.

War Office Papers. The National Archives, Kew, U.K.

Washington, George. *The Writings of George Washington: Being His Correspondence, Addresses, Messages and Other Papers, Private and Public.* Vol. 8. Edited by Jared Sparks. Boston: Russell, Odiorne, and Metcalf, 1835.

Woodmason, Charles. *The Carolina Backcountry on the Eve of the Revolution.* Edited by Richard J. Hooker. Chapel Hill: University of North Carolina Press, 1953.

## Secondary Sources

### *Books and Chapters*

Alden, John R. *John Stuart and the Southern Colonial Frontier: A Study of Indian Relations, War, Trade, and Land Problems in the Southern Wilderness, 1754–1775.* Ann Arbor: University of Michigan Press, 1944.

———. *The South in the Revolution, 1763–1789.* Baton Rouge: Louisiana State University Press, 1957.

Alexander, Bevin. *How Great Generals Win.* New York: W. W. Norton, 1993.

Allen, Thomas B. *Tories: Fighting for the King in America's First Civil War.* New York: Harper, 2010.

Arthur, Robert. *The Sieges of Yorktown 1781 and 1862.* Fort Monroe, Va.: Coast Artillery School, 1927.

Babits, Lawrence E. *A Devil of a Whipping: The Battle of Cowpens.* Chapel Hill: University of North Carolina Press, 1998.

Babits, Lawrence E., and Joshua B. Howard. *Long, Obstinate, and Bloody: The Battle of Guilford Courthouse.* Chapel Hill: University of North Carolina Press, 2009.

Bailyn, Bernard. *The Ideological Origins of the American Revolution.* Cambridge, Mass.: Harvard University Press, 1967.

Baker, Norman. *Government and Contractors: The British Treasury and War Supplies, 1775–83.* London: Athlone, 1971.

Bargar, B. D. *Lord Dartmouth and the American Revolution.* Columbia: University of South Carolina Press, 1965.

Bass, Robert D. *The Green Dragoon*. Orangeburg, S.C.: Sandlapper, 2003.
———. *Swamp Fox: The Life and Campaigns of General Francis Marion*. New York: Holt, 1959.
Billias, George A. *George Washington's Generals and Opponents*. Cambridge, Mass.: Da Capo, 1994.
———, ed. *George Washington's Opponents: British Generals and Admirals in the American Revolution*. New York: William Morrow, 1969.
Black, Jeremy. *The British Seaborne Empire*. New Haven, Conn.: Yale University Press, 2004.
———. *Parliament and Foreign Policy in the Eighteenth Century*. Cambridge, U.K.: Cambridge University Press, 2004.
———. *War for America: The Fight for Independence, 1775–1783*. New York: St. Martin's, 1991.
Borick, Carl P. *A Gallant Defense: The Siege of Charleston, 1780*. Columbia: University of South Carolina Press, 2003.
Bowler, R. Arthur. *Logistics and the Failure of the British Army in America, 1775–1783*. Princeton, N.J.: Princeton University Press, 1975.
Brewer, John. *The Sinews of Power: War, Money, and the English State, 1688–1783*. New York: Alfred A. Knopf, 1989.
Brinkley, W. David. *Back to the Future: The British Southern Campaign, 1780–1781*. Fort Leavenworth, Kans.: School of Advanced Military Studies, U.S. Army Command and General Staff College, 1998.
Brown, Gerald S. *The American Secretary: The Colonial Policy of Lord George Germain, 1775–1778*. Ann Arbor: University of Michigan Press, 1963.
Brown, Marion Marsh. *The Swamp Fox*. Philadelphia: Westminster, 1950.
Brown, Robert W., Jr. *Kings Mountain and Cowpens: Our Victory Was Complete*. Charleston, S.C.: History Press, 2009.
Brown, Wallace. *The King's Friends: The Composition and Motives of the American Loyalist Claimants*. Providence, R.I.: Brown University Press, 1965.
Brumwell, Stephen. *Redcoats: The British Soldier and the War in the Americas, 1775–1763*. Cambridge, U.K.: Cambridge University Press, 2002.
Buchanan, John. *The Road to Guilford Courthouse: The American Revolution in the Carolinas*. New York: Wiley, 1997.
Carpenter, Robert C. *Carpenters a Plenty*. Baltimore: Gateway, 1982.
Carpenter, Stanley D. M. *Military Leadership in the British Civil Wars, 1642–1651: "The Genius of This Age."* London: Frank Cass, 2005.
Clausewitz, Carl von. *On War*. Edited and Translated by Michael Howard and Peter Paret. Princeton, N.J.: Princeton University Press, 1976.
Coker, William S., and Robert R. Rea. "Anglo-Spanish Confrontation on the Gulf Coast during the American Revolution." Paper presented at the Gulf Coast History and Humanities Conference, 1982.
Cook, Don. *The Long Fuse: How England Lost the American Colonies, 1760–1785*. New York: Atlantic Monthly Press, 1995.
Corbett, Julian S. *Some Principles of Maritime Strategy*. 1911. Reprint, Annapolis: Naval Institute Press, 1988.
Crow, Jeffrey J., and Larry E. Tise, eds. *The Southern Experience in the American Revolution*. Chapel Hill: University of North Carolina Press, 1978.

Dameron, David. *Kings Mountain: The Defeat of the Loyalists October 7, 1780*. Cambridge, Mass.: Da Capo, 2003.

Davis, Burke. *The Campaign That Won America: The Story of Yorktown*. New York: Eastern Acorn, 1989.

———. *The Cowpens-Guilford Courthouse Campaign*. Philadelphia: University of Pennsylvania Press, 2002.

Davis, Robert S., Jr. *Georgians in the Revolution: At Kettle Creek (Wilkes Co.) and Burke County*. Easley, S.C.: Southern Historical, 1986.

DeMond, Robert O. *The Loyalists in North Carolina during the Revolution*. 1930. Reprint, Baltimore: Clearfield, 2009.

De Vorsey, Louis, Jr. *The Indian Boundary in the Southern Colonies, 1763–1775*. Chapel Hill: University of North Carolina Press, 1966.

Donoughue, Bernard. *British Politics and the American Revolution: The Path to War, 1773–75*. London: Macmillan, 1964.

Draper, Lyman C. *King's Mountain and Its Heroes: History of the Battle of King's Mountain, October 7th, 1780, and the Events Which Led to It*. 1881. Reprint, Charleston, S.C.: Nabu, 2010.

Edgar, Walter. *South Carolina: A History*. Columbia: University of South Carolina Press, 1998.

Fenn, Elizabeth A. *Pox Americana: The Great Smallpox Epidemic of 1775–82*. Boston: Hill and Wang, 2002.

Ferling, John. *Almost a Miracle: The American Victory in the War of Independence*. Oxford: Oxford University Press, 2007.

———. *A Leap in the Dark: The Struggle to Create the American Republic*. New York: Oxford University Press, 2003.

———. *Whirlwind: The American Revolution and the War That Won It*. London: Bloomsbury, 2016.

Fischer, David Hackett. *Washington's Crossing*. New York: Oxford University Press, 2004.

Fortescue, Sir John. *A History of the British Army*. 20 vols. London: Macmillan, 1902. Reprint, East Essex, U.K.: Naval and Military Press, 2004.

———. *The War of Independence: The British Army in North America, 1775–1783*. 1911. Reprint, London: Greenhill Books, 2001.

Gilbert, Alan. *Black Patriots and Loyalists: Fighting for Emancipation in the War for Independence*. Chicago: University of Chicago Press, 2012.

Gleig, G. R. *Lives of the Most Eminent British Military Commanders*. London: Longman, 1831–32.

Golway, Terry. *Washington's General: Nathanael Greene and the Triumph of the American Revolution*. New York: Henry Holt, 2005.

Gordon, John W. *South Carolina and the American Revolution: A Battlefield History*. Columbia: University of South Carolina Press, 2003.

Greene, Jerome A. *The Guns of Independence: The Siege of Yorktown, 1781*. New York: Savas Beatie, 2009.

Griffin, Clarence W. *The History of Old Tryon and Rutherford Counties, North Carolina, 1730–1936*. Spartanburg, S.C.: Reprint Company, 1982.

Gruber, Ira D. *The Howe Brothers and the American Revolution*. Chapel Hill: University of North Carolina Press, 2014.

Hagan, Kenneth J., and William R. Roberts, eds. *Against All Enemies: Interpretations of American Military History from Colonial Times to the Present.* New York: Greenwood, 1986.

Hairr, John. *Guilford Courthouse: Nathanael Greene's Victory in Defeat, March 15, 1781.* Cambridge, Mass.: Da Capo, 2002.

Hart, Basil H. Liddell. *The British Way in Warfare.* New York: Macmillan, 1933.

———. *Strategy.* 2nd rev. ed. New York: Meridian, 1991.

Hibbert, Christopher. *Redcoats and Rebels.* New York: W. W. Norton, 1990.

Higginbotham, Donald. *Daniel Morgan: Revolutionary Rifleman.* Chapel Hill: University of North Carolina Press, 1979.

———, ed. *Reconsiderations on the Revolutionary War: Selected Essays.* Westport, Conn.: Greenwood, 1978.

———. *The War of American Independence: Military Attitudes, Policies, and Practices, 1763–1789.* Bloomington: Indiana University Press, 1971.

Higgins, W. Robert, ed. *The Revolutionary War in the South: Power, Conflict, and Leadership, Essays in Honor of John Richard Alden.* Durham, N.C.: Duke University Press, 1979.

Holmes, Richard. *Redcoat: The British Soldier in the Age of Horse and Musket.* New York: W. W. Norton, 2001.

Jasanoff, Maya. *Liberty's Exiles: American Loyalists in the Revolutionary World.* New York: Alfred A. Knopf, 2011.

Johnson, William. *Sketches of the Life and Correspondence of Nathanael Greene.* 2 vols. 1822. Reprint, New York: Da Capo, 1973.

Johnston, Henry P. *The Yorktown Campaign and the Surrender of Cornwallis, 1781.* 1881. Reprint, Spartanburg, S.C.: Reprint Company, 1973.

Katcher, Philip R. N. *Encyclopedia of British, Provincial, and German Army Units, 1775–1783.* Harrisburg, Pa.: Stackpole Books, 1973.

Ketchum, Richard M. *Victory at Yorktown: The Campaign That Won the Revolution.* New York: Holt, 2004.

Lambert, Robert Stansbury. *South Carolina Loyalists in the American Revolution.* Columbia: University of South Carolina Press, 1987.

Landers, H. L. *The Battle of Camden.* Washington, D.C.: Government Printing Office, 1929.

———. *The Virginia Campaign and the Blockade and Siege of Yorktown, 1781: Including a Brief Narrative of the French Participation in the Revolution Prior to the Southern Campaign.* Washington, D.C.: U.S. Army War College, 1931.

Lanning, Michael. *African Americans in the Revolutionary War.* New York: Kensington, 2000.

Leckie, Robert. *George Washington's War: The Saga of the American Revolution.* New York: Harper Perennial, 1993.

Lumpkin, Henry. *From Savannah to Yorktown: The American Revolution in the South.* Columbia: University of South Carolina Press, 1981.

Lunt, James. *The Duke of Wellington's Regiment (West Riding).* London: Leo Cooper, 1971.

Machiavelli, Niccolo. *Discourses on Livy.* Translated by Harvey Mansfield and Nathan Tarcov. Chicago: University of Chicago, 1996.

Mackesy, Piers. *The War for America, 1775–1783.* Lincoln: University of Nebraska Press, 1992.

Magill, Frank N., ed. *Great Lives from History: British and Commonwealth Series*. Vol. 2. Pasadena, Calif.: Salem, 1987.

Mahan, Alfred Thayer. *The Influence of Sea Power upon History, 1660–1783*. New York: Hill and Wang, 1957.

———. *The Major Operations of the Navies in the War of American Independence*. London: Sampson Low, Marsten, 1913.

Maier, Pauline. *From Resistance to Revolution: Colonial Radicals and the Development of American Opposition to Britain, 1765–1776*. London: Routledge and Keegan Paul, 1973.

Marlow, Louis. *Sackville of Drayton*. Totowa, N.J.: Rowman and Littlefield, 1973.

Marshall, P. J. *The Making and Unmaking of Empires: Britain, India, and America, c. 1750–1783*. Oxford: Oxford University Press, 2005.

Mattern, David B. *Benjamin Lincoln and the American Revolution*. Columbia: University of South Carolina Press, 1995.

McIntyre, James R. *The Development of the British Light Infantry, Continental and American Influences, 1740–1765*. Point Pleasant, N.J.: Winged Hussar, 2015.

Messick, Hank. *King's Mountain: The Epic of the Blue Ridge "Mountain Men" in the American Revolution*. Boston: Little, Brown, 1976.

Meyer, Duane. *The Highland Scots of North Carolina, 1732–1776*. Chapel Hill: University of North Carolina Press, 1987.

Middlekauff, Robert. *The Glorious Cause: The American Revolution, 1763–1789*. Rev. and exp. ed. New York: Oxford University Press, 2005.

Murray, Williamson, and Peter R. Mansoor. *Hybrid Warfare: Fighting Complex Opponents from the Ancient World to the Present*. New York: Cambridge University Press, 2012.

Nelson, Paul David. *Francis Rawdon-Hastings, Marquess of Hastings: Soldier, Peer of the Realm, Governor-General of India*. Madison, N.J.: Fairleigh Dickinson University Press, 2005.

———. *General Horatio Gates: A Biography*. Baton Rouge: Louisiana State University Press, 1976.

Nester, William R. *The Frontier War for American Independence*. Mechanicsburg, Pa.: Stackpole Books, 2004.

O'Donnell, James H. *Southern Indians in the American Revolution*. Knoxville: University of Tennessee Press, 1973.

O'Shaughnessy, Andrew Jackson. *The Men Who Lost America: British Leadership, the American Revolution, and the Fate of the Empire*. New Haven, Conn.: Yale University Press, 2013.

Padfield, Peter. *Maritime Supremacy and the Opening of the Western Mind: Naval Campaigns that Shaped the Modern World, 1588–1782*. London: John Murray, 1999.

Palmer, Dave Richard. *George Washington's Military Genius*. Westport, Conn.: Greenwood, 1975.

Parks, Virginia, ed. *Siege, Spain, and Britain: Battle of Pensacola, March 9–May 8, 1781*. Pensacola: Pensacola Historical Society, 1981.

Patterson, Benton Rain. *Washington and Cornwallis: The Battle for America, 1775–1783*. Boulder, Colo.: Taylor, 2004.

Pearson, Michael. *Those Damned Rebels: The American Revolution as Seen through British Eyes*. Cambridge, Mass.: Da Capo, 2000.

Peckham, Howard H. *The War for Independence: A Military History*. Chicago: University of Chicago Press, 1958.

Pengelly, Colin. *Sir Samuel Hood and the Battle of the Chesapeake*. Gainesville: University Press of Florida, 2009.

Piecuch, Jim. *The Battle of Camden: A Documentary History*. Charleston, S.C.: History Press, 2006.

———. *The Blood Be upon Your Head: Tarleton and the Myth of Buford's Massacre, The Battle of the Waxhaws: May 29, 1780*. Lugoff, S.C.: Woodward Corp., 2010.

———. *Three Peoples, One King: Loyalists, Indians, and Slaves in the Revolutionary South, 1775–1782*. Columbia: University of South Carolina Press, 2008.

Raab, James W. *Spain, Britain, and the American Revolution in Florida, 1763–1783*. Jefferson, N.C.: McFarland, 2007.

Rankin, Hugh F. *Greene and Cornwallis: The Campaign in the Carolinas*. Raleigh: North Carolina Office of Archives and History, 1976.

———. *The North Carolina Continentals*. Chapel Hill: University of North Carolina Press, 1971.

———. *North Carolina in the American Revolution*. Raleigh: Historical Publications Section, Division of Historical Resources, Office of Archives and History, North Carolina Department of Cultural Resources, 1959.

Rodger, N. A. M. *The Insatiable Earl: A Life of John Montagu, Fourth Earl of Sandwich, 1718–1792*. New York: W. W. Norton, 1993.

Rush, N. Orwin. *Spain's Final Triumph over Great Britain in the Gulf of Mexico: The Battle of Pensacola, March 8 to 8 May, 1781*. Tallahassee: Florida State University, 1966.

Schwoerer, Lois G. *"No Standing Armies!": The Anti-Army Ideology in Seventh-Century England*. Baltimore: Johns Hopkins University Press, 1974.

Searcy, Martha C. *The Georgia-Florida Contest in the American Revolution, 1776–1778*. Tuscaloosa: University of Alabama Press, 1985.

Selby, John M. *The Road to Yorktown*. New York: St. Martin's, 1976.

Shaw, Helen L. *British Administration of the Southern Indians, 1756–1783*. 1931. Reprint, Norwalk, Conn.: AMS, 1981.

Sherrill, William L. *Annals of Lincoln County, North Carolina, Containing Interesting and Authentic Facts of Lincoln County History through the Years 1749 to 1937*. 1937. Reprint, Baltimore: Regional Publishing, 1972.

Shy, John. *A People Numerous and Armed: Reflections on the Military Struggle for American Independence*. Rev. ed. Ann Arbor: University of Michigan Press, 1990.

Smith, Paul H. *Loyalists and Redcoats: A Study in British Revolutionary Policy*. Chapel Hill: University of North Carolina Press, 1964.

Spring, Matthew. *With Zeal and with Bayonets Only: The British Army on Campaign in North America, 1775–1783*. Norman: University of Oklahoma Press, 2010.

Starr, J. Barton. *Tories, Dons, and Rebels: The American Revolution in British West Florida*. Gainesville: University Press of Florida, 1976.

State of Georgia. *Kettle Creek: The Battle of the Cane Brakes, Wilkes County*. Atlanta: Historic Preservation Section, Office of Planning and Research, Department of Natural Resources, 1975.

Stoker, Donald, Kenneth J. Hagan, and Michael T. McMaster, eds. *Strategy in the American War of Independence: A Global Approach*. London: Routledge, 2010.

Stone, Lawrence, ed. *An Imperial State at War: Britain from 1689 to 1815*. London: Routledge, 1994.

Sun Tzu. *The Art of War*. Edited and Translated by Samuel B. Griffith. New York: Oxford University Press, 1963.

Swisher, James K. *The Revolutionary War in the Southern Backcountry*. Gretna, La.: Pelican, 2008.

Syrett, David. *The Royal Navy in American Waters, 1775–1783*. Aldershot, U.K.: Scolar, 1989.

———. *Shipping and the American War, 1775–83: A Study of British Transport Organization*. London: Athlone, 1970.

Thayer, Theodore. *Nathanael Greene: Strategist of the American Revolution*. New York: Twayne, 1960.

———. *Yorktown: Campaign of Strategic Options*. Philadelphia: J. B. Lippincott, 1975.

Tilley, George L., and Thomas Crane. *The British Navy and the American Revolution*. Columbia: University of South Carolina Press, 1987.

Treacy, M. F. *Prelude to Yorktown: The Southern Campaign of Nathanael Greene, 1780–1781*. Chapel Hill: University of North Carolina, 1963.

Tsouras, Peter G., ed. *Warrior's Words: A Quotation Book: From Sesostris III to Schwarzkopf, 187 B.C. to A.D. 1991*. London: Cassell, 1992.

Tuchman, Barbara W. *The March of Folly, from Troy to Vietnam*. New York: Alfred A. Knopf, 1984.

Urban, Mark. *Fusiliers: The Saga of a British Redcoat Regiment in the American Revolution*. New York: Walker, 2007.

Valentine, Alan. *Lord George Germain*. Oxford: Clarendon, 1962.

Van Creveld, Martin. *Command in War*. Cambridge, Mass.: Harvard University Press, 1985.

Van Tyne, Claude Halstead. *The Loyalists in the American Revolution*. New York: Macmillan, 1902.

Wickwire, Franklin, and Mary Wickwire. *Cornwallis: The American Adventure*. Boston: Houghton Mifflin, 1970.

Willcox, William B. *Portrait of a General: Sir Henry Clinton in the War of Independence*. New York: Knopf, 1962.

Wilson, David K. *The Southern Strategy: Britain's Conquest of South Carolina and Georgia, 1775–1780*. Columbia: University of South Carolina, 2005.

Wood, Gordon. *The Radicalization of the American Revolution*. New York: Alfred A. Knopf, 1992.

Wood, William J. *Battles of the Revolutionary War, 1775–1781*. Cambridge, Mass.: Da Capo, 2003.

Wright, J. Leach, Jr. *Florida in the American Revolution*. Gainesville: University Press of Florida, 1975.

Wylie, J. C. *Military Strategy: A General Theory of Power Control*. Annapolis: Naval Institute Press, 1989.

### *Articles, Chapters, and Papers*

Atkinson, C. T. "British Forces in North America, 1774–1781: Their Distribution and Strength, Part 1." *Journal of the Society for Army Historical Research* 16 (1937): 3–23.

Babits, Lawrence E. "Greene's Strategy in the Southern Campaign, 1780–1781." *Air Force Journal of Logistics* 8, no. 1 (Winter 1984): 10–14.

Bayse, Arthur Herbert. "The Secretary of State for the Colonies, 1768–1782." *American Historical Review* 28, no. 1 (1922): 13–23.

Bennett, Thomas B. "Early Operational Art: Nathanael Greene's Carolina Campaign, 1780–1781." School of Advanced Military Studies, U.S. Army Command and General Staff College, Fort Leavenworth, Kans., 1993.

Berg, Richard H. "The Southern Campaigns: The British Effort to Retake the South, 1778–1781." *Strategy and Tactics* 104 (1985): 14–23.

Black, Jeremy. "British Military Strategy." In Stoker, Hagan, and McMaster, *Strategy in the American War of Independence*, 58–72.

Bowler, R. Arthur. "Logistics and Operations in the American Revolution." In Higginbotham, *Reconsiderations on the Revolutionary War*, 53–71.

Breen, Kenneth. "Graves and Hood at the Chesapeake." *Mariners' Mirror* 66 (1980): 63–64.

Brown, Gerald S. "The Anglo-French Naval Crisis: A Study of Conflict in the North Cabinet." *William and Mary Quarterly*, 3rd ser., 9, no. 3 (July 1952): 317–37.

Burne, A. H. "Cornwallis at Yorktown." *Journal of the Society for Army Historical Research* 17 (Summer 1938): 71–76.

Carpenter, Charles F. "The Southern Loyalists in British Strategic Military Planning for the American War of Independence." Honors thesis, University of North Carolina at Chapel Hill, 1979.

Carpenter, James L. "The Army of Cornwallis: A Study of Logistics Inadequacies." *Logistics Spectrum* 10, no. 3 (Fall 1976): 5–13.

Carpenter, Stanley D. M. "Army." In *Britain in the Hanoverian Age, 1714–1837*, edited by Gerald Newman. New York: Garland, 1997.

———. "The British Army." In *A Companion to Eighteenth-Century Britain*, edited by H. T. Dickinson. Oxford: Blackwell, 2002.

———. "Patterns of Recruitment of the Highland Regiments of the British Army, 1756 to 1815." Master's thesis, University of St. Andrews, Scotland, 1978.

Carpenter, William L. *The Battle of Ramsour's Mill*. Lincolnton, N.C.: Lincoln County Historical Association and Lincoln County Museum of History, 1995.

Cavanaugh, John C. "The Military Career of Major General Benjamin Lincoln in the War of the American Revolution." Ph.D. dissertation, Duke University, 1969.

Clover, J. P. "The British Southern Campaign in the Revolutionary War: Implications for Contemporary Counter-Insurgency." U.S. Army War College, Carlisle, Pa., 2006.

Comtois, Pierre. "Virginia under Threat." *Military History* 11, no. 4 (1994): 54–60.

Conway, Stephen. "The Politics of British Military and Naval Mobilization, 1775–83." *English Historical Review* 112, no. 449 (November 1997): 1179–1203.

———. "To Subdue America: British Army Officers and the Conduct of the Revolutionary War." *William and Mary Quarterly*, 3d ser., 43, no. 3 (1986): 381–407.

Crawford, Michael J. "New Light on the Battle off the Virginia Capes: Graves vs. Hood." *Mariner's Mirror* 103, no. 3 (2017): 337–40.

Davis, Andrew M. "The Employment of Indian Auxiliaries in the American War." *English Historical Review* 2, no. 8 (October 1887): 709–28.

Davis, Robert S., Jr. "The British Invasion of Georgia in 1778." *Atlanta Historical Journal* 24 (1980): 5–25.

Dukes, Richard Sears, Jr. "Anatomy of a Failure: British Military Policy in the Southern Campaign of the American Revolution, 1775–1781." Ph.D. dissertation, University of South Carolina, Columbia, 1993.

Farley, M. Foster. "The 'Old Wagoner' and the 'Green Dragoon.'" *History Today* 25, no. 3 (1975): 190–95.

Frasché, Louis D. F. "Problems of Command: Cornwallis, Partisans and Militia, 1780." *Military Review* 57, no. 4 (April 1977): 60–74.

Graham, William A. "The Battle of Ramsaur's Mill, June 20, 1780." *North Carolina Booklet* 4, no. 2 (June 1904).

Gruber, Ira D. "Britain's Southern Strategy." In Higgins, *Revolutionary War in the South,* 205–38.

———. "British Strategy: The Theory and Practice of Eighteenth-Century Warfare." In Higginbotham, *Reconsiderations on the Revolutionary War,* 14–31, 166–70.

———. "The Origins of British Strategy in the War for American Independence." In *Military History of the American Revolution: The Proceedings of the Sixth Military History Symposium, United States Air Force Academy, 10–11 October 1974,* edited by Stanley J. Underdal, 38–51. Washington, D.C.: Office of Air Force History, Headquarters USAF and U.S. Air Force Academy, 1974.

Hamer, Philip M. "John Stuart's Indian Policy during the Early Months of the American Revolution." *Mississippi Valley Historical Review* 17, no. 3 (December 1930): 351–66.

Hatch, Charles E., Jr. "Gloucester Point in the Siege of Yorktown, 1781." *William and Mary Quarterly,* 2nd ser., 20 (April 1940): 265–84.

Hoffer, Edward E. "Operational Art and Insurgency War: Nathanael Greene's Campaign in the Carolinas." School of Advanced Military Studies, U.S. Army Command and General Staff College, Fort Leavenworth, Kans., 1988.

Johnson, Donald F. "The Failure of Restored British Rule in Revolutionary Charleston, South Carolina." *Journal of Imperial and Commonwealth History* 42, no. 1 (2014): 22–40.

Kyte, George W. "Strategic Blunder: Lord Cornwallis Abandons the Carolinas, 1781." *Historian* 22, no. 2 (1960): 129–44.

Larrabee, Harold A. "A Near Thing at Yorktown." *American Heritage* 12, no. 6 (1961): 56–64, 69–73.

Lawrence, Alexander A. "General Robert Howe and the British Capture of Savannah in 1778." *Georgia Historical Quarterly* 36 (1952): 303–27.

Lumpkin, Henry. "The Battle off the Capes." *Virginia Cavalcade* 31, no. 2 (1981): 68–77.

Lutnick, Solomon M. "The Defeat at Yorktown: A View from the British Press." *Virginia Magazine of History and Biography* 72, no. 4 (1964): 471–78.

Mackesy, Piers. "British Strategy in the War of American Independence." *Yale Review* 52, no. 4 (1963): 539–57.

Mallahan, Richard A. "The Siege of Yorktown: Washington vs. Cornwallis." Air Command and Staff College, Air University, Maxwell Air Force Base, Ala., 1985.

Massey, Gregory De Van. "The British Expedition to Wilmington, January–November, 1781." *North Carolina Historical Review* 66, no. 4 (1989): 387–411.

Nelson, Paul David "Horatio Gates in the Southern Department, 1780: Serious Errors and a Costly Defeat." *North Carolina Historical Review* 50, no. 3 (1973): 256–72.

Olson, Gary D. "Thomas Brown, Loyalist Partisan and the Revolutionary War in Georgia, 1777–1782." *Georgia Historical Quarterly* 54 (1970): 1–19.

Pearson, Jesse T. "The Failure of British Strategy during the Southern Campaign of the American Revolutionary War, 1780–81." U.S. Army Command and General Staff College, Fort Leavenworth, Kans., 2005.

Rankin, Hugh F. "*The Moore's Creek Bridge Campaign, 1776.*" *North Carolina Historical Review* 30 (1953): 23–60.

Rhinesmith, W. Donald. "October 1781: The Southern Campaign Ends at Yorktown." *Virginia Cavalcade* 31, no. 2 (1981): 52–67.

Rogers, Shelly. "Francis Marion. The Swamp Fox: American Military in Low Intensity Conflict." Marine Corps Command and Staff College, Quantico, Va., 1988.

Selig, Robert. "Francois Joseph Paul Comte de Grasse, the Battle off the Virginia Capes, and the American Victory at Yorktown." *Journal of the Colonial Williamsburg Foundation* 21, no. 5 (October–November 1999): 26–32.

Shy, John. "British Strategy for Pacifying the Southern Colonies, 1778–1781." In *The Southern Experience in the American Revolution,* edited by Jeffrey J. Crow and Larry E. Tise, 155–73. Chapel Hill: University of North Carolina Press, 1978.

Smith, Bradley W. "Decision at Wilmington: Cornwallis Abandons the Carolinas, 1781." School of Advanced Military Studies, U.S. Army Command and General Staff College, Fort Leavenworth, Kans., 1982.

Smith, Michael. "Lord Charles Cornwallis: A Study in Strategic Leadership Failure." U.S. Army War College, Carlisle, Pa., 2001.

Smith, Paul H. "The American Loyalists: Notes on Their Organization and Numerical Strength." *William and Mary Quarterly,* 3rd ser., 25, no. 2 (April 1968): 259–77.

Tokar, John R. "Redcoat Resupply: Strategic Logistics and Operational Indecision in the American Revolutionary War, 1775–1783." School of Advanced Military Studies, U.S. Army Command and General Staff College, Fort Leavenworth, Kans., 1999.

Urwin, Gregory J. W. "Cornwallis and the Slaves of Virginia: A New Look at the Yorktown Campaign." *International Commission of Military History Proceedings* (2002): 172–92.

Weddle, Kevin J. "A Change of Both Men and Measures: British Reassessment of Military Strategy after Saratoga, 1770–1778." *Journal of Military History* 77, no. 3 (July 2013): 837–65.

Wight, Frank R. "Nathanael Greene, Major General of the American Revolution." Air Command and Staff College, Air University, Maxwell Air Force Base, Ala., 1965.

Willcox, William B. "The British Road to Yorktown: A Study in Divided Command." *American Historical Review* 52, no. 1 (October 1946): 1–35.

Wright, John W. "Notes on the Siege of Yorktown in 1781 with Special Reference to the Conduct of a Siege in the Eighteenth Century." *William and Mary Quarterly,* 2nd ser., 12 (October 1932): 229–49.

Zais, Mitchell M. "Strategic Vision and Strength of Will: Imperatives for Theatre Command." In *The Challenge of Military Leadership,* edited by Lloyd J. Matthews and Dale E. Brown, 85–89. Washington, D.C.: Pergamon-Brassey's, 1989.

# INDEX

Page numbers in *italics* indicate an illustration.